The Nation Should Come First

WARSAW STUDIES
IN CONTEMPORARY HISTORY
Edited by Dariusz Stola / Machteld Venken

VOLUME 1

Bibliographic Information published by the Deutsche Nationalbibliothek
The Deutsche Nationalbibliothek lists this publication in the Deutsche Nationalbibliografie; detailed bibliographic data is available in the internet at http://dnb.d-nb.de.

This publication was financially supported
by the Ministry of Science and Higher Education
- National Programme for the Development of Humanities.

 NARODOWY PROGRAM ROZWOJU HUMANISTYKI

Library of Congress Cataloging-in-Publication Data
Górny, Maciej, 1976-
 [Przede wszystkim ma byc naród. English]
 The nation should come first : Marxism and historiography in East Central
Europe / Maciej Górny ; translated by Antoni Górny ; editorial assistance Aaron Law.
  pages cm. – (Warsaw studies in contemporary history, ISSN 2195-1187 ; volume 1)
 Includes bibliographical references and index.
 ISBN 978-3-631-64512-3 – ISBN 978-3-653-03538-4 (e-book) 1. Europe,
Eastern – Historiography. 2. Europe, Central–Historiography. 3. Marxian
historiography. I. Górny, Antoni, translator. II. Title.
 DJK32.G6713 2013
 947'.0072--dc23
                                                                              2013030186

Cover image: © Mikołaj Górny

ISSN 2195-1187
ISBN 978-3-631-64512-3 (Print)
E-ISBN 978-3-653-03538-4 (E-Book)
DOI 10.3726/978-3-653-03538-4

© Peter Lang GmbH
Internationaler Verlag der Wissenschaften
Frankfurt am Main 2013
All rights reserved.
Peter Lang Edition is an Imprint of Peter Lang GmbH.

Peter Lang – Frankfurt am Main · Bern · Bruxelles · New York ·
Oxford · Warszawa · Wien

www.peterlang.de

Maciej Górny

The Nation Should Come First

Marxism and Historiography in East Central Europe

Translated by Antoni Górny
Editorial assistance Aaron Law

Contents

made similar development decidedly harder to achieve, but even there one could find scholars who combined Marxist thought with an interest in comparative history and international cooperation.

Before this Marxism-inspired intellectual ferment began, each Eastern bloc country went through a more or less prolonged period of forcible, swift Sovietisation. Marxism ceased to be just one of the many options that could be embraced in one's methodology or worldview. Reframed as Marxism-Leninism, or historical materialism, it became the publicly endorsed doctrine that defined the boundaries of history, as well as science. This book discusses four Marxist-Leninist historiographies in three real-socialist countries: Poland, Czechoslovakia and the GDR. My attention will focus on the way these historiographies dealt with the tradition of national historiography. Approaching revolutionary manifestos and projected institutional or methodological changes with caution, I inquire how Czech, Slovak, Polish and East-German self-declared Marxist historians approached dominant national discourses about the past. To what lengths were they prepared to go in reinterpreting the Romantic framework in a Marxist vein (as described by Monika Baár)? And if the two were irreconcilable, were historians ready to leave tradition behind or subordinate Marxist terminology and a materialist philosophy of history to a traditional way of thinking about the past?

There is, then, at least one reason why a comparative analysis suits Marxist historiographies better than historiographies of the early 19th century. Here, the similarities are not limited to traits generally common to all Western historiographies. The correspondences, perhaps enforced, but nonetheless, real, also grew out of the region's existing political situation and the imposition of a singular methodology. This makes the dearth of actual comparative research on the Communist era even more unusual. The "singularity" of the GDR's historical narrative, which Matthias Middell observed at the turn of the millennium, often proves to have been made up of elements common to history writing in other Eastern Bloc countries as well.[2]

This attempt to partially fill the gap is based on a set of straightforward assumptions. Two of them seem to be of key importance in the context of my research. At the same time, they rather pointedly illustrate the problems faced by comparative history, bound up as they are with a specific practical example.

First, the comparison in question must not fail to take account of mutual influences, the interactions between different historiographies, as well as the influence of Soviet historiography on East Central European historians. Otherwise

2   Matthias Middell, "Kulturtransfer und Historische Komparatistik – Thesen zu ihrem Verhältnis," *Comparativ* 10 (2000), 1, 30.

Introduction
Writing Comparative Histories
of Historiography

In her recently published, brilliant book about Romantic-era historiographies of Central and Eastern Europe, the Hungarian historian Monika Baár comes to the conclusion that the presumed differences between these historiographies and their supposed detachment from dominant Western European historiographies were not as compelling as had been heretofore believed. Similarities are so frequent, and so deeply ingrained, that "on closer inspection the historical narrative reveals the existence of a general template of national historiography in our era, which comprised a core story and numerous omnipresent tropes."[1] Not only do national historiographies share similar narrative patterns – they also relate to the same myths and images. For example, one of the things they share is the belief in the uniqueness of their own story.

Romantic-era historiography, which in Central and Eastern Europe is associated with founding father figures or innovators who reframed the task of the historian, shaped our ways of thinking about the past. In time, Romantic narratives came to be criticised and opposed, but the voices rejecting the domination of national historiography by the Romantic idea can often be seen singing the same tune. While taking positions similar to the ones chosen by Romantic historians, the critics also employed similar arguments. At first, Marxism served as an inspiration for a research attitude opposed to the early 19th century modes of historical thinking. Since the late 19th century, it has inspired social scientists. Its influence in Central and Eastern Europe peaked in the 1960s. Polish and Hungarian historians especially enjoyed success in using their methodological backgrounds and local competencies in cooperative work with the foremost scholars of France or the United States. In general, the encouraging climate for comparative research in economic and social history of the region and beyond contributed to what may have been the most productive period in the modern history of Polish and Hungarian historiography. The more austere regimes in other Eastern bloc countries – such as the GDR or Czechoslovakia –

---

1   Monika Baár, *Historians and Nationalism: East-Central Europe in the Nineteenth Century*, Oxford 2010, 295.

PRL   – Polska Rzeczpospolita Ludowa (People's Republic of Poland)
PTH   – Polskie Towarzystwo Historyczne (Polish Historical Society)
PZPR   – Polska Zjednoczona Partia Robotnicza (Polish United Workers'
         Party)
SAV   – Slovenská Akadémie Vied (Slovak Academy of Sciences)
SAVU   – Slovenská Akademia Vied a Umeni
SD   – *Soudobé Dějiny*
SED   – Sozialistische Einheitspartei Deutschlands (Socialist Unity Party of
         Germany)
SHS   – Slovenská Historická Spoločnost (Slovak Historical Society)
SNP   – Slovenské Národné Povstanie (Slovak National Uprising)
U.S.   – United States (of America)
TDP   – Towarzystwo Demokratyczne Polskie (Polish Democratic Society)
VHD   – Verband der Historiker Deutschlands (Association of Germany's
         Historians)
VŠPHV – Vysoká škola politických a hospodářských věd (School of Politics
         and Economy)
ZfG   – *Zeitschrift für Geschichtswissenschaft*
ZfO   – *Zeitschrift für Ostforschung*
ZfO-F – *Zeitschrift für Ostmitteleuropa-Forschung*

List of Abbreviations

AK	– Armia Krajowa (Home Army)
BUW	– Biblioteka Uniwersytetu Warszawskiego (Warsaw University Library)
CISH	– Comité International des Sciences Historiques
CPSU	– Communist Party of the Soviet Union
ČAVU	– Česká Akadémie Věd a Umění (Czech Academy for Sciences and Arts)
ČČH	– *Český Časopis Historický*
ČMM	– *Časopis Matice Moravské*
ČSAV	– Československá Akademie Věd (Czechoslovak Academy of Sciences)
ČSHS	– Československá Historická Společnost (Czechoslovak Historical Society)
DAW	– Deutsche Akademie der Wissenschaften (German Academy of Sciences)
DHG	– Deutsche Historiker-Gesellschaft (German Historians' Society)
DN	– *Dzieje Najnowsze*
FRG	– Federal Republic of Germany
GDR	– German Democratic Republic
GLP	– Gromady Ludu Polskiego (Communes of the Polish People)
GOSR	– Great October Socialist Revolution
GWU	– *Geschichte in Wissenschaft und Unterricht*
HČSAV	– *Historický Časopis Slovenskej Akademii Vied*
HZ	– *Historische Zeitschrift*
JfGO	– *Jahrbücher für Geschichte Osteuropas*
KH	– *Kwartalnik Historyczny*
KPD	– Kommunistische Partei Deutschlands (Communist Party of Germany)
KSČ	– Komunistická Strana Československa (Communist Party of Czechoslovakia)
NKVD	– Peoples Commissariat for Internal Affairs
NSDAP	– Nationalsozialistische Deutsche Arbeiterpartei
NSZ	– Narodowe Siły Zbrojne (National Armed Forces)
PAN	– Polska Akademia Nauk (Polish Academy of Sciences)
PH	– *Przegląd Historyczny*
PPR	– Polska Partia Robotnicza (Polish Workers' Party)
PPS	– Polska Partia Socjalistyczna (Polish Socialist Party)

At the same time, historians gave substance to the fundamental myths undergirding these communities. As a rule, they aimed to make their compatriots happy rather than forcing them to critically rethink their own positions or self-evaluations. If we focus on the themes that recur throughout different national cultures, the myths that tell the same old story with the support of different details, then chronological turning points will prove to be of secondary importance. Instead of rigidly comparing Marxist interpretations of specific epochs, I begin my analysis by examining the role particular historical phenomena played in the collective memory as well as in the historiography of a given nation, which is important because historiography comprises both a part of that memory and a medium for its dissemination. I believe that this kind of functional comparison can yield many positive results, even if it often leads one to connect ostensibly unrelated facts. The reader of this book will easily notice that this functional comparison is used, for instance, to set the Czech and Slovak national revival against the Polish uprisings. The Medieval expansion of East German feudal lords or the battle of the Teutoburg Forest, that pitted Germanic barbarian tribes against the Roman legions, are seen simply as different examples of the same historiographical narrative. Looking for instances of social revolt against growing feudal oppression, Marxists from different countries of the Eastern bloc traversed national histories with apparent ease, building analogies between events as far apart as the Great Peasant Revolt and the activities of the Carpathian robbers. Such unusual juxtapositions grow out of Thomas Welskopp's Max Weber-inspired idea of fashioning comparative models that can prove useful in describing different circumstances.[5] The goal is not to come up with a universal schema, but rather – as Welskopp and Weber claim – to lend substance to an idea of how things would have developed had history taken a different route. A comparative study produces data about *potential* possibilities of historical development, which, while speculative, are still more realistic than pure speculation.

The history of historiography in general, and particularly the history of Marxist historiography, can benefit greatly from this kind of comparative study, or *histoire croisée*, and not only because new facts might be uncovered, relations between different countries highlighted, and mutual inspirations and borrowings underlined. In my opinion, however, the greatest premium which this kind of approach can provide us is the rare chance to take temporary leave of our own backyard and look at it from the outside, through the eyes of another. In this

---

5   Thomas Welskopp, "Stolpersteine auf dem Königsweg. Methodenkritische Anmerkungen zum internationalen Vergleich in der Gesellschaftsgeschichte," *Archiv für Sozialgeschichte* 35 (1995), 365-367.

the image resulting from the comparison would amount to nothing more than a schematic juxtaposition. According to Michael Werner and Bénédicte Zimmermann, this is one of the major dangers of comparative study. However, it can be averted if the comparative study is informed by knowledge gained from the study of cultural transfers. Werner and Zimmermann propose a *histoire croisée*, which „breaks with a one-dimensional perspective that simplifies and homogenizes, in favour of a multidimensional approach that acknowledges plurality and the complex configurations that result from it. Accordingly, entities and objects of research are not merely considered in relation to one another but also *through* one another, in terms of relationship, interactions and circulation."[3] In relation to Marxist historiographies discussed in this book, this translates into the necessity not only to take mutual influences into account, but also to reflect on the relationships between these countries and other states beyond East Central Europe. The image of Slovak historiography – whether Marxist or not – is never complete if it does not reflect on its relationship to the work of Hungarian historians. A similar focus is necessary when studying the works from GDR historians, whose attitude toward West German historians and historical narratives is particularly relevant to the study of East German historiography. As I also believe, it is important to note that no transfer of ideology or interpretative framework culminates in a state of total domination or the formation of one historiography by another. This observation is particularly useful when considering the relationships between any one of the Eastern bloc historiographies and Soviet historical sciences. Even if one could never treat them as equal, to describe any one of these relationships in terms of unilateral domination would be fundamentally inaccurate. Middell's idea of comparative history moving from bilateral toward multilateral perspectives finds an apt illustration in the comparative study of Marxist-Leninist historiographies.[4] By juxtaposing two examples "cleansed" of non-bilateral influences, not only would we produce a distorted image, we would also make it more difficult to develop a proper reading of the complex processes behind the adoption of intellectual currents, ideologies or even systems of science.

Second, I believe that a comparison should not be "rigid," i.e., limited to an analysis of the way each historiography treats a specific, narrowly defined topic. Already in its heroic period during the early 19th century, historiography was both an inspiration for the study of problems faced by the community and a source of answers to such problems – concerning questions of the community's genealogy, its rightful territory, or characteristics of its collective psychology.

---

3   Michael Werner, Bénédicte Zimmermann, "Beyond Comparison: Histoire croisée and the Challenge of Reflexivity," *History and Theory* 45 (2006), 38.
4   Middell, "Kulturtransfer," 39-40.

light, what once was considered exceptional often proves extremely typical and schematic, that which seemed dangerously pathological becomes the grim norm, and that which looked quite obvious seems suddenly inexplicable. The comparative approach is therefore useful outside of comparative studies as well. Some of its tools appear to be indispensable if we are to advance any reliable historical claims that go beyond stating obvious facts.

***

The circle of people to whom I owe a debt of gratitude for the help and inspiration they offered during my work on this book is very broad and continues to expand. To all those whom I thanked in the Polish (2007) and German (2011) editions, I would like to add the employees of my home institution, the Institute of History at the Polish Academy of Sciences, without whose aid this considerable undertaking would not have gained the necessary financial support. The translator, editor and publisher know how highly I value their involvement in our common work. Finally, at the risk of sounding ingratiating, I would like to thank the quite sizeable group of reviewers of previous editions of my book. The differences between the successive editions are to a significant extent due to their critical observations.

The notion of discontinuity, as it is being used in the post-1989 history of historiography, refers not only to the scientific policy of Communist regimes, but also to dominant historical narratives. As Rafał Stobiecki puts it, Marxists – rather unwittingly – destroyed elemental social ties of historical continuity linking state and nation.[9] The East Central European Marxism of the 1950s was thus clearly perceived as a gap in the development of historical science. In the historical debates that arose immediately after the collapse of Communism in East Central Europe, the notion of "white spots" (among others) was intended to represent the difference between 'Communist' historiography and the new, truly scientific, non-ideological historical science. The debates submitted to the logic of the totalitarian paradigm. Whereas Polish historians discussed the status of the People's Republic of Poland (Polska, Rzeczpospolita Ludowa, PRL), describing it variously as a case of Soviet occupation or limited independence, of a totalitarian or authoritarian regime etc.;[10] in Czechoslovakia the Communist regime was declared unlawful and criminal; the thematic rupture, coupled with an increased interest in the history of political resistance and dissent, automatically brought on criticism of pre-1989 historiography.[11] One of the interesting effects of this process was a sudden popularity of source literature, epitomising the "historical truth."

To historians of historiography, the events of 1989 brought open access to archives, including the archives of the Communist party. It allowed them to study issues such as the balance of power in historical institutions, ways in which authorities influenced historians, personal connections, interdependences and conflicts, which were previously more or less known, but had no available evidentiary support in the documentary record. These new possibilities aroused an immense interest in the history of historiography in 1990s, especially in Germany. Dozens of historians (most prominently Konrad Jarausch, Matthias

---

in: *Past in the making. Historical revisionism in Central Europe after 1989*, ed. Michal Kopeček, Budapest 2008, 78-80.

9   Rafał Stobiecki, *Historia pod nadzorem. Spory o nowy model historii w Polsce (II połowa lat czterdziestych – początek lat pięćdziesiątych*, Łódź 1993, 182. See also his article, "Between Continuity and Discontinuity: A Few Comments on the Post-War Development of Polish Historical Research," *Zeitschrift für Ostmitteleuropa-Forschung* 2001/2, 214-229.

10 The 1990s public debate over the nature of the Communist regime in Poland is analysed by Anna Magierska, *Dylematy historii PRL*, Warszawa 1995. For an international perspective, consult *Obrachunki z historią*, ed. Włodzimierz Borodziej, Warszawa 1997.

11 For the post-1989 East Central European debates on the legacy of Communism, consult the collective volume: *Narratives unbound. Historical studies in post-communist Eastern Europe*, eds. Sorin Antohi, Balázs Trencsényi, Péter Apor, Budapest 2007.

Chapter I
Method

One of the most intriguing characteristics of the history of Marxist historiography in the last twenty years is its separation from the agenda of a "general" history of historiography. It is, on the one hand, a somewhat-"natural" side effect of the largely unchallenged position that the year 1945 is a turning point in recent history. But it is also, on the other hand, a reflex of post-1989 historical and political debates which spread their influence over historical science. Polish, Slovak, Czech, and German authors decisively distinguish between the historiography of the 19th century and that of the interwar period on the one side, and postwar Marxist-Leninist historical science on the other. Attempts at unifying both periods are rare and, even if they meet in the same book, the qualitative difference between them is emphatically marked. One of the most frequent oppositions discussed after 1989 was embodied in the contrast: "continuity or discontinuity." Whereas the answer seems to be more than obvious: Marxism of the Soviet type has nothing to do with "normal" historiography. It was an attempt – to use the formulation of Polish historian of science Piotr Hübner – to decapitate the intellectual elite.[6]

This post-1989 narrative identifies Marxist methodology as a part of an external attempt to subordinate and control the historians' milieu. As soon as the deepest incursions of Stalinism had abated, historians were able to go back to their previous ideals, running their business more or less as usual.[7] Even when – as happened after 1968 in Czechoslovakia – there was a backlash of a strong dictatorship and a revitalisation of Stalinist narratives, the dichotomised picture remains dominant: a clear division between historians on one side and Communist party functionaries on the other.[8]

---

6   Piotr Hübner, "Stalinowskie 'czystki' w nauce polskiej," in: *Skryte oblicze systemu komunistycznego. U źródeł zła*, ed. Roman Bäcker & Piotr Hübner, Warszawa 1997, 220.

7   See Maciej Górny, "'Przełom metodologiczny' na łamach 'Przeglądu Historycznego' na tle wybranych czasopism historycznych w Europie Środkowowschodniej," *Przegląd Historyczny* 2006/1, 39-48.

8   See Michal Kopeček, "In search of 'national memory.' The politics of history, nostalgia and the historiography of communism in the Czech Republic and East Central Europe,"

scholar Martin Nodl adopted a majority of them to Czech historiography).[15] These were, to name but a few: relations between East German historians and their ideological opponents from the Bundesrepublik,[16] opposition to and collaboration with the authorities, and relations between power and historical science, or censorship. The same topics are discussed at least to an extent in Polish, Czech and Slovak historical works.

The same *Sonderheft* included a text by Frank Hadler and Georg Iggers, discussing the possibility of a comparative analysis of various Communist historiographies.[17] John Connelly's analysis of Polish, Czechoslovak and East German universities under Stalinisation is without a doubt a prominent example of the advantages offered by such an approach.[18]

The first appeals for the use of postmodernism in research on Marxist historiography were made in Germany. In the aforementioned special issue of *Historische Zeitschrift* from 1998, Konrad Jarausch proposed postmodernism as a tool for interpreting East German historical science.[19] In 2000, during a congress of German historians in Aachen, the issue was debated by Jarausch, Matthias Middell and Martin Sabrow, among others.[20] Their postulates were almost immediately – at least in a formal sense – put into practice, with contemporary German authors analysing the *Meistererzählung* (master

15   Martin Nodl, "Možné přístupy ke studiu dějin české historické vědy v letech 1945-2000," *Soudobé Dějiny* 2001.

16   Martin Sabrow, "Die Geschichtswissenschaft der DDR und ihr 'objektiver Gegner'"; Rainer Eckert, "Die Westbeziehungen der Historiker im Auge der Staatssicherheit"; Wolfgang Mommsen, "Die DDR-Geschichtsschreibung aus westdeutscher Perspektive," all in: *Die DDR-Geschichtswissenschaft als Forschungsproblem....*

17   Frank Hadler & Georg Iggers, "Überlegungen zum Vergleich der DDR-Geschichtswissenschaft mit den 'gespaltenen' Historiographien Ostmitteleuropas nach 1945," in: *Die DDR-Geschichtswissenschaft als Forschungsproblem...*

18   John Connelly, *Captive University. The Sovietisation of East German, Czech and Polish Higher Education 1945-1956*, Chapel Hill – London 2000.

19   Konrad Jarausch, "Historische Texte der DDR aus der Perspektive des linguistic turn," in: *Die DDR-Geschichtswissenschaft als Forschungsproblem....*

20   Konrad Jarausch & Martin Sabrow, "Das Konzept der 'historischen Meistererzählung' als Maßstab eines deutsch-deutsches Historiographievergleichs," in: *43. Deutscher Historikertag Aachen 2000. Skriptheft 2 Eine Welt – eine Geschichte?*, eds. Max Kerner, Peter Droste, Angelika Ivens & Cornelia Kompe, Aachen 2000; Matthias Middel, "Historische Meistererzählung und Institutionalisierung in der Geschichtswissenschaft," in: ibidem; Martin Sabrow, "Bauformen einer erneuerten nationalen Meistererzählung in der DDR: das Lehrbuch der deutschen Geschichte," in: ibidem.

Middell and Martin Sabrow) agreed concerning the end of these political debates: "To escape from the vicious circle of mutual accusations and egoistic self-admiration, we need to critically historicise GDR historiography."[12] From this perspective, new research should focus on a comparison between East German and other historiographies of the East Bloc as well as historical science in Nazi Germany.

This approach became a wholeheartedly embraced practice in Poland, in the Czech Republic, and in Slovakia. Polish works devoted to this aspect of history focus on such phenomena as the conference in Otwock (1951-52, planned as an official imposition of Marxism on Polish historiography), the Party-governed colleges, or the Institute of History at the Polish Academy of Sciences (founded in 1953 under Marxist auspices). Research on Czechoslovak historiography develops more or less along the same lines. The turning points in this case are: the last democratic congress of Czech historians in 1947, the purges accompanying the Communist takeover in 1948, and institutional changes concomitant with the persecution of professors and students. German and Polish historians were the first to analyse the impact of political censorship on historical writings.[13] The main research question for all the scholars in this field is whether continuity was maintained in historical sciences, or if Stalinism did cause a personnel and institutional break.

The *Verwissenschaftlichung* (which in this context means "professionalisation") of research on GDR historiography became the topic of a special issue of *Historische Zeitschrift* in 1998.[14] Some of the texts it includes may be treated as research suggestions for the near future (and in fact Czech

---

12   Konrad Jarausch & Matthias Middel, "Einleitung. Die DDR als Geschichte: Verurteilung, Nostalgie oder Historisierung?," in: *Nach dem Erdbeben. (Re-)Konstruktion ostdeutscher Geschichte und Geschichtswissenschaft*, eds. Konrad Jarausch & Matthias Middel, Leipzig 1994.

13   Zbigniew Romek, "Cenzura w PRL a historiografia – pytania i problemy badawcze," in: *Metodologiczne problemy syntezy historii historiografii polskiej*, ed. Jerzy Maternicki, Rzeszów 1998; *Cenzura w PRL – relacje historyków*, ed. Zbigniew Romek, Warszawa 2000; idem, *Cenzura a nauka historyczna w Polsce 1944-1970*, Warszawa 2010; Siegfried Lokatis, "Die Zensur historischer Literatur in der DDR unter Ulbricht," in: *Die DDR-Geschichtswissenschaft als Forschungsproblem*, eds. Georg Iggers, Konrad Jarausch, Matthias Middel & Martin Sabrow, München 1998; idem, "Die Zensur historischer Literatur in der DDR," in: *Geschichte als Argument. 41. Deutscher Historikertag in München 17. bis 20. September 1996. Berichtband*, eds. Stefan Weinfurter & Frank Siefarth, München 1997.

14   *Die DDR-Geschichtswissenschaft als Forschungsproblem...*

narrative) and the *Herrschaftsdiskurs* (discourse of power) within the GDR.[21] The best practical example of the advantages and disadvantages of this method is Martin Sabrow's book *Das Diktat des Konsenses. Geschichtswissenschaft in der DDR 1949-1969.*[22] It is based on broad archival research and describes not only various aspects of party dictate, but also the initiatives of historical circles. Sabrow analyses (in a very detailed, but somewhat tiring manner) mechanisms for the creation of rules in GDR historical discourse. The image he comes up with is much more complicated than a one-way model of the subordination of science to politics. Sabrow points to the moments when historians themselves disciplined their colleagues, creating an efficient system of self-control and thus reducing the need for direct political intervention. But, surprisingly, Sabrow devotes relatively little attention to a seemingly vital problem – the analysis of historical narratives, rhetoric, style or strategies of argumentation. Thus, his analysis is not a deconstruction of the content of GDR historiography but a description of historical sciences in the GDR. Because of this, one might wonder whether postmodernist notions are truly useful in this type of analysis. Nevertheless, Sabrow's influence on later international research cannot be denied. In some cases – as in the recent monograph of Slovak Marxist historiography by Adam Hudek – the outcome may be a well-balanced mix of institutional and textual analysis.[23]

Sabrow's interesting attempt has one more feature that seems characteristic of the new type of German research into the history of science in the GDR. The question whether or not East Germany was a totalitarian state hinges upon the issue of research professionalisation. German authors generally relate to contemporary definitions of totalitarianism, concluding that none of them fully describes the GDR: the dictatorship of the Communist Party (Sozialistische Einheitspartei Deutschlands, SED) was seriously limited, *ergo*, the GDR could not have been a totalitarian state. This explains why John Connelly's claims concerning the Sovietisation of Central European universities met with a rather cold response in Germany.[24] Instead of referring to abstract models, Connelly compared the reality of scholarly work in the GDR to the situation of

---

21 See *Die historische Meistererzählung. Deutungslinien der deutschen Nationalgeschichte nach 1945*, eds. Konrad Jarausch & Martin Sabrow, Göttingen 2002 (herein especially: Martin Sabrow, "Auf der Suche nach dem marxistischen Meisterton. Bauformen einer nationalen Gegenerzählung in der DDR").

22 Martin Sabrow, *Das Diktat des Konsenses. Geschichtswissenschaft in der DDR 1949-1969*, München 2001.

23 Adam Hudek, *Najpolitickejšia veda. Slovenská historiografia v rokoch 1948-1968*, Bratislava 2010.

24 See Konrad Jarausch's review in *Zeitschrift für Ostmitteleuropa-Forschung* 2002/2.

scholarship under Polish and Czechoslovak Stalinism. Such a comparison inevitably leads to the conclusion that, even if none of these countries was actually totalitarian, East Germany came surely the closest to clear-cut totalitarianism.

In the programmatic article cited above, Konrad Jarausch opposed deconstructivism in the history of historiography to a simplified formula, within which Marxist historiography is analysed exclusively in its legitimising function. Jarausch noted that "The common critique of the instrumentalisation of historiography in the GDR leads to the tricky question: what to do with all those libraries full of East German intellectual heritage." Postmodern analyses are supposed to yield as broad an image of historiography as possible, and not be restricted only to one function of it (regardless of its importance). Nevertheless, despite all the conceptual differences, those two different approaches often lead to similar effects. Characteristically, a number of recent works on the historical legitimisation of political power in East Central Europe show a solid background in theories of sociology, visibly exceeding the typical level of engagement with sociological theory for each of the respective historiographies.[25] Although historiography is not always accorded a central position (for instance, by Marcin Zaremba), it is always referred to as an important legitimising tool. In most cases, however, historians dealing with the process of legitimisation through historiography look at the problem from the perspective of rulers and their need for history (or their fear of history) rather than considering historiography as a science or art with its own tradition. Furthermore, the period researched (whether it is a Communist or Nazi dictatorship) is often treated in isolation from the rest of national history, as an abnormality contrasting with the supposedly "normal" before and after.[26] All this leads back to the simplified ascriptions of totalitarianism. The paradox is even more striking if we consider that those works commonly conclude that Communists eagerly borrowed nationalist ideas – in other words, that they borrowed a lot from their predecessors.

Opposition towards the tendency to treat Marxist historiography, or, more generally, the culture of the Communist period, in isolation may have different reasons behind it. According to Jarausch and Sabrow, Marxist historical science should not be compared to "normal" historiographies of the democratic, liberal West. They believe that the research on historiography in the GDR should be conducted without reference to what was happening simultaneously in the

25   Marcin Zaremba, *Komunizm, legitymizacja, nacjonalizm. Nacjonalistyczna legitymizacja władzy komunistycznej w Polsce*, Warszawa 2001; Michal Kopeček, "Ve službách dějin, ve jménu národa. Historie jako součást legitimizace komunistických režimů ve střední Evropě v letech 1948-1950," *Soudobé Dějiny* 2001/1.
26   See Marcin Zaremba, *Komunizm, legitymizacja, nacjonalizm...*, 398.

Federal Republic of Germany.[27] Within this scheme, historiography is perceived as a part of the *Herrschaftsdiskurs*, but it is also a science, so East German historians should not be judged in the same way as journalists of *Neues Deutschland*. GDR historiography is supposed to be analysed only as an aspect of the SED's dictatorial rule.

Another German-American historian Georg Iggers seems to be of a different opinion. He questions sharp distinctions between historiography under dictatorial and democratic rule. In both cases, history serves non-scientific purposes. From this point of view, Marxist historians of the Eastern Bloc may stand in line with Michelet, Droysen or Palacký.[28] Iggers obviously believes that "objective historiography" is a purely normative term, but as Karl Popper said, historians may try to show *wie es eigentlich nicht gewesen*.[29]

The idea of supporting the treatment of the history of historiography as a continuous effort, without subjecting the 45 postwar years to exclusive treatment, seems very appealing. The works of John Connelly and others highlight the fascinating encounters between tradition and "Sovietisation," including the pressures applied and concessions made in view of creating a new compromise. To answer the question whether historical science maintained continuity during the era or not, we should refer not only to the dimension of personal or institutional politics; of equal importance are the questions whether Marxist historiographies follow in the footsteps of their bourgeois predecessors, and if so, how. The title of one of Sabrow's books, *Das Diktat des Konsenses*, could be used to describe relations not only between historians and authorities but also between Marxist historical narratives and the national traditions in Poland, the GDR and Czechoslovakia.

Assuming that a broader perspective on the analysis of Marxist historiographies is useful and needed, we should draw methodological inspiration from at least a small part of the history of "classic" historiography. In the process, we will probably notice that scholars researching 19th century historiography have already raised a number of questions that are still untouched

---

27 Martin Sabrow, "Die DDR-Geschichtswissenschaft im Spiegel ihrer Gutachterpraxis," in: *Geschichte als Argument. 41. Deutscher Historikertag in München 17. bis 20. September 1996. Berichtband*, eds. Stefan Weinfurter & Frank Siefarth, München 1997, 198.

28 See *Proceedings Actes. 19th International Congress of Historical Sciences. University of Oslo 6-13 VIII 2000*, Oslo 2000, 87-88; *Die Mauern der Geschichte. Historiographie in Europa zwischen Diktatur und Demokratie*, eds. Gustavo Corni & Martin Sabrow, Leipzig 1996; idem, "Historiography in the 20th century," in: *The Misuse of History. Symposium on "Facing Misuses of History,"* Oslo 28-30 June 1999, Strasbourg 2000.

29 Idem, "Geschichtsschreibung und Politik im 20, Jahrhundert," in: *Die Mauern der Geschichte...*, 33.

or have only been addressed recently by historians of Marxist historiography. For instance, manipulations of historical memory were discussed in a well-known essay by Herbert Butterfield, *The Whig Interpretation of History*, published in 1931.[30] Links between past heroes and current political trends were characteristic of Marxist historiographies as well.

In mid-1950s, Butterfield postulated that historians should raise the heretofore neglected question of the impact of historical science on European nations over the previous 150 years.[31] This area was visited not only by Butterfield himself, but also by numerous other scholars. In East Central Europe, this question was researched as well, primarily by the most eminent representatives of the so-called Łódź school of the history of historiography: Marian Henryk Serejski and Andrzej Feliks Grabski. Both analysed various forms of historical thought, without restricting themselves to the so-called scientific discourse. Both also held historiography in high regard as a science concentrating on a broad complex of problems, including considerations of organisational structures, theoretical foundations and interpretations of the past.[32] According to Serejski and Grabski, a historian of historiography should be interested in both historical institutions and the content of historical books – a far from obvious statement for many contemporary historians dealing with the Communist period. This perspective not only accepts but demands an interest in everything that shapes popular historical knowledge.

Both postulates were fulfilled in detailed works by the two historians of the Łódź school. Where Serejski wrote about references to "nation" and "state" in Polish historical thought,[33] Grabski described phenomena occurring on the margins of professional historiography, such as the works of Franciszek Duchiński, the 19th century Polish-Ukrainian author of the theory of the Russians' non-Slavic origin, or of the political aspects of 19th century historical

---

30   Herbert Butterfield, *The Whig Interpretation of History*, London 1968 (reprint of the 1931 edition).

31   "An aspect of the history of historiography which has been somewhat neglected is the examination of the role which historical study and historical thinking played in the development of European nations during the last one hundred and fifty years" – Herbert Butterfield, *Man on His Past. The Study of the History of Historical Scholarship*, Cambridge 1955, 30.

32   Rafał Stobiecki, "Wprowadzenie," in: Andrzej F. Grabski, *Dzieje historiografii*, Poznań 2003, XIII.

33   Marian H. Serejski, *Naród a państwo w polskiej myśli historycznej*, Warszawa 1973; *Historycy o historii. Od Adama Naruszewicza do Stanisława Kętrzyńskiego 1775-1918*, ed. Marian H. Serejski, vol. I, Warszawa 1963, *Historycy o historii 1918-1939*, vol. II, Warszawa 1966.

competitions.[34] A similar approach can be found in the writings of other Polish authors, such as Andrzej Zahorski's or Andrzej Wierzbicki's works on 19th century historical culture.[35] The latter wrote a short book *Konstytucja 3 Maja w historiografii polskiej*, which is of particular interest for the present study.[36] Wierzbicki describes the 19th century debates on the 1791 Polish Constitution, but then moves on to a discussion of Marxist authors. Zahorski follows a similar pattern in his writings. Neither of the two authors introduces any division between the "normal" pre-1945 historiography and its "Stalinist" incarnation; by doing so, they achieve a clear and coherent narrative of specific intellectual debates.

The idea of a history of historiography as a broad panorama of concepts and events shaping an image of the past is surely not new. This kind of approach is familiar to the history of ideas and collective memory. With respect not only to the history of historical science, but also to the culture of Bohemia (including German Bohemian historiography) and Slovakia, it can be found in the brilliant work of synthesis by František Kutnar and Jaroslav Marek.[37] *The German conception of history*, one of the early books by Georg Iggers, offers a similar perspective.[38] Iggers applies ideas of German historicism to the German national awakening, especially the *Befreiungskriege*, which – according to him – played for Germany a role equivalent to that of the French revolution.[39] Josef Macůrek's book on East European historiographies since 1946, although devoted for the most part to professional science, deals with politics and culture, and may be perceived as a powerful and continuously appealing manifesto of

34   Andrzej F. Grabski, "Na manowcach myśli historycznej. Historiozofia Franciszka H. Duchińskiego," in: idem, *Perspektywy przeszłości. Studia i szkice historiograficzne*, Lublin 1983; idem, *Historiografia i polityka. Dzieje konkursu historycznego im. Juliana Ursyna Niemcewicza 1867-1922*, Warszawa 1979; idem *Kształty historii*, Łódź 1985; idem *W kręgu kultu Naczelnika. Rapperswilskie inicjatywy kościuszkowskie (1894-1897)*, Warszawa 1981.
35   See Andrzej Zahorski, *Spór o Stanisława Augusta*, Warszawa 1990 (2nd edition); Andrzej Wierzbicki, *Naród-państwo w polskiej myśli historycznej dwudziestolecia międzywojennego*, Wrocław 1978; idem, *Wschód-Zachód w koncepcjach dziejów Polski*, Warszawa 1984; idem, *Historiografia polska doby romantyzmu*, Wrocław 1999.
36   Andrzej Wierzbicki, *Konstytucja 3 Maja w historiografii polskiej*, Warszawa 1993.
37   František Kutnar & Jaroslav Marek, *Přehledné dějiny českého a slovenského dějepisectví. Od počátků národní kultury až do sklonku třicátých let 20. století*, Praha 1997 (2nd ed.).
38   Georg G. Iggers, *The German Conception of History. The National Tradition of Historical Thought from Herder to the Present*, Middletown 1968.
39   Ibidem, 7.

European cultural unity.[40] Macůrek strongly opposed submitting European historiography to geopolitical divisions: it is singular and should be treated as such. In addition, such a division would be very problematic for Macůrek himself, as his book on Eastern European historiography does not discuss either Czech or Slovak historiographies. Should they be placed in the West, or did Macůrek perceive them as being somewhere in-between the two poles?

There seems to be enough evidence not to doubt the usefulness of the research frames of older historiography for the analysis of East Central European Marxist historiographies. On the contrary: they may help to develop a complex picture including not only institutions and the scientific policy of party and state, but also all the interconnections between historiography and historical tradition, the imaginings of the national past, the history of ideas and collective memory, and, finally, historical myths.

In 1986, Jerzy Jedlicki formulated the idea that "Nations which in their history experienced (and still experience) mostly failures and humiliation and which still share the same feeling of unfulfilled individual and group aspirations, those nations search in their history not so much for learning, but for compensation."[41] It is worth mentioning that in other conditions the same "creative" attitude towards history may be found also among those who win, as was the case with the aforementioned Whigs. Already in the Middle Ages, the imagined ethnogenesis of European nations was based on myths that proved surprisingly durable. The 19th and 20th century debate between the "Latin school," which claimed that Romanians were descendants of the Romans, and historians who stressed their Dacian and Daco-Roman heritage should suffice as an example. Both intellectual strains shared the conviction that Romanians, whether they derived from Romans or Dacians, were the first inhabitants of Moldavia, Wallachia and Transylvania, a contention by which they demonstrate their difference from Hungarians or Slavs. Such "political" myths belong in the broad "margins" of historiography researched by Grabski and other aforementioned Polish, Czech, and German historians (I put "margins" into quotation marks because, in fact, the myth is often more important – and no less true – than the fact on which it is built).[42]

The 19th century is a particularly rich research field in this respect as the period saw the birth of many "historical traditions," not only in the nations

---

40   Josef Macůrek, *Dějepisectví evropského východu*, Praha 1946.
41   Jerzy Jedlicki, *Źle urodzeni czyli o doświadczeniu historycznym. Scripta i postscripta*, Londyn-Warszawa 1993, 166.
42   See Petr Čornej, *Lipanské ozvěny*, Praha 1995 a reception history of the Medieval battle of Lipany and a companion to the book *Lipanská křižovatka, Příčiny, průběh a historický význam jedné bitvy*, Praha 1992.

discussed in this study. The problem was illustrated by Lucian Boia in the example of Mihal Viteazul, who is said to have united Romanian lands and who in fact ruled over Moldavia, Wallachia and Transylvania, albeit for one year only (1599-1600). This fact did not prevent him from playing the role of a national hero in the works of Mihail Kogălniceanu and Nicolae Bălcescu in mid-19th century.[43] Other "national rebirths," "awakenings," and "renaissances" could yield many analogous examples. The Czech "national awakening" is the best known and, to some extent, universal example because – due to the path-breaking research by Miroslav Hroch – it is used as a referential frame for other equivalent phenomena.[44]

Vladimír Macura authored a very concise analysis of the Czech "national awakening." He believed that the very idea of comparing the efforts of a national movement to an awakening is connected with a mythical, non-linear understanding of time.[45] Macura's works offer a catalogue of various strategies used by Czech patriots to "discover" (or construct) a national past, sometimes resulting in brand new national traditions.[46] He also raised the question of the imagined traditions originating in the 19th century, claiming that "we were made of illusions, myths and mystifications."[47] The task of the scholar is not to demystify ideas of the past, even in a just cause, but rather to discover the origins of the social or national imagined past and the mechanisms governing it.[48]

As already mentioned, the "Czech" perspective is also applied by non-Czech authors, sometimes even in a much sterner manner, as in the case of Maria Bobrownicka, who stressed the cultural infertility of the Slavic myth in Central and South-eastern Europe, especially in Bohemia and Slovakia.[49] Boia's book showed that attempts to describe national myths using historical categories can meet with a violent reaction.[50] Maria Janion and Maria Żmigrodzka analyse the

---

43   Lucian Boia, *History and Myth in Romanian Consciousness*, Budapest 2001, 39.

44   Miroslav Hroch, *Social Preconditions of National Revival in Europe*, Cambridge 1985.

45   Vladimír Macura, *Znamení zrodu. České národní obrození jako kulturní typ*, Praha 1995, 79-80.

46   See Vladimír Macura *Český sen*, Praha 1998 as well as Robert Burton Pynsent, *Questions of Identity (Czech and Slovak Ideas of Nationality and Personality)*, Budapest 1994.

47   Vladimír Macura, *Masarykovy boty a jiné sem(o)fejetony*, Praha 1993, 16.

48   See Jiří Rak, *Bývali Čechové... České historické mýty a stereotypy*, Praha 1994, 7.

49   Maria Bobrownicka, *Narkotyk mitu. Szkice o świadomości narodowej i kulturowej Słowian zachodnich i południowych*, Kraków 1995, 39.

50   Lucian Boia describes the violent critiques of his approach which followed the publication of his *Istorie şi mit în conştiinţa românească*, Bucureşti 1997 – see. Boia, *History and Myth*, 1-2.

myths of Polish Romanticism in an only slightly different manner, with relation to literature.[51]

The formation of nations in the 19th century has become one of the most popular topics of comparative research over the past few decades. Christoph Conrad and Sebastian Conrad stress that this approach is useful also for work in fields that are traditionally considered "untranslatable," i.e. national in a very strict sense. In other words, the belief in the uniqueness of nations is one of the most common forms of faith.[52]

Vladimír Macura analysed 19th century patriotic culture, as well as Czech myths of the Communist period.[53] There are undoubtedly serious differences between Communist ideology and the "national awakening," starting with a completely different definition of time. While the reborn Czech nation saw itself in an eternal cycle, socialist culture was based on the notion of a new beginning and perceived time as running toward a strictly defined goal along the lines of progress.[54] This might raise some doubts as to the concept of a continuity of ideas between the 19th century and the Communist period. To eliminate those doubts, I propose to forego theoretical considerations for a moment and to concentrate on the phase of development of Soviet historiography which was supposed to set the tone for East Central European historical sciences after 1945.

The Bolshevik takeover was not directly followed by any general change in Russian historiography. It was only in 1926 that a Marxist Historical Society was created, and a new methodological orientation was officially approved at an historical congress in 1928-1929. The new interpretation of Russian history was inspired mainly by Mikhail N. Pokrovsky. He attacked Russian historiography, criticising particularly all attempts at portraying Russia as a unique and special case of a country following its own *Sonderweg*. According to Pokrovsky, Russia had developed just as any other country, it was simply backward. Traditionally crucial elements of Russian history, such as the country's territorial expansion, were seen not as any particular tsar's success, but as a result of the development of trade (by this token even Alexander Nevsky was a servant to capital). The christianisation of Russia was deemed "an incident" and wars against the Tatars were viewed as a struggle between two cultures at the same stage of development. Pokrovsky accused tsardom of imperialism, and interpreted the

---

51   Maria Janion & Maria Żmigrodzka, *Romantyzm i historia* (2nd edition), Gdańsk 2001.
52   Christoph Conrad & Sebastian Conrad, "Wie vergleicht man Historiographien?," in: *Die Nation schreiben. Geschichtswissenschaft im internationalen Vergleich*, eds. Christoph Conrad & Sebastian Conrad, Göttingen 2002, 19-20.
53   Vladimír Macura, *Šťastný věk – Symboly, emblémy a mýty 1948-89*, Praha 1992.
54   See Rafał Stobiecki, *Bolszewizm a historia. Próba rekonstrukcji bolszewickiej filozofii dziejów*, Łódź 1998, 65.

Polish-Russian wars of the early 17th century not as Polish aggression but as a social struggle against the tsar. Even more strikingly, Pokrovsky claimed that Russians were most likely of Finnish origin, which likened his approach to Franciszek Duchiński's fantastic theories formed in the mid-19th century.[55]

The domination of Pokrovsky's interpretation of history did not last long. He died in 1932, and his theories were rebuked only two years later. They were characterised as abstract, unusable in school education, and indebted to inappropriate sociological frameworks. But in fact – as foreign commentators noted – it was Pokrovsky's hostility towards Russian national traditions that invited the most disapproval.[56] His sociological leanings were soon displaced by a Stalinist model of historiography, referring in many respects to earlier interpretations of Russian history.[57] The new narrative of national history was to be filled with a Russian-Soviet patriotic spirit, and was indebted to the Russian heirs of German historicism in its method. Like Ranke, Karamzin and others, Soviet historians referred to the state as a focal point of history. The importance of each state was estimated according to its military power. Even the term "historicism" was adapted in the USSR as "Marxist-Leninist historicism," letting it survive the next crisis of historiography in 1945 when "western" notions fell out of fashion.[58] Russian nationalism achieved its peak in Soviet historiography during World War II. Josef Macůrek noted almost immediately after its end that "You could see everywhere that the Russian past was viewed not in Marxist, but in patriotic terms, as a fight for independence and freedom against numerous aggressors and plunderers, above all 'against the German element'; it was described as the Russian people's eventual rise to power, the development of outstanding military skills, but was simultaneously also a struggle for freedom only, which hugely affected the universal culture. Russian science elevated the moral and spiritual forces in Russians, and we may say that it contributed to this historical victory in the defence of Russia, civilisation, and the national existence of many nations conquered by the Germans."[59]

The victory of "national values" over Pokrovsky's interpretation was not easy, with some Russian Marxist historians seriously fearful of a relapse of nationalism. During the Russian offensive of May 1944, Anna Pankratova

---

55   See Macůrek, *Dějepisectví*, 259-264.
56   Ibidem, 260.
57   Н. В. Иллерицкая, "Становление советской историографической традиции: наука, не обретшая лица," in: *Советская историография*, ed. Ю. Н. Афанасьев, Москва 1996, 165-170.
58   Por. Eduard Thaden, "Marxist Historicism and the Crises of Soviet Historiography," *Jahrbücher für Geschichte Osteuropas* 2003/1, 17-20.
59   Macůrek, *Dějepisectví*, 264.

issued a letter to the Central Committee of the Communist Party of the Soviet Union, criticising the re-evaluations of historical figures such as Ivan the Terrible, Peter the Great or Alexander I. She observed that Soviet historians (and Soviet propaganda) had lost sight of the fact that the masses were the subject of history, not the leaders. In late May and early June 1944, a meeting took place in Moscow between representatives of the two tendencies of interpretation of national history, all aspiring to be Marxist. While they came to no final solution, Pankratova was later punished for distributing material pertaining to the meeting.[60]

An interesting variant of the same evolution occurred in Ukraine. The situation of historians there was even more uncertain than in Russia. Not only did they not know whether they should interpret the history of Ukraine from a "class" or "national" perspective, but they also had to determine the role played in it by Russia. Soviet Ukraine had its own Pokrovsky in a young historian, Matvyi Yavorsky. His theses on national history competed with the dominant "national" interpretation of Mikhailo Hrushevsky. Javorsky rejected the idea of the nation as the driving force of history; at the same time, he was not at all pro-Russian. In his interpretation of the Bolshevik revolution in Ukraine, he underlined its peculiar characteristics which were dissimilar to those of the Russian Revolution. Javorsky's success – the official condemnation of Hrushevsky's interpretation - was almost immediately followed by his own fall. Javorsky was arrested in 1933; Hrushevsky, who had been recognised as 'fascist', died a year later. During the war, the historical policy in Ukraine bowed to the necessity of boosting confidence in national values, but still without any clear guidelines. *Zhdanovshchyna*, which for Russians meant the campaign against "Occidentalism" and liberalism, for Ukrainians was also a fight against nationalism. This increased the chaos in the Marxist interpretation of Ukraine's history. Finally, as in Russia, Ukrainian Marxist historiography similarly adopted the Hrushevskyian "national" paradigm, combining it with elements of historical materialism.

By the second half of the 1940s, other, newly conquered nations were expected to adjust multiple professions, including those related to the historical sciences, to the Soviet model. However, Marxism, soon to become the only acceptable methodology, was no longer understood in the same way in Bolshevik Russia. Its Soviet variation borrowed heavily from the tradition of Russian historiography and the Russian national tradition. The variations formulated in the satellite countries were also less likely to break away from

---

60   Maureen Perrie, *The Cult of Ivan the Terrible in Stalin's Russia*, Houndmills 2001, 99-
      102.

existing traditions than to revise and re-evaluate them, along with the perspectives on Russia's role in the history of Central and Eastern Europe.

This current work attempts for the most part to find an answer to one question: how did the Marxist historians of Poland, Czechoslovakia and the GDR employ national historical and historiographical traditions? The reader will likely spot the differences between the mode of analysis of Marxist-Leninist historiographies proposed herein and their previous evaluations. Outlining the relationships between different Marxist-Leninist historiographies, I usually (though not without exceptions) put stress on "lateral" relations (between Polish, Czech, Slovak and East German historians) more than on "vertical" relations (between each satellite historiography and Soviet historiography). Analysing the content of Marxist works, I rarely depend on Party publications (though statements on historical matters from relevant directorships will be frequently referenced). I strive to maintain a focus on historical publications without tampering with the facts, if possible, even if the works in question fail to retain a proper scientific profile. Finally, in my analysis of the views of Marxists, I put greater stress on elements of continuity and on references to non-Marxist historiographical traditions – that is, while conscious of a lack of continuity in numerous aspects of scholarly life, I focus on the signals of a continuity of historical thought. All these factors of my analysis constitute a deliberate attempt at presenting a different, and, in my opinion, more complete, perspective on Marxist historical sciences in Central and Eastern Europe. It is more of an invitation to debate than a closing remark on a past discussion.

The extent and propriety of using the terms "Marxist" and "Stalinist" with reference to the intellectual or cultural phenomena of the Stalinist period remains questionable. Georg G. Iggers points to differences between "Western Marxism" and the official Marxist philosophy of international Communist parties. Leszek Kołakowski, on the other hand, claims that Stalinism was in a certain sense a form of Marxism: Marxism-Leninism of the Soviet type was deeply dependent on "classic" Marxist thought. This view naturally does not indicate that Stalinism as such was the only possible and logically necessary extension of Marx's thought.[61]

There is, on another note, no specifically original concept behind the time frame which I have chosen for this study. The dates differ between the countries under discussion – I accept the boundary dates specified by Polish, Czech, Slovak and German scholars. In the case of Poland, these are 1948 or 1949 and

---

61   See Georg G. Iggers, *Historiography in the Twentieth Century. From Scientific Objectivity to the Postmodern Challenge*, Middletown, Conn. 1997, 78-79; Leszek Kołakowski, *Main Currents of Marxism: The Founders, The Golden Age, The Breakdown*, New York 2000, 1110-1118.

1956; with respect to Czechoslovakia, the years 1948 and 1963 are assumed to mark the beginning and end of the Stalinist period. Allowing for lengthy publication processes, I used 1965 as a final boundary date for my research, and in some cases went as far as 1968. In the history of the GDR, the starting date of the Stalinist period is widely assumed to be 1949 (which is, by the way, also the date of the country's formation itself), and the closing date is put at the end of the 1960s, a period which saw an ongoing centralisation of schooling, an introduction of another school reform, as well as generational changes in scholarly circles.[62]

---

62   These dates refer to the generally applied chronology of cultural history and, as such, are not always accepted by historians of historiography. Nevertheless, they represent not only the main turning points in the scientific policy in the Soviet bloc but also prove to be flexible enough to reflect specific features of historiography (i.e., the time needed for the publication and reception of a given publication). For the criticism of my approach, see Martin Nodl, *Dějepisectví mezi vědou a politikou. Úvahy o historiografii 19. a 20. století*, Brno 2007, 106.

Chapter II
The Organisation of Historical Sciences
and the Creation of Early Postwar Narrations

The impact of war and occupation between 1939 and 1945 on historical scholarship varied considerably from country to country. Polish historiography suffered heavy losses in academic personnel. Moreover, with the death of Marceli Handelsman in 1945, postwar historiography was deprived of its most innovative theoretician. However, the reorganisation of research and education progressed even in an almost totally devastated Warsaw. Influential figures in the field of history, such as Tadeusz Manteuffel, the first postwar director of the Historical Institute of Warsaw University and, in subsequent decades, the first director of the Institute of History within the Polish Academy of Sciences, were also in contact with the new political leaders from the Communist Party.

None of the other historiographies examined here had to deal with such a drastic collapse of infrastructure and such devastating human losses. Slovak historians actually profited from the violent dissolution of Czechoslovakia. The subsequent expulsion of Czech professors from the only Slovak university in Bratislava opened positions for their Slovak colleagues during wartime. After 1945 only a small group of nationalist historical propagandists fled the country to avoid the approaching Soviet army. The rest proved to be much more self-confident and sceptical towards the idea of Czechoslovak unity than had been the case during the interwar period.

Though the Czech universities were closed under German occupation, historians were allowed to perform research and publish their findings, and the Czech Academy for Sciences and Arts (Česká akademie věd a umění, ČAVU) operated unperturbed. Losses in scholarly personnel were limited to the few murdered and tormented at the concentration camps.[63] Paradoxically, the casualties sustained both before and just after the war proved much more significant. Josef Pekař, one of the most outstanding Czech historians, died in 1937. That same year saw the death of his rival in the dispute over the meaning of Czech history, the first president of Czechoslovakia, Tomáš Garrigue

---

63   Peter Heumos, "Geschichtswissenschaft und Politik in der Tschechoslowakei," *Jahrbücher für Gechische Osteuropas* 1978/4, 543.

Masaryk; while not a historian, he often took part in discussions on Czech history and formed the outlook of numerous Czech scholars. Kamil Krofta, a survivor of the Terezin camp, died in 1945, while Josef Šusta, accused by an overeager "patriot's opinion" of being a collaborator with the Germans, committed suicide the same year. As a result, the historical community was robbed of a number of scholars distinguished not only by the extent of their output, but also by their potential for being leaders, capable, like Poland's Tadeusz Manteuffel or Stanisław Lorenz, of acting as representatives of the scholarly world before the authorities.

In occupied Germany, the key task was to deal with scholars who collaborated with the National-Socialist regime. In the eyes of many students, especially those expelled from universities during Hitler's reign, the steps that rectors took to denazify the schools were not radical enough. At any rate, administrators from the occupying states soon took control over personnel matters. They worked hard to perform a thorough denazification, leading to an actual break in continuity in personnel in the scholarly departments of the Soviet occupation zone: over 80% of professors active before 1945 could not continue to occupy their posts after the war.[64] In spite of denazification and the Soviet army administration's strict supervision, new universities and scientific institutions began to form swiftly in the Eastern part of the country as well. All decisions concerning the scientific policy were made by the Soviet military administrators, with the aid of the Deutsche Zentralverwaltung für Volksbildung (German Central Administration for National Education), serving as a German "conveyor belt."[65]

Throughout the first postwar years, the work of the Polish, Czech, Slovak and German historians concentrated on reconstructing scientific institutions, replenishing archives and libraries, and reinstating regular study programs at universities. In Poland and Czechoslovakia, scholars clearly maintained ties to the prewar period, putting stress most of all on the independence of research. Though it seems that for Czech historians, as for most of their native society, the

---

64   Connelly, *Captive University*, 4.
65   Stefan   Ebenfeld,   *Geschichte   nach   Plan?   Die   Instrumentalisierung   der Geschichtswissenschaft in der DDR am Beispiel des Museums für Deutsche Geschichte in Berlin (1950 bis 1955)*, Marburg 2001. 30. During the first post-war years, the conditions in which German universities operated were rather unusual, also because of the constant but unpredictable Soviet control. The university archives at Leipzig include a description of an unexpected visit at the university by a Soviet major. The author of the document responded with utter surprise to the major's offer that he would decide which of the university employees dismissed for being members of the NSDAP should be allowed to get back to work. – Universitätsarchiv Leipzig, R. 219, Bd. 2 [Microfilm 1101].

Communist Party did not constitute a threat (in any case, Communists won over 43% of the popular vote in Bohemia during the free elections of 1946.). In this context, Alexej Kusák writes of the irrationality of the Czech intelligentsia, which traced "Fascism" in petit bourgeois behaviour, while at the same time, failing to see it at work in Communist-supported state control, collectivism, and anti-German nationalism.[66] In these circumstances, the Czech historians' relations with their Slovak counterparts could indeed seem to be the biggest problem to tackle. Having suffered a far worse fate and – even more importantly – having had a chance to observe the Communist *Machtübernahme* at work, the Poles seem to have looked to the future of their profession with more caution. In the Soviet occupation zone in Germany, scholars were effectively barred from any attempt at self-government; all decisions concerning programs and personnel were issued by the Soviet occupational government in the form of military orders.

In the process of achieving power, various national Communist parties searched for legitimacy. The broad social support the Czech Communists enjoyed was an exception rather than the rule. Even in the Slovak part of the state the Communist Party lost sympathy during the early postwar years. In this situation, the Communists looked in the first instance to national culture and national history for support in the assumption of power. All attempts to reshape the preexisting Communist historical narratives were marked by this necessity. The interwar Communist movements were extremely critical of national traditions of any kind, offering an internationalist counter-narrative in opposition to dominant nationalist interpretations. This changed partly during the second half of the 1930s and certainly during the war, evolving along with the Soviet historical narrative. Thus the adoption of the Soviet paradigm in 1945 did not mean adopting the native Communist tradition of historical thought but rather searching for a new interpretation that would be "national in form and socialist in content."

In their first attempts to attract the sympathy of the "common people" Polish, Czech, and Slovak Communists invoked recent history. A strong anti-German sentiment was common currency in postwar Europe, not restricted to its eastern parts. Poland and Czechoslovakia were among the countries that expelled German populations from their older or newly "reunited" western areas. Both states referred to a long history of conflicts with Germans, stressing

---

66   Alexej Kusák, *Kultura a politika v Československu 1945-1956*, Praha 1998, 208.

at the same time the importance of Slavic brotherhood in past and future battles.[67]

The need for a widely accepted national Communist policy was responsible for the development of a network of Polish research institutes, the most prominent of which was the Western Institute (Instytut Zachodni) in Poznań. Under the directorship of Medievalist Zygmunt Wojciechowski, Instytut Zachodni was a significant landmark on the Polish historiographic landscape, publishing its own periodical *Przegląd Zachodni* (The Western Review) and opening branches in several Polish cities. Wojciechowski was not only a gifted historian, but also a nationalist politician. In the interwar period he had been a proponent of the concept of 'Polish maternal lands,' a national geography including more or less the lands that were transferred from the collapsed Third Reich to Poland after 1945. Wojciechowski's book *Polska—Niemcy: Dziesięć wieków zmagania* (Poland and Germany: A Thousand Years of Struggle), first published in 1933, reappeared in 1945 in a new edition, considerably more critical of Germany than the first one. According to Wojciechowski, the whole western branch of the Slavic world had been shaped by constant military struggle against German aggression. The Germans, he contended, were unable to cohabit peacefully with Slavs, since they 'biologically' hated everything Slavic. Now, after 1945, "A new epoch of the Slavic march to the west has begun, replacing the German *Drang nach Osten*. Those who cannot comprehend that, will not understand the new era and will not recognize the true role of Poland in the new international reality."

The *Przegląd Zachodni* vividly supported Wojciechowski's view of Polish–German relations. At the same time, the editors of the journal expressed their loyalty to the Communist leadership and their gratitude to Stalin for the new and, in their view, legitimate western border of Poland. As a mixture of political and scholarly arguments, this so-called Polish western idea was a mirror image of the German *Ostforschung* with a pan-Slavic sentiment. As such, it had no Czechoslovak counterpart. Although the German problem was crucial for the Czech national movement from its beginnings (and perhaps because it was so important), there was no separate Czech or Slovak "western idea." Consequently, no person could embody such a movement in the manner of Wojciechowski, who provided a face for this political tendency in Poland. The expulsion of Germans from Czech lands was accompanied by texts that questioned the moral and cultural values of the defeated enemy. Historical

---

67   See Edmund Dmitrów, *Niemcy i okupacja hitlerowska w oczach Polaków. Poglądy i opinie z lat 1945–1948*, Warszawa 1987 and *Obraz Němců, Rakouska a Německa v české společnosti 19. a 20. století*, eds. Jan Křen & Eva Broklová, Praha 1998.

writings described a thousand years of Czech-German struggles and an evil innate in the national character of Germans whose aggressive inclinations had led inexorably to the emergence of the Nazi dictatorship. However, in contrast to the Polish situation, postwar Czechoslovak historiography did not view Germans as a popular topic.[68] But there was another motif that attracted the attention of Czech and Slovak historians: the idea of Slavic brotherhood. An editorial in the first issue of the postwar *Český Časopis Historický* (Czech Historical Journal) claimed that "the Slavic idea in its new Russian understanding makes us sure that our motherland will never be a part of Greater Germania and, with all our frank sympathy for Europe, we will be allowed to develop as an independent nation."[69] One of the most important animators of this Slavophile campaign was Zdeněk Nejedlý, musicologist, minister of education, first president of the Czechoslovak Academy of Sciences, and the unquestioned leader of Czech Marxist historical sciences.

As in the Polish example, some Czech historians, who were rather far removed from the Communist camp, nonetheless supported the pan-Slavic and anti-German line. In 1947 a liberal Moravian historian, Ladislav Hosák, published his history of the Czech lands,[70] a rather typical example of interwar Czech historiography. Nevertheless, it introduced nationalist elements that argued against the more general liberal line. The Hussites were, according to Hosák, "cleansing our country of a religious and national enemy." Lajos Kossuth was characterised as a "denationalised Slovak."[71] But the most critical remarks were reserved for Germans, who were characterised as having chosen since 1848 a path of hostility towards everything Czech, a path which led straight to Munich and the Second World War, and which culminated in the expulsion of the incurably traitorous Germans. The book ends with an affirmation of the belief in the "Slavic orientation" of Czechoslovak policy and with predictions of a glorious future for Czechoslovak-Russian brotherhood.

A largely similar picture was drawn by František Bokes, the Slovak author of a history of Slovakia and the Slovaks (published in 1946).[72] Both Hosák and Bokes mixed the language of interwar geopolitics with radical new ideological

---

68   Ferdinand Seibt, "Die Deutschen in der tschechischen Historiographie 1945–1990", in: *Im geteilten Europa: Tschechen, Slowaken und Deutsche und ihre Staaten 1948-1989*, eds. Hans Lemberg, Jan Křen & Dušan Kováč, München 1992, 43.

69   Václav Chaloupecký, "Pozdrav nové svobodě", *Český Časopis Historický*, 47 (1946), 2.

70   Ladislav Hosák, *Nové československé dějiny*, Praha 1947.

71   Ibidem, 421.

72   František Bokes, *Dejiny Slovenska a Slovákov od najstarších čias po oslobodenie*, Bratislava 1946.

tendencies. Traditional references to Slavic mutuality gained new meanings when uttered in a new political context.

In the late 1940s when both Poland and Czechoslovakia entered a period of Stalinisation, the orthodox historical outlook underwent a rapid change. During a conference in Wrocław in 1950, Zygmunt Wojciechowski was condemned for his anti-German chauvinism. A local Marxist historian Ewa Maleczyńska commented: "I think that those who understand the postwar changes according to the dictum that once they beat us and now it's their time to be beaten—those who want to replace the German *Drang nach Osten* with the Slavic 'Drang nach Westen'—I think that those people don't understand the meaning of recent developments." [73] As a consequence, though Polish, Czech, or Slovak Marxist historical writings never lost their anti-German undertones, the candid blend of nationalist and Communist perspectives on the past was for a time marginalised.

In the postwar period, the "revolutionary" was sometimes combined with the "national" even at the cost of reproducing explicitly nationalistic interpretations. Though short, this period was then indicative of the Communist politics of history as well as of the reaction of historical communities in East Central Europe. The Communists learned how to approach a wider audience with a popular vision of the national past; the historians learned how to retain at least a part of their freedom in exchange for close cooperation with the new power.

***

In each of the aforementioned cases, the authorities introduced a number of solutions that stripped universities of their autonomous status and expanded the state's importance to the fashioning of academic careers. The properties owned by academic institutions were nationalised. In Poland and Czechoslovakia, the Soviet system of collective institutional leadership and central planning in research was introduced; the former was implemented in the GDR in 1968. The plan was enforced by basic party cells at every university. New, Soviet-inspired academic titles were introduced. [74] The work conducted in historical

---

73   Ewa Maleczyńska, "Problem polsko-niemiecki w dotychczasowej historiografii polskiej," in: *Historiografia polska wobec problemu polsko-niemieckiego. Referaty i dyskusja na konferencji międzyśrodowiskowej we Wrocławiu 6 lipca 1950*, Wrocław 1951, 15.

74   See Connelly, *Captive University*, 58-69; Ralph Jessen, *Akademische Elite und kommunistische Diktatur. Die ostdeutsche Hochschullehrschaft in der Ulbricht-Ära*, Göttingen 1999, 52-64; Teresa Suleja, *Uniwersytet Wrocławski w okresie centralizmu stalinowskiego 1950-1955*, Wrocław 1995, 19-24; Józef K. Szłapczyński, *Zarząd szkołą wyższą w Polsce Ludowej*, Warszawa 1968, Janusz Tymowski, *Organizacja szkolnictwa*

departments, both at the universities and at the academies of science (newly formed in the early 1950s), was expected to embrace the ruling ideology, not only through the choice of a uniform methodology, but also through "worldview-affecting" activities: academic gatherings and ideological instruction. The scientific candidate exam, introduced as a result of the implementation of new academic titles, focused on testing one's basic knowledge of Marxism. To be able to tackle it, younger tenured scholars were expected to attend special preparatory lectures. Though the exam was mandatory only for the younger cadres, all scholars employed at scholarly institutions were expected to attend the exam preparations.

Yet, the changes involving structure, schedule, political education, academic titles and planning were not at all sufficient in transforming schools into institutions capable of propagating the achievements of Marxism-Leninism. While Polish, Czech and Slovak Communists gradually tightened the noose over their respective countries, borrowing heavily from reservoirs of nationalist interpretations of history along the way, they also made their first attempts at changing the social profile of students. The goal of the ruling caste in each of the countries under discussion was a "proletarianisation" of the universities, that is, effecting a situation in which card-carrying Communist professors of worker and peasant origins would teach the youth of worker and peasant classes to be good citizen and Party members.

The authorities ultimately failed to transform universities into a power base in Poland. John Connelly, who has studied this problem, stressed the importance of the strong relationship binding Polish professors and their students, which was a characteristic feature of scholarly life in Poland, and which made it impossible to drive a wedge between the two groups (a feat accomplished in the GDR). This failure was not only a result of the ineffectiveness of authorities, but also a consequence of differences among the scholarly traditions of Poland, Germany and Czechoslovakia. In the two latter countries, modern universities never became an autonomous community of scholars and students. On the contrary: they were deeply rooted in the structures of the state and therefore susceptible to its dealings. Polish universities were renowned for their curious, "lateral" structure of half-formal and informal relations which helped build a dense and broad network, observable even to this day. It played a seminal role in the struggle for control over the peoples' minds. University employees were accountable most of all to their own community of intelligentsia; contrarily, in

wyższego w Polsce, Warszawa 1980; Bolesław Krasiewicz, *Odbudowa szkolnictwa wyższego w Polsce Ludowej w latach 1944-1948*, Wrocław 1976.

Germany and Czechoslovakia universities were not as distinguishable from the rest of society and much more dependent on the Party.

Despite the limitations which could not have been overcome through scientific policies introduced by the PPR and the PZPR, the struggle for "proletarianisation" of the universities could be said to have yielded one definite result. Though neither professors nor students joined the Party *en masse*—and those of them who did never severed ties with the community—the authorities managed to ensure that a significant number of the youth of authentic worker-peasant origin studied at universities. During the 1950s, these students amounted to about 50% of all admitted first year students.[75] However, youth with an "appropriate" background did not necessarily act as puppets of the authorities – having found themselves at the universities, they were influenced by a cadre that was indifferent, and at times even unsympathetic toward the government. According to Connelly, "With the doors to seminar rooms or lecture halls shut, the Party was left alone in the corridor."[76] As a result, after 1956 the situation was returned to the state prior to the "Stalinisation of the universities."[77] Besides, even the problematic success of "proterianising" efforts is questionable; Connelly seems to give undue credit to admission politics. Looking at the social stratification of those admitted, as well as all candidates, it is apparent that already in 1949 workers-peasants made up a third of the Warsaw candidates, while "working intelligentsia" was responsible for half of all applications; moreover, this breakdown persisted throughout the Stalinist period. It would seem, then, that the long-term effects described by John Connelly were secured as much through the Stalinisation of the universities as through accelerated social advancement, the migration of numerous peasant families into towns and the pauperisation of society. One could therefore hazard the claim that, at least as far as the Stalinist period is concerned, the significant rise in the percentage of students of worker-peasant origins in Poland was not caused by Party policies

---

75   According to the data collected by Connelly for the academic year 1949-50, there were
      as many as 45.6% of first-year students of the kind in the entire country. However,
      already in the following year, as much as 62.2% were admitted. In subsequent years, the
      percentage steadily lowered, reaching in 1956-57 a value near to that of 1949-50
      (48,5%). John Connelly, "Szkolnictwo wyższe w Europie Środkowej i Wschodniej w
      epoce stalinizacji," in: *Skryte oblicze...*, 227-228.
76   Ibidem, 227.
77   Jan Uher, "Kampaň proti tzv. buržoáznemu nacjonalizmu," in: *Od diktatúry k diktatúre.
      Slovensko v rokoch 1945-1953 (Zborník materiálov z vedeckej konferencie v
      Smoleniciach 6. – 8. Decembra 1994)*, ed. Michal Barnovský, Bratislava 1995, 105-113;
      Grzegorz Gąsior, *Stalinowska Słowacja. Proces „buržuazyjnych nacjonalistów" w 1954
      roku*, Warszawa 2006.

toward universities; in fact, it was an effect of huge social changes brought about not by the authorities (though they played a part), but rather by the war. A far larger proportion of candidates of worker-peasant background became students after the war simply because so many more of them applied.

The efforts of Central European Communist Parties to transform universities politically and socially yielded divergent results. Authorities showed the greatest consistency in this regard in the Soviet occupation zone in Germany, and later in the GDR. Here, universities were turned into "proletarian" outposts controlled by the SED. The reaction of the majority of the East German intelligentsia to the worker's uprising in Berlin in 1953 already proved the value of this policy. Neither in Czechoslovakia, nor in Poland did the governments succeed in winning the genuine support of the intelligentsia. In fact, the opposite was the case: it was the intelligentsia that served as the breeding ground for the leaders of social revolts up until and including 1989. The Polish Communists' policy toward the universities did not yield the desired effects. Though the social base of the student community broadened, the authorities and government's role in the achievement of this goal is debatable. The Polish universities avoided purges, and their staff did not join the Party *en masse* – which had occurred in Czechoslovakia, where the government managed to put the universities under Communist control, but failed to fill them with representatives of the urban and rural proletariat.

The defeats and victories of the academic politics of the Communist states and parties had crucial significance for the communities of historians in each of the countries under discussion. In the late 1940s in the GDR, after denazification and another purge, this community almost had to form anew. Communist historians enjoyed a numerical superiority over their "bourgeois" colleagues, growing with every new batch of graduates from "proletarianised" universities. In Czechoslovakia, where purges were not as thorough and occurred only after 1948, the community of historians was also shaped for the most part by Communists. Representatives of the "bourgeois" academy were pushed to the margins, relocated to universities outside Prague, and sometimes even barred from teaching altogether. In Poland, the community was led by "bourgeois" historians, forced to endlessly negotiate with the authorities. Over the long term, their position was reinforced by the fact that, at the expense of PZPR, they retained control over schooling of the younger generations of scholars.

Despite numerous differences among the communities of historians in 1950s' Poland, Czechoslovakia and the GDR, the government of each of these countries set similar goals for the scholars to meet. They were supposed to create a new, Marxist historical science, and record it in magazines and in general works on national history. Deviations from the established norms were unacceptable, and individualities were condemned. The historians worked in a fearful climate caused by the terror aimed against enemies of the new order, whether real or "objective" (who learned of their guilt only during interrogations). At times, it affected education and science in a highly direct manner. The so-called campaign against bourgeois nationalism, begun in Slovakia in 1950, started out as an effort to locate the Czechoslovak "supporters" of Tito, but, with the arrest of the commissioner of education (an equivalent of a minister in the Slovak government) Ladislav Novomeský, many teachers – historians as well – were removed from schools.[78]

Despite obvious examples of Stalinist terror in each of the countries under discussion, we should also pose the question: is the monochromatic image of the 1950s really representative of what occurred outside prison walls and camp fences? Or, if we are talking about the intelligentsia – was the dictatorship of new governments and "faithful" artists and scientists an absolute rule? In each case, we are dealing with a process which took years to complete, a process of bringing together authorities' demands and historians' responsiveness.

Social scientists discuss and exchange opinions in scientific journals as well as at a variety of conventions, conferences and congresses. Obviously, quite a few of these occurred at locations and times which are the focus of this study. To describe the circumstances in which historians performed their work, however, it is advisable to distinguish those meetings that played a crucial role in shaping the views and actions of their community. Some of those "special" conferences are vividly remembered, almost as symbolic events, and memories of them are held to this day; in the case of Poland, one such event was definitely the First Methodological Conference of Polish Historians in Otwock, at the turn of 1952. A similar role can be ascribed to historical associations' conventions and to international historians' congresses (which were especially well-suited to perform the role). Each such event, to an extent, provides insight into dominant intellectual currents, the contemporaneous political situation, and the interpersonal relations within the organised historians' guild. As far as my own interests are concerned, of highest importance will be the conferences, conventions, etc., during which the representatives of "bourgeois"

---

78   Josef Hanzal "Čeští historici před únorem 1948," *Český Časopis Historický* 1993, 279-281. See Antonín Kostlán, "K vývoji českého dějepisectví v letech 1945-1948," *Český Časopis Historický* 1994; Jaroslav Čechura & Jana Šetřilová, "Josef Klik a II. sjezd československých historiků," *Český Časopis Historický* 1994; Antonín Kostlán, *Druhý sjezd československých historiků (5.-11. října 1947) a jeho místo ve vývoji českého dějepisectví v letech 1935-1948*, Praha 1993.

historiography clashed with Marxists in a struggle that serves as the focal point of the current study.

The intellectual and personal continuity between prewar and postwar Czech historiography was symbolically confirmed at the II Convention of Czechoslovak Historians in 1947. The convention was at the same time a portent of coming radical changes. Its organisers, the Czechoslovak Historical Society (Československá Historická Společnost), led by Karel Stloukal, invited some 800 guests (including a negligible Slovak contingent). Foremost among the topics were historical materialism and other methodological novelties, the German question, the question of Slavic cooperation, and the problem of Czech-Slovak relations.[79] Even before the proceedings began, a conflict arose between the organisers and a group of representatives of Marxism. The latter demanded that the paper on the October Revolution and the Slavic world be presented by Zdeněk Nejedlý rather than Jan Slavík, a well-known opponent of the Soviet Union. After a discussion with the leadership of the historians' union, Slavík agreed to give the topic away to Nejedlý, but one would be excused for doubting that this concession resolved tensions. As Josef Hanzal observed, the key problem was that most of the active proponents of Marxism in its Soviet incarnation were closely connected to Slavík before the war as collaborators on the *Dějiny a přítomnost* magazine. After the war, Václav Husa, Jaroslav Charvát, Václav Čejchan, Jan Pachta, Oldřich Říha and Jaroslav Vávra found themselves among the ranks of KSČ, while their "spiritual father" became an "inveterate enemy" of the first country ruled by workers and peasants.[80]

The convention proceeded in due course until Zdeněk Nejedlý, then-current Minister of Labour and Social Affairs, took the stage to present his paper. His text sketched in a very raw outline the leading role of Soviet Union among the states and nations of the Slavs. The reaction of the public present to his talk was reserved to the utmost – some of the listeners already heard that Nejedlý's presence at the convention was practically forced upon the organisers. When Nejedlý finished his presentation, Jan Slavík took the floor with a critical response, exceeding the time allotted; among other things, he described to the congregated the methods of Stalin's dictatorial rule.[81] Instead of countering, Nejedlý left the convention in a fury, stating that the old generation was evidently unable to comprehend him (in fact, Nejedlý was Slavík's senior by 7 years). The convention concluded with a double visitation at the graves of Josef Šusta and Tomáš Garrigue Masaryk. As Josef Hanzal rightly observed,

---

79   Josef Hanzal, *Cesty české historiografie 1945-1989*, Praha 1999, 58-61.
80   Ibidem, 69.
81   Hanzal, "Čeští historici," 281.

"Reading the proceedings of the convention today, we may be surprised at the fact that just before the February catastrophe historians could allow themselves to be so carefree, at ease, and fail to see the signs of an impending threat."[82] At the same time, the conflict between the Marxist group (self-proclaimed representatives of the Slovak historians) and Karel Stloukal presaged a coming storm.[83]

As is well known, the danger materialised several months after the historians' convention, in the shape of a political upheaval with utterly dramatic consequences for Czech historians. In the following years, the authorities stepped cautiously through the field of historical sciences, avoiding a direct confrontation between Marxist and non-Marxist historians; instead, administrative decisions were carried out, and debates were replaced by purges in historical departments. The gradual liberalisation of cultural life that began in the first half of the 1960s was also not the work of "bourgeois" academics, but of card-carrying Marxists, including personages so vital to the shape of the 1950s as František Graus or Josef Macek. This is the reason why, until the early 1960s, meetings in which Czech historians took part were for the most part manifestations of the community's ideological unity. Executive decisions by the Party took a special importance for the period's historians; for instance, in May, 1951, the Central Committee of the KSČ accepted the motion that works on Czech history should include a broader focus on the most recent events. As Nejedlý put it, scholars should become interested in Lenin's Prague rather than the Baroque Prague.[84] Yet none of the other similar ideologically-charged conferences became such a visible focal point – their results were known well before they occurred, and they served more as conveyor belts for motions that had already been accepted behind closed doors. No "mass conversions" were expected, since they were proclaimed before the fact: people who did not appear likely to cooperate were robbed of the power to affect either the scholarly community or students.

The ground-breaking moment in Czechoslovak historiography, which also attained the rank of a symbolic event, was the involvement of 200 Czech and Slovak historians in the international congress of historical sciences in Vienna in 1965. At that point, the thaw had already arrived: cultural and artistic personalities had abandoned Socialist-Realist patterns, the Prague Spring had just begun, and heretofore "hardliner" Marxists like Graus or Macek were backing away from Party orthodoxy. Historians arrived at the congress on a

---

82   Ibidem, 282.
83   Heumos, "Geschichtswissenschaft", 547-548.
84   Kostlán, "Druhý sjezd," 276-278.

small, rented ship. Both in Vienna and during the following year's conference on the problem of nation in the Habsburg monarchy, scholars from the West were surprised to see that they were dealing with actual historians, and not Party functionaries.[85] The attitudes of Czechoslovak historians must have seemed surprising, since other participants were often quite aloof toward them. Henryk Wereszycki, barred from working with students during the Stalinist period, was also expected to attend the conference, but his passport application was rejected. In a letter to Piotr Wandycz, Wereszycki commented acerbically on the differences between himself and historians from other countries of the Soviet bloc, who were allowed to attend the venue: "they travel with ease," he wrote with irony – "their luggage is small."[86]

In Slovakia, the situation developed largely along the same lines as it did in Bohemia. During the first plenary meeting of the community of Slovak historians (Slovenská Historická Spoločnost, SHS) in April 1946 in Piešťany, participants focused primarily on the problem of normalising relations with their Czech colleagues. The newly-formed Slovak Historical Society, led by Daniel Rapant, enjoyed the support (including financial) of the Slovak government. The meeting featured speeches from then-commissioner for education, Ladislav Novomeský, as well as A.J.P. Taylor.[87] No Marxist minority appeared because none had existed at the time.[88] The second plenary meeting, scheduled for 1947, was cancelled. Several weeks after the scheduled meeting, one of the secretaries of the union of historians, Vendelin Jankovič, was arrested for allegedly taking part in an anti-government conspiracy.[89] Then, several months before a further meeting, scheduled for 1948, Czechoslovakia underwent a political coup.

The most important changes within the Slovak historical community took place during the process of "verifying" university personnel, just like in Bohemia.[90] Purges affected the historians' society as well. The discharge of Daniel Rapant as the president of SHS (and a professor at the University of

85   Jiří Kořalka, "Czechosłowacja," in: *Historiografia krajów Europy Środkowo-Wschodniej*, eds. Jerzy Kłoczowski & Paweł Kras, Lublin 1997, 51.

86   Piotr Wandycz, "Między starymi a nowymi laty," in: *Henryk Wereszycki (1898-1990). Historia w życiu historyka*, eds. Elżbieta Orman & Antoni Cetnarowicz, Kraków 2001, 265.

87   Lýdia Kamencová, "Vznik Slovenskej historickej spoločnosti a prvá etapa jej činnosti (1946-1950)," *Historcký Časopis SAV* 1991, 183-188.

88   Marek Havrila, *Slovenská historiografia v rokoch 1945-1968*, Prešov 2004, in: www.pulib.sk/elpub/FF/Havrila1, chapter „Slovenská historická spoločnosť v rokoch 1946-1968."

89   Ibidem.

90   Ján Mlynárik, *Diaspora historiografie. Štúdie, články a dokumenty k dejinám československej historiografie v rokoch 1969-1989*, Praha 1998, 15.

Bratislava), a man commonly named to this day as the greatest Slovak historian, became a symbolic event. Several other historians were ousted from their posts as well, and threateningly charged with anti-state activities.[91] After the "victorious February," SHS joined in with the official support of the Communist Party. The third plenary meeting of the organisation in October 1948 became one of the last occasions for expressions of protest against the changes taking place in the country as well as in the historians' union. This occasion was used by an archivist, Maria Jeršová, who declined an invitation to take part in the meeting, since her husband, a hero of the uprising of 1944, was at that point locked up in jail.[92] At any rate, this was the penultimate meeting of the SHS. Between 1950 and 1957, the organisation was practically inoperative.

The postwar historical consciousness of the Slovaks was significantly affected by the Slovak National Uprising (Slovenské Národné Povstanie, SNP), an assault on the German occupiers as well as on the pro-German Slovak government. Shifts in the official interpretation of that event render various symptoms of Stalinisation, and then of the thaw, eminently more visible. The Stalinist reinterpretation of the Uprising was related to the fact that contemporaneous Communist leaders, Gustáv Husák and Ladislav Novomeský, were accused of rightist-nationalist leanings and spent the whole Stalinist period in prison, awaiting, in all likelihood, death penalties. In this context, the yearly conferences devoted to the uprising achieved a symbolic status: in a way, they sketched out the current disposition of Slovak historiography. Jozef Jablonický compares two such conferences: The first, organised in 1953 by the Institute of History of the Slovak Academy of Science (Historický Ústav Slovenskej Akadémie Vied, HÚ SAV) shared the same outlook as Czech conferences on cosmopolitanism. There was no discussion involved other than the postulate, presented by the director of the Institute, that the presenters "unmask" the connections between the leaders of the Uprising and foreign intelligence—the Intelligence Service in particular—with more daring.[93] Another conference, in June 1964, occurred in the dramatically changed atmosphere of the "Slovak Spring."[94] The Slovak National Uprising was returned to official memory, and

---

91   Referring to L. Čulen, J. V. Gajdoš und V. Jankovič. See Havrila, *Slovenská*, chapter
      „Slovenská historická spoločnosť v rokoch 1946-1968."

92   Kamencová, „Vznik," 191.

93   Jozef Jablonický, *Glosy o historiografii SNP. Zneužívanie a falšovanie dejín SNP*,
      Bratislava 1994, 32.

94   Agneša Kalinová, "Z redakčného zákulisia Kultúrného života čiže príbeh o desiatich
      malých černoškoch," in: *Kultúrny život a Slovenská jar 60. rokov*, Bratislava 1998, 94.

while its Communist leaders were rehabilitated, there was enough room for the non-Communist majority involved also to be recognised.[95]

The cultural and political thaw in Slovakia began, like in Bohemia, around 1963. In June of that year, a plenary meeting of the Slovak Historical Society took place in Bratislava. The participants performed a special kind of self-criticism, seeking out traces of the "cult of personality" in their own works of the preceding years. They also criticised the influence of Party functionaries, show trials and falsifications of history. Participants also raised an issue of a more general nature: Whether historians guilty of all those shortcomings were still worthy of the name, or that they should be treated exclusively as propagandists.[96] The 6th convention of Slovak historians in Martin became a sort of a high-water mark for the "Slovak Spring." The very choice of location for the convention was significant – during the 1950s, Martin, the birthplace of the Slovak national movement and the seat of Matica Slovenská, was closely symbolic of Slovak clerical-fascist nationalism.[97] Presentations devoted to the state of historiography of the previous 20 years bore special importance. Ľubomír Lipták observed a lack of foreign relationships along with efforts at breaking the generational continuity of Slovak historiography and its generally poor state.[98] Ján Mlynárik spoke with even greater vehemence: he underlined the decline in the quality of instruction of historians after 1948 and spoke up for Daniel Rapant (who had been previously ousted from all public positions).[99] However, Ľudovít Holotík, then-president of the historians' association and director of the SAV's Institute of History, distanced himself from papers presented at the convention, claiming that they criticised the "past period" too vehemently.[100]

The self-definition of Marxist historiography of the GDR was significantly affected by the fact that it was in a constant dispute with other German historiography. Relations between neighbours and ideological opponents were dependent to a large extent on the political climate, which sometimes fostered

---

95   Jablonický, *Glosy*, 54. See Ľubomír Lipták, "Slovakia: History and Historiography," in: *A Guide to Historiography in Slovakia*, eds. Elena Mannová & David Paul Daniel, Bratislava 1995, 13; Jozef Jablonický, "Slovenské národné povstanie v historiografii v rokoch totality," in: *SNP v pamäti národa. Materiály z vedeckej konferencie k 50. výročiu SNP, Donovaly 26.-28. apríla 1994*, Bratislava 1994, 88-91.

96   Havrila, *Slovenská,* chapter: Slovenská historická spoločnosť v rokoch 1946-1968.

97   "VI. Zjazd slovenských historikov roku 1968," *Historický Časopis SAV* 1990, 844.

98   Ľubomír Lipták, "Úloha a postavenie historiografie v našej spoločnosti," *Historický Časopis SAV* 1969.

99   Ján Mlynárik, "Vzťah politiky a historiografie," *Historický Časopis SAV* 1990, 864-865.

100   "VI. Zjazd slovenských historikov roku 1968," 845.

limited cooperation, but at other times turned ice cold. Common, all-German historical conventions, involving scholars from the GDR up until 1958, gave the Marxists a special opportunity to meet representatives of "bourgeois" historiography. East-German conferences and scientific meetings did not offer this opportunity, since as a rule, they did not allow for an exchange of divergent opinions or the persuasion of the resistant, being more akin to the manifestations of an already-achieved Marxist unity as had been the case in Stalinist Czechoslovakia.

The first postwar conventions of the Verband der Historiker Deutschlands (VHD) involved very few Marxist scholars. The sole representative of the GDR was typically Walter Markov, a Marxist from Leipzig, who was valued in the West as well (he fell victim to hunts for Tito's supporters in the GDR in 1951).[101] East-German historians invited to the 1951 convention in Marburg did not receive passports and were unable to take part in the proceedings.[102] A breakthrough occurred in 1953, in Bremen. The government decided to send a sizeable contingent, including non-Party specialists. GDR historians constituted about 10% of all participants (ca. 700), and took active part in the discussions and lobby conversations. In his report from the convention, published in *Zeitschrift für Geschichtswissenschaft*, Fritz Klein joyfully observed that only a few West-German historians approached the Marxists with hostility (which they did in a highly unpleasant manner, denying them the right to call themselves historians).[103] The general, official response to the event was therefore mildly positive.[104] Still, the aggressive statements of Heinz Kamnitzer and Joachim Streisand, reproaching some of their Western colleagues for their national-socialist past, could suggest a different interpretation.[105]

---

101 Matthias Middell, "Jenseits unserer Grenzen? Zur Trennung von deutscher und allgemeiner Geschichte in der Geschichtswissenschaft und Geschichtskultur der DDR," in: *Nach dem Erdbeben*, 101.

102 Martin Sabrow, "Ökumene als Bedrohung. Die Haltung der DDR-Historiographie gegenüber den deutschen Historikertagen von 1949 bis 1962," in: *Historikertage im Vergleich*, eds. Gerald Diesener & Mattias Middell, Leipzig 1996 178-179.

103 Fritz Klein, "Erinnerungen an die ersten Jahre der Zeitschrift für Geschichtswissenschaft 1953-1957," in: *Historische Zeitschriften im internationalen Vergleich*, Leipzig 1999, 338.

104 Fritz Klein, "Der Bremer Historikertag 1953," *Zeitschrift für Geschichtswissenschaft* 1953, 906.

105 Heinz Kamnitzer, "Zum Vortrag von Th. Schieder Das Verhältnis von politischer und gesellschaftlicher Verfassung und die Krise des bürgerlichen Liberalismus," *Zeitschrift für Geschichtswissenschaft* 1953; Joachim Streisand, "Zum Vortrag von O. Brunner Das Problem einer europäischen Sozialgeschichte," *Zeitschrift für Geschichtswissenschaft* 1953; Alfred Meusel, "Zum Vortrag von G. Ritter Das Problem

Another confrontation with non-Marxist German historiography took place three years later, during a VHD congress at Ulm. The young GDR historiography had already made its international début by that time at the congress of the Comité International des Sciences Historiques in Rome, though, on that occasion none of the contingents from people's democracies managed to overcome the image of a manipulated, centrally controlled and politicised academy.[106] At Ulm, the GDR was represented by a tight group of Party functionaries. The discussion spots were entirely orchestrated. A scant description of the proceedings in *Zeitschrift für Geschichtswissenschaft* lauded a sober German-German discussion and observed with satisfaction that historians from GDR were quite visible at Ulm.[107] The subsequent number of the magazine offered an even more optimistic representation of the event. The GDR historians wrote that Marxism was rejected by mostly the elder generation from the West, while the young doubted the cognitive capabilities of bourgeois historiography and were much more open to cooperation with the GDR.[108]

The year 1956 was at the same time the final period of a more or less peaceable exchange of opinion between the two German historiographies. The 20th convention of the CPSU, the Hungarian Uprising and the Polish October, and then the anti-revisionist campaign in the GDR (including the persecution of Jürgen Kuczynski and the ousting of Fritz Klein and Joachim Streisand as editors of *Zeitschrift für Geschichtswissenschaft*) radically altered this picture. If Marxist historiography was to retain its dominant position in the country, it had to eschew direct confrontation with other methodological and political currents. The ideological organ of the SED, *Einheit*, published a fundamental critique of the politics of a direct exchange of opinions: "Scientific debate, a fruitful exchange of views, and a national meeting between German historians from the West and the East – all of these can work to the advantage of a progressive science, peace and international understanding, as long as they remain grounded in an inexorable struggle against imperialist historiography. On this ground, every contact with West German historians can prove fruitful and desirable."

---

des 'Militarismus' in Deutschland," *Zeitschrift für Geschichtswissenschaft* 1953; E. Werner, "Zum Vortrag von B. Spuler Hellenismus und Islam," *Zeitschrift für Geschichtswissenschaft* 1953.

106   Karl Dietrich Erdmann, *Die Ökumene der Historiker. Geschichte der Internationalen Historikerkongresse und des Comité International des Sciences Historiques*, Göttingen 1987, 316-319.

107   "23. Versammlung deutscher Historiker in Ulm," *Zeitschrift für Geschichtswissenschaft* 1957, 125-127.

108   Sabrow, "Ökumene," 189.

The final joint convention of German historians took place in September 1958 at Trier. The GDR delegation was on that occasion organised by the Deutsche Historiker-Gesellschaft (DHG), which formed several months before under the leadership of Ernst Engelberg, and was approved by the Department of Science of the Central Committee of the SED. This new association of East German historians vowed to struggle against militarism and neo-fascism for the victory of socialism in the whole of Germany.[109] Alfred Meusel's proposition that DHG members should also join VHD was rejected; more than that – members of the East German association were expressly forbidden to join VHD.[110] Even before the convention began, *Zeitschrift für Geschichtswissenschaft* published an assault on some West German historians, branding them as imperialists.[111] In addition, the number of GDR historians escaping to the West rose rapidly in the months directly preceding the convention; VHD filed a protest against the GDR government's attempts to suppress this wave. The affair of Willy Flachs added insult to injury: Flachs, a scholar who could not endure the oppressive atmosphere of East Germany, fled to FRG and committed suicide.[112] The GDR side vehemently rejected the notion that his decision was in any way affected by a period of imprisonment or by being stripped of all his titles.[113]

An official severing of ties with West German historiography was for the most part a pure formality. At Trier, West German historians reacted to the pre-planned performances by their Eastern colleagues by taking away their right to speak.[114] From that point on, the East German scholars treated their Western colleagues exclusively as ideological enemies, an attitude reflected in more and more denounciations in the *Zeitschrift für Geschichtswissenschaft*.[115] The death of Alfred Meusel, a proponent of relative openness toward the Western scientific community, just before the 11th Congress of CISH in Stockholm, gained a symbolic meaning. Without him among the ranks, the GDR prepared an

---

109 E. Hoffmann, "Über Tendenzen, die den weiteren Fortschritt unserer Geschichtswissenschaft hemmen," *Einheit* 1957/12, 1151, quoted in: ibidem, 190.

110 "Aufruf zur Gründung der 'Deutschen Historiker-Gesellschaft' in der DDR," *Zeitschrift für Geschichtswissenschaft* 1958, 217.

111 Sabrow, "Ökumene," 191-192.

112 Heinz Heitzer, "Über unser Stellung zu den westdeutschen bürgerlichen Historikern," *Zeitschrift für Geschichtswissenschaft* 1958.

113 Sabrow, "Ökumene," 192-193.

114 "Zu den Zwecklügen des Herrn Thiedeck (Interview der Redaktion mit G. Schilfert und G. Pretsch)," *Zeitschrift für Geschichtswissenschaft* 1958, 1355.

115 "Zu den Vorfällen auf der 24. Versammlung des westdeutschen Historiker-Verbandes in Trier," *Zeitschrift für Geschichtswissenschaft* 1958, 1134.

independent contingent, focused around an "ideological struggle" against their peers from the U.S., the FRG, Yugoslavia as well as against Polish émigrés.[116] East German historians no longer tried to win anyone over. Enclosed in their own milieu, they no longer needed to, or indeed could, confront their beliefs with adherents of other worldviews.

Poland differed from Czechoslovakia and the GDR in that the Stalinist "Sturm und Drang" lasted relatively shorter there. Before 1956, the Party failed to secure total control in terms of ideology or personnel, and criticism of the Stalinist schematism in historiography began to appear even before the Polish October. Hence, the Stalinisation of the Polish historiography proved to be an unfinished process, which makes it all the more interesting. In Poland, the confrontations between Marxists and "bourgeois" historians spread out over several years, with milestones occurring at conventions and conferences of great value and importance to the community. As a result, conferences were not pure formalities, as in the case of Czechoslovakia or the GDR, even though they did not foster a free and unrestrained exchange of opinions.

The first public appearance of an organised group of Polish Marxist historians occurred at the 7th General Convention of Polish Historians in Wrocław, which took place on September 19-22, 1948. Among the invited were a delegation of Soviet historians (Fyodor Tretyakov, Arkady Sidorov and Ivan Udaltsov, each delivering a paper). On the other hand, though, invitations were also extended to Charles Morazé, representing the CISH, and Josef Macůrek from Brno, a historian out of favour with Czechoslovak Communist authorities. One of the papers was presented by another historian who soon became *persona non grata*, Henryk Wereszycki (1898-1990).[117] A motion by Wanda Moszczeńska "for the necessity of including an up-to-date course on the methodology of history, and specifically historical materialism, in the regular university curriculum in history," won unreserved approval.[118] The convention

---

116 See Felix-Heinrich Gentzen, J. Kalisch, G. Voigt & E. Wolfgramm, "Die 'Ostforschung' – ein Stoßtrupp des deutschen Imperialismus," *Zeitschrift für Geschichtswissenschaft* 1958; Karl Obermann, "Bemerkungen über die bürgerliche Metternich-Forschung," *Zeitschrift für Geschichtswissenschaft* 1958; Manfred Unger, "Bernhard von Clairvaux und der Slawenkreuzzug 1147. Bemerkungen zu einem Aufsatz von W. Schlesinger," *Zeitschrift für Geschichtswissenschaft* 1959; Percy Stulz & Siegfried Thomas, "Zur Entstehung und Entwicklung der CDU in Westdeutschland 1945-1949," *Zeitschrift für Geschichtswissenschaft* 1959.

117 Rolf Rudolph, "XI. Internationaler Historiker-Kongreß in Stockholm," *Zeitschrift für Geschichtswissenschaft* 1960, 1790-1794. See. Sabrow, *Das Diktat*, 305-312.

118 Elżbieta Orman, "Historyk i jego historia. Próba biografii Henryka Wereszyckiego," in: *Henryk Wereszycki*, 56-57.

occasioned the official formation of a group of Marxist historians (under the name of the Marxist Association of Historians), which was supposed to coordinate the actions and enhance the skills of the very few proponents of the new methodology.

At the convention, the achievements of Marxists were judged to have been rather limited.[119] Worse than that – talks given by Polish Marxists did not earn the approval of the Soviet guests.[120] Hopes for the future were mostly associated with the emergence of an organised group promoting the new methodology. The Marxist Association of Historians (Marksistowskie Zrzeszenie Historyków) was expected to perform this role, but it needed the government's trust and support to operate efficiently. At the same time, it became evident early on that this Marxist organisation had a rather negligible effect on the Polish historiography. The Marxists spent several months intensively preparing for the CISH Congress in Paris in 1950.[121] It soon turned out that the profile of the Polish delegation for the Congress was dependent on the composition of the German contingent. The French organisers sent out a list of the German participants to all concerned, asking for any critical comments or reservations. In Poland, the reservations were quickly voiced by the Western Institute (Instytut Zachodni), which protested against the participation of several German scholars in the Congress.[122] Soon enough, Party historians came up with their own list of objections to the arrangement of the German delegation. During a meeting at the Department of Science of the Central Committee of the Party in January, Żanna Kormanowa pointed out that "There are [in the German delegation] only three people from Berlin, and [Jürgen] Kuczynski isn't there. The organisers are apparently trying to smuggle in the imperialist historians.... They obviously want Poland to be their dummy. The Party authorities will have to decide this matter."[123] Not long thereafter, Żanna Kormanowa handed to Manteuffel a list of representatives of "the German democratic historical science," who should have been invited to the Parisian Congress. By April, Tadeusz Manteuffel prepared a list of Polish delegates to the Congress for the

---

119 *Kwartalnik Historyczny* 1948, 580. See Tadeusz Paweł Rutkowski, *Polskie Towarzystwo Historyczne w latach 1945-1958. Zarys dziejów*, Toruń 2009, 31-41.

120 Stobiecki, *Historia*, 97.

121 Quoted in Zbigniew Romek, "Historycy radzieccy o historykach polskich. Uwagi o zjeździe wrocławskim i konferencji otwockiej (1951/1952)," *Polska 1944/45-1989. Studia i materiały*, 4 (1999), 197.

122 Dział Rękopisów BUW, Spuścizna Niny Assorodobraj, VII/2, Protokół z posiedzenia partyjnej grupy historyków przy Wydziale Nauki KC PZPR, 7 I 1950.

123 Archiwum PAN, sygn. III 192 Materiały Tadeusza Manteuffla, j. 38 Akta Delegata PTH do stosunków międzynarodowych – List sekretarza Wydziału Naukowego Instytutu Zachodniego Zdzisława Kaczmarczyka do Tadeusza Manteuffla, 2 I 1950.

Ministry of Education, but "Party authorities" had already been forced to decide to boycott the event. Tadeusz Manteuffel was told to draft a letter to the organisers, rejecting the invitation in the kindest of terms.[124]

The manner in which the authorities chose to settle the issue of the Polish involvement in the Congress of Historical Sciences exemplifies not only the attitude of the government toward historians as such, but also toward Marxist historians who, just like all the others, had already prepared their presentations, with some, like Żanna Kormanowa, putting quite an effort into organising the event and giving it an appropriate ideological resonance. The government's decision, whether it was taken at Moscow's behest, or in response to the composition of the German delegation, or even resulted from the increasingly strained post-1949 Polish-French relations, illustrates the disdain with which it treated historians, whether or not they were card-carrying Party members.

While the question of the Polish participation in the Parisian Congress of Historical Sciences was still up in the air, more and more Party-members began to voice their demands of serious changes in personnel and organisation of the field. According to the preliminaries of a Party group at the Department of Science of the Central Committee, the Congress was meant to serve as an opportunity to prove the qualifications of a group of leading Polish Marxists and to illustrate its cohesion. What's more, the guidelines for the content of the presentations, delivered to the Polish Historical Association (Polskie Towarzystwo Historyczne), demanded that non-Party historians reference works of "progressive" science, at least in footnotes, just like Marxists. Had those plans succeeded, their creators' works would have gained a fantastic opportunity to enhance their scientific standing. However, with the trip to Paris called off, administrative repressions and a "closing of the ranks" seemed to the Marxists a more viable method of exerting control over the community. In this climate, preparations for the 1st Congress of Polish Science, originally drafted by the late Jerzy Borejsza, took place.

The participants of the meeting of the Subsection of History were presumably impressed the most by a paper which summarised their debates, presented by Żanna Kormanowa. Kormanowa began by stressing the role of history as one of the most Party-bound social sciences, heretofore exploited with relish by the possessor classes. A brief outline of the history of Polish historiography before 1918 was complemented by a broader section devoted to the interwar period. With all the positives (sometimes deemed questionable) of the period, Kormanowa found ample room for a scathing critique of some still

---

124 Dział Rękopisów BUW, Spuścizna Niny Assorodobraj, VII/2 – Protokół z posiedzenia partyjnej grupy historyków przy Wydziale Nauki KC PZPR, 7 I 1950.

active colleagues and several academic institutions.[125] Then, she stated that the Western Lands have officially been incorporated into the fatherland, which in her view meant that the Western Institute lost its *raison d'être*.[126] Among the postulates of the Subsection, the presenter named the formation of corporate departments in the manner characteristic of the Soviet Union, a deeper centralisation of academic publishing, and the formation of an Institute of History at the Polish Academy of Sciences.[127]

Kormanowa's presentation made a lasting impression on her audience primarily because of her use of a rather primitive language when describing the achievements of widely known historians. This certainly did not bode well for the quality of the future Marxist scholarship in the history of historiography. One could hazard that the proceedings of the 1st Congress of the Polish Science were the final wake-up call for non-Party historians, alerting them to the dangers they faced, both personally and as a community. This was not because of a "totalitarian structuring" of the proceedings (according to Piotr Hübner), but rather thanks to fairly clear signals from card-carrying scientists, such as the philosopher Adam Schaff, or, in historiography, Żanna Kormanowa. The positions of non-Party professors who failed to submit to the new policies were now under threat. Partly independent scientific institutions, deemed obsolete already at that stage, were also in danger; according to Kormanowa, they included the Polish Academy of Learning (Polska Akademia Umiejętności) or the Western Institute. One could also expect the newly-formed, centralised scientific structures of the Polish Academy of Sciences to be handed over to historians who, like Kormanowa, acted for the government in regards to their colleagues. This was not a welcome development, especially in light of the fresh memory of a fragment of her presentation, in which she stated that, in the struggle for the completion of the 6-year plan, "we, historians, failed to keep the pace of the miner, the steelworker, the founder, the weaver."[128] It soon transpired that some historians were conscious of these developments and drew the right conclusions.

The next opportunity for a meeting of numerous Marxist and so-called "liberal-democratic" historians came with the First Methodological Conference of Polish Historians in Otwock between December 28th, 1951 and January 12th, 1952. The Otwock conference inarguably has an exceptionally bad reputation.

---

125 Archiwum PAN, sygn. III 192, Materiały Tadeusza Manteuffla, j. 38 Akta Delegata PTH do stosunków międzynarodowych – Projekt listu 7 VII 1950.

126 Żanna Kormanowa, "Referat podsekcji historii sekcji nauk społecznych i humanistycznych I KNP," *Kwartalnik Historyczny* 1951, 317.

127 Ibidem, 297.

128 Ibidem, 325.

Its main goal was to prove the superiority of card-carrying historians over their non-Party colleagues. The conference was rescheduled several times to give the young Marxists enough time to prepare for it.[129] The venue was visited by a huge number of historians from all the major research centres and many younger tenured scholars. No invitation was sent to, among others, Władysław Konopczyński or Zygmunt Wojciechowski, both of whom were criticised by Kormanowa at the 1st Congress of Polish Science.

The participants were to be evaluated not only by representatives of the Party and state authorities, but also by a delegation of Soviet historians: the director of the Institute of History of the Soviet Academy of Sciences, Boris Gryekov, Yevgeni Kosminsky, Arkady Sidorov and Fyodor Tretyakov. The non-Party historians could derive comfort from the way the Soviet guests carried themselves. They did not offer support to the proponents of Stalinism, never allowed themselves to be isolated from their Polish colleagues, and spoke competently and courteously, emphasising the high qualifications of their hosts.[130] The leader of the delegation, Boris Gryekov, won the Polish participants over when he asked the organisers to take him to one of the villages near Otwock, where he quartered during the First World War. This led to a meeting with an aged landowner, who supposedly kept fond memories of the erstwhile officer.[131] When the conference ended, the Soviet guests were entertained by Bolesław Bierut, who expressed a great interest in the proceedings, and most of all, in the evaluation of the Polish academic cadres. The guests spoke highly of the non-Party historians, a fact which, as Leonid Gorisontov claimed, had very sad consequences for some of the Soviet delegates (back in their home country, Anna Mikhailovna Pankratova, a member of the Academy and an acquaintance of Żanna Kormanowa,[132] accused them of yielding to the influence of the Polish bourgeois academy).[133]

The evaluation presented by the Soviet guests was expected to frame the government's decision on the leadership of the future Institute of History at PAN.[134] Appeased by it, Tadeusz Manteuffel could safely pass on the resolution recommending the formation of the Institute to Prime Minister Cyrankiewicz.[135]

---

129   Ibidem, 297.
130   Ibidem, 195-197.
131   Andrzej F. Grabski, *Zarys historii historiografii polskiej*, Poznań 2000, 205.
132   Based on the account by Prof. Janina Leskiewiczowa (in a conversation, February 2002).
133   Żanna Kormanowa, *Ludzie i życie*, Warszawa 1982, 199.
134   Juliusz Bardach, "Trudne początki," in: *Instytut Historii Polskiej Akademii Nauk 1953-1993*, ed. Stefan K. Kuczyński, Warszawa 1993, 69.
135   Stobiecki, *Historia*, 109; Romek, "Historycy radzieccy," 193.

The likelihood of the Institute's being handed over to someone like Żanna Kormanowa decreased. However, before the cadre of the future Institute of History at PAN took shape, the Otwock conference also brought about a number of events that inevitably worsened the non-Party historians' mood. These were the assaults of Roman Werfel, Tadeusz Daniszewski and Józef Kowalski on Henryk Wereszycki, the author of *Historia Polityczna Polski w dobie popowstaniowej 1864-1918* (The Political History of Poland in the Post-Uprising era, 1864-1918, Warszawa 1948), a book they deemed pernicious, as a result of which it was withdrawn from bookshops. Asked to present a self-criticism, Wereszycki explained that he had not known nor applied the rules of Marxism-Leninism while working on the book. The assailants judged this self-criticism insufficient and renewed their assaults during subsequent sessions. The atmosphere became stressful not only for the victim of the assaults, but also for the other participants. Wereszycki himself thought that an arrest during the proceedings might be in the cards.[136]

The Otwock conference is the last in a series of events that, in the eyes of both contemporaneous and current scholars, led to the Stalinisation of the Polish historiography. What did this Stalinisation consist of? A comparison of the proceedings of historical conventions and major conferences in each of the countries under discussion suggests that Stalinisation begins when the historical community is taken over by card-carrying Marxists, who then gradually force all members of the historical community to join the Party. This goal was fully achieved in the GDR, where authorities were greatly helped both by the denazification that decimated departments of the humanities at East German universities, and by the availability of an escape route to the West, chosen by many a dissident historian. In Czechoslovakia, the goal was actually achieved twice before 1989: first during the 1950s, and then after a period of "normalisation" that followed the Prague Spring. In Poland, neither of the stages crucial to its attainment were completed. Not only were the Marxists unable to achieve a numerical and qualitative advantage over the "bourgeois" historians; they even failed to come up with Marxist candidates for leadership of the community who would be capable of representing Polish historiography abroad. As a result, the Soviet guests at Otwock, for instance, expressed their esteem of Tadeusz Manteuffel or Aleksander Gieysztor (1916-1999), and not Żanna Kormanowa or Celina Bobińska. A comparison of the form, character and progress of the major conferences and conventions of historical societies shows that, in contrast to the other countries under discussion, in Poland the new

---

136 Tadeusz Manteuffel, *Historyk wobec historii. Rozprawy nieznane. Pisma drobne. Wspomnienia*, Warszawa 1976, 358.

methodology had to be introduced repeatedly. It is not inconceivable that these attempts would eventually have yielded a definite result, and that both the Polish "liberal-bourgeois" historians and their students would have embraced a role similar to that of the university elites in the GDR. Still, the fact that the pressure to unify historiography lessened palpably already before 1956 undermined such an evolution of attitudes, and Polish historians were spared the fate shared for decades by their colleagues from the GDR or Czechoslovakia.

Every Central European Marxist historiography aimed to produce a comprehensive and useful synthesis of national history. A new textbook was meant to displace the old, "bourgeois" history books, entirely changing the perspective from which history was to be written; the popular masses were now supposed to become its subject. The production of this new "grand narrative" was also meant to exemplify a new approach toward historical work, treated as a collective endeavour. In most countries under discussion the task of the textbook's creation was handed over to historical institutes formed at the newly-created academies of sciences. The structure of these institutes (broken down into chronologically ordered departments) roughly corresponded to the structure of the planned textbooks. Research queries as well as writing and editing duties for each of the volumes were delegated to numerous employees whose involvement in the work was not always marked by the inclusion of their names on the title pages of its final product. The work on the final versions of the textbooks took a long time – in the case of Poland, it was never completed – so the published books played their designated role only rarely and briefly. The effort put into their preparation turned out to be disproportionate to the effect.

Though the necessity of producing a Marxist textbook seemed obvious both in Poland, in the GDR, and in Czechoslovakia, the scheduling of the work and the hierarchy of goals to be achieved along the way to the final product were open to debate. Sometimes even card-carrying scientists were not entirely in agreement as to the type of textbook whose publication should be prioritised. In both Czechoslovakia and Poland, priority was eventually given to works of smaller volume, which could be of use for the final years of high school and at universities, and primarily the kind that would be easy to prepare and publish quickly.[137] The story of the publication process of a certain Polish university history textbook is most instructive in this regard. During a session of the scientific committee of the Institute of History at PAN in September 1953, a controversy arose between Leon Grosfeld and Żanna Kormanowa with respect to

---

137   See František Kavka, Josef Polišenský & František Kutnar, *Přehled dějin ČSR v epoše feudalismu (1526-1781)*, Praha 1956, František Kutnar, *Přehled dějin Československa v epoše kapitalismu*, Praha 1957.

the choice of the first book to be prepared for publication. Grosfeld believed that the academic textbook should receive an absolute priority; Kormanowa, on the other hand, supported the idea of focusing on a textbook for the later high school classes first.[138] In this dispute, Kormanowa had the upper hand at all times. Polish history schoolbooks were prioritised by the authorities even a few years before the formation of the Institute of History at PAN. In 1951, a textbook written by Gryzelda Missalowa and Janina Schoenbrenner, and edited by Kormanowa herself, arrived in print.[139] The work was a highly critical portrayal of national history, comparing the self-induced (by the gentry) collapse of the Polish–Lithuanian Commonwealth to the defeat of September 1939. During debates over this textbook, which engaged prominent historians, Party members and non-members alike, the book was criticised for evident deficiencies, among them for its all-too-critical approach to the national traditions.[140]

The authorities, as much as the leading Polish historians, wanted the new Polish history textbooks to represent an advance in quality both in terms of content and attitude toward national history. General history offered no such problem, since translated Soviet textbooks were in wide use.[141] Before the publication of the especially important textbook intended for the final years of high school (classes 9 to 11), a range of consultations were organised – a practice observed after each re-edition of the work.[142] The textbook for classes 9 to 11, eventually published in 1952, did not quite meet all the original guidelines.[143] Several weeks after the meeting of the Academic Council of the Institute of History at PAN that revealed the split between Kormanowa and Grosfeld, a session of the Department of Polish History at the Institute of the Education of Scientific Personnel (Instytut Kształcenia Kadr Naukowych, an institution devoted to teaching Party specialists), centered on the problem of the

---

138 Jerzy W. Borejsza, "Henryk Wereszycki czyli optymizm słusznych tez," in: *Henryk Wereszycki*, 210.

139 Archiwum Instytutu Historii PAN, sygn. 5/27, Protokoły Rady Naukowej – Protokół nr 3 z posiedzenia Rady Naukowej IH PAN, 25 IX 1953.

140 Gryzelda Missalowa & Janina Schoenbrenner, *Historia Polski*, Warszawa 1951.

141 Dział Rękopisów BUW, Spuścizna Witolda Kuli, p. 27, t.: Podręcznik – programy nauczania, zwłaszcza historii gospodarczej - T. Manteuffel, Materiał do recenzji pierwszych 50 lekcyj (str. 3-132) podręcznika "Historii Polski" G. Missalowej i J. Schoenbrenner; Ibidem: B. Leśnodorski, Marksistowski zarys dziejów Polski; Ibidem: W. Kula, Tezy do dyskusji nad podręcznikiem G. Missalowej i J. Schoenbrenner "Historia Polski," 11 II 1952.

142 E. Kosminski, *Historia wieków średnich*, Warszawa 1953.

143 Dział Rękopisów BUW, Spuścizna Witolda Kuli, p. 27, t.: Podręcznik – programy nauczania, zwłaszcza historii gospodarczej, Projekt tez dla autorów podręcznika historii Polski.

textbook, took place. During her presentation on that occasion, Żanna Kormanowa conducted a self-criticism for herself and her collaborators on the book, claiming that its deficiencies resulted from "our insufficient familiarity with theory."[144] According to her, the errors were partially explained by – paradoxically – the absence of a university textbook which could serve as a basis for authors of textbooks designed for high-school students. The responses of other participants in the session were highly critical. In their view, the book was simply poorly prepared, "Particular authors wrote their pieces, others did not read what they wrote, and as a result the book includes a horrendous amount of repetitions, including repeated citations and dates, while numbers do not always add up," observed Sylwester Zawadzki, a doctoral student at the Institute for the Education of Scientific Personnel, "the textbook should be appealing, it should foster a love for the workers' movement.... But because it was written in such dry tones, one could even say: scribbled in a kind of – if you excuse the term – Marxist jargon, it does not appeal, it does not foster love.... Furthermore, I have to say," Zawadzki continued, "that I don't enjoy its criticism of the PPS.[145] The major error consists in the fact that the authors apparently criticise the PPS constantly for struggling for an independent Polish state. Instead of attacking their anti-national attitudes, the authors choose an entirely opposite route."[146] According to this speaker, "the textbook at times resembles Party minutes," particularly irritating by its sectarian view of Polish history, according to which "if there's such a thing as an honest man, he must be a Communist.... There are no Poles if not Communist.... I'm not talking about the superstructure, ... but ... there's no Żeromski, Prus, Konopnicka, Orzeszkowa, there's no Matejko, none of our painters, there's no room for those who protested." Zawadzki's arguments were accepted by Zygmunt Modzelewski, who identified the major flaw of the textbook as "its narrowing down of the object of analysis to the history of the workers' movement." "The textbook itself," he concluded, "may finally prove the frailty of our historical front. At this point, our Polish Marxist historiography is still rather feeble, and this is obviously visible in the product of our writing, in what we now receive.... The main point of this textbook is to raise our youth in the spirit of love toward the Polish nation, the masses who created Polish history, and they need to be represented in this book.

---

144 *Historia Polski 1864-1945. Materiały do nauczania w klasie XI*, ed. Żanna Kormanowa, Warszawa 1952.

145 PPS – Polish Socialist Party – the biggest socialist organisation in Poland until 1948, when it forcibly joined the Communist PPR.

146 Dział Rękopisów BUW, Spuścizna Witolda Kuli, p. 27, t.: Dyskusja nad podręcznikiem szkolnym 1864-1945 – Stenogram posiedzenia Katedry Historii Polski IKKN odbytego w Warszawie, 3 XI 1953.

And they aren't. We heard it said here that the man has disappeared. Because of humanism and the Renaissance, we talk of the man, but I think we should rather be speaking of a nation as well – this is the background against which we will see the leaders. The nation should come first at all times."[147]

The experience of the debates on school textbooks had a definite influence on the organisation of work on the university textbook on Polish history. The work on Polish, Czechoslovak and Slovak textbooks progressed according to patterns so similar that one could use these examples to illustrate the specific rules of production for Marxist syntheses. It was assumed that the textbooks should result from a broad discussion, which was to take place before the publication of their final versions. After the publication, texts of a canonical or normative character were expected to attract controversy no longer. For this reason, the publication of the final versions of particular volumes was preceded by lengthy discussions over periodisation, the evaluation of specific events, and finally the printing of extracts from selected fragments of the textbook. Another important stage consisted in the publishing of "theses" and "drafts" meant to serve as a basis for discussion, both with national and international (primarily Soviet) historians.[148] Central historical magazines widely distributed news of the progress of successive stages of the work.

Work on Marxist textbooks proceeded at a slow pace. The draft of the first volume of *Přehled československých dějin* was published in 1958.[149] The first volume of the Polish "Draft" saw print in 1955 (in two parts), while *Dejiny Slovenska* (the idea of having a "draft" printed first was in that case dropped) went to press in the early 1960s.[150] The whole endeavour may have been ambitious, but there were also other, more mundane reasons for the slow progress of the work. It quickly transpired that despite sincere dedication of all involved in the work, a quality synthesis was hard to come by in the absence of

---

147 Ibidem.
148 "Rozmowa z Czesławem Madajczykiem (not. Zbigniew Romek)," in: *Cenzura w PRL*, 134; Havrila, *Slovenská*, chapter: „Historický ústav SAV v rokoch 1953-1968"; Roman Ferstl, "František Graus v počátcích Historického ústavu ČSAV" in: *František Graus – člověk a historik. Sborník z pracovního semináře Výzkumného centra pro dějiny vědy konaného 10. prosince 2002*, eds. Zdeněk Beneš, Bohumil Jiroušek & Antonín Kostlán, Praha 2004, 52-53; Jiří Jílek, "František Graus a „Maketa," ibidem, 57-68.
149 *Přehled československých dějin*, vol. 1, eds. Josef Macek, František Graus & Ján Tibenský, Praha 1958.
150 *Historia Polski*, vol. 1, part 1, ed. Henryk Łowmiański (project editors Tadeusz Manteuffel, Leon Grosfeld & Bogusław Leśnodorski), Warszawa 1955; *Historia Polski*, vol. 1, part 2, ed. Henryk Łowmiański, Warszawa 1955; *Dejiny Slovenska* (tézy), ed. Ľudovít Holotík, Bratislava 1955; *Dejiny Slovenska*, vol. 1, eds. Ľudovít Holotík & Ján Tibenský, Bratislava 1961.

monographic works. The first "draft" saw print in Poland, and yet its editor, Tadeusz Manteuffel, was rumoured to have purposefully slowed the progress of the work, especially the part devoted to the latest period, which was by nature given to the most severe political deformations. I was unable to verify this claim, but as far as the earlier volumes were concerned, Manteuffel hardly needed to apply any pressures of the kind. Quite the contrary: he expended a lot of energy trying to put authors who were running late with commissioned texts back on track. The Archives of the Institute of History at PAN have collected a number of more or less coarse admonitions, including dispatches categorically demanding the submission of delayed works.[151] The entire endeavour was to an extent unfortunate; some of the delays were caused by the theft of collected materiel.[152] The progress of the work was also greatly slowed by debates concerning matters of key importance from the perspective of Marxist historiography. In the case of Poland, the most important problem was the characterisation of the achievements of national and foreign historiographies. Josef Macek and František Graus, who chaired sessions devoted to the first volume of the Czechoslovak "draft" in February 1959, faced mostly hundreds of small remarks and claims about particular historical facts, to which they repeatedly responded that the textbook was not meant to replace the nonexistent monographs on particular subjects.[153]

The lack of clarity over criteria for evaluation of "bourgeois" historiography is reflected in the debate on the historiographical chapters of the following volume of the Polish textbook, which took place in April 1955. Marian Serejski criticised the views maintained by Celina Bobińska, who claimed that conservative historians of the Kraków school, and especially Michał Bobrzyński, stood out from the other "imperialist" historians because they "saw through the patterns of history." Since the conservative Bobrzyński was supposedly a comparatively progressive moderate – responded Serejski – how should we evaluate the progressive liberals, Wacław Tokarz, Bolesław Limanowski or even Marceli Handelsman?[154]

Slovak Marxists also faced numerous obstacles in interpretation, sometimes of an entirely essential nature. A traditional problem, encountered already in the works of Július Botto and František Sasinek, was the determination of the object of history (beside the obvious, though hardly specific assumption that history should always speak primarily of the popular masses). Should the Marxist

---

151 Archiwum Instytutu Historii PAN, sygn. 12/60, Podręcznik Historii Polski. Protokół z dyskusji, preliminarz, korespondencja.
152 Ibidem – Pismo Wacława Urbana, Kraków, 24 I 1954.
153 Jílek, "František Graus," 67.
154 Ibidem.

synthesis be a history of the Slovak ethnic grouping, or of the territories it inhabited? How should one approach the problem of Slovak-Hungarian and Slovak-Czech relations? The authorial collective attempted to merge national and territorial perspectives, making itself susceptible to criticism. Commenting upon the "Theses," František Bokes pointed precisely to the fact that they were concerned more with "Slovak history" than with "history of Slovakia," which stood in contradiction to the title of the work.[155] Still, *Dejiny Slovenska* was in later years valued more than any of the other Marxist syntheses. The most basic reason for this was the fact that this unprecedented and daring attempt could not rely on any pre-existing sources, which meant that its authors had to conduct a series of pioneering inquiries. It was impossible for them to rely extensively on analyses and sources published by native historians of the 19th century, as the Czech Marxists among others did.[156]

The work on the university textbook on the history of Poland and the reception of the first published volumes of the "Draft" both perfectly illustrate the political transformations of Stalinist Poland. The first critical reactions to contemporaneous policies toward historians were heard at the General Assembly of the Polish Historical Society in 1956. The final meetings prior to the publication of the "Draft" did not lead to any significant debate over the form of Marxist interpretation of national history. The coming political thaw is perfectly visible in comments on the debate over the first volume of the "Draft," published in the mid-year *Kwartalnik Historyczny*.[157] The authors of the report optimistically concluded that "the synthesis marked an attempt ... – mostly successful – to avoid committing the errors of the previous epoch when being schematic equalled being in the right, and when some historians, entangled in dogmas and their own opportunism, were given to describing events according to an ideal pattern – 'the way they should appear,' not taking into account the abundant original sources."[158] The same yearbook of *Kwartalnik Historyczny* included an assessment written by Witold Kula, entitled *W sprawie naszej polityki naukowej* ("On our scientific policy"). The piece was a printed version of a presentation given at a session of the Academic Council of the Institute of History at PAN in June 1956, in which the author evaluated the achievements of Polish historiography after 1945. Describing the initial postwar period, he noted "a flood of rubbish, often imbued with undisguised nationalism" rising against the gradually strengthening influence of the *Annales* school. For Kula, the

---

155 Havrila, *Slovenská*, chapter: Historický ústav SAV v rokoch 1953-1968.
156 Helena Třísková, "Synthesis," in: *A Guide*, 40.
157 Ryszard Kiersnowski, Tadeusz Lalik, Janusz Tazbir & Andrzej Wyczański, "Dyskusja nad makietą I tomu Historii Polski," *Kwartalnik Historyczny* 1956.
158 Ibidem, 4.

Wrocław convention was a failure, not so much for card-carrying historians, as for their "progressive" non-Party colleagues denounced both by "traditional" historiography and by the decision-makers. The period from 1949 to 1952 was marked by the rule of the iron fist, which resulted in a total stagnation as well as a flight from history into related disciplines: archaeology, history of art or economics. At Otwock, "Representatives of the Party and state authorities saw that, in spite of what their informers had said, most of the Polish historians were in fact people, living, thinking and feeling, respondent to the enormous scientific perspectives opened up by Marxism, wanting to be and capable of being of use to the country."[159] Further on, Kula claimed that the first postwar decade brought a multitude of disappointments. Marxism was at times applied in a primitive manner: "It sufficed to prove the 'constantly worsening' lot of the peasant, it sufficed to say anything bad about the relations between Poland and any western country in any century – and one was already deemed a Marxist. It sufficed to juggle the term 'objective progressiveness' to be thought of as a dialectician."[160] Kula criticised the sorry state of research into recent history, stemming from the self-delusion of Party representatives: "It is time to end with making a secret (strictly guarded, but remembered by elder people and known to younger historians through documents) of the Party position, which was either faulty for its time, or, if right, no longer remains valid."[161] The article also included mentions of falsifications of historical sources, "a censor's attitude toward the past," and also of a certain "pessimism" of the history of Poland as viewed in this Marxist light (a motif of high importance to later "thaw" debates). The same problem was discussed in the final volume of *Kwartalnik Historyczny* published in 1956, in the report *Z prac organizacji partyjnej w Instytucie Historii PAN*, compiled by Krystyna Zienkowska and Jerzy Jedlicki.[162]

Paradoxically, Witold Kula combined these exceptionally critical remarks with a generally positive evaluation of the achievements of the first decade under Communism: "We can claim with full responsibility that there does not seem to have been, in the history of Polish science, another decade as progressive."[163] Nevertheless, some changes in academic policy seemed

---

159   Witold Kula, "W sprawie naszej polityki naukowej," *Kwartalnik Historyczny* 1956, 154.
160   Ibidem, 156.
161   Ibidem, 158.
162   Krystyna Zienkowska & Jerzy Jedlicki, "Z prac organizacji partyjnej w Instytucie Historii PAN," *Kwartalnik Historyczny* 1956, 530.
163   Kula, „W sprawie," 155.

necessary even to Kula who gave a lot of weight to the freedom of scientific debate and highlighted the importance of research trips abroad.[164]

Even before Kula's article appeared in print in *Kwartalnik Historyczny*, it sparked a heated debate during a session of the Academic Council of the Institute of History at PAN. Its primary participants, Marian Małowist (1909-1988) and Leon Grosfeld opted to cushion the blow Kula delivered, pointing to the "problem of a dangerous tendency toward reverse dogmatism" and the undesirability of a complete rejection of Marxist methodology.[165] Aleksander Gieysztor made a much harsher statement; he spoke for the hasty organisation of a general convention of historians. "It should have a impetuous character to it – he added – as a kind of vote of no confidence."[166] "We should also," he continued, "demand to be told about employed scholars who were dragged into the archives." When Małowist commented that, compared to other fields of study, historiography did not plummet so low under Stalinism, Gieysztor replied that "while it didn't suffer the worst, it doesn't mean it's doing well." Gieysztor's statement unleashed a flood of criticism toward the scientific policies of the Communists. Stefan Kieniewicz raised the issue of censorial interferences and obligations to tamper with historical truth.[167] Marian Henryk Serejski made a statement that could have informed Witold Kula's later claim that Polish Marxist historiography was stretched between Communism and nationalism. Serejski reminded the congregation that during the "past period," questions of a national nature were treated in a highly unusual manner: "for instance, it was said that Suvorov was a Russian patriot, while Batory was nothing but a reactionary Pole." Years later, Kula concluded that "Traditional historians accuse Polish historiography of the years 1948-1955 of excessive revisionism and deprecating national traditions. For proof, elements such as a critical evaluation of Batory, depictions of the armies of the old *Rzeczpospolita* as an instrument of class repression, or putting stress on the reactionary character of Czartoryski's milieu, and so on, suffice. Historians who have been tied to the progressive movement for years were surprised by the exact opposite of that: pressures toward apologetics, the untouchability of 'national sanctities,' a hagiographic streak."[168] This difference of opinion remains valid in today's evaluations of Polish historiography under Stalinism.

---

164 Stefan Żółkiewski, "Uwagi o postępie metodologicznym nauki polskiej w minionym dziesięcioleciu," *Studia z dziejów nauki polskiej* 3/1955, 13.
165 Archiwum Instytutu Historii PAN, sygn. 5/26, Protokoły Rady Naukowej 1956-1959 – Protokół z posiedzenia Rady Naukowej IH PAN, 25 VI 1956.
166 Ibidem.
167 Ibidem.
168 Witold Kula, *Wokół historii*, Warszawa 1998, 101.

The wave of "reverse dogmatism," which Leon Grosfeld feared, was not a purely imagined danger. Some of the reactions to ever more visible signs of the coming thaw could make card-carrying historians quite apprehensive, and in time, they were also found to be distasteful even to some of their non-Party colleagues. The Marxist textbook on the history of Poland, both in its "Draft" edition and in its final incarnation, was one publication which, due to its importance, met with very stern appraisal from the reviewers. In 1957, Henryk Wereszycki delivered a crushing, though tactful, analysis of its second volume for *Kwartalnik Historyczny*.[169] Early in his review, he lauded the authors of the "Draft" for clearly striving to avoid a vulgarisation of history. Later on, though, he criticised the crucial, most important aspect of the book: the vision of national history that it represented. "After reading some thousand and more pages of post-Partitions history," he asserted, "I was overcome by an irresistible feeling that we were presented with a clearly pessimist image of our nation's past."[170] Wereszycki did not agree with this pessimist outlook. He pointed to several sources for the authors' pessimism. First, he named the "pessimism of the historian's workshop": "The authors of the draft seem to have somehow lost faith in their own vocation. Skimming through chapters of the first part of the second volume, I noted that, some fairly important issues related to the period of the Partitions are quite often resolved with recourse to the authorities of Marx and Engels – scholars whose views on matters of Polish history took shape a hundred years ago. Throughout these hundred years, Polish historiography worked diligently, particularly with regard to the period of the Partitions. But for the authors of this textbook, scholars of a hundred years ago remain the highest authority on the matter. Therefore, the whole scholarly effort of those hundred years of work by Polish historians has come, to an extent, to waste. For a Polish historian writing in our times, whose teachers belong precisely to the lineage of that century, teachers who schooled him in that century's context, whom he valued in his youth, and sometimes even revered – it must fill him with pessimism and lack of faith."[171] There was also another kind of pessimism, which depressed Wereszycki even more. Since the synthesis which he reviewed was apparently supposed to serve as a kind of "justification" of the People's Republic of Poland, it inevitably became an apotheosis of the people and a condemnation of the possessing classes. According to Wereszycki, these basic assumptions were justified in the textbook by recourse to two claims: "The first claim, that all anti-feudal movements were *eo ipso* movements for the freedom

---

169   Henryk Wereszycki, *Niewygasła przeszłość*, Kraków 1987.
170   Ibidem, 250.
171   Ibidem, 251.

of the nation. And the second claim, that every counter-revolutionary idea, every idea defending feudalism was also anti-national. These claims draw us to the very depths of pessimism. The peasant who struggles against the feudal oppression is the driving force of the liberation movement: that is an oft-repeated phrase. Yet, the textbook is scientifically sound, and hence, specific facts stand in constant contradiction to this main claim. As a result, the peasants' movement in Galicia in 1846 [aimed against Polish insurrectionists – MG] becomes the greatest Polish anti-feudal movement of the era. If that is a liberation movement, and particularly the greatest of the era, then the main claim is surely awash in pessimism."[172] Wereszycki argued that in the 19th century, the achievements of the higher classes were necessarily of a much higher importance for Polish culture and the national cause; yet these classes were deplored by the authors of the textbook. It was an obvious mistake to evaluate the past anachronistically, through the lens of contemporary politics. The authors should have reminded themselves that their work was addressed primarily to the young reader. "Therefore, if the authors want to make the minds of the youth more susceptible to the ideas they propagate, they need to take their feelings into account as well. If the feelings of the youth are offended, the youth will be inclined to reject all that the textbook offers."[173]

Wereszycki's statement was only one among many critical evaluations of the "Draft." In April 1957, during a debate over its second volume, the number of critical comments rose so high that a resigned Witold Kula scribbled in his notebook: "What I'm not going to talk about: 1) How the same people judged the same things in January 1956; 2) How those responsible avoided criticism in January 1956."[174] When he finally got to speak, he conceded that though the Marxist historians set numerous historical falsities straight, they created a spate of new ones themselves, thereby risking losing the confidence of their readers. According to Kula, the thaw was sometimes understood in historiography in an unwise manner, veering dangerously close to nationalism. This was not the result he had envisioned from the work of correcting the Stalinist period's errors. And yet, after 1956, it was becoming customary to shrug off the entire output of the previous decade, without making any efforts at distinguishing between its virtues and its vices.[175]

The authors of the textbook tried to apply all the necessary (and possible) corrections to their work before its final version saw print. The brunt of those

---

172   Ibidem, 252.
173   Ibidem, 276.
174   Dział Rękopisów BUW, Spuścizna Witolda Kuli, p. 9, t.: Udział w konferencjach – Dyskusja nad makietą II tomu UPHP, Sulejówek, 14-17 IV 1957.
175   Ibidem.

corrections was in fact borne by several people, primarily Witold Kula, Tadeusz Manteuffel, elected as the solitary editor of the entire work in 1956 (up until that point, in accordance with the rules promoting at least formally collective work, the book was edited by a team of several people), and finally Stefan Kieniewicz, who had, for instance, made corrections to chapters on the 19th century, which were prepared by Celina Bobińska.[176] Despite their efforts, the reaction to early volumes of the final version of the textbook was hardly positive. In June 1958, *Twórczość* magazine published an article by Paweł Jasienica, an author one would hardly associate with the Marxist methodology.[177] Of course, Jasienica had a number of reservations with regard to the university textbook on the history of Poland as well (mostly related to the selection of boundary dates for the particular volumes), yet it was the way other critics had lambasted the book's authors that elicited his firm protest. "The work on *The History of Poland* began in Autumn 1952," Jasienica wrote, "In subsequent years, many things changed for the better, and it made the work of this team of scholars decidedly more complex. The outposts of 'schematism, dogmatism and one-sided distortions,' at first dismantled piece by piece with great effort, started falling one by one in 1956. Life took on an insane pace, and the heavy machine working on the *History* at full-steam had to adjust to rapidly changing conditions."[178] The team working on the textbook did all they could – Jasienica continued. After the thaw, the only way to make everybody happy was to call a halt to all work on the project and "linger, keeping one's ears to the ground." However, in his eyes, such behaviour would be simply foolish.

Jasienica also believed some of the reactions to the work betrayed ill will: "The printing process for the *History* ended in November 1957, and the book reached the readers only in January. Yet already on December 17th, *Polityka* carried an extensive piece entitled 'Adult prose.' Its author scoffs loftily: 'A serious work, an effect of a collective effort, perhaps a bit untimely, but fairly ambitious, a synthesis of a representative character, claims that Władysław II Wygnaniec "became an agent of foreign intervention." We are talking about a prince from the second quarter of the 12th century, a son to Bolesław Krzywousty.' The statement could likely be found in the 'draft' of the work, but sounds much different in the final version of *History*: 'Władysław II, later called Wygnaniec, quickly followed the route chosen by numerous disinherited rulers, bringing foreign intervention into his homeland.' It's beyond my

---

176 Dział Rękopisów BUW, Spuścizna Witolda Kuli, p. 13, t.: Bieżące funkcjonowanie zawodowe – Stefan Kieniewicz to Kula on February 26 1956: "I'm returning the final 3 chapters by Bobińska … The historiography now looks decidedly better."
177 Paweł Jasienica, *Tylko o historii*, Warszawa 1992.
178 Ibidem, 73.

comprehension, this tendency to put spokes in others' wheels, to a public condemnation of faults in the project that were actually *mended*! I wouldn't tussle over any given piece if it wasn't for the fact that one can hear sometimes caustic remarks about *History* from people who have not seen or read it. This bad credit of faith – inevitably inflated by some personal scuffles – hurts people who performed a hard, necessary and useful work. It isn't free of errors and faults, but I doubt that anyone could have done it better in the complicated conditions of the past few years. It's very likely that the final fruit of the work of the authors of *History* is in reality fairly close to a best possible performance in these circumstances."[179]

The authors of the textbook took the critical comments of the readers of the "Draft" very seriously. This is well illustrated by an analysis of the introduction to the first part of the second volume of the book, published in 1958 (edited by Stefan Kieniewicz and Witold Kula).[180] The editors started the book off by informing the readers that, as a result of the debate over the "Draft," the meeting in Sulejówek, and the article by Henryk Wereszycki, "It can be said that some chapters were written anew."[181] The highly controversial issue of the boundary dates chosen for the volume – 1764 and 1864 instead of the traditional choices of the Third Partition (1795) and – e.g. – the insurrection of 1863 – was treated in detail (these were the boundary dates both Wereszycki and Jasienica questioned). The authors of the preface underlined with force that "The rules of periodisation ... were approved ... in the years 1953-54, and have been maintained in the same general shape without changes. These rules are entirely debatable by definition."[182] The period discussed in the volume was characterised by the authors as the crisis of feudalism, yet it is hard not to think that by 1958 such "Marxist" periodisations, based on the theory of formations, were typically cast aside, to make room for reinstated traditional caesuras. This is where the following hint, included in the preface, comes from: "The first part of the second volume, together with the two parts of the first volume, forms a three-volume history of independent Poland, while the second and third parts of the second volume are a beginning of a four-volume history of post-Partition Poland."[183]

Compared to the Marxist syntheses of national histories published in Poland and Czechoslovakia, the GDR's *Lehrbuch der deutschen Geschichte* stands out

---

179   Ibidem, 74.
180   *Historia Polski*, vol. 2, 1764-1864, part 1, 1764-1795, eds. Stefan Kieniewicz & Witold Kula Warszawa 1958.
181   Ibidem, 4.
182   Ibidem, 1.
183   Ibidem, 3.

already by its appearance. Both the "Drafts" and the final versions of the other textbooks are typically bulky volumes marked by the names of several editors and even more collaborators, co-authors of specific fragments and authors of studies used to create the textbooks. In the case of the textbook written in the GDR, we are dealing with a series of slim books of a smaller size, distinctly marked with the name of a single author (or sometimes two). The collective that was involved in the preparatory work remained in the shadow of the seminal figures of East German historiography, a practice which marked something akin to a revision of the otherwise commonly embraced egalitarian methodological and organisational guidelines.

The decision to publish the Marxist synthesis of the history of Germany at a faster pace, until 1953, was taken by the Central Committee of the SED in October 1951. Alfred Meusel, the only card-carrying historian in the GDR who could boast a pre-World War II professorship, was named chief editor of the project. Having returned from exile in Great Britain in 1946, Meusel taught at Humboldt University in Berlin, where he was also appointed Dean of the Department of Philosophy. In 1947, he became the first Marxist full professor, and then was appointed director of the Museum für Deutsche Geschichte. The authors of the particular volumes of the Marxist textbook benefited from rich aid provided by the employees of the Museum für Deutsche Geschichte and the Institut für die Geschichte des deutschen Volkes of the Humboldt University in Berlin. Among the authors, one could also find formidable figures of East German historiography, such as Ernst Engelberg, Gerhard Schilfert, Heinz Kamnitzer, Karl Obermann or Albert Schreiner. Outlines of particular chapters were discussed at the publishing committee meetings and published in *Zeitschrift für Geschichtswissenschaft*.[184]

The ambitious undertaking faced numerous obstacles, some of the kind reminiscent of the work on the Polish "Draft" and some entirely singular. The composition of the team of authors changed constantly – suffice it to say that seven names "fell out" of the initial list. Despite pressure from Walter Ulbricht, the work on the textbook became a protracted effort, and the deadline for its completion was inevitably pushed back. After 1956, the publishing committee was torn by an open conflict. First, Alfred Meusel's position was weakened when his close friend Jürgen Kuczynski fell out of favour with the authorities. Then, as a result of a discussion on the character of *Novemberrevolution*, Albert Schreiner was deposed from the committee. The personal and aspirational conflict between Meusel and Ernst Engelberg, however, proved the most fateful.

---

184   Mario Kessler, *Exilerfahrung in Wissenschaft und Politik. Remigrierte Historiker in der frühen DDR*, Köln-Weimar-Wien 2001, 85-86.

It was, to an extent, a struggle over the interpretation of national history. Alfred Meusel, an ardent supporter of German unity, believed that the forcible unification of the country and the formation of an empire in 1871 was a progressive event, despite its limitations. Engelberg, who was to become Bismarck's biographer and the co-author of the "Prussian renaissance" in the GDR, was at that time far more critical toward this part of the national tradition, and considered Meusel's interpretation unacceptable. The conflict between the two historians played itself out through internal reviews, memoranda to the authorities and conversations with employees of the Abteilung Wissenschaften of the Central Committee of the SED rather than in professional magazines or even the popular press, but Meusel, who at first had enjoyed a higher standing as an editor reviewing Engelberg's text, made some exceptionally vicious comments, also with regard to the writing style of his competitor – he stated that professors should not demand of their pupils that they write in good German as long as they cannot do it themselves.[185]

At the point when the work on the textbook (and the attendant conflict between Engelberg and Meusel) were progressing at an ever-increasing pace, Alfred Meusel was one of the leaders of the community of historians of the GDR. This was also how he was seen within the Party: the very fact that he was given the task of overseeing the publication of a key work proved it beyond doubt. Engelberg, on the other hand, was a "greenhorn" Marxist, struggling both to gain acceptance for his interpretations and to achieve a position that would match his personal ambitions. Tried and imprisoned in the Third Reich, he had later emigrated to Switzerland. After the war broke out, when the Swiss authorities began to persecute antifascists, he had agreed to take up a job as a German teacher at the Istanbul University. After his return to Leipzig in 1948, Engelberg gave lectures on German history at the local university and was appointed director of the Institut für Deutsche Geschichte. Despite alleged connections with Rudolf Slánský, Engelberg's career proceeded apace. Luck was apparently on his side, as Meusel's position began to wane in the later 1950s. The dissolution of remnants of unity between German historians on both sides of the border, as well as the anti-revisionist campaign, both worked to Engelberg's benefit.

Meusel's position became precarious as a result of an affair that gave East German historiography a bad name abroad. Meusel had high hopes for a younger colleague he ardently promoted – the émigré Heinz Kamnitzer (1917-2001). Having returned from England, Kamnitzer joined the SED and, since 1947, lectured at Humboldt University. Between 1952 and 1954, he headed the

---

185   Ibidem, 242.

university's Institute of History (Institut für Geschichte des Deutschen Volkes) and was the Dean of the University, and between 1953 and 1955, he co-edited the *Zeitschrift für Geschichtswissenschaft*. In 1952, Meusel's monograph, *Thomas Müntzer und seine Zeit*, appeared in print; Kamnitzer selected source materials for the publication. In his introduction, he professed that the texts he chose were completely new to historians. In reality, however, the selection consisted of texts that had already come out in print and were familiar to historians. The damage to his reputation was all the more significant for the fact that, as a Communist and Jew, he eagerly castigated West German historians with a national-socialist past. Now, it was their time to exact their revenge on the moralist. In later years, Kamnitzer left history behind and devoted himself to literature.

Meusel and Engelberg's struggle consisted of sending letters to Party authorities. Ignoring the rules of collective work (as well as many other rules), Engelberg contacted the Department of Science of the Central Committee of the SED in February 1958 with a proposal for the publication of a volume under his editorship, *Deutschland von 1849 bis 1871*.[186] He complained that because of Meusel he fell victim to indiscriminate attacks from the publishing committee and hence suggested that the committee be bypassed in this case. The authorities accepted his suggestion, and the volume, devoted to the years 1849 to 1871, saw print as the first of the series, despite being scheduled to appear as only the seventh of the sequence. What is more, because of his steadfast rejection of any kind of cooperation with West German historiographers, Engelberg earned himself the position as head of the newly-formed association of GDR historians, the DHG.

This was not the end of Engelberg's assaults on his elder colleague though. In subsequent letters to the Central Committee of the SED, Engelberg demanded that Meusel be removed from his position as chief editor in the author's collective. He accused Meusel of espousing liberal views, criticised his interpretation of history, and finally charged him with a deviation from the ruling methodology. He concluded that their conflict was a "clash between a warring Marxism on the one side, and a just as combative and conscious non-Marxism on the other."[187] More importantly from the perspective of the work on Marxist synthesis, Engelberg expressed the belief that Meusel's activities robbed the author's collective of any ability to act further. Therefore, he advocated that the collective be disbanded and individual agreements signed with particular authors.[188]

---

186   Ernst Engelberg, *Deutschland von 1849 bis 1871*, Berlin 1959.
187   Quoted in: Kessler, *Exilerfahrung*, 243.
188   Ibidem, 244.

The ruthless struggle over the main historical undertaking of the East German academy ended only with Alfred Meusel's death in September 1960. Eventually, as Martin Sabrow remarked with irony, this erstwhile seminal figure of East German historiography did not get his name on any of the textbook's volumes.[189] His idea that "Drafts" of the subsequent volumes of the textbook be printed first, like in other people's democracies, to spark a broader, national debate, was also dropped. Though the textbook did eventually appear in print, it hardly qualifies as a monument to a collective effort. It was found wanting in terms of its professional status, reliability, and level of detail. The final shape of this East German historical synthesis largely bears out the character of the community of local card-carrying historians, whose main and most representative example was the efficient tactician, experienced political player, and also historian, Ernst Engelberg.

In each of the countries that interest us here, scientific associations of historians, academies of learning and professional societies boasted an old and rich tradition. However, the decision of Communist authorities to introduce deep organisational changes, leaving behind old scientific traditions, should not be thought of as an act of reckless vandalism; in fact, it was an outcome of reasoned calculation (as far as the authorities were concerned). Of course, historical institutes of the Party, focused on the history of local organised workers' movements and filled with deserving Party activists, had already been in place at that time. The goal was not to counterbalance the existing structures, but rather to form and control an institution that would oversee the entire historiographical effort of each nation and would command the respect of society as well as the esteem of the historical community. The formation of Academies, tasked solely with research activities and a representative role, facilitated control over the historians and made it possible to create elevated offices for leading card-carrying scholars, who could then devote their time to writing, at a remove from teaching obligations. Additionally, a structure created from the ground up could be easily shaped and politically controlled.

The centralisation of scientific societies was universally opposed – the opposition, however, did not utterly and fundamentally reject the policy of centralisation, but rather resisted the shape of reforms that were expected to occur sooner or later in any case. The members of several Czech scientific societies conducted extended negotiations with authorities, hoping that the

---

189 Martin Sabrow, "Auf der Suche nach dem materialistischen Meisterton. Bauformen einer nationalen Gegenerzählung in der DDR," in: *Die historische Meistererzählung. Deutungslinien der deutschen Nationalgeschichte nach 1945*, eds. Konrad H. Jarausch & Martin Sabrow Göttingen 2002, 55.

projected Czechoslovak Academy of Sciences (Československá Akademie Věd, ČSAV) would turn out to be merely a "cap" over the other organisations, a formalised centre for a federation of independent entities. Their hopes turned out to have been futile.

From the very beginning, both Polish and other academies of science were all expected to attain two seemingly contradictory goals. On the one hand, they were supposed to introduce the new methodology, setting an example for scientists all over their respective countries. On the other hand, though, as the authors of the Polish Party's internal document wrote, "For political reasons, it [wa]s necessary that PAN t[ook] over from the Polish Academy of Learning and other general associations the serious and recognised scholars not currently engaged in academic work; though they may often be ideologically foreign to us, [because] they [we]re well known to have been of great service to the Polish academy."[190] PAN was therefore conceived as a Marxist institution as well as a refuge for scientists who exerted a pernicious influence on the youth. This characteristic befit the Institute of History at PAN as well.[191]

Consequently, traditional scientific associations and the newly-founded academies of science based on the Soviet model recruited their personnel in highly similar ways. Even members of old associations, who – as in Czechoslovakia – questioned the sensibility of the government's centralisation policy, were typically inducted into the academies of science.[192] The new academies were even open to those scientists whose credentials were in doubt due to the Party cells at their home departments.[193] To an extent, then, academies acted as a preserve for those who were refused the right to teach. In the case of Poland, the two spheres in fact never separated entirely, as scholars of the Institute of History at PAN could often enjoy double employment: both at the academy and at a university. As a rule, academic institutions benefited from

---

190   Archiwum Akt Nowych, sygn. 237/XVI – 27, KC PZPR Wydział Nauki i Szkolnictwa Wyższego – Uchwała BP KC PZPR w sprawie PAN. Tajne. Projekt, 1951.

191   Stefan Kieniewicz, "Kilka słów o Instytucie Historycznym," in: Instytut Historii, 74; Frank Hadler, „Geschichtsinstitute an ostmitteleuropäischen Wissenschaftsakademien. Budapest, Prag und Warschau im Vergleich," in: *Historische Institute im internationalen Vergleich*, eds. Matthias Middell, Gabriele Lingelbach & Frank Hadler, Leipzig 2001, 302-303.

192   Magdalena Pokorná, "Sjednocením proti jednotě. Spor o budoucí podobu akademie věd," in: *Věda v Československu v letech 1945-1953. Sborník z konference*, eds. Blanka Zilynská, Petr Svobodný & Blanka Šachová, Praha 1999, 120.

193   Alena Míšková, "ČAVU a ČSAV: Otázky kontinuity a diskontinuity II. (Vytvoření sboru členů ČSAV a jeho vztah k členské základně ČAVU a KČSN)," in: *Česká akademie věd a umění 1891-1991. Sborník příspěvků k 100. výročí zahájení činnosti*, eds. Jiří Pokorný & Jan Novotný, Praha 1993, 107.

a decidedly more friendly atmosphere than the universities, and were much more welcoming to "bourgeois" scholars.[194]

At the same time, in both the Czech and Slovak scholarly communities a far greater role was played by a sizeable group of younger scholars, steadfastly supportive of government policies and in most cases belonging to the Party. Lýdia Kamencová writes of sections of SAV in which the "young," ardent supporters of the Communist ideology, were paired with the "old," typically opportunist scholars, seeking only to adapt to the new situation.[195] At times, conflicts erupted between these two groups.

Polish, Czech and Slovak institutes of history at the national academies of science, established between 1952 and 1953, shared a similar structure and an identical set of goals. The research units which comprised them were divided according to chronology – in Czechoslovakia, they owed their names to the theory of formations, while in Poland, the boundary dates between the great epochs served as official titles. In the early 1960s, when its personnel was already fully established, the Institute of History at PAN employed over 180 people; toward the end of the 1950s, its Czech counterpart employed just over 70 people.[196] At the time of its formation, the Institute of History at SAV employed 16 people, but that number grew steadily.[197] The Institute of History at PAN stood out among other equivalent institutions because of its decentralised structure: nearly half of its personnel worked in affiliate institutes (the Prague Institute had only two branches; the idea of creating branches was only considered at the SAV in the 1960s).

Aside from the production of monographs, the institutes were tasked with popularising Marxist methodology through the publication of central historical magazines, the creation of Marxist syntheses of national history, documentary and bibliographic work, as well as the schooling of younger cadres. In terms of work organisation, they were expected to introduce collective methods (exemplified by university textbooks on the histories of Poland, Czechoslovakia and Slovakia). The employees, task groups and entire institutes were supposed

---

194 Jindřich Schwippel, "ČAVU a ČSAV: otázky kontinuity a diskontinuity I.," in: *Česká akademie*, 95.

195 Lýdia Kamencová, "Rozvoj spoločenských vied na Slovensku v rokoch 1953-1963 v materiáloch Ústredného archívu SAV," in: *Věda v Československu v letech 1953-1963. Sborník z konference (Praha 23.-24. listopadu 1999)*, eds. Hana Barvíková, Marek Ďurčanský & Pavel Kodera, Praha 2000, 325.

196 Frank Hadler, "Geschichtsinstitute an ostmitteleuropäischen Wissenschaftsakademien. Budapest, Prag und Warschau im Vergleich," in: *Historische Institute*, 307.

197 *Slovenská akadémia vied 1953-1973*, eds. Milan Repaš, Vojtech Filkorn, Ján Gouda, Vojtech Kellö, Miroslav Murín & Alexander Ujváry, Bratislava 1974, 73.

to draft yearly plans, and then report on their completion.[198] In practice, planning was a real nuisance, especially in the early years of the new academies. The new model of work organisation raised issues which are well illustrated in the debate over a project of a general plan for the entire Institute of History at PAN, presented by Witold Kula at the third meeting of the Academic Council, in November 1953. The project was criticised by the auditorium for having missed questions that particular members of the Academic Council deemed vital, or for devoting insufficient space to the work of regional branches that these members oversaw. Celina Bobińska protested against the exclusion from the project of the Kraków unit she directed which was devoted to researching class conflict in Lesser Poland. She underlined the political weight of the plan, which in its current shape had "st[olen] all support from the only combative Marxist department, already working in adverse circumstances."[199] Nearly all participants in the meeting agreed that the plan was chaotic and overlooked too many issues of prime importance. The director of the Institute was forced to explain to his audience the meaning of planning in science: "Planning isn't easy," he said, "we're still learning from those more experienced than us. Actually, though planning in science has been introduced in the Soviet Union over 20 years ago, no one dares to suggest a general, national plan for science. Each institute has its own plan, but there's no national plan. We need to draw conclusions from this fact. We shouldn't forget that both PAN and the Institute of History are productive establishments that plan their output and claim responsibility for it. Planning means committing oneself. A failure to complete a plan leads to very serious consequences. We can't plan to meet all guidelines for essential research tasks. These guidelines are meant to act as indicators whether financial aid should be offered for a given research proposal or not. This current debate, despite its advantages, leads us down a very dangerous alley. We can't and would invite ridicule for having the whole plan disqualified."[200]

Marxist research centres were expected to address new questions and come up with interpretations that would contest the products of "bourgeois" historiography. During a session of the Academic Council of the Institute in January 1954, Stanisław Arnold proposed that young academic employees focused solely on the most recent history. His proposal was supported by Stanisław Okęcki, who named several key topics of concern: "the necessity of shaping a 'historical' answer to Adenauer's revisionist propaganda. ... There's a

---

198   Hadler, "Geschichtsinstitute," 295-296.

199   Archiwum Instytutu Historii PAN, sygn. 5/27 Protokoły Rady Naukowej – Protokół nr 3 z posiedzenia Rady Naukowej IH PAN, 25 IX 1953.

200   Ibidem.

campaign going on to vindicate AK, NSZ[201]," Okęcki complained, "During the
past two months, [Radio] 'Free Europe' broadcast 85 programs devoted to topics
from Polish history. We have nothing with which to oppose this. This problem
should be addressed in our press, in our historical publications. We need to lend
more focus to counteracting enemy ideology."[202]

Until the early 1950s, decisions concerning the scholarly life in the Soviet
occupation zone of Germany were taken exclusively by the military
administration of the Red Army and its German auxiliary, the Deutsche
Zentralverwaltung für Volksbildung. A drastic shortage of scholarly employees,
dismissed as a result of denazification, forced the authorities to allow numerous
"bourgeois" scholars to maintain their posts to keep universities running. By the
end of the 1940s, the government policies in science were becoming more
stringent. As a part of the *Sturm auf die Festung Wissenschaft* (Assault on
Fortress Science), announced in 1951, historical institutes in half of East
German universities were liquidated. Until a sufficient number of Marxist cadres
was schooled, only institutes of the history of the German people (Institute für
Geschichte des deutschen Volkes) in Berlin, Leipzig and Halle, were
maintained.[203] In October 1951, the Central Committee of the SED proclaimed
the formation of a museum of German history, and then also of an institute of
history at the academy of sciences.[204]

At first, the museum was to be devoted to the history of the German
workers' movement, but eventually, it assumed the decidedly more neutral name
of the Museum für Deutsche Geschichte (Museum of German History). It began
operating in 1950. Describing its goals, Wilhelm Pieck said that until that point,
museums "still devote[d] too much space and attention to some mediocre
princelings. I believe that we should put an end to that and give that space to the
real German people, the workers and the peasants, thinkers and poets fighting
for freedom, to all who are entitled to this space on merit."[205] The museum was
supposed to discover and commemorate the progressive traditions of the
German nation from the German Peasants' Revolt until Ernst Thälmann.[206]
Among the museum's employees one could find "bourgeois" historians ("big
names") as well as Party members; gifted graduates of historical departments

---

201 AK – Armia Krajowa, NSZ – Narodowe Siły Zbrojne – organisations of non-
    Communist resistance during the Second World War.
202 Archiwum Instytutu Historii PAN, sygn. 5/27 Protokoły Rady Naukowej – Posiedzenie
    Rady Naukowej 26 I 1954 r.
203 Sabrow, *Das Diktat*, 40-41.
204 Ebenfeld, *Geschichte*, 41-42.
205 Quoted in: Kessler, *Exilerfahrung*, 79.
206 Ebenfeld, *Geschichte*, 63.

were also sought after with intent, since the museum was supposed to become a central research institute for East Germany as well, an equivalent of an academic institute of history.

The enlistment of employees for the new institution turned out to be a problematic task. Historians working at universities, or even the Party's Marx-Engels-Lenin-Stalin Institute (M-E-L-S-Institut) at the Central Committee of the SED, were loath to leave their jobs. Alfred Meusel also failed to show any enthusiasm upon receiving his nomination for the post of museum director (throughout an almost two-year initial phase, the organisation was temporarily directed by an associate of the Marx-Engels-Lenin-Institut, Eduard Ullmann).[207] This choice exemplified a tendency toward shaping the museum as a separate institution not associated with the Party, but rather with the unitary German nation, in accordance with the views espoused by Meusel, a tireless militant for a united, socialist Germany. The museum was also supposed to train young Marxist cadres. To ensure the proper quality of the training, however, it had to employ a tremendous percentage of "bourgeois" scholars. Their employment at an institution that was also responsible for visual and printed propaganda led to conflicts and violent divisions. Incidentally, these conflicts did not arise solely between the Party-members and non-Party employees.[208]

Keeping the museum working day in, day out gave its directors quite a headache. Personnel shortages translated into a dearth of middle-aged scholars, while young graduates and students closer to graduation were represented in throngs. Almost no one (including the director himself) had any experience in museum work; most employees were only learning the basics of scholarly work. The first exhibitions were scheduled to open on May 1st, 1952, but were running late by over two months. The museum operated under continuous and very strict control from the Central Committee, which sanctioned exhibition plans and evaluated their completion. Stefan Ebenfeld quotes an exemplary intervention of the Central Committee of the SED, concerned with the period from 1918 to 1945: "While exhibiting the fascist terror, the use of the poem *Kinderschule* by J.R. Becher is advised" (Johannes R. Becher was an officially approved prominent poet of the GDR),[209] and Fritz Haecker's painting was to be remade because the members of the Political Office "look[ed] too thin."[210]

---

207   Ibidem, 91-96.

208   Karen Pfundt, "Die Gründung des Museums für Deutsche Geschichte", in: *Historische Forschung und sozialistische Diktatur. Beiträge zur Geschichtswissenschaft der DDR*, eds. Martin Sabrow & Peter Th. Walther, Leipzig 1995, 101-102.

209   Manfred Jäger, *Kultur und Politik in der DDR. Ein historischer Abriß*, Köln 1982, 1-9.

210   Ebenfeld, *Geschichte*, 120-121.

The work of the museum was also troubled by internal conflicts between its director and Albert Schreiner. The latter, a veteran of the *Novemberrevolution* and a Party apparatchik, became the chief of the museum's department concerned with the 1918-1945 period and pushed it to approach that era from a strictly Party perspective, with special attention to the November Revolution, which in his eyes was a proletarian affair. Meusel did not accept that vision. "This script," he wrote, "represents a story of a German failure, illustrated – or even better – identified with the history of the KPD. It's a story about the good who are always right, but unfortunately always lose, while the bad, who are always wrong, unfortunately always win. Had the script not ended with the victory of the Socialist Soviet Union during the Second World War and the Potsdam Treaty, I'd be forced to call it one of the saddest stories I've ever read."[211] With regard to the general character of the exhibition, the Party authorities lent Schreiner their support; however, the *Novemberrevolution* was re-evaluated in accordance with the guidelines of the *Short course*....[212]

The ambiguity of the position of the museum was also exposed in the fact that, beside the didactic and museum work, its employees were also expected to prepare a Marxist textbook on German history. The fact that Alfred Meusel became the chief editor of the entire work was in no way a coincidence: the production of the textbook was expected to engage the "human resources" found at the museum, and the directors of particular departments were to act as (and, to an extent, became) authors of particular volumes of the projected work. More than that: despite there being no formal connection between the *Zeitschrift für Geschichtswissenschaft* and the museum, the central historical magazine of East Germany was commonly assumed to have been yet another outlet of the Museum für Deutsche Geschichte.[213]

With both the museum and the historical departments at several East German universities in place, the formation of a central academic historical institute turned out to be a rather daunting challenge. Each of the existing institutions came with its own set of card-carrying, well-connected directors. This system did not favour centralisation, as it would have been concomitant with renouncing personal privileges, submitting to another leading historian, or losing part of one's independence. The choice of the first director of the Institut für Geschichte at the DAW was a question of compromise: though Karl Obermann was a Communist returnee, he was not as significant as Leo Stern, Alfred Meusel or Jürgen Kuczynski (nor as competitive as Ernst Engelberg). He

211   Quoted in: ibidem, 142. See. Pfundt, "Die Gründung," 109.
212   Kessler, *Exilerfahrung*, 81.
213   Ebenfeld, *Geschichte*, 144-148.

was, however, one of the first scholars researching the workers' movement and 19th century workers' history. As we shall see, this curious compromise with regard to personnel did not hold too long.

The newly-established (in March 1956) Institute took over the main task of the Museum für Deutsche Geschichte: the creation of a Marxist textbook on German history. Among the ranks of the academic institute of history were numerous employees of the museum, with prominent historians of the museum's Academic Council topping the list. During its first year, the Institute recruited over sixty people for its five chronologically divided departments.[214] Though the Institute was located in Berlin, the directors of its particular departments transferred their work to cities in which they held professorial or administrative positions. Because of that, the Institute of History of the DAW became as decentralised as its equivalent at PAN, the main difference being that its decentralisation was a result of a power play between prominent Marxists of the GDR, rather than an attempt at empowering provincial research centres. Compared to academy institutes in other people's democracies, the East German incarnation of the institution was also distinguished – as Martin Sabrow points out – by a very strict, quite organic politicisation.[215]

The Institute of History at DAW was imagined as the ground-breaking institution for the new science. A year after it officially opened, both the Institute and the Museum für Deutsche Geschichte publicly condemned Jürgen Kuczynski, who was suspected of harbouring revisionist sympathies. This moment marked a distinct caesura in the history of the Institute: the authorities and some card-carrying historians used this opportunity to vehemently criticize what they perceived as the excessively high standing of their "bourgeois" colleagues. Heinrich Scheel called for a reorganisation of the Institute into a strictly Party-bound research centre.[216] In September 1958, director Obermann was assaulted by Rolf Dlubek, who discerned remnants of positivism and "factology," an "archival fetishism" and objectivism in the part of the *Lehrbuch* Obermann was tasked with preparing.[217] Prominent directors of several departments of the Institute of History at DAW – Ernst Engelberg, Albert Schreiner, Leo Stern and Jürgen Kuczynski – also spoke out against Obermann. Though engaged in mutual argument, they were all in perfect agreement in their critical evaluation of the director. Party leadership took up an interest in

---

214   Sabrow, *Das Diktat*, 55-71.

215   Martin Sabrow, "Parteiliches Wissenschaftsideal und historische Forschungspraxis. Überlegungen zum Akademie – Institut für Geschichte (1956-1989)," in: *Historische Forschung*, 202.

216   Ibidem, 81-82.

217   Kessler, *Exilerfahrung*, 215.

Obermann, assuming that his political qualifications were not sufficient for performing such a prominent function.[218]

However, Obermann's critics were unable to reach a compromise as to his prospective replacement. The basic Party organisation at the Institute reserved the seat for Leo Stern, who directed the department of the museum tasked with researching the Second World War. However, while Obermann was characterised by an insufficient political commitment in the eyes of the Party activists, Stern was charged with even heavier crimes. The erstwhile would-be director of the Institute of History at DAW, Leo Stern (born Jonas Leib), hailed from Austria. He was the only East German émigré historian to have taken part in the Second World War on the side of the Soviets (he fought in the Battle of Stalingrad). In 1945, he lectured at the University of Vienna, but his Austrian career was soon broken by a fatal coincidence. As a delegate of the Austrian Communist Party to the celebrations of May 1st at the provincial town of Kleinpöchlarn, he was assaulted and wounded by unrecognised drunks. The Soviet soldiers, who were summoned to the location, shot several random participants in the celebrations, incidentally Communists. From that event on, Stern was labelled a NKVD spy. Because of this, he joyfully accepted an invitation to take over the department of modern history at the University of Halle. As a professor since 1950, and three years later as a rector of that university, he presided over the task group *Dokumente und Materialien zur Geschichte der deutschen Arbeiterbewegung*. The group was composed mostly of "bourgeois" historians, some of them even burdened with a national-socialist past. This made Stern susceptible to political assaults. The first of these took place in 1954, when one of Stern's collaborators, Werner Frauendienst was accused of glorifying Prussia. Corrections sent to the editors of *Neues Deutschland* did not improve his situation, and Frauendienst opted not to wait for the story to unwind and fled to West Germany.[219] Four years later, the University of Halle was afflicted by a series of escapes to the West; among the escapees was yet another assistant professor, Ernst Klein, and Stern was summoned by the Rütten&Loening publishing house to provide an explanation for the fact that a collection of documents concerning the Great Socialist October Revolution would not appear as scheduled after several of his collaborators on the project permanently left the country.[220]

Stern's rival to the seat of director of DAW's Institute of History, Ernst Engelberg, was fully capable of ruthlessly exploiting all of Stern's mishaps. As a

---

218   Ibidem, 215.
219   Ibidem, 271-273.
220   Sabrow, *Das Diktat*, 101.

member of the younger generation of historians of the GDR, he steadfastly opposed all kinds of collaboration with "bourgeois" scholars. At the point when he took over the leadership of the East German historical association, having pushed Alfred Meusel from his position as the chief editor of the Marxist synthesis of German history, and took up the position the director of the Institute of History at DAW, East German historiography entered a new phase of development.[221] Ernst Engelberg was at the same time the last "great" among GDR historiographers. After him, no one ever played as seminal a role: the new education system, shaped in part by Engelberg himself (as well as his rivals), did not foster such exceptional individuality.

The struggle for the position of director of the Institute of History at the East German Academy of Sciences was unprecedented in either of the other countries under our consideration. In the case of Czechoslovakia, the competition ended with the equivalent position at the Czech Academy handed to Josef Macek (1922-91), a young historian of the Mediaeval era. According to Bohumil Jiroušek, this was a surprising decision, since the design of the structure of the Institute of History at ČSAV was the brainchild not of Macek, but of Václav Husa. Going forward, Macek's eventual victory proved to have affected the frigid relations between the academy of sciences and the philosophical department of Charles University in Prague, where Husa led the Czechoslovak history section.[222] At the same time, it was just another stage in a career that led the former student of Zdeněk Kalista to considerable heights. Macek became not only the director of the Institute of History at ČSAV, but also a representative in the National Assembly, and even a member of the Central Committee of the KSČ.[223] Right after his nomination as director of the Institute, he was also appointed a regular member of the ČSAV – and all at the age of only 31![224] At the dawn of this stunning career stood a national award the young historian received in 1952 for his work entitled *Husitské revoluční hnutí*.

What could have prompted such swift promotion? Petr Čornej, who questioned Macek about the circumstances of the award's presentation, recounts the following story: "Right after 1948 [when Macek passed his M.A. exam – MG], he devoted himself to researching the beginnings of Tábor in a broad work entitled *Tábor v husitském revolučním hnutí*. Sadly, no one was interested in publishing the book; every publishing house pointed to the specialist nature of the work and suggested that the author submit a piece that could explain to 'the

221   Ibidem, 112.
222   Bohumil Jiroušek, *Josef Macek. Mezi historií a politikou*, Praha 2004, 38-40.
223   Ibidem; See also Hanzal, Cesty, 104-105; *In memoriam Josefa Macka (1922-1991)*, eds. Miloslav Polívka & František Šmahel, Praha 1996.
224   Hadler, "Geschichtsinstitute," 293-294.

working people' the Marxist views on the role of the Hussite movement in Czech and European history. This is supposedly how *Husitské revoluční hnutí*, the work that paved the way to the highest positions and a strong political standing for the thirty-year-old Macek, came into being. It hardly needs to be added that it took personal ambition and good connections in the Communist leadership to make such a brilliant career possible. By a twist of fate, Macek's history of the Hussite movement was published while a prominent Communist functionary overseeing the formation of the Czechoslovak Academy of Sciences, Ladislav Štoll (1902-81), was recovering in a hospital. He killed time reading the latest books – that is how he happened upon Macek's *Husitské revoluční hnutí*, a book he found enchanting. It was Štoll who put the young historian on the road to success, bringing him his national prize."[225]

Ambitious, intelligent, and enjoying the support of Party leadership, Josef Macek cut a figure reminiscent of his senior of 13 years, Ernst Engelberg. Yet, his later career followed a much different route. Macek took an active part in the liquidation of the remnants of Czechoslovak Stalinism. Following his involvement in documenting the 1968 intervention of Warsaw Pact forces in Czechoslovakia, he was ousted from his position and rejected the right to publish his works in the country by the Husák regime. This did not prevent him from enjoying worldwide renown as a specialist on the Renaissance, or from publishing in foreign languages.

There was no ruthless struggle for the position of director in the new institute in Slovakia either. In this particular case, the Communist authorities simply had no candidates on hand that could offer a proper scientific quality as well as guarantee faithfulness and loyalty to the cause. While the German occupation was still in place, Alexander Markuš seemed an option, but he died prematurely while being transported to a concentration camp.[226] At the turn of the 1940s, the position of director of the Institute of History at SAVU was held by, among others, Jaroslav Dubnický (1916-79, born Jaroslav Honza), a Marxist historian of art and an official of the Plenipotentiary for Education and Culture ("plenipotentiary" was an equivalent of the 'ministry in Prague, tasked with representing the central government of Slovakia). Dubnický was briefly preceded in his directorial position by three "bourgeois" historians: František Bokes, Alexander Húščava (1906-69) and Branislav Varsik (1904-94). Dubnický also took over lectures in the history of Slovakia for students at Komenský University in Bratislava from the expelled Daniel Rapant (in 1950-

---

225 Čornej, *Lipanské*, 168.
226 Anton Špiesz, "K problematike starších dejín Slovenska," *Historický Časopis SAV* 1990, 683; Hudek, *Najpolitickejšia*, 50.

51, Dubnický was the Dean of the Philological Department at the university). He was one of the few Slovak scholars in the humanities who had any knowledge of Marxist methodology, which is why he was tasked with the heavy burden of teaching it to other Slovak historians.[227] His ties to the KSČ dated back to before the war; he formally joined the Party in 1945, and three years later, he oversaw purges in the Slovak historical association.[228]

With an excess of responsibilities on his hands, Dubnický was replaced as director of the newly-formed Institute of History at SAV by Ľudovít Holotík (1923-85; he was already the director of the Institute of History at SAVU since 1951). Holotík was an alumnus of the Prague School of Politics and Society (Vysoká škola politická a sociální, which preceded VŠPHV). After graduation, he worked at the School as an assistant and conducted classes in Marxism-Leninism at the Medical Department of Charles University. Following his return to Slovakia, he also became the chief editor for *Historický Časopis SAV* and edited the Marxist synthesis of national history. Despite his apparent prominence, Ján Mlynárik describes Holotík as a tragic figure in his role as one of the leading representatives of Slovak historiography. Too intelligent to gain the trust of Slovak Party apparatchiks, Holotík became a "buffer": for the historical community (as well as the reading public), he became the face of the Stalinisation of historical sciences, slandering the heroes of the Slovak National Uprising and condemning the sins of interwar Czechoslovakia, both real and imagined. He was evidently unable to stay in tune with the times: his book "unmasking" the real face of Milan Rastislav Štefánik appeared only in 1958, well after the 20th Congress of the Communist Party of the Soviet Union, at a time when such publications were already dated. In 1968, this work stood as a symbol of the Stalinisation of Slovak science and was publicly burned in effigy by students protesting against this repressive policy. A year later, Holotík published a text in which he claimed the ephemeral Slovak Soviet Republic, far from being an example of proletarian internationalism, was actually a Hungarian attempt at violating the territorial integrity of Czechoslovakia. Meanwhile, card-carrying scholars were mostly of the persuasion that the Slovak Soviet Republic represented a "progressive tradition of the Slovak nation." As a result of these interpretative mistakes, a lack of both a political sense and the support of sufficiently powerful friends, Holotík, the director of the Institute of History at SAV and the editor of the central historical magazine as well as the synthesis, never became a full-time member of either the SAV or the ČSAV. On the

---

227   Havrila, *Slovenská*, chapter: "Hlavné pracoviská slovenskej historickej vedy."
228   See *Slovenský historický slovník (od roku 833 do roku 1990)*, eds. Vladimír Mináč et al., vol. 1, Martin 1986.

contrary: 1968 de-Stalinisation deposed him from all posts (he ceded his position as director terminally, and resigned from his editorship duties temporally). A suicide committed in 1985, at the height of Husák's normalisation, provided a tragic ending to his story.[229]

The Institute of History at PAN differed significantly from other equivalent institutes of the newly-formed academies; some scholars see this difference as an aftermath of the Otwock conference.[230] However, the final decision to offer the seat of director of the Institute to a non-Communist widely recognised both at home and abroad, Tadeusz Manteuffel, actually occurred only after the Otwock conference. The Central Archives of Modern Records in Warsaw store several variants of the directing cast of the Institute, all framed by the Department of Science of the Central Committee of the PZPR between 1951 and 1952. Neither proposed Tadeusz Manteuffel as the director. Initially, the cast was supposed to be formed entirely of "Party elements." Henryk Jabłoński was the first prospective director, while Żanna Kormanowa, Nina Assorodobraj, Stanisław Arnold and Roman Heck were to act as his deputies. Positions within the Institute's sections were also supposed to be filled with Party members. The project left the issue of the post of director of the section of Polish history between 1795 and 1917 unresolved (the rivalling options were Celina Bobińska and Stefan Kieniewicz, but Kieniewicz's name came with an annotation stating that he was a Catholic).[231] Another plan of the personal cast for the Institute of History at PAN, appended to the previously mentioned projected resolution about the tasks of the Institute, suggested that Henryk Jabłoński become the Institute's director, while Stanisław Arnold and perhaps Natalia Gąsiorowska-Grabowska would act as his deputies, and Żanna Kormanowa would become an assistant on scientific matters. Manteuffel was included in the cast as one of the director's deputies.[232] This shows that the first corrections had already been applied, raising the number of non-Party historians involved in governing the Institute.

The findings of the Otwock conference were assessed by a special commission formed by the Office of the Political Bureau. Its work bore fruit in the shape of a resolution which, beside calls for improved efforts in the swift formation of the Institute of History and for the promotion of Marxist methodology, also included a motion to "promote to directorial positions non-

229 Mlynárik, *Diaspora*, 18-28.
230 Dział Rękopisów BUW, Spuścizna Niny Assorodobraj, VII/2 – Protokół konferencji organizacyjnej MZH...; Rafał Stobiecki, „Pierwsza Konferencja Metodologiczna," 208.
231 Archiwum Akt Nowych, sygn 237/XVI – 43 Wydział Nauki i Szkolnictwa Wyższego – Projekt obsady personalnej.
232 Archiwum Akt Nowych, sygn 237/XVI – 43 Wydział Nauki i Szkolnictwa Wyższego – Projekt obsady personalnej IH.

Party historians who showed a sufficient command of the Marxist-Leninist method and whose faithfulness to the People's Republic of Poland is beyond doubt."[233] The resolution also included another projected cast for the Institute of History at PAN, this time suggesting Natalia Gąsiorowska-Grabowska as the prospective director. Manteuffel was presented as her projected deputy, as were two further historians, Henryk Łowmiański and Bogusław Leśnodorski (1914-85); the position of the scientific assistant was reserved for Witold Kula or Juliusz Bardach.[234] This particular project was sent to Tadeusz Manteuffel for evaluation: he criticised it from top to bottom. He pointed out the overgrown directorial cadre, explaining the inevitable fragmentation of responsibilities that would result from it. It is hard to assess the extent to which his evaluation affected the academic policies of the authorities; it seems more instructive to read between the lines of his opinion. Manteuffel wrote: "Fully accepting the necessity of handing the position of the director to a Party member, we see two possible ways to make this course acceptable – a) to offer the position to a candidate of a younger age and essentially active, b) to offer it to an older candidate with a high political standing, who would only outline the general direction of the work of the Institute, while relying on a deputy to substitute for him on a regular basis."[235]

Obviously, the decision-makers eventually ceased to consult on the proposed cast for the Institute of History at PAN with Tadeusz Manteuffel and simply nominated him for the post of director of the Institute. Manteuffel differed in every possible way from the typical official leaders of Marxist historiography chosen in other countries discussed in the present study. He was not a member of the Party; he had studied in the West. He gained recognition already before the war, particularly as the organiser of the 1933 congress of Comité International des Sciences Historiques in Warsaw. During the occupation, he helped organize underground education, and right after the war, as we already know, he was involved in recreating the Historical Institute at the University of Warsaw. Consequently, as director of the Institute, he depended on his academic standing and organisational abilities. In 1950, he became elected president of the Polish Historical Society (PTH), his victory serving as proof of having gained the trust of the community. The fact that he was able to successfully negotiate the tendencies of the authorities to intrude into the lives of historians resulted also from a peculiar personal trait, unequivocally asserted by

---

233 Archiwum Akt Nowych, sygn 237/XVI – 43 Wydział Nauki i Szkolnictwa Wyższego –
     Uchwała Sekretariatu BP KC PZPR w sprawie nauk historycznych.
234 Archiwum Akt Nowych, sygn 237/XVI – 43 Wydział Nauki i Szkolnictwa Wyższego –
     projekt obsady IH PAN, no date.
235 Ibidem.

numerous witnesses who had the chance to make his acquaintance. He was endowed with a veritable charisma – he exuded trustworthiness while being quite fearsome.[236] In Party circles his comportment won him the nickname of the "wooden prince."[237] His authoritative standing is well illustrated by an anecdote recounted by Henryk Samsonowicz. During the 1956 elections for the new government of the historical society, the only candidate proposed and approved by the authorities, Natalia Gąsiorowska-Grabowska, lost out. Having long been connected with the Left (she belonged to the Parisian section of the PPS in 1904, sided with the party's left wing after it split, and during the interwar period, until 1922, was a member of the group that later reformed into the Polish Communist Party), she moved away from it after 1922, and did not join the KPP or the PPR. She did join PZPR in 1949, however. The authorities saw her for a while as a candidate for the editorship of *Kwartalnik Historyczny*, as well as a prospective director of the Institute of History at PAN; later, she presided over the Academic Council of the Institute, was a member of the Board of the PAN, and the president of the Polish Historical Society.[238] Gąsiorowska-Grabowska's defeat in the elections perplexed and scared the General Board of the Society, which then decided to call on Manteuffel, who was absent from the convention due to an illness. Manteuffel listened to a report by telephone, and then calmly asked: So what? His reaction prompted the Board to call for another election, this time with no candidates set for an instant victory.[239]

***

An in-depth analysis of the Communist scientific policies and their effect on historians would necessarily take much more room than we can afford to give it. The overview of the most important problems presented above is supposed to act as an introduction to the main part of this book – an analysis of the relationship between Marxist historiographies and national traditions, including the traditions of national historiographies. It delineates circumstances in which works quoted later on were written, and specifies the names of the historians engaged in the aforementioned scientific and political struggles. As we shall see,

---

236 Robert Jarocki, *Opowieść o Aleksandrze Gieysztorze*, Warszawa 2001, 233; also in verbal comunication with Marcin Kula.

237 Reminiscences of Stanisław Trawkowski at the celebration of the 100th anniversary of Tadeusz Manteuffel's birthday at the Institute of History at PAN, March 5th 2002.

238 See Ireneusz Ihnatowicz, "Natalia Gąsiorowska (1881-1964)," in: *Historycy warszawscy ostatnich dwóch stuleci*, eds. Aleksander Gieysztor, Jerzy Maternicki & Henryk Samsonowicz, Warszawa 1986, 252-256.

239 Reminiscences of Henryk Samsonowicz at the celebration of the 100th anniversary of Tadeusz Manteuffel's birthday at the Institute of History at PAN, March 5th 2002.

some of the traits of particular historical sciences discussed in this chapter are reflected in the shape and character of historical publications. Simplifying the astonishingly complex situation as much as humanly possible, one might say that Czech and Slovak Marxist historiographies were centralised and unified to a far larger extent than Polish and East German historiographies. Hence the question: can a unification (or lack thereof) be observed in publications emerging in the 1950s, affecting, for example, the variety of the Marxist opinions being formulated? On the other hand, taking into account the origins of the most politically, intellectually and socially important Marxists, we would be excused for assuming that the superiority of the historiography of the GDR in that regard should result in the greater methodological maturity of its output – or, in other words, that Marxism should have had a greater role to play in its historiography than in all the other historiographies discussed.

There are also similarities that should be accepted before we attempt to comprehend the mechanics of the process for creating Marxist interpretations of history. Obviously, the manner in which scientific debates were conducted in each of the countries under discussion differed from country to country (suffice it to remind one of the differences between Poland and the GDR in that regard). Still, some traits were shared. In each of the countries of interest to us, Marxist historians aimed not so much to convince their opponents and readers, or even to present their views in a compelling way, but rather to dominate and monopolize a fragment of the commonly accepted interpretation of history. There could be only one interpretation – only one reading of the classics was right. A multiplicity would suggest a weakness and a lack of discipline among Marxists, which was downright unacceptable. The subsequent chapters will show, among other things, how historians more or less successfully performing their work attempted to break out of those narrow boundaries.

Chapter III
On the Lookout for Progressive Traditions

The Marxist vision of national history tended to focus attention on a specific category of historical events that were – or could be – understood as a nation's "progressive traditions." According to the ruling methodology, this category included all social and political upheavals as well as attempted coups. Upheavals were believed to mark a society's advance to another, higher level of development, in accordance with Marxist theory of formations. Debates over that theory among Russian historians were cut short by Joseph Stalin, whose last word on the matter was that transitions from one formation to another occurred by way of revolutions.[240] The task of Marxist historians was therefore to locate such revolutions in order to rewrite the national history according to the framework set by their Russian peers. All revolutionary movements – even those which, as so often was the case in East Central Europe had usually ended in failure – could count, provided one interpreted them the right way. Marxist historians worked diligently to properly emphasise their social importance. Sometimes a historical breakthrough could hardly be located at a distinct point in time (such was the case with early feudalism, whose origins were consigned to oblivion.). In these cases historians often entered disputes over chronology and nomenclature; hence, for instance, the Czechoslovak historians' quarrels over the form of government in Greater Moravia. Elsewhere, the breakthrough points were more or less obvious, as in the case of the Hussite Wars in Bohemia, the Great Peasants' Revolt in Germany, the Miners' Revolt in Slovakia, the Central European upheavals inspired by the French Revolution, as well as national movements, uprisings, and revolutions of the 19th century, or finally the Great October Socialist Revolution (in this last case, the influence of the event was traced in countries neighbouring the Soviet Union, but also in countries further away).[241]

---

240 Stobiecki, *Bolszewizm*, 100-101.
241 Marcin Kula shared some interesting thoughts on the role of the GOSR in the history of Latin America and the debates that took place between local historians and Soviet scholars. Fritz Klein, on the other hand, discussed his disputes with scholars of the Abteilung Wissenschaften ZK SED, who insisted on referencing 1917 (rather than 1918) as the turning point in the history of Germany. His inquiry whether the caesura of

These issues were often popular with historians before the 1950s as well; some contributors to earlier historiography believed revolutionary movements to have a national character. Such was the case with Hussites. Similarly, the onset of the feudal era was bound up with an emerging state structure that was also of interest to "bourgeois" historiography. Furthermore, 19th century nationalist movements played a significant role in shaping the cultures, national self-definitions, and interpretations of the past in each of the countries in question. In these circumstances, Marxist historiography entered into dialogue with existing, fixed historical traditions. As we shall learn further on, the results of this dialogue were extremely varied. The new, "Stalinist" interpretations of the national history were by no means bound to differ from past assessments. In the following analysis of key tropes, I pay special attention to yet another aspect of continuity: a reference to a historicist methodology particularly visible in the evaluation of state structures.

Finally, one should observe the similarities and differences between historical events that have become familiar to historians and were deemed common knowledge before 1945 or 1948, and those that entered the popular consciousness, in a way, when a nation's "progressive traditions" were found lacking when compared to those of its neighbours. Few knew (or had heard) of the robust Polish Hussite movement until Ewa Maleczyńska made it a focus of her specialist works. In a similar vein, Peter Ratkoš played a seminal role in "discovering" the great miners' revolt of 1525-1526 for Slovak historians. The interconnections between such freshly "invented" traditions and the established image of Hussites' revolt in Bohemia or the Great Peasants' War in Germany speak volumes about the Marxist historians' way of thinking about history.

At the Dawn of Feudalism

According to basic Marxist methodological assumptions, the feudal state could only emerge from a sufficiently developed base. Jan Baszkiewicz elaborated on this idea by naming three elements facilitating the emergence of the early feudal state: "a swift rise of feudal relations of production and deepening forms of dependence, from which followed – deepening class antagonisms."[242] At a slightly different angle, the Polish state could be seen to have been invented out

---

1917 should also apply to an analysis of the history of, say, the Eskimo people, was replied in the affirmative. Cf Fritz Klein, *Drinnen und draussen. Ein Historiker in der DDR. Erinnerungen*, Frankfurt am Main 2000, 205.

242   Jan Baszkiewicz & Bogusław Leśnodorski, *Materiały do nauki historii Polski. Historia Polski od wspólnoty pierwotnej do drugiej połowy XVIII wieku*, Warszawa 1953, 20.

of necessity: "The rise of the Polish early feudal state played a crucial role in the progressive development of our country. It made it possible to effectively defend the Polish lands against foreign aggression, especially that of feudal Germany, and it secured the political independence of those lands."[243] Greater Moravia played the same role with regard to Frankish aggression.[244] The circumstances leading to the rise of the German state, obviously free from the threat of German assaults, were explained in a slightly different fashion. What mattered here were the class conflicts between free peasantry on one side, and knighthood and aristocracy on the other. Hence, the early feudal state was seen to have emerged as a product of the possessor classes' fear of the ever-threatening eruption of discontent among the oppressed strata.[245]

According to Stalin, when socio-economical development has reached a level sufficient for the creation of a political organisation, the requirements have been met for the emergence of a nation in its infant shape, that is, of a nationality.[246] The rise of the state was seen both as a result of the processes responsible for the rise of nationality, and as its direct cause.[247] Having recorded numerous manifestations of a national consciousness in the Gallus' chronicle, Stanisław Piekarczyk asked: "How far back from Gallus' times can the emergence of a Polish nationality be moved into the past?" The historian opined that the nationality must have been developing well before the turn of the 11th century.[248] In this, Piekarczyk agreed with the Soviet authors of *Istoriya Polshi* (*История Польши*), who dated the emergence of the Polish nation to the turn of the 7th century.[249] Meanwhile, Czech historians had no doubts that the Lands of the Crown of St. Wenceslas should simply be treated as a Czech state. On the other hand, they entirely rejected the claim that the Přemyslid state could simply be a successor to Greater Moravia.[250]

It's interesting to set the claims of East German Medievalists against this backdrop. Throughout the period in question, they approached the issue of the

---

243 *Historia Polski. Makieta*, vol. 1, part 1, ed. Henryk Łowmiański, Warszawa 1955, 133.

244 *Přehled československých dějin*, vol. 1, 46-48.

245 Leo Stern & Hans-Joachim Bartmuß, *Deutschland in der Feudalepoche von der Wende des 5./6. Jh. bis zur Mitte des 11. Jh.*, Berlin 1963, 132.

246 See Józef Wissarionowicz Stalin, *Marksizm a kwestia narodowa. Kwestia narodowa a leninizm*, Warszawa 1949, 5-13.

247 *Historia Polski. Makieta*, vol. 1, part 1, 147.

248 See S. Piekarczyk, "Kilka uwag w sprawie kształtowania się i rozwoju narodowości polskiej," *Kwartalnik Historyczny* 1955, 107-111.

249 В. Д. Королюк, И. С. Миллер, П. Н. Третьяков, *История Польши*, vol. 1, Москва 1954, p. 9.

250 *Přehled československých dějin*, vol. 1, 72.

development of German nationality with utmost caution, if only because accusations of nationalism carried more weight in post-war Germany than anywhere else. For this reason, they were more inclined to write on the history of the state, rather than the nation formation process; the emergence of a German nation was customarily associated with the rise of the Saxon dynasty.[251] However, the difference between Polish or Czech historians, embroiled in the task of detecting signs of the emergence of nations even before the rise of Medieval states, and their East German peers amounted to nothing more than a question of style. Although Leo Stern and Hans-Joachim Bartmuß wrote that the unification of different Germanic tribes under Frankish rule was a condition for the later emergence of the German state, they probably meant the rise of the German nation, despite never using the phrase.[252] In Volume One of their *Lehrbuch der deutschen Geschichte*, one can also find an interesting discussion of the nation-building potential of the Saxons, brutally subordinated by Charlemagne. Stern and Bartmuß claimed that Saxons were no strangers to the feudal system and were in fact in the process of forming their own feudal state before the Frankish conquest.[253] Hence, the Saxons were already in the process of raising a German feudal state, when the Franks destroyed it. At that stage, the Saxon aristocracy betrayed their own people by pinning their hopes for expanding their control over the rest of society on the Franks. "Only the peasants of Saxony continued to defend their freedom against the yoke of oppression from the Frankish feudal state and its Saxon allies."[254] These peasants clearly represented German progressive traditions, and as victims of Western aggression they were, in effect, represented in a style characteristic of GDR propaganda two years after the rise of the Berlin Wall.

While Polish and Czech historians had no doubts over the national character of their Medieval states, similar claims would prove hard to defend for Slovak scholars. This was not a new state of affairs. Before 1918, Czech history was taught as the history of Austria, then as the history of Czechoslovakia, and nowadays, with few alterations in terms of factual data, it is taught simply as Czech history.[255] At each of those stages, the past of the nation was imagined as a state-territorial continuum: Greater Moravia gave way to a Czech state which

---

251 Andreas Dorpalen, "Die Geschichtswissenschaft der DDR", in: *Geschichtswissenschaft in Deutschland. Traditionelle Positionen und gegenwärtige Aufgaben*, ed. Bernd Faulenbach, München 1974, 125-126.

252 Stern & Bartmuß, *Deutschland*, 71.

253 Ibidem, 95.

254 Ibidem, 99.

255 Jan Rychlík, "České, slovenské a československé dějiny – problém vzájemného vztahu v různých historických dobách", *Česko-slovenská historická ročenka* 2000, 21-22.

suffered from severe Habsburg oppression since 1620, but was reborn in 1918. It was much harder to review the history of Slovakia in a similar manner due to a lack of continuity. Hence, nationalist historiographers developed the idea (which in many respects continues to hold sway) that all early Medieval state formations emerging on Slovak lands were essentially Slovak.[256] The staunchest defender of this claim – František Hrušovský – emigrated from Slovakia in 1945.[257] Because of its tainted origin, Slovak Marxists could never simply embrace it; besides, their Czech peers also staked a claim to Greater Moravia.[258] As a result, Czechoslovak publications customarily referred to it as "the first joint country of Czechs and Slovaks."[259] Claims of its unanimously or partially Slovak provenance reappeared in mid-1960s due in part to the political thaw and a new opening in the debates over Czech-Slovak relations.[260] During the Stalinist era, the question of Medieval nation-building processes on Slovak territories was often raised in historical journals, leading to rather animated debates.[261] A draft of a university textbook on the history of Czechoslovakia

256   Dušan Kováč, "Slovensko-české vzťahy v historickom vedomí slovenskej spoločnosti", *Česko-slovenská historická ročenka* 2000, 57-58.
257   Stefan Albrecht, *Geschichte der Großmährenforschung in den Tschechischen Ländern und in der Slowakei*, Praha 2003, 83 & 114.
258   See Maciej Górny, *Między Marksem a Palackým. Historiografia w komunistycznej Czechosłowacji*, Warszawa 2001, 67. Similar claims can be found in e.g.: *Dejiny Slovenska (tézy)*; Peter Ratkoš, "Počiatky feudalizmu na Slovensku (K problematike raného feudalizmu v našich krajinách)," *Historický Časopis SAV* 1954, 253.
259   *Dejiny Slovenska (tézy)*, 100.
260   See Peter Ratkoš, "Postavenie slovenskej národnosti v stredovekom Uhorsku," in: *Slováci a ich národný vývin (Sborník materiálov z V. sjazdu slovenských historikov v Banskej Bystrici)*, ed. Július Mésároš, Bratislava 1966, 9.
261   In 1956, Jozef Kudláček put forward the possibility of a Greater-Moravian nationality (Jozef Kudláček, "K otázke o vznikaní národnosti na našom území," *Historický Časopis SAV* 1956), a claim he developed a year later (Jozef Kudláček, "K novším názorom o vznikaní ranofeudálnych národností na našom území," *Historický Časopis SAV* 1957). Cf. also other positions in the debate: Lubomír Havlík, "K otázce národnosti na území Velké Moravy," *Historický Časopis SAV* 1957; Peter Ratkoš, "Velkomoravské obdobie v slovenských dejinách," *Historický Časopis SAV* 1958; Jozef Kudláček, "K začiatkom slovanského osídlenia na území Československa," *Historický Časopis SAV* 1958; Jan Dekan, "Skutočnosť a mýtus v bádaní o vzniku ranofeudálnych národností (Odpoveď dr. J. Kudláčkovi)," *Historický Časopis SAV* 1958; Eugen Paulíny, "Poznámky k vzniku slovenskej národnosti zo stanoviska historickej jazykovedy," *Historický Časopis SAV* 1959; Ján Tibenský, "Problémy výskumu vzniku a vývoja slovenskej feudálnej národnosti," *Historický Časopis SAV* 1961; Branislav Varsik, "Vyznam výskumu osídlenia východnęho Slovenska pre otázku vzniku a rozvoja slovenskej národnosti," *Historický Časopis SAV* 1961; O. R. Halaga, "K otázke vzniku slovenskej národnosti,"

professed that the Slovak nationality had formed already after the dissolution of Greater Moravia, under the rule of the Kingdom of Hungary.[262]

When Greater Moravia fell victim to a Hungarian invasion, the future of the Slovaks was bound with Hungary for the next thousand years. This posed numerous problems to historians who accorded extraordinary significance to the institutions of a national state since there were few sources that could serve as a basis for a singularly Slovak political history. They tried to bridge this gap by discussing the history of culture, especially folk culture. Still, this only allowed one to draw very general conclusions that "the Slovak people, separated from the ruling classes by an unbreakable divide of language, led its own cultural life. The wandering musicians, folk singers of the time and of later centuries, travelled from town to town, from village to village, and the people itself constantly enriched the cultural heritage, passing it on from one generation to another."[263] Within the Hungarian state, Slovaks were assumed to represent a folk element. At a Hungarian historians' congress in 1953, Ľudovít Holotík simply stated that the "neighbouring nations" fought for true independence side by side with the Hungarian folk: "In the olden days in Hungary, the Slovaks were an oppressed nation, but the Hungarian working people faced conditions just as troubling. The Slovak and Hungarian people were naturally drawn together against common native and foreign exploiters."[264] Even if the relations between Slovak and Hungarian historians grew colder in later years, the image of Slovaks as allies and collaborators in most of the progressive undertakings in Hungarian history retained its vitality.

With Marxist historians putting so much stress on the problem of the emergence of the state and (their particular) nation, the question of identification of early state-like entities with particular formations gained in importance. Already when discussions over the history of Poland began, the Marxist scholars encountered an obstacle concerning nomenclature: did the newly-formed state truly amount to a feudal entity, and if so, was it fully developed or only in early stages of development? An initial suggestion for periodisation from Stanisław Arnold, who dubbed the state of the early Piasts pre-feudal, was criticised by

---

Historický Časopis SAV 1962; Peter Ratkoš, "K diskusii o vznikaní národností na našom území," Historický Časopis SAV 1963.

262 *Přehled československých dějin*, vol. 1, 102.

263 Ibidem, 104-105.

264 Ľudovít Holotík, "Z výsledkov kongresu maďarských historikov," *Historický Časopis SAV* 1953, 317.

Soviet scholars and consequently rebuked.[265] Such was the general tendency at that time: a similar critique was levelled against Jürgen Kuczynski, who protested against what he saw as a premature staking out of new eras.[266] The propositions of Polish scholars were not unaffected by the wording chosen by the Medievalists of neighbouring countries. At several points, including the Otwock conference, Karol Maleczyński pointed out that František Graus saw "in the 10th century a fully-formed feudal system in a not yet entirely organised Czech feudal state." Meanwhile, Ibrahim Ibn Yaqub, in his reminiscences from travels through this part of Europe dating from the very period, claimed that Mieszko's state was the most powerful in the region, which meant that it had to be more powerful than the Czech state of the same epoch. This comparative analysis proved that, already in the 10th century, there was a developed feudal state on Polish soil.[267]

Czech and Slovak historians were deeply concerned about the proper classification of the form of government predominant in Greater Moravia. František Graus and Václav Husa's initial suggestions, deeming it a pre-feudal state, were rejected, as were analogous proposals put forward by Stanisław Arnold with regard to Poland.[268] According to a contending interpretation, Greater Moravia was an early feudal state. In the case of Slovakia, Peter Ratkoš observed that the concepts of periodisation proposed by Ľudovít Holotík left no room for any questions regarding the Greater Moravian state formation. Holotík claimed that Slovakia became a feudal state in the 10th century, but did not comment on the form of government in the country prior to that historical stage.[269] According to Ratkoš (as well as later theses on the history of Slovakia, edited by Holotík, and also the Czechoslovak university history textbook),

---

265 Stanisław Arnold, "Niektóre problemy periodyzacji dziejów Polski," in: *Pierwsza Konferencja Metodologiczna Historyków Polskich. Przemowienia, referaty, dyskusja,* eds. Stanisław Herbst, Witold Kula & Tadeusz Manteuffel, vol. 1, 168-174.

266 Kuczyński claimed: "Weder eine einzelne Schwalbe noch ein ausgegangener Ofen sind Merkmale des Frühlings, was nicht ausschließt, daß sie ihn ankündigen können" – Jürgen Kuczynski, „Zum Aufsatz von Johannes Hichtweiß über die zweite Leibeigenschaft", *Zeitschrift für Geschichtswissenschaft* 1954, 471. The reply to the critique can be found in: Johannes Nichtweiß, „Antwort an Jürgen Kuczynski," *Zeitschrift für Geschichtswissenschaft* 1954.

267 See Karol Maleczyński, "Zróżnicowanie społeczne i powstanie państwa polskiego w IX w.," in: *Pierwsza Konferencja,* vol. 1, 259; idem, review of František Graus, *Dějiny venkovského lidu v Čechách,* vol. 1, *Kwartalnik Historyczny* 1953, 285.

268 František Graus, "Pokus o periodisaci českých dějin," *Československý Časopis Historický* 1953.

269 Ľudovít Holotík, "K periodizácii slovenských dejín v období feudalizmu a kapitalizmu," *Historický Časopis SAV* 1953.

Greater Moravia was the first instance of a feudal formation in the region.[270] For
the authors of *Dejiny Slovenska*, this suggested a kinship to the Kievan Rus, a
native, Slavic early feudal formation.[271]

The debates over periodisation of the feudal era among Polish, Soviet,
Czech and Slovak historians appear to be marked by a particular ambitious
streak. Karol Maleczyński precisely captured the essence of these discussions: it
was simply unacceptable that Polish feudal relations should be less developed
than those prevalent in Bohemia in the same historical period.[272] On the other
hand, interpretations which suited the suppositions of Soviet historians with
regard to the history of the Kievan Rus were promoted. These two features of
the historical debate are vividly registered in the so-called Norman theory.

This theory, according to which the Kievan Rus was formed by Scandinavians,
was criticised both in view of its scientific viability and the political role ascribed to
it. According to Aleksander Gieysztor, Normans did traverse Ruthenia "as
merchants or enlisted in mercenary troops formed by the Ruthenian princelings.
Yet, they did not – and could not – play the role of an independent political
agent."[273] At the Otwock conference, one of the members of the Soviet delegation,
Yevgeni Kosminsky, proposed a less measured opinion: "Don't the western
historians stick to the rubbish they call the theory of Norman conquest, whose
essence lies in denying Slavs the ability to form their own states?" – he asked
rhetorically.[274] In V. Mavrodin's pamphlet, published in Poland as well,
"Normanism" was characterised as a rhetorical weapon of western reactionaries in
their struggle against the Soviet Union.[275] Violent assaults on the theory abated
only after 1956, and not in every country of the eastern bloc. In a book published in
1957, Henryk Łowmiański admitted that "The theory of the Norman origins of Rus
and its statehood was, so to speak, a proper historiographic phenomenon only so far
as the interest in political history prevailed and the historical process was viewed as
an outcome of actions taken by individuals and dynasties, with mass processes

---

270   Peter Ratkoš, "Počiatky feudalizmu na Slovensku (K problematike raného feudalizmu v
      našich krajinách)," *Historický Časopis SAV* 1954, 253-276; *Přehled československých
      dějin*, vol. 1, 49; *Dejiny Slovenska (tézy)*, 31.
271   *Dejiny Slovenska (tézy)*, 31.
272   See Maleczyński, "Zróżnicowanie," 259.
273   Juliusz Bardach, Aleksander Gieysztor, Henryk Łowmiański & Ewa Maleczyńska,
      Historia Polski do r. 1466, Warszawa 1953, 27.
274   Eugeniusz Kosminski, "Aktualne zagadnienia mediewistyki marksistowsko-
      leninowskiej," in: *Pierwsza Konferencja*, vol. 1, 352.
275   W. Mawrodin, *Walka z "teorią normańską" w rosyjskiej nauce historycznej*, Warszawa
      1951.

thoroughly neglected."[276] Łowmiański's book faced criticism in the GDR for an all-too-tame approach to the subject, while the debate over the beginnings of Ruthenia was assumed to have been finally and decisively resolved in accordance with the Party's "anti-Normanist" views.[277]

Unquestionably, Poland (whether feudal or early feudal), like Bohemia, faced foreign aggression from its inception, especially from the Germans – so much so that Polish borders seemed to have been threatened from one side only. According to Marxist writers, Poland's relations with Ruthenia were the opposite of Polish-German relations.[278] Soviet authors promoted similar views.[279] The belief in an essential and perennial Polish-German enmity, on the other hand, resembled quite closely the beliefs of Zygmunt Wojciechowski. The fact that Wojciechowski himself was castigated as a nationalist in no way affected West Germany's bad press in Poland. For Poles, wars against the Germans were "just wars, conducted in defence of our own country and Western Slavs threatened with complete extermination at the hands of German feudal lords."[280] The point of the struggles against German aggression was maintenance of the country's natural boundaries – boundaries which, from the very beginning, matched national divisions.[281]

The concept of the Polish motherland was naturally supported by historians associated with the Western Institute. During the Otwock conference, Michał Sczaniecki took part in a discussion on the issue, proposing a thorough focus in scientific texts on "borders whose existence we owe to the Soviet Union, and which so faithfully replicate the boundaries of the Polish motherland."[282] At that point in time, East German historians also offered unqualified support for historically-grounded Polish borders in the West.[283]

---

276 Henryk Łowmiański, *Zagadnienie roli Normanów w genezie państw słowiańskich*, Warszawa 1957, 183.

277 Bruno Widera, "Zur Normanenfrage in Osteuropa. Überblick über 230 Jahre Forschung", *Zeitschrift für Geschichtswissenschaft* 1959, 210-216.

278 See Bardach, Gieysztor, Łowmiański, Maleczyńska, *Historia*, 53; *Historia Polski. Makieta*, vol. 1, part 1, 141.

279 See W. Koroluk, "Przyczynek do zagadnienia stosunków polsko-ruskich w X w.," in: *Historycy radzieccy o Polsce. Wybór prac*, ed. Stefan Gwich, Warszawa 1953, 16-17.

280 Bardach, Gieysztor, Łowmiański, Maleczyńska, *Historia*, 53.

281 See *Historia Polski. Makieta*, vol. 1, part 1, 98.

282 Michał Sczaniecki, "Stosunek periodyzacji ogólnej do specyficznej periodyzacji historii poszczególnych dziedzin nadbudowy. Rejonizacja periodyzacji czyli uwzględnienie w periodyzacji specyficznego rozwoju w ramach terytorialnych," in: *Pierwsza Konferencja*, vol. 1, 286.

283 See Felix Heinrich Gentzen, "Polskie Ziemie Zachodnie – historyczne ziemie polskie," *Nowe Drogi* 1952/7, 71.

The German *Expansionspolitik* became a major issue for East German Medievalists. While they found little redeemable value to it, they stressed the connection between the brutal conquest of the Polabian Slavs and the criminality of the Prussian state,[284] as well as chancellor Adenauer's equally repulsive foreign policy.[285] At times, East German authors even accused their Polish counterparts of underappreciating the political effect of the phenomenon.[286] The said conquest proceeded in a manner reminiscent of the way Charlemagne's Saxon Wars were described. Slavic possessor classes collaborated with German aggressors, gradually embracing a German identity. The broad, popular masses, however, responded to the foreign invasion with fierce resistance which was broken with an unprecedented brutality.[287] While much Medieval German expansion was of a pacific nature, even German law settlements were deemed to have brought more harm than good.[288] *Ostexpansion*, whether military or economic, caused "German-Slavic relations to become poisoned for centuries, until modern times, and the Revanchists of Bonn continue to stir anti-Polish, anto-Czech and anti-Russian resentments, whether openly or under the cover of anti-Communism; they hope to use them to win the masses over for their criminal purposes."[289] Historians from the GDR posed the actions of their Western brethren in opposition to the tradition of German-Slavic cooperation, for instance the Polish-German brotherhood in arms during the fight against the Tartars at Legnica in 1241.[290]

Czech writers, whether Marxist or not, persistently referenced the Germans, beginning with the Franks, who had posed a constant threat to the Greater Moravia by military means as well as through propaganda, i.e. the Catholic Church. Hence Marxist historiography assigned a mostly defensive role to the

---

284 Leo Stern, "Disposition des Hochschullehrbuches der Geschichte des deutschen Volkes (1. Bd.)", *Zeitschrift für Geschichtswissenschaft* 1953, 643.

285 Ingrid Hagemann, "Die mittelalterliche deutsche Ostexpansion und die Adenauersche Außenpolitik", *Zeitschrift für Geschichtswissenschaft* 1958, 814-816.

286 Ingrid Hegemann made that accusation against Gerard Labuda – ibidem, 816.

287 Leo Stern & Horst Gericke, *Deutschland in der Feudalepoche von der Mitte des 11. Jh. bis zur Mitte des 13. Jh.*, Berlin 1964, 171-180; Stern & Bartmuß, *Deutschland*, 191.

288 Stern & Gericke, *Deutschland*, 205.

289 Ibidem, 206.

290 Leo Stern, "Disposition des Hochschullehrbuches der Geschichte des deutschen Volkes (1. Bd.)," *Zeitschrift für Geschichtswissenschaft* 1953, 641. The claim of a Polish-German brotherhood of arms at Legnica was criticised by Aleksander Gieysztor and Ewa Maleczyńska, who questioned East German estimates of the size of the troops in particular (according to historians from the GDR, Polish and German troops were of a more or less equivalent size); see Leo Stern, "Erste Zwischenbilanz einer wissenschaftlichen Kritik (III)", *Zeitschrift für Geschichtswissenschaft* 1955, 221.

Saints Cyril and Methodius, who sought to guard the state from the infiltration of German clergy.[291] Czech sovereigns were assessed according to their ability to maintain a political and spiritual independence from the Empire. Even the latest representatives of the Přemyslid dynasty, during whose reign Medieval Bohemia enjoyed its heyday, did not enjoy much appreciation on account of the fact that, along with their courts, they underwent cultural Germanisation.[292]

Slovak historians focused on German feudal aggression only insofar as it concerned Greater Moravia, for obvious reasons. The Hungarian invasion, however, received a different interpretation; unsurprisingly, given that one of the axioms of Slovak historical consciousness is the claim that Magyars were "civilised" by the Slavic inhabitants of Greater Moravia, who were also partially responsible for the formation of the Kingdom of Hungary.[293]

As already mentioned, East German scholars could not use the threat of feudal aggression to justify the formation of a state-like entity on their lands, since Germany posed precisely such a threat to other countries in East Central Europe. Still, even German history includes a period when the fragmented forces of the country joined to rebuke Western expansion, with much success. Nevertheless, this happened long before the formation of early feudal state-like entities. According to Karl-Heinz Otto, in the first years A.D., Romans crossed the Rhine, decisively changing the nature of their struggles with the Germans. From that point on, the latter were fighting a war of liberation.[294] Meanwhile, the Roman slave system suffered a deep crisis, illustrated by increasingly frequent slave uprisings, including the War of Spartacus, the foremost rebellion (which, as Otto added, also involved slaves of German origin).[295] In this light, neither side of the Roman-German conflict represented a higher stage of social development, but the Germans could claim the moral high ground. As Otto observed, "The great triumph over the superior forces of Rome was the fruit of a true struggle for freedom. The result of this struggle proves the historical fact that when an organised liberation struggle is elevated as the highest of values, the forces of the oppressed popular masses are released, making them stronger than the better equipped mercenaries serving the dominant power. ... German

---

291 *Přehled československých dějin*, vol. 1, 46-47.
292 Ibidem, 118.
293 See Daniel Rapant, "Słowacy w historii. Retrospektywa i perspektywy (Przyczynek do filozofii i sensu słowackiej historii)," in: *Kwestia słowacka w XX wieku*, ed. Rudolf Chmel, transl. Piotr Godlewski, Zofia Jurczak-Trojan, Maryla Papierz, Gliwice 2002, 408.
294 Karl-Heinz Otto, *Deutschland in der Epoche der Urgesellschaft (500000 v. u. Z. bis zum 5./6. Jh. u. Z.)*, Berlin 1961, 114.
295 Ibidem, 114.

warriors were morally superior to Roman mercenaries because they were struggling to free their homeland from Roman occupation."[296]

The triumph over Romans in the Teutoburg Forest also had a singular hero. Hermann, the chieftain of the Cherusci, whose memorial near Detmold became a symbol of German nationalism, was referred to in East German historical works exclusively by his Latin name, Arminius. The authors stressed that the historical image of the leader of German resistance was falsified to serve a chauvinist version of history. Meanwhile, all his qualities notwithstanding, one should not forget that the Romans were vanquished primarily by the German popular masses.[297]

This interpretation of Roman-German conflict met with critique from Polish scholars. Kazimierz Tymieniecki observed that, by exaggerating the importance of the Battle of the Teutoburg Forest, his colleagues from the GDR were closely following the traditional, popular, nationalist reading of national history. In his opinion, the battle, though bloody indeed, had very little political effect – it could hardly be credited, for example, with having brought about the withdrawal of Roman forces behind the Rhine. The response to this statement, given by Leo Stern, left no room for doubt as to the importance of this element of German progressive traditions: "the Battle of the Teutoburg Forest was, as Engels put it, one of the turning points in history, and we should not allow ourselves to be misled by the fact that this statement was echoed in popular literature. ... The German working class has to summon all of its traditions of liberation to reinforce the will to resist American imperialism with its 'European idea,' destructive of the national consciousness, as well as the West German bourgeoisie with its 'European integration'. W. Ulbricht spoke in the same spirit at the 2nd Congress of the SED: 'Our professors of history remain silent about the Battle of the Teutoburg Forest, where, as Engels writes in his *Der Ursprung der Familie, des Privateigentums und des Staats*, the Romans were beaten because Germans were free people whose personal courage and discipline far exceeded those of the Roman troops. They were fighting for the freedom of their country'."[298] Tymieniecki's critique left no mark on the East German interpretation of the battle.

As far as the Polish history was concerned, the key event, not only from a Marxist standpoint, was the baptism of the state. Neither in Germany, nor in Czechoslovakia was so much weight attached to analogous events. Polish

296 Ibidem, 119.
297 Ibidem, 119-120.
298 Leo Stern, "Erste Zwischenbilanz einer wissenschaftlichen Kritik (II)," *Zeitschrift für Geschichtswissenschaft* 1955, 55 & 64.

historians underscored the ambiguous nature of the acceptance of Christianity: the baptism had positive as well as negative effects. Historians steadfastly opposed the traditionally accepted view of its anti-German meaning. Henryk Łowmiański agreed that "the baptism solidified Poland's international position in the Christian world," but at the same time stressed that "Bourgeois historians moved this less important moment to the foreground, claiming that Poland accepted the baptism to fend off the danger of German assaults, when, undoubtedly, the essential aim of assuming Christianity was strengthening the rule of the feudal lords."[299] For Czech historians, state baptism had more vices than virtues, while at the same time, it did play a progressive part insofar as it sped up the feudalisation of society.[300] Nevertheless, it did not elude their attention that Christianity in general supported existing social relations – at one point even upholding the system of slavery.[301] Yet, even in Marxist works, one can find surprising deviations from the rule proclaiming that events hastening the onset of a subsequent social formation have at least a partly progressive character. According to Jan Baszkiewicz, "The acceptance of Christianity aided the further development of feudalism, strengthened and justified the class rule of the feudal lords over the feudally dependent peasantry. Christianity of the time was no longer the progressive Christianity known from the first centuries A.D."[302]

This difference of opinion between Medievalists echoes the dispute over whether phenomena which accelerate the advance toward subsequent formations (feudal or capitalist) are by necessity objectively progressive, or, in the opposite case whether all popular, anti-feudal and anti-capitalist movements are always progressive, even when they objectively delay historical advance (according to the criteria of a given epoch). Henryk Łowmiański and Jan Baszkiewicz gave contradictory answers to this question: Christianity and the Church structure certainly hastened the development of feudalism, but while this was interpreted as a virtue by Łowmiański, Baszkiewicz saw it as a vice. In time, Baszkiewicz's views prevailed and Henryk Łowmiański partially revised his view on the Baptism of Poland, while stressing its long-term negative effects.[303]

This difference of opinion should not be taken as proof of any essential rift among Marxist Medievalists as to the role of the Baptism. All authors were in perfect agreement as to the negative effects of the decision. First of all, the

---

299 Bardach, Gieysztor, Łowmiański, Maleczyńska, Historia, 40; see also, Maleczyńska, *Problem*, 20.
300 *Přehled československých dějin*, vol. 1, 49.
301 Ibidem.
302 Baszkiewicz & Leśnodorski, *Materiały*, 22.
303 *Historia Polski. Makieta*, vol. 1, part 1, 136-137.

acceptance of Western Christianity tied Poland to the Vatican. Another important drawback of the Baptism was that it arrested the development of national literature and the Polish language, which, in turn, impeded the formation of the Polish nation. The claim that the introduction of the Church accelerated the development of the country was refuted. At the same time, "the negative impact of Christianisation in the Latin creed was reflected in the erection of a cultural division between the Polish and the Southern and Eastern Slavs."[304]

This last aspect drew Polish historians closer to positions taken by their Slovak and Czech colleagues. It is fairly obvious that Christianity was accorded two different readings, depending on the rite. The activities of Saints Cyril and Methodius usually received a far more favourable appraisal than those of the German clergy, or even the patron saint of Bohemia. Due to the fact that early modern reactionaries used him as a symbol of opposition to the progressive Hussite tradition, the cult of Saint Wenceslas received a critical evaluation from Czech Marxists.[305] The development of the "national" cult of Saint Stanislaus in Poland received a similar treatment. The particularly negative attitude the Marxists had toward this specific figure naturally translated into a rather positive treatment of Bolesław the Bold, the bishop's killer, who stood up against the Empire (though this also meant that he sided with the Papacy), allied himself with Yaroslav the Wise, and finally killed Saint Stanislaus – all of which received positive evaluations from the Marxists. Still, the authors of the "Draft" claimed that Bolesław erred in letting himself be coronated as a king "as this meant the submission of Poland to the Papacy which arrogated to itself superiority over all Christian states; the coronation thereby gave the Pope the right to interfere in Polish affairs."[306] Apparently, the selfsame antipathy toward the Vatican in particular and all ecclesiastical undertakings in general is responsible for the inconsistency inherent in evaluations of Christianity in the Middle Ages. As one of the areas where a Marxist evaluation could not rely solely on the authority of the classics, it was to a significant extent shaped by the Soviet Union's current politics.

It is plain to see that Marxist Medieval studies attached particular attention to matters related to the creation and formation of states. Syntheses of national histories opened with ruminations on the origins of particular states, the reasons for their emergence, and the stage of development they reached, as well as the

---

304 Ibidem.
305 *Přehled československých dějin*, vol. 1, 73-74; see also, Václav Husa, *Historia Czechosłowacji*, Praga 1967, 42.
306 *Historia Polski. Makieta,* vol. 1, part 1, 184.

influence they had on the formation of national consciousness. Of vital importance was the ability to trace the political history of the states in question back to an appropriate development of the indigenous forces of production, rather than foreign invasions or personal achievements of individuals. It was the state that faced German aggression (in the case of Germany, the state-forming Saxons struggled against the invading Franks). Christianity, on the other hand, attracted the interest of historians only insofar as it facilitated the consolidation of feudal structures and/or limited the independence of the states by subordinating them, to an extent, to the Papacy. Marxist methodology was also open to other topics, as long as they worked to highlight the importance of the state as the most revered of all accepted values. Each of the historiographies under discussion introduces numerous examples corroborating this conviction. For example, historians of the GDR justified their critique of Germany's Eastward expansion by means of a moral argument as well as through analyses of internal politics: like Italian campaigns, Eastward expansion weakened central power while improving the position of the magnates, opening the way to a splintering of the state.[307] This feudal breakup, in turn, had dire consequences for the people as well as the state – both of which sufficiently corroborate the predominant interest of the popular masses in the unification of Germany.[308] Successive stages of decline and reinforcement of the *Zentralgewalt* form an axis for weaving the history of Medieval Germany in the *Lehrbuch der deutschen Geschichte*. Marxist works revived the theory of the German *Sonderweg*: the feudal victory over the centralised power prevented the Empire from becoming the crystallisation of the German nation, as it had been in France or England.[309] This vision of German history also includes motifs present in works of authors belonging to the Prussian school: the elevation of the state to the rank of an absolute good because it was the entity designated to bring about the idea of national freedom for the Germans. Interestingly, German historians differed from their Soviet or Polish colleagues in their evaluation of the splintering of their respective states. Outside of Germany, historians agreed that it was a natural phenomenon, characteristic of a certain stage of historical development, and in this sense positive. "In the changed circumstances of a well-grounded feudal regime," wrote Juliusz Bardach, "the power of the central prince was hardly of any use to the feudal lords."[310] From Jan Baszkiewicz's

---

307 Stern & Bartmuß, *Deutschland*, 187 i 200; see also Erik Hühns, „Die politische Ohnmacht des Reiches (1250-1500)," *Zeitschrift für Geschichtswissenschaft* 1954, 71-73.

308 Erik Hühns, "Die politische Ohnmacht des Reiches 1250-1500 (II)," *Zeitschrift für Geschichtswissenschaft* 1954, 238.

309 Stern & Gericke, *Deutschland*, 119.

310 Bardach, Gieysztor, Łowmiański & Maleczyńska, *Historia*, 81.

perspective, the feudal breakup (a term commonly used in the 1950s) was not only progressive – it actually led to an even stronger unification of Polish territories.[311]

Though the feudal breakup was not by itself a regressive, or even a troubling phenomenon to Polish historians, Marxist Medievalists commended the princes of the Piast lineage for attempting to reunite the country. As a fragmented Poland progressed socio-economically, feudal fragmentation ceased to be considered opportune and turned into a regressive event, "a check on further economic development."[312] As in Germany, the peasantry was supposedly the group which held the most interest in reunification. Polish society also included groups which did not support reunification or tried to prevent it. Marxist analyses often remind the reader that "neither all the Polish clergy, nor all the Catholic hierarchy supported the unification of Poland."[313] In these circumstances, Marxist Medievalists had also to reevaluate the cult of Saint Stanislaus. Jan Baszkiewicz characterised "the use of the cult of Stanislaus – regardless of the extremely harmful, negative role the figure played in Polish history in relation to the concepts of renewing the crown and unifying the country as well as popularising these ideas. It (using the cult of Stanislaus) played an *objectively* [Baszkiewicz's italics] crucial and positive role for the unification of Polish lands. Objectively, that is, irrespective of the intentions of the creators of the cult of bishop Stanislaus (beginning with Wincenty Kadłubek) and the advocates of his canonisation; more than that – perhaps even in spite of their intentions."[314] The author did not explain the subjective goals of the creators of the cult, but his explication found its way into the "Draft" of the university textbook on Polish history: "The positive attitude of the Papacy toward the canonisation of Saint Stanislaus is justified by its contemporaneous, intensive attempts – failed, as we know today – at subordinating the Orthodox Church in ... Red Ruthenia. The canonisation reinforced the position of the Church in Poland as Catholicism's outpost closest to Ruthenia."[315] Among the social groups that did not support the unification of the country, the clergy was joined by feudal magnates, primarily the district princelings with a personal interest in retaining an independent control over their respective principalities.[316]

---

311 Jan Baszkiewicz, *Powstanie zjednoczonego państwa polskiego na przełomie XIII i XIV wieku*, Warszawa 1954, 39.

312 Ibidem, 147; Baszkiewicz & Leśnodorski, *Materiały*, 47.

313 Ibidem, 427.

314 Ibidem, 445.

315 *Historia Polski. Makieta*, vol. 1, part 1, 327-328.

316 Baszkiewicz, *Powstanie*, 283-284.

Marxist monographs, especially those about Polish or German history, can easily serve as a basis for an analysis of a phenomenon similar to that which occurred in the Soviet Union in the mid-1930s. There, after a period of domination by a rigorous Marxist vision of history framed by Mikhail Pokrovsky, the previous interpretation was reinstated. It diverged from Pokrovsky's views in ascribing instrumental value to the tsarist state, whose strength, external and internal development, and military victories were thenceforth to be celebrated with solemnity befitting the successes of the Bolshevik regime. Historians previously castigated for nationalism, idiographic tendencies, and other offences against Marxist methodology (like Evgeni Tarle), were allowed to return to work. Their scientific approach, in turn, was rooted in the tradition of German historiography. This vision of national history, which reconciled the claim to freedom with the concept of a strong state, going so far as to find its embodiment in the firmly centralised state of Prussia, was precisely a product of the Prussian school and its key contributors such as Heinrich von Sybel, Heinrich von Treitschke or Hermann Baumgartner. According to them, the state played the political, as well as ethical role assigned it by Hegel.[317] This particularly German variation of liberalism, mediated by the historians of the Russian Empire, proved equal to Marxism as an ideological tool for the interpretation of Medieval history, which did not prevent Marxist scholars from criticising historians of the Prussian school. Perhaps the two trends in methodology were joined by the idea of submitting the individual to a higher power – to the state in German historicism, and to historical processes in Marxism. Therefore, Marxist historians did not need to borrow directly from representatives of the Prussian school – they could refer to Karl Marx as a mediator, since his ideas were formed at the same time and place as those of Johann Gustav Droysen, an effervescent, talented national-liberal activist from the period preceding the Springtime of the Peoples. At the point when Marxist Medievalists transferred their interests from the popular masses to structures of the state, they moved closer to Sybel or Treitschke. Their description of Western feudal (or "slavish" in the case of ancient Romans) aggression, on the other hand, moved toward beliefs espoused by Joachim Lelewel, who perceived Slavic peoples as being marked by a drive to freedom of a more or less democratic nature, and as subjected to Germanic aggression. When referring to the same tropes of national historiographies, Marxist scholars stressed the state-building abilities of the Slavs (or the Saxons), abandoning the idea of their cultural superiority to the West. Instead, they focused on the equality of both worlds in terms of culture and civilisation, while maintaining the belief in the moral superiority of their own ancestors over the aggressors.

317 Iggers, *The German*, 91-93.

In this respect, Andrzej Feliks Grabski's claim of an antinomy between the dominant methodology in the Stalinist model of historiography and the political demands set before historians needs to be reevaluated.[318] The claim that the demands of current politics in the 1950s were more important than Marxist methodology is obviously true for the most part, but it does not significantly alter our knowledge of the historiography of that period, or of historiography in general. This lends a certain poignancy to the image of a historiography whose thin veneer of Marxism fails to preclude elements of an older methodological tradition, at times fairly distant from said Marxism. If Marxist historiography is, then, truly incoherent, it is not due to the collisions between Marx's "theory" and the contemporary political interests of the Soviet Union, but rather to the fact that changes in politics uncover and introduce other, competing interpretations of history, ruled by their own internal logic and therefore seldom in agreement with Marxist orthodoxy.

There is a minor, but interesting divergence between different Marxist interpretations of Medieval history – it pertains to the evaluation of feudal fragmentation. The fact that it received divergent appraisals from country to country can be explained in two different ways, both of which seem acceptable to me. On the one hand, in the case of the Holy Roman Empire, other than in Bohemia or Poland, the unification did not occur swiftly. An historical fact, which was of transitory interest to Czech and Polish scholars, was for the Germans an event of enormous significance that in time rose to the rank of a stumbling block on the way toward implementing the program of the national movement. On the other, one can see the divergence as a result of the employment of two different methods of Marxist interpretation. Polish and Czech historians treated feudal fragmentation as one of the laws of history, corroborated by other examples (e.g. from the history of Russia). This led them to assume the historical process as a certain continuous whole. One can also discern another source of inspiration at work in this decidedly Marxist view: it likewise agrees with Leopold Ranke's understanding of historical processes as the result of forces and phenomena which could have affected the balance of history if they were to achieve solitary dominance. According to this optic, it is illogical to reproach the Empire for having fallen apart, and its unity can no longer be seen as a dogma by which one can measure and evaluate historical events. East German historians, favouring a different approach, more often than not looked to the tradition of the German national movement for inspiration, interpreting this section of the Medieval period in a manner deeply akin to that of the historians of the Prussian school.

---

318 Grabski, *Dzieje historiografii*, 690-691.

The Anti-Feudal Social Revolution

At its inception in the Central and Eastern Europe, feudalism was a progressive phenomenon. However, as already shown, its vices were on display even prior to that – as seen, for instance, by the fact that it was introduced by force, or that the Church facilitated its introduction. Hence, one can hardly be surprised by the fact that Marxist historians searched for signs of this formation's decline at very early periods. The so-called crisis of feudalism in Bohemia was dated to the 14th-15th century, that is, before the Hussite Wars. At the same time, analogous structures were uncovered by Polish, as well as, East German historians (in this case, the crisis predated the eruption of the Great Peasants' Revolt.). According to Stalin's thesis on the revolutionary character of inter-formational phases, every crisis paving the way to another capitalist formation should be followed promptly by a revolution. Such crises were treated as progressive events solely because they catalysed other formations. As a result, previous uprisings and revolts could not be deemed progressive, having occurred during feudalism's heyday – i.e., while it was still responsible for the progress of history, rather than for pegging it back. This diagnosis caused much pain to historians who believed their main task to be describing the history of the struggle of the popular masses against the possessor classes – because Marxist historians typically sympathised with the weak and poor.

From the point of view of this new methodology, potentially the most arresting event of the early Piasts' reign was the pagan revolt, which figured in works of the 1950s as a popular uprising. Still, even this case posed serious methodological questions. Just as with the Baptism of Poland, Henryk Łowmiański noted that "The popular uprising broke out at a time when feudalism was at a stage of ascension and corresponded to the existing state of creative forces."[319] The popular uprising, conducted with the intent to bring the country back to the pagan tradition, could not relate to the contemporary socio-economic situation and therefore was not likely to be treated as a progressive movement. Again, as in the case of the Baptism of Poland, Jan Baszkiewicz presented an opinion radically different from that of Łowmiański: "The pagan slogans," he wrote, "like the movement's ideology, were an expression of a struggle against feudal oppression. ... Rejecting the openly brutal forms of feudal dependence, the popular uprising played an objectively progressive role, regardless of the intentions of the peasants who took part in the uprising and doubtless pushed for a return to the past community. ... [W]ith the popular uprising quashed, the reactionary elements of slavery, and the elements of a

---

319   Bardach, Gieysztor, Łowmiański & Maleczyńska, *Historia*, 60.

slave system in Poland, were put to serious question."[320] Łowmiański's claim was criticised at the Otwock conference by Marian Serejski, who recounted the positive evaluation granted feudal-era popular uprisings in Soviet scholarly works. Though Łowmiański attended the venue, he did not venture to respond in his presentation. The version of national history presented in the "Draft" agreed with Baszkiewicz's interpretative claims.[321]

East German and Czechoslovak historians approached the early feudal peasants' revolts with much more caution. In 1965, the *Zeitschrift für Geschichtswissenschaft* published a debate between Siegfried Hoyer and Hans Mottek, concerning the peasants' uprising of 1336-1339. Mottek vehemently debunked Hoyer's all-too-favourable view of the event and even went so far as to state that it was not a popular uprising at all, merely feudal-inspired anti-Jewish riots.[322] Czech historians, on the other hand, treated the early-feudal pagan reaction as a phenomenon characteristic of the previous formation, hence ill-suited to play a progressive part. This was reserved for phenomena like the more "mature" heresy, and, in particular, the revolutionary Hussite movement.[323]

As we will see presently, the Hussite movement played a very special role in Czechoslovak Marxist historiography (in part because of the fact that earlier historians also believed the period of the movement's existence to have been the most important in the history of Bohemia).[324] The fact that two leading young Czech Marxist historians of the 1950s – Josef Macek and František Graus – were interested in this movement also played a part. The new Marxist interpretation of the Hussite period was subjected to a tripartite division, suggested by Graus, into phases of the supremacy of the poor, the supremacy of the bourgeoisie, and the final phase which culminated in the Battle of Lipany and the victory of the nobility.[325] Nevertheless, the numerous works of Josef Macek and other Marxist Medievalists often make the reader feel as if the transformation of religious movements into revolutionary ones did not constitute the axis of their narratives, and consequently, that the tracing of the progress of

---

320 Baszkiewicz & Leśnodorski, *Materiały*, 28-29.
321 *Historia Polski. Makieta*, vol. 1, part 1, 176.
322 Siegfried Hoyer, "Die Armlederbewegung – ein Bauernaufstand 1336/1339," *Zeitschrift für Geschichtswissenschaft* 1965; Hans Mottek (letter to the editor, *Zeitschrift für Geschichtswissenschaft*), *Zeitschrift für Geschichtswissenschaft* 1965, 695-697.
323 *Přehled československých dějin*, vol. 1, 71.
324 Mor on the subject in: František Šmahel, *Idea národa v husitských Čechách*, Praha 2000; see also Čornej, *Lipanské*.
325 František Graus, "Pokus o periodisaci českých dějin," *Československý Časopis Historický* 1953, 202-213.

revolution hardly constituted an enterprise worthy of the effort. Of far greater import seems the appraisal of individual and mass actors involved in the events described. This is primarily due to the fact that the Hussite movement is analysed not only as a historical event, but also as a myth. On the one hand, it is a national myth, for centuries a hallmark of Czech culture. On the other, due to its chronological precedence, the movement became a crucial link in the chain of so-called "progressive traditions" through a partially competitive re-reading of the myth by Marxist historiography.

In spite of Marxist demands for a "deheroisation" of historiography, the Czech interpretation of the Hussite revolution reserved the main roles in the event for two heroic figures of the period – Jan Hus and Jan Žižka. Hus was described as a dedicated internationalist, hostile to all nationalist obstinacy. This image was particularly affected by his attitude toward Germans. His internationalism did not go so far as cosmopolitanism. Quite the contrary: he was a staunch patriot, open to calls for Slavic cooperation.[326] Hence "Our socialist patriotism and proletarian internationalism finds a living specimen and exemplar in Hus" even at so late a time.[327] Hus' social background was also found highly commendable – he was born to a poor family, and earned his post as a university teacher thanks to his hard work and ability.

However, Czechoslovak Marxist historians soon discovered that they faced a crucial problem of interpretation. Not only was Hus a preacher whose teachings translated into the language of programs for political and social revolution only with great difficulty. They also did not include any revolutionary elements, but only calls for a return to the real faith, chastity and an expiation of the sins of the Church. These problems were recognised.[328] The solution implemented consisted of claims that Hus' moderate ideology achieved revolutionary implications in the context of his fate.[329] Hus's death as a martyr, which transformed him into a national and religious symbol, was not the only reason for treating him as a revolutionary. He was said to have undergone an evolution well before his demise. According to Josef Macek, this evolution consisted of a "dialectical coupling" of the exceptional individual with the revolutionary people. Hus's teachings, having become more and more "optimistic," gained a progressive resonance.[330]

---

326   *Přehled československých dějin*, vol. 1, 176.
327   Josef Macek, *Jan Hus*, Praha 1963, 142.
328   See Josef Macek, *Ktož jsú boží bojovníci*, Praha 1951, 14; idem, *Husitské revoluční hnutí*, Praha 1952, 50.
329   Macek, *Ktož jsú*, 14.
330   Macek, *Husitské*, 49-50.

Hus was not the only one to undergo the translation of his reformatory religious postulates into the language of political programs – the same treatment was applied to preachers who spread his teachings. They were to play the role of his political tribunes: "The ideological struggle against the Church could only be conducted by those who were properly armed for it with sufficient education – and these were typically petty, impoverished priests, preachers. Yet their struggle could only be conceived in the same frame which the Church used to veil its class dogmas. ... Popular preachers could urge the people to war from the pulpit."[331] According to Marxist scholars, the Hussites were not propelled by love of God or a desire for salvation, but by humanism, anti-clericalism, and a belief in the progress of humanity – features found in later progressive movements as well.[332] There were other common, timeless traits shared all across this broad spectrum, such as the desire to destroy the forces of reaction, as well as the exploiters and the entire feudal system.[333]

Jan Žižka was as troubling a figure for Marxist historiography as he was for historians of the 19th century. His noble birth and troubled past (he was said to have dabbled in banditry in his youth) were usually left unsaid or dismissed as fabrications of bourgeois historians.[334] Josef Macek played down the problem of Žižka's noble birth, claiming that "the Trocnov warlord did not differ that much from any of the richer peasants." In Tábor, however, Žižka formed ties with the middle bourgeoisie instead of bonding with radical sectarians. However, given the economic situation of the time, he was forced to rely on towns to be able to operate effectively. Had he sided with the poor, he would have lacked sufficient resources to succeed militarily. In the end, Marxist scholars decided to take Žižka's side. Like Hus, he was said to have won the support of the "progressive poor" with his uncompromising approach; like Hus, he was believed to have undergone an evolution through his experience with the simple folk-revolutionaries whom he commanded.

The positive appraisal of the Hussite leader seems to be primarily due to his extraordinary military talents. According to Marxist historians, Žižka was far more nationalist than Hus. Philosopher Milan Machovec named him "the inheritor of Hus's torch." In this role, he became "the favourite of the Czech nation."[335]

For the Communists, Žižka's image was tarnished by his ruthless dealings with the Hussite sectarians – the Adamites. As opposed to the earlier,

---

331   *Přehled československých dějin*, vol. 1, 171.
332   Timoteus Čestmír Zelinka, *Husitskou Prahou*, Praha 1955, 10.
333   See Macek, *Husitské*, 11 & 79.
334   Josef Macek, *Tábor v husitském revolučním hnutí*, Praha 1956, vol. 2, 34.
335   Milan Machovec, *Husovo učení a význam v tradici*, Praha 1953, 250.

historically "immature" heretics, the Adamites "were by no means religious fanatics, they struggled for the rights and victory of the poor. ... Their common sense and healthy reason and the conclusions drawn thereupon assailed Medieval obscurantism and fostered a primordial atheism."[336] Still, there was no chance for the realisation of such a radical program. Czech historians thus faced a problem analogous to the appraisal of the pagan revolt in the Piast state, and responded to it by showing less sympathy for the popular movement with no chance of hastening the arrival of another formation.[337] The example of Žižka and the Adamites shows with striking clarity how the national-liberal patriotic tradition and the struggle for a Marxist historiography intermingled, even if they tended to accentuate different moments. Milan Machovec seemed to favour a more nationalist form of Marxism than Macek. His views on the Adamites were fairly straightforward: "If during the Hussite revolution the popular masses would have succumbed to similar errors and dependence on aid from above, it would have disarmed the people and made it believe in Jesus Christ more than in the flails."[338] Ewa Maleczyńska accused Macek of awarding the Adamites undue recognition. In her opinion, they were not as significant as Macek believed, but she showed understanding of the "Marxist historian's emotional attachment to those most oppressed and persecuted."[339] Interestingly, the university textbook on the history of Poland, published in 1957 and co-authored by Maleczyńska, included a highly similar appraisal of a different radical religious group – the Polish Brethren of the 16th and 17th century. According to the textbook, their ideology, "though utopian at the time, was in social terms the most progressive program of the Polish Renaissance." Like the Adamites, the Brethren were not "impoverished, disorganised and shapeless in class terms": "The Arian left propagated a utopian Communism, endemic to plebeian political programs of the period, and far ahead of contemporary socio-economic relations." The author of that portion of the textbook, Kazimierz Lepszy, actually identified only two serious weaknesses in the Arian ideology: that the Arian gentry oppressed the peasantry as much any other gentry did, and that the Brethren's pacifism could prove to be pernicious. "The Polish Brethren's position, denouncing all wars, whether aggressive or defensive, is understandable. However, this noble disposition against wars carried in itself a serious danger. On the one hand, it led to an abstention from conflicts as such, even if the independence of the fatherland was at stake. On the other, by throwing away their arms, the Brethren

---

336 Ibidem, 202.
337 Macek, *Husitské*, 98.
338 Machovec, *Husovo*, 250.
339 Ewa Maleczyńska, review of: Josef Macek, *Tábor v husitském revolučnim hnutí, Praha 1955-1956, Kwartalnik Historyczny* 1958.

renounced all struggle for social justice if conducted by sword."[340] Apparently, then, the heretic movements could be interpreted in two divergent ways: one could either imbue their theology with a sense of progressive political ideology, and bring out the social content hiding behind religious phrases – as did Josef Macek; or, one could accept the religious character of the heretic movements, but only as an error, a deviation from proper revolutionary ideology. In both cases, Czech Marxists were particularly prone to tie themselves to a traditional interpretation of national history, for which the Hussite movement was much more than just a heresy, and the theological questions it posed were deemed irrelevant to its character.

As was the case with tracing the beginning of Medieval states, the history of the Hussite movement was subjected to a thorough "influence-ological" analysis: both external influences affecting the particular revolution and Hussite currents in other countries were taken into account (the latter with a far more considerable dose of enthusiasm). Within this frame, Josef Macek wove his ruminations, reminiscent of the debate over the "Norman theory": "The revolutionary ideology of the popular heresy was therefore not condemned to transfer the 'idea' from one sect to another, from one country to another, but it could rise on its own in a local environment, from the depths of humiliation, oppression and exploitation experienced by our kinsfolk. If, then, the numerous heretic errors share so many similarities, this is due to a (qualitatively) identical level of exploitation of the peasant folk in our country, Southern France, Austria or England, and to the similar identity of the enemy, the exploiter-Church."[341] Robert Kalivoda, whose work won recognition from Western Medievalists as well, offered another view. Having set out from the same Marxist basis, he traced the influence which European heresies had on the Hussite movement.[342] The contrast between these two perspectives serves as yet another illustration of the extent of changes that took place in Czechoslovak scholarly life between the mid-1950s, the time of Macek's writing, and the early 1960s, when Kalivoda published his work.[343]

By far the most spectacular manifestation of the Hussite influence abroad was evident in the military expeditions called "rejza." In historiography, these raids were represented primarily as propaganda efforts. For Marxist scholars, the reactions of the West, so fearful of the Hussites they resorted to slander, seemed akin to anti-Bolshevist propaganda of the interwar period.[344] Czech and German

---

340   *Historia Polski*, vol. 1, part 2, 288-289.
341   Macek, *Tábor*, vol. 1, 153.
342   Robert Kalivoda, *Husitská ideologie*, Praha 1961.
343   See Ferdinand Seibt, *Hussitica. Zur Struktur einer Revolution*, Köln 1965, 8-10.
344   Jan Durdík, *Husitské vojenství*, Praha 1954, 19.

"bourgeois" historiography treated the Hussite raids as typical wars of plunder. This view was summarily rejected by the Marxists, who endorsed an opposite view: "The Hussites subscribed to an age-old dream of stirring the peoples of neighbouring countries crushed by feudal oppression and binding them together in a struggle against a common enemy, the Church, which was the cornerstone of feudalism."[345] This new concept was bound up with widespread research into the resonance the movement enjoyed in East Central European countries, of which we will yet speak further.

From the perspective of Czech historians, the problem of the Hussite movement's reception turned out to have been quite simple. As a rule, scholars assumed that the popular masses of neighbouring countries were friendly toward the Hussites, while the feudals responded with hatred. This comes as no surprise, given the oft-repeated claim that the Hussites solely pillaged feudal possessions.[346] On the other hand, historians underlined the military efficacy of the Hussites and the fear they inculcated in the surrounding areas – even though the latter and former claims were completely at odds.[347]

Understandably, the foreign reception of the Hussite movement was of considerable interest to Marxist historiographies of Czechoslovakia's neighbouring countries. The readership of East German historical literature were offered unlimited access to the interpretation of the Hussite movement provided by Czech Marxists through translations published both in the GDR and in Czechoslovakia.[348] Scholars of the GDR often referenced the findings of their Czech colleagues, sometimes tempering their enthusiasm on the subject of Hus. On the other hand, though, they thoroughly agreed with claims about a vivid response to the Hussite movement in Germany, acting on the assumption that the Czech revolution was joined by numerous Germans, among them the "German Hussite" Friedrich Reiser.[349] Nevertheless, German scholars attached primary importance to the effect the Hussite revolution had on the participants and leaders of the Great Peasants' Revolt, Thomas Müntzer most of all. Asserting this influence was hardly a straightforward or uncontroversial matter. As late as 1955, in an unprecedentedly virulent review of Heinz Kamnitzer's work on the beginnings of the Great Peasants' Revolt, Rosemarie Müller put one of the axioms of Czech historiography

---

345 Ibidem, 15.
346 Choc, *Boje*, 341.
347 Josef Macek, *Husité na Baltu a ve Velkopolsku*, Praha 1952, 17.
348 See Alois Míka, "Die wirtschaftlichen und sozialen Folgen der revolutionären Hussitenbewegung in den ländlichen Gebieten Böhmens," *Zeitschrift für Geschichtswissenschaft* 1959; Josef Macek, *Die Hussitenbewegung in Böhmen*, Praha 1958.
349 Horst Köpstein, "Über den deutschen Hussiten Friedrich Reiser," *Zeitschrift für Geschichtswissenschaft* 1959, 1069-1070.

to question, writing that both the Hussite movement and the anti-feudal movements in Germany followed the example of peasants' uprisings in France and England. This amounted to a rejection of the thesis concerning the overwhelming influence the Hussite movement had on Germany. Furthermore, Müller disagreed with Kamnitzer's appraisal of Müntzer, whom she saw as hardly matching the brilliance of the figure described by Kamnitzer.[350] In the early 1960s, Bernhard Töpfer debated Václav Husa in the pages of the *Zeitschrift für Geschichtswissenschaft*, accusing the latter of overestimating the influence which a short stay in Bohemia had had on Müntzer's revolutionary beliefs.[351] Still, the prevailing claim dictated that just as the Hussite revolution had influenced the Great Peasants' Revolt, so Hus had influenced Müntzer.

The research into the reception of the Hussite movement abroad played a particularly important role in Slovak Marxist historiography. As in Bohemia, the Hussites counted among the most crucial local progressive traditions. Already in the first pages of the inaugural number of the *Historický Časopis SAV*, Ľudovít Holotík named as a significant task set before Slovak Marxist historical science the investigation of the influence of the Hussite movement, an issue to that point tendentiously avoided by bourgeois scholars.[352] A more detailed analysis of the attitudes toward the Hussite movement prevailing among Slovak historians was presented by Peter Ratkoš. In his view, while their stance was generally negative (e.g. in describing the Hussite raids as pillage expeditions), there was a vivid tradition of Hussite thought in Slovakia, which, in the 19th century, became a foundation for the Slovak national movement.[353]

According to Marxist scholars, Slovak Hussitism was both an imported ideology and an indigenous anti-feudal current. While the Czechs organised raids into Upper Hungary, the area eventually began to house permanent bases of the so-called *bratríci*, a group led by Jan Jiskra of Brandýs and Petr Aksamit. According to Ratkoš, the *bratríci* movement was already imbued with a national spirit.[354] The outbreak of the Hussite revolution in neighbouring Bohemia significantly strengthened the Slovak bourgeoisie in its confrontation with the German patricians, and solidified its feelings of kinship with the Czechs, thereby

---

350   Rosemarie Müller, review of: Heinz Kamnitzer, *Zur Vorgeschichte des Deutschen Bauernkrieges, Berlin 1953*, *Zeitschrift für Geschichtswissenschaft* 1955, 133-135.

351   Bernhard Töpfer, review of: Václav Husa, *Tomáš Müntzer a Čechy, Praha 1959*, *Zeitschrift für Geschichtswissenschaft* 1960, 1690.

352   Ľudovít Holotík, "K sedemdesiatym piatym narodeninám akademika Zdeňka Nejedlého," *Historický Časopis SAV* 1953, 23.

353   Peter Ratkoš, "Husitské revolučné hnutie a Slovensko," *Historický Časopis SAV* 1953, 28.

354   Ibidem, 39.

laying foundations for the modern Slovak nation.[355] This did not mean, however, that Slovaks joined the Hussites in large numbers. On the contrary, the powerful gentry and patricians were fully capable of preventing a revolt among the poor townsfolk. In view of this fact, historians contented themselves with stating that news from the West generally aggravated class warfare in Slovak towns and villages. An unambiguously positive appraisal of a key portion of Czech progressive traditions often contrasted with the sources which the Slovak Medievalists were condemned to use. For example, a very soundly prepared 1965 re-edition of Branislav Varsik's interwar work, replete with citations from original sources, almost exclusively registered the devastation the Hussites caused during their raids (specifically, the estimated numbers of buildings burned). Although Varsik observed that "Today we can have no doubt that the Hussite period was the only moment since the collapse of the Greater Moravia when the clouded skies of Slovakia's past cleared somewhat," the reader of his work will likely miss this bright moment of improvement concealed as it is behind the smoke of Bratislava's burned outskirts.[356] Varsik's book may have been based on a doctoral dissertation defended way back in 1928, yet the author had ample time and opportunity to "colour" somewhat the image of the Hussite influence in Slovakia. The progressive role of Czech cultural influence – linguistic, musical, etc. – was also described in fairly general terms.

The works of the Polish Medievalist Ewa Maleczyńska, the founder of the centre for Hussite study in Wrocław, Poland, constitutes a special case in the reception of the Marxist interpretation of the Hussite movement. As Wojciech Iwańczak observed, this particular topic has always suffered from a strong infusion of ideology, but Maleczyńska's writings surpassed even the notoriously one-sided analyses dating back to the 19th century in the ease with which she formed broad historical claims.[357] The choice of Hussitism as one of the objects of particular interest to the Silesian Medievalists was also connected to the contemporaneous political situation. Ewa and Karol Maleczyński, as well as other scholars from Wrocław, realised that the history of that region, which merely moments ago had belonged to Germany, was rich with memories of Polish-German and Polish-Czech conflicts. As a common ground for Polish-

---

355 *Přehled československých dějin*, vol. 1, 223.

356 Branislav Varsik, *Husitské revolučné hnutie a Slovensko*, Bratislava 1965, 5 & passim.

357 Wojciech Iwańczak, "Polskie badania nad wpływami husyckimi w Polsce," in: *Polskie echa husytyzmu. Materiały z konferencji naukowej, Kłodzko, 27-28 września 1996*, eds. Stanisław Bylina & Ryszard Gładkiewicz, Warszawa 1999, 25-26 & 31. See also idem, "Rewolucja husycka w historiografii polskiej XIX w.," *Sobótka* 1996/4.

Czech cooperation, the Hussite movement represented a research opening into Medieval history that was devoid of dreadful spectres from the past.[358]

The Wrocław Medievalists attached the most importance to researching Polish involvement in the Hussite movement. Hussite ideology was said to have had a particular influence on Silesia. "In Silesia, the Hussite troops were joined by local peasants. Some castles … were inhabited by Hussite leaders, mostly Poles."[359] The Hussite movement was particularly strong among Polish inhabitants of Wrocław.[360] These, in turn, "dragged" the German city rabble and peasants into the movement.[361] Although less pronounced than in Silesia, the influence of the Czech Hussite revolution in other Polish regions still played a role of some significance. Historians recounted how, during the Constance council, the Polish delegation stood up for Jan Hus against accusations of heresy, and his demise caused all of Poland to "reverberate with powerful slogans of Slavic bonds."[362] The calls elicited a particularly strong response in Ruthenia, where even "The inquisition began to track Hussite agitators."[363]

The Hussite movement on Polish lands was as revolutionary as the one in Bohemia. However, there were no real grounds for the victory of a social revolution in the 15th century. This phenomenon was explained at the Otwock conference by Evgeni Kosminsky: "Why didn't the peasant movement win? Because it couldn't. We know well enough that a peasant movement … won't win if it is not led by a hegemonic class. … The bourgeoisie of the period could not exert this kind of influence. It only reached that stage during the era of bourgeois revolution, which is when it matured enough to claim that role."[364] Hence, it is hardly surprising that the Polish revolutionary Hussites often had to seek sanctuary beyond the borders of their country. For them, Bohemia

---

358   See Marek Cetwiński & Lech Tyszkiewicz, "Prawda historii i racja stanu (mediewiści wrocławscy o średniowiecznym Śląsku. Pół wieku badań)," *Sobótka* 1999.

359   Bardach, Gieysztor, Łowmiański & Maleczyńska, *Historia*, 236.

360   See *Teksty źródłowe do dziejów chłopa śląskiego*, part 1 up to 1945, eds. Zbigniew Kwaśny, Józef Leszczyński, Mieczysław Pater, Anna Skowrońska & Józef Gierowski, Wrocław 1956, XIII; *Teksty źródłowe do historii Wrocławia, 1. Do końca XVIII w.*, eds. Karol Maleczyński, Jan Reiter & Ewa Maleczyńska, Wrocław 1951, 45.

361   See Ewa Maleczyńska, "Ruch husycki na ziemiach polskich i jego znaczenie społeczne," in: *Pierwsza Konferencja*, vol. 1, 448.

362   *Historia Polski. Makieta*, vol. 1, part 1, 528 and 533.

363   Ibidem, 539.

364   Eugeniusz Kosminski, "Postępowość i wsteczność folwarku pańszczyźnianego. O przezwyciężenie okcydentalizmu. Historyczne znaczenie Słowian," in: *Pierwsza Konferencja*, vol. 1, 521.

embroiled in revolutionary flames, seemed like a natural destination. This movement developed until reaching its apogee in the 1430s.[365]

Due to these translocations, Poles became a significant force within the Czech Hussite movement, especially in its radical wing.[366] The collapse of that wing of the Czech Hussite movement at the Battle of Lipany was said to have caused an increase in migration to Poland, and the subsequent rise of a radical ideology in the country. These phenomena brought about the confederacy of Spytko of Melsztyn, interpreted by Ewa Maleczyńska as "an openly Hussite revolt in Poland."[367] Her thesis was approved by Polish Marxist Medievalists.[368] Spytko's defeat – like the failure of the Czech movement – was caused by a "class" betrayal of a section of the gentry, which, "just when it faced ... the radical, plebeian current of Hussitism," switched sides: "Just as the treason of the utraquists [led] to Lipany, so in Poland the majority of the participants in Spytko's confederacy of noble birth [left] the camp in Grotniki on the eve of the battle."[369]

Polish Medievalists engaged in cooperative work with their Czechoslovak counterparts, a partnership which helped produce, among other publications, another book by the leading Czech scholar of the epoch, Josef Macek (*Husyci na Pomorzu i w Wielkopolsce*, Warszawa 1955, orig. publ. 1952). The work in question was devoted to a description of the Czech mercenaries' involvement in the service of the Polish king in his wars against the Teutonic Order, as well as to Polish-Czech exchanges in radical thought. In time, though—especially after the publication of Ewa Maleczyńska's *Ruch husycki w Czechach i w Polsce*— scholarly cooperation faced substantial obstacles, and Czech Medievalists began to view their neighbour's attempts to co-opt their native progressive traditions into the catalogues of the Polish national history with more scepticism. Maleczyńska's claims were more and more vocally opposed. She was accused of an unwarranted overinflation of the role of Polish Hussitism and of attempting to paint it as even stronger and more radical than the Czech Hussite movement itself.[370]

Similar reservations toward revelations about the strength of the Polish Hussite movement were voiced by Polish Medievalists as well (though in this

365 Bardach, Gieysztor, Łowmiański & Maleczyńska, *Historia*, 242.
366 See Maleczyńska, "Ruch husycki," 447.
367 Bardach, Gieysztor, Łowmiański & Maleczyńska, *Historia*, 243.
368 Baszkiewicz & Leśnodorski, *Materiały*, 74.
369 Maleczyńska, "Ruch husycki," 450; *Historia Polski. Makieta,* vol. 1, part 1, 533.
370 See Ewa Maleczyńska, *Ruch husycki w Czechach i w Polsce*, Warszawa 1959. The Czechoslovak reactions to the theories of a robust Polish Hussite movement are discussed in my *Między Marksem a Palackým*, 90-95.

case, the motivation may well have been different than with the Czechoslovak Marxists). In a review of one of Maleczyńska'a earlier works, Karol Górski stated, among other criticisms, that she "endeavours to prove that the Hussite movement enjoyed a broad reception in Poland, using as proof, among other things, accusations raised by foreign preachers, while failing to test their veracity."[371] For a historian, it was clear that Maleczyńska transposed phenomena described by Czech Medievalists onto a Polish environment without bothering to find sufficient support for her claims. As late as 1968, in *Kwartalnik historyczny*, she published an article in which she clearly and unambiguously defined her own understanding of historical truth. She found it essential "to ensure that the historian who engages in an analysis of particularly dense material is fully morally committed to building socialism; that, if the material leads him to critical conclusions, he will formulate them not to attack this reality, but to mend it, to point the way toward mending it."[372] The manner in which the author of these words approached her research problems might serve as ample proof of her genuine belief in the subservience of history to politics. According to this logic, the Polish Hussites had a double use for propaganda: as a native progressive tradition and an example of a Polish anti-feudal movement strictly bound to the "Recovered Territories," Silesia in particular. In this light, it comes as no surprise that the Party historian's status remained unshakeable well into the 1960s.[373]

Research into responses to the Hussite movement in Bohemia's neighbouring countries was grounded in a shared belief in the movement's progressive role. Furthermore, Czech historians were convinced of the movement's exceptional character. An astute reader of Slovak and East German scholarship would likely notice that their opinion was not a universally accepted truth. Both historians of the GDR and Slovak Marxists researched their native anti-feudal revolutions and created separate catalogues of progressive traditions.

Czech Marxists overlooked several competing traditions, first and foremost the Great Peasants' Revolt, whose importance for German history was described already by Engels. For historiography in the GDR, this tradition was of key importance. In Alexander Abusch's *Der Irrweg einer Nation*, the failure of the people's movement was already identified as an early origin for the *Deutsche Misere*. Abusch described the Peasants' Revolt through a conflict between two

---

371 Karol Górski, review of: Ewa Maleczyńska, *Społeczeństwo polskie pierwszej połowy XV wieku wobec zagadnień zachodnich. Studia nad dynastyczną polityką Jagiellonów, Wrocław 1947, Przegląd Historyczny* 1948, 458.

372 Ewa Maleczyńska, "O społecznej użyteczności historii," *Kwartalnik Historyczny* 1968, 669-700, quoted in: Stanisław Bylina, "Dorobek czterdziestolecia," in: *Instytut*, 12.

373 See Jerzy Serczyk, "Kilka uwag w sprawie cenzury w PRL," in: *Cenzura w PRL*, 185.

exceptional personalities, representatives of mutually hostile socio-political camps: Thomas Müntzer and Martin Luther. In his view, Müntzer was "the greatest revolutionary figure of his day."[374] Still, his revolution failed; and, according to Abusch, Luther was at fault for this failure. He was the one who had prevented the formation of a durable alliance between the bourgeoisie and the peasantry, and his teachings essentially solidified the people's belief in the righteousness of their subservience in the feudal system.[375]

The Great Peasants' Revolt was "the first act of a European anti-bourgeois revolution."[376] To be more precise, it was a stage of an early-bourgeois revolution. Max Steinmetz, who attempted to redefine this historical event in 1960, established the boundary dates for this revolution as spanning 1476 to 1535. The movement drew its inspiration from the Hussites, from the ideology of György Dózsa's Hungarian revolt, as well as from the beginnings of Reformation.[377] The latter became a catalyst for the people's rebellion, somewhat in spite of the will of its creators. As Leo Stern observed, "the great figures of the religious reformation: John Wycliff, Jan Hus and Martin Luther were drawn into political and social conflicts of their day against their will, caught in the revolutionary movements of the peasantry fighting the existing feudal order."[378] Yet, the Marxist appraisal of Hus differed significantly from that of Luther. While Czechoslovak scholars fully recognised the progressive character of their native reformer's ideas, for decades Luther remained a symbol of the *Deutsche Misere*. Abusch stated that "The German reformation is to blame for the failure of the peasants and for the fact that urban and rural communities could not come together under a common program. ... Martin Luther became the key figure of the German counter-revolution, and went on to claim that status for centuries."[379] When, in the 1950s, the hyper-critical interpretation of national history fell out of favour, historians opted to change their views on the Reformation as an event, rather than on its instigator. Their

---

374 Abusch, *Der Irrweg*, 20.

375 Ibidem, 21.

376 Gerhard Schilfert, review of: Wilhelm Zimmermann, *Der Große deutsche Bauernkrieg, Berlin 1952, Zeitschrift für Geschichtswissenschaft* 1953, 152.

377 Max Steinmetz, "Die frühbürgerliche Revolution in Deutschland (1476-1535). Thesen zur Vorbereitung der wissenschaftlichen Konferenz in Wernigerode vom 20. bis 24. Januar 1960," *Zeitschrift für Geschichtswissenschaft* 1960, 113-116.

378 Leo Stern, "Martin Luther und Philipp Melanchton – ihre ideologische Herkunft und geschichtliche Leistung. Eine Studie der materiellen und geistigen Triebkräfte und Auswirkungen der deutschen Reformation," *Wissenschaftliche Zeitschrift der Martin-Luther-Universität   Halle-Wittenberg,   1952/53/6   Gesellschafts-   und schprachwissenschaftliche Reihe*, 32.

379 Abusch, *Der Irrweg*, 21.

only courtesy toward Luther being that they granted him that, until 1521, his ideas had a desirable (negative, in this instance) effect on his compatriots' attitude toward the Papacy.[380] In Alfred Meusel's *Thomas Müntzer und seine Zeit*, published in 1952, the author recounted Friedrich Engels' opinion that the Reformation was a part of the early-bourgeois revolution. The Great Peasants' Revolt supposedly formed yet another part of the same historical event.[381] The Reformation, the oft-repeated claim went, should not be treated as a religious or cultural phenomenon, but primarily as a stage that resulted from class warfare.[382] Initially, the Swiss "progressive-bourgeois" Reformation received a positive appraisal in comparison with its German "feudal-absolutist" counterpart.[383] Noteworthy changes in the evaluation of Luther's role began to take place in the 1960s, beginning with Max Steinmetz's presentation at a conference in Wernigerode which sparked a renewed interest in the Reformation among GDR historians.[384] The increasingly positive image of the reformer was an outcome of political shifts – the resignation from calls to reunify German and the formation of a new concept of an East German nation. Eventually, it was agreed, as Josef Foschepoth wrote, that, "without the reformer of Wittenberg, Thomas Müntzer would not have been possible."[385] By the early 1980s, Luther was already firmly ensconced in the catalogue of the GDR's progressive traditions, so much so that, in 1983 when West Germany celebrated his jubilee, East Germans hosted a competing celebration.[386]

Thomas Müntzer did not pose as many problems of interpretation as Luther, and, consequently, his image in the historiography of the GDR did not undergo as significant an evolution. The German historiographic tradition formed two opposing interpretations of the figure. For Georg Sartorius or Leopold Ranke, he was a bane to the social order, a dangerous individual threatening the state itself.

---

380 Thomas Vogtherr, "'Reformator' oder 'frühbürgerlicher Revolutionär'? Martin Luther im Geschichtsbild der DDR," *Geschichte in Wissenschaft und Unterricht* 1988/39, 596.

381 Por. Josef Foschepoth, *Reformation und Bauernkrieg im Geschichtsbild der DDR. Zur Methodologie eines gewandelten Geschichtsverständnisses*, Berlin 1976, 33.

382 Max Steinmetz, review of: Alfred Meusel, *Thomas Müntzer und seine Zeit. Berlin 1952*, *Zeitschrift für Geschichtswissenschaft* 1953, 971.

383 Hanna Köditz, "Die gesellschaftlichen Ursachen des Scheiterns des Marburger Religionsgesprächs vom 1. bis 4. Oktober 1529," *Zeitschrift für Geschichtswissenschaft* 1954, 70.

384 Thomas A. Brady Jr., *The Protestant Reformation in German History*, Washington 1998, 19-20.

385 Foschepoth, *Reformation*, 110.

386 Jan Herman Brinks, *Die DDR-Geschichtswissenschaft auf dem Weg zur deutschen Einheit. Luther, Friedrich II. und Bismarck als Paradigmen politischen Wandels*, Frankfurt am Main – New York 1992, 12.

For the same reasons, Müntzer was revered by scholars of a liberal-democratic persuasion, such as Karl Hammerdörfer or (before the revolution of 1848) Wilhelm Zimmerman.[387] Until the mid-1960s, East German historiography saw in Müntzer essentially the progressive antithesis to Luther. While Czechoslovak authors discussed kinship between the enemies of the radical Hussites and the "reactionaries" of the 20th century, East German historians construed two historical lineages: "namely, the lineage which proceeds from Müntzer to the national politics of the working class (that is, a tradition of radical progress); and the other tradition, spanning from the anti-national alliance between Luther and the princelings up until the anti-national policies of the West German bourgeoisie, a tradition of reaction and betrayal."[388] Müntzer's image was reminiscent in a myriad of ways to that of Hus, the difference being that East German scholars attached even less importance to the religious underpinnings of Müntzer's beliefs. Although the German revolutionary was named as an heir to Hus,[389] he was not treated merely as the executor of a program for social revolution developed in Bohemia. The German reviewer of Václav Husa's book *Tomáš Müntzer a Čechy* stressed that, contrary to Husa's claims, Müntzer's stay in Prague did not bring about his detachment from Lutheranism, which was destined to happen anyway and in no way predicated on the influence of the Czechs.[390] Like Hus, Müntzer was said to have undergone an evolution from a moderate reformer to a revolutionary.[391] But, most of all, Müntzer was said to have been a propagandist and campaigner for an early-bourgeois revolution. As a "conservative" revolutionary, he was, therefore, to some degree better than Hus. Ernst Werner consequently compared Müntzer to Želivský, the most radical of the Hussite preachers. "Müntzer's teachings," he wrote, "were a genial anticipation of a history that was already in the making, and of a budding class that did not originate in any of the existing social strata of the 16th century – neither the peasantry, nor the common folk. Still, this new class found its

---

387 Günther J. Trittel, "'Thomas Müntzer mit dem schwerte Gedeonis' – Metamorphosen einer "historischen Metapher," *Geschichte in Wissenschaft und Unterricht* 1991, 551-559.

388 Foschepoth, Reformation, 109. See also: Manfred Bensing, "Thomas Müntzer und Nordhausen (Harz) 1522. Eine Studie über Müntzers Leben und Wirken zwischen Prag und Allstedt," *Zeitschrift für Geschichtswissenschaft* 1962, 1105.

389 Horst Köpstein, "'Die revolutionäre Hussitenbewegung' – eine Ausstellung des tschechoslowakischen Nationalmuseums in Berlin," Zeitschrift für Geschichtswissenschaft 1958, 1133.

390 Bernhard Töpfer, review of: Václav Husa, *Tomáš Müntzer a Čechy*, Praha 1957, *Zeitschrift für Geschichtswissenschaft* 1960, 1690. Husa emphasised ties between Müntzer's beliefs and the radicalism of the Taborites. Cf. Václav Husa, *Tomáš Müntzer a Čechy*, Praha 1957, 2.

391 Foschepoth, *Reformation*, 90.

necessary support in the lowest strata of urban and rural people. It created and revolutionised the movement, forming an alliance between the poor of the city and the poor of the country, and establishing objectives for future general upheaval."[392]

What made the appraisal of the revolutionary even more celebratory was the fact that he "could only summon a hazy precognition of what was already established knowledge to Marx and Engels – that the most oppressed class was precisely the one endowed with an historical mission."[393] One could hardly be surprised, then, that Müntzer became so hated and was slandered by reactionaries. The early 1950s image of Müntzer – as an incendiary revolutionary – retained validity outside of GDR historiography as well.[394] In time, especially toward the early 1960s, East German historians began to think of Müntzer no longer in terms of Hus or Želivský, but in terms of Žižka, a doer, an experienced revolutionary politician far removed from all, even noble, utopias.[395] "We fulfil the ideas of Thomas Müntzer" counted among the most common phrases summoned by East German propaganda, and the ideas in question had decidedly nothing to do with religion.[396]

Despite this high esteem for its leader, the early-bourgeois revolution in Germany (incidentally, just like everywhere else) failed. The reasons given for this defeat also shared a distinct similarity to the theses of Czechoslovak Marxists who analysed the defeat of the radical Hussites. Though the revolution worked in the interest of a still non-existent bourgeoisie, the class which resembled it the most, the Medieval townsfolk, not only did not support the peasants' movement, but actually rose against it. The "revolutionary alliance between the country and the city" proved to have been still lacking.[397] Josef Foschepoth proposed two ways of interpreting this problem: one could either assume that the popular masses objectively acted in the interest of the townsfolk, which at that point in time opted to join the counter-revolution (and hence acted against its own interest); or one could divide the townsfolk into a progressive

392 Ernst Werner, "Messianische Bewegungen im Mittelalter, Teil 2," *Zeitschrift für Geschichtswissenschaft* 1962, 605.
393 Ibidem, 616.
394 The same year (1952) which saw the publication of Albert Meusel's *Thomas Münzer und seine Zeit* (including the selection of "previously unknown" sources edited by Heinz Kamnitzer), also saw publication, in Russian and German, of M. M. Smirin's *Die Volksreformation des Thomas Münzer und der große Bauernkrieg* (Berlin 1952).
395 Foschepoth, *Reformation*, 110-111.
396 Ibidem, 151.
397 Helmut Hesselbarth, "Eine Flugschrift aus dem Großen Deutschen Bauernkrieg," *Zeitschrift für Geschichtswissenschaft* 1953, 551.

(consciously or not) section that worked for the revolution and its reactionary counterpart.[398] East German historiography used both explanations, either of which, like the evaluation of the Hussite radicals, amounted to a simple enough assertion: the revolution had broken out several hundred years too early.

The structural similarities between Marxist interpretations of the Great Peasants' Revolt and the Hussite movement are hardly accidental. Rather they are the result of both events having performed a similar function in the schematic interpretations of history. At stake in both were traditions that existed prior to 1945 or 1948-1949. While Marxist historiography's task was to reinterpret them, it was not forced to single-handedly "invent" them – the Peasants' Revolt was a topic broached by Engels, and the Hussites had been discussed already by Palacký. Liberal historians took note of the anti-feudal nature of the heretic movements even prior to the Springtime of the Peoples, as did the conservatives, who viewed the movements as cases of upheaval against social stability and attempts at rousing the dormant destructive powers of the common folk. In a way, Ukrainians and Poles could relate to one similar event from their national traditions, namely Khmelnytsky's Uprising (whose goal, according to Soviet historiography, was the incorporation of Ukraine into Russia).[399] Attempts at a "takeover" of the progressive Hussite tradition and its adaptation to Polish history, made by Wrocław Medievalists, resulted from a belief (justified or not) that an analogous native tradition was not available. In the final analysis, Ewa Maleczyńska's works proved the "superiority" of the history of Bohemia over that of its neighbours. But adaptation was not the only means of picking out native anti-feudal revolutions. One could also attempt to fabricate them from raw elements, and this is precisely what Slovak historians did.

A significant portion of the Czechoslovak university history textbook is devoted to a description of the most powerful Slovak anti-feudal effort: the 1525-1526 revolt of the miners of Banská Bystrica against the owners of the mines, the Fugger and Thurz families. The uprising began with a strike instigated by the miners, dissatisfied with a diminished payment for their work. The upheaval was exacerbated by the formation of the religious "Brotherhood of the Body of Christ," founded by the miners, which sparked a new conflict. In time, however, "The miners' uprising transformed from a struggle for daily wages into a revolutionary combat under admittedly vague calls for a classless society."[400] The progression from a religious conflict and a battle over wages to

398 Foschepoth, *Reformation*, 72.
399 Emilián Stavrovský, "Rešenie otázky vzťahu dejín Ukrajiny k dejinám SSSR v Istorii URSR, zv. I.," *Historický Časopis SAV* 1955, 281-282.
400 *Přehled československých dějin (Maketa)*, vol. 1, 311.

a veritable revolution was explained in several ways. The Brotherhood was designated as an example of the reception of the radical reformation's slogans, like those of Thomas Müntzer, whose stay in neighbouring Bohemia attracted genuine interest from Czechoslovak historians. Historians interpreted it as an attempt to revive the program of the Tábor and bring about another revolution. The Brotherhood was also a vivid testament to the crisis of feudalism, which reached Slovak territories at the turn of the 16th century.[401] The miners' wage demands, which proved eventually to have been their only stated grievance, were not supposed to be treated literally. According to Peter Ratkoš, "it would be a mistake to treat the content of their proclamations as the final postulates of the revolutionary struggle. Written manifestos and demands are merely their tempered reflection. The real programs of anti-feudal struggles, such as the miners' uprising, ... have to be construed by the historian from the military clashes and court minutes; he must take note of wage issues as well as costs of living, ideological currents and political events, in order to be able to draw the right conclusions."[402] So, the revolutionary program of the insurgents was said to have been hiding behind economic and religious considerations, and found its most perfect expression in the general idea of "weeding out all the lords."[403]

The question of nationality was another interesting problem with regard to the uprising. In the early 1950s, when Slovak historians "discovered" this part of their native history, they often stressed the uprising's progressive, internationalist resonance. It is worth quoting at length from an article by Gustáv Hackenast, published in 1954, that went the furthest in stressing the internationalist agenda of the miners: "The heroic legacy of the Slovak and German miners' uprising in Banská Bystrica marks a fitting beginning to the centuries-long struggle of Hungarian miners for humane living conditions, for freedom. It fills us with pride, and it inspires even more dedication to work, and an ever more heroic attitude befitting the rightful heirs of this tradition: the Slovak and Hungarian miners in their successful endeavour to build socialism, the Hungarian and Slovak working class and Hungarian and Czechoslovak people, will forever be bound with the bonds of brotherhood."[404] Within the next few years, Marxist authors abandoned the idea that the rebellious miners of the 16th century should be treated as an example for the strike workers of the 1950s,

401 Ľudovít Holotík, "K periodizácii slovenských dejín v období feudalizmu a kapitalizmu," *Historický Časopis SAV* 1953, 54.
402 Peter Ratkoš, *Povstanie baníkov na Slovensku roku 1525-1526*, Bratislava 1963, 11.
403 Peter Ratkoš, "Predohra baníckeho povstania v našich banských mestách v rokoch 1525/1526," *Historický Časopis SAV* 1953, 353.
404 Gustáv Hackenast, "Banskobystrické banícke povstanie (1525-1526)," *Historický Časopis SAV* 1954, 104.

but they also removed all mentions of Hungarians and verified the involvement of the Germans in the rebellion. In Ratkoš's essential monograph devoted to this subject, *Povstanie baníkov na Slovensku roku 1525-1526*, published in 1963, the national question took centre stage. The author claimed that the German miners were likely more ideologically enlightened, acting as a conduit for passing the slogans of the Great Peasants' Revolt on to the Slovaks.[405] At the same time, though, he observed: "the fact that the manifestos of the rebellious miners' camp were written in German should not be taken as proof that the uprising was an action comprised solely of the German element."[406] Ratkoš also stressed that the miners were opposed by German patricians and moderate German reformationists. The interpretation that remained largely unchallenged was the thesis that the political program of the miners' uprising was an extension of the aims of the Great Peasants' Revolt as well as Dózsa's uprising in Hungary.

The miners' uprising in Banská Bystrica has indeed been a recognised fact for years, but until the 1950s no one attached any importance to it. Its emergence as a topic for research is unequivocally tied to Peter Ratkoš, who played the same role in Slovak Medievalism which Josef Macek played in the Czech part of the country.[407] At first, Ratkoš attempted to shed some positive light on the influence the Czech Hussites enjoyed in Slovakia – a daunting enough task given the conviction, commonly held in sources from the era and replicated by earlier Slovak and Hungarian historiography, that the *rejzas* were nothing more than brutal plundering expeditions. The miners' uprising was a less controversial, and more importantly, native Slovak source for progressive traditions, even if, as contemporary Slovak historians believe, Ratkoš not only decidedly overestimated its importance, but also romanticised the progression of the events he described.[408]

The ease with which Peter Ratkoš introduced the 16th century miners into Slovak history was quite uncommon among attempts at positioning newly uncovered progressive traditions as key links in the chain of historical progress and as sources of national pride. It is far easier to cite examples of anti-feudal movements which, despite the efforts of some Marxist scholars, retained a marginal status and failed to garner the kind of attention accorded the Hussite movement or the Great Peasants' Revolt. One such case was highlander banditry, linked in Slovak tradition primarily to Juraj Jánošík, a figure well-

---

405 Ratkoš, *Povstanie*, 271.
406 Ibidem, 10.
407 Anton Špiesz, "K problematike starších dejín Slovenska," *Historický Časopis SAV* 1990, 683.
408 Ibidem, 684.

known in Czechoslovakia and beyond who was sometimes called the Slovak Robin Hood.

Jánošik was exploited already by the ideology of interwar Czechoslovakia as a symbol of the struggle against the monarchy and the nobles. It was only after the war, however, that the bandits of the Carpathian Mountains became protagonists not only of children's schoolbooks and popularising efforts, but also Czechoslovak historiography. In several of his works devoted to Jánošik, Andrej Melicherčík provided a general characterisation of the phenomenon of highlander banditry, judging it to have been an effective form of fighting feudalism. Banditry was not an outgrowth of a highlander mentality nor of the folk's living circumstances, as previously believed, but was a reflection of class relations. Melicherčík listed numerous similarities between Polish, Ukrainian, Slovak and Hungarian highwaymen. In his opinion, the great peasant revolts of the 16th and 17th centuries, typically devoid of political programs and the support of townsfolk, were doomed to failure. Banditry, on the other hand, was considered to be an effective method of harassing class opponents.[409] Jánošik also retained legendary status among the Slovak common folk as late as the 19th century when banditry had already faded away as a result of the rise of social consciousness among the working class.[410] According to Melicherčík, the memory of the highlander bandits became a sort of bandit messianism, deftly illustrated by the example of Oleksa Dovbush: "And yet the Ukrainians of yore believed more than anything in the coming of a new Dovbush. Their faith was confirmed by the legend that the gun which Oleksa Dovbush buried deep in the ground before his death draws closer to the surface every year, and that, when it emerges completely, the new Dovbush will arrive. That hope of the Ukrainian people, tied in literary practice to Oleksa Dovbush's name, has already materialised."[411]

The problem of banditry affected Poland to a rather large extent, which meant that Polish Marxist historiography, comparatively, devoted the most attention to it. The authors of the draft of the university textbook on the history of Poland wrote: "The finest bandit commanders ... became the stuff of legend for the people well before their death. Banditry served as fuel to the fire of class warfare, but at the same time was also a playground for developing the peasantry's military skills and partisan tactics."[412] In a way, it made up for the

---

409 Andrej Melicherčík, *Juraj Jánošík. Hrdina protifeudálniho odboje slovenského lidu*, Praha 1956, 78.

410 Jozef Butvin, *Slovenské národno-zjdenocovacie hnutie (1780-1848) (K otázke formovania novodobého slovenského buržoázneho národa)*, Bratislava 1965, 281.

411 Ibidem, 41.

412 *Historia Polski. Makieta*, vol. 1, part 2, 530.

absence of a native early-bourgeois revolution, since, as Bohdan Baranowski complained, "In Poland, there were no anti-feudal peasant revolts of proportions similar to those in some other European countries ... Struggles as vehement and dramatic as those which took place, for instance, in Germany, England or Russia, were unheard of in Poland."[413] For most Marxist scholars, though, bandits were far less unambiguous than for Slovak historians. The authors of the "Draft" recognised that "while their activities to an extent assumed the shape of a class war against the oppressive feudals, they quite swiftly transformed into something completely different, being restricted to simple robbery of not only noblemen's properties, but also peasants' huts."[414] In the early 1950s, bandits became the topic of several works (mostly collections of original sources).[415] Some of them reframed the highwaymen in the manner of folktales. As Baranowski observed, "The bandits of the time were characterised by a specific code of ethics. One could only assault and rob the manors of the gentry or corrals belonging to rich landowners who made their wealth from another's misery. No self-respecting bandit would take anything from the poor – he would rather divide the riches stolen from the wealthy among the impoverished."[416] Claims like these, though generally supportive of the "good cause," met with critical responses from reviewers at specialist journals. Janina Bieniarzówna, writing in *Przegląd Historyczny*, criticised the "idealisation of bandit groups, whose unquestionable class disposition cannot erase evidence of the common robberies that took place."[417] In an even sterner response to a work on highlander banditry, Juliusz Bardach pointed out "the class line distortion in banditry."[418]

A special type of banditry developed in the Ukrainian territories of the Polish-Lithuanian Commonwealth. The area was located at the crossroads of class, religious and national conflicts. The resulting mixture was far more complex than was the case with Polish highlander bandits. The leadership of this collection of bandits was assumed by the Zaporizhian Cossacks, and it found its most significant manifestation in Khmelnytsky's Uprising.

---

413 Bohdan Baranowski, *Powstanie Kostki Napierskiego w 1651 r.*, Warszawa 1951, 8.
414 *Historia Polski. Makieta*, vol. 1, part 2, 362.
415 See *Materiały do powstania Kostki Napierskiego*, ed. Adam Przyboś, Wrocław 1951; W. Ochmański, *Zbójnictwo góralskie. Z dziejów walki klasowej na wsi góralskiej*, Kraków 1950.
416 Baranowski, *Powstanie*, 56.
417 Janina Bieniarzówna, review of: *Materiały do powstania Kostki Napierskiego*, ed. Adam Przyboś, Wrocław 1951, *Przegląd Historyczny* 1953, 217.
418 Juliusz Bardach, review of: W. Ochmański, *Zbójnictwo góralskie. Z dziejów walki klasowej na wsi góralskiej*, Kraków 1950, *Przegląd Historyczny* 1952, 154-155.

The Cossack Uprisings formed the portion of Rzeczpospolita's history which was subjected to the most thorough reinterpretation after 1945. In works by members of the Kraków School, the analysis of Khmelnytsky's revolt already included more criticism of the Polish gentry than of the rebels.[419] Still, the popular understanding of the war, shaped by Henryk Sienkiewicz's novels, determined the society's way of thinking about the events. The problem decidedly warranted an explanation. This need was recorded by Jan Micigolski, a reader of the journal *Nowe Drogi* who posed the following question in a letter to the editor: "I was taught in middle school about the so-called rebellion of Bohdan Khmelnytsky in the Ukraine. In 1946, I read H. Sienkiewicz's *With Fire and Sword*. I feel that my previous knowledge of peasant rebellions in the Ukraine was insufficient. My stay at the Party-governed school in Kielce in 1949-1950 helped very little in this regard. I often travel around the Kielce voivodship and I can see that many people lack a clear vision of the problem, especially those who finished their schooling before the war. Therefore, I ask for a clarification of this problem in the pages of *Nowe Drogi*."[420]

The editors' explanation, like the new interpretation of Khmelnytsky's uprising included in Marxist works, painted a decidedly favourable image of both the Cossacks and Khmelnytsky himself. The rebellious leader "felt the misery of the Cossacks and the suffering of the Ukrainian nation, the more so since he too had fallen victim to the licentiousness of the Polish feudal lords and their retainers."[421] Because of the complex nature of the uprising, commingling social, national and religious issues, its social basis was very broad: "Khmelnytsky's standards were carried not only by the peasants, but also by Ukrainian townspeople, as well as by a section of the Ukrainian gentry and the Orthodox clergy; in other words, the rebel forces formed a united front of Ukrainian social and national forces against the rule of the Polish magnates."[422] At the 2nd Congress of the PZPR in March 1954, Nikita Khrushchev, speaking as a guest, advanced an audacious claim that the rebel army included a significant contingent of Polish peasants.[423] The Ukrainian uprising received disinterested aid from Russia, but other neighbours of Ukraine were animated by completely different designs toward the rebels. In the "Draft" of the university

---

419 See Andrzej Stępnik, "Historia a literatura. Kontrowersje wokół powstania Chmielnickiego na przełomie XIX i XX w.," in: *Historia poznanie i przekaz*, ed. Barbara Jakubowska, Rzeszów 2000, 152-163.

420 "Listy do redakcji," *Nowe Drogi* 1952/7.

421 *Historia Polski. Makieta*, vol. 1, part 2, 557.

422 Ibidem.

423 "Przemówienie powitalne I Sekretarza KC KPZR towarzysza N. S. Chruszczowa," *Nowe Drogi* 1954/3, 85.

textbook on the history of Poland, Turkey was mentioned as Khmelnytsky's ally only in inverted commas. The Tartars received a similar appraisal.[424] The Polish-Lithuanian Commonwealth represented the interests of the magnates who wanted to continue their oppression of the Ukrainian folk. For this reason, all later attempts at a compromise between the warring sides were doomed to fail. Consequently, the section of the Cossack elders who chose to support an agreement with Poland were seen as traitors to their own nation.[425]

The Treaty of Pereyaslav, binding Ukraine to Russia, received a dramatically different evaluation. In the Soviet Ukraine, its tricentennial was celebrated as a holiday honouring the "immovable" unity of two brotherly nations, with the ethnic and cultural proximity of Ukrainians and Russians emphasised heavily.[426] In Polish Marxist historiography, the treaty's incorporation of a part of Ukrainian territory into the Russian state was praised as a step that fostered Ukrainian autonomy.[427] The authors of the "Draft" phrased this claim in an even more radical manner, stating that "For a long time, the broad Ukrainian popular masses drifted toward Russia, to which they were bound by historical tradition." In their view, within the Polish Republic of feudal nobles, "the very existence of Ukrainian nationhood was threatened with extinction in such circumstances, and its only hope was to merge with Russia."[428] The Treaty was said to have had a positive effect on the peasants' daily lives.[429]

No less progressive than the fortuitous development of Ukrainian nationality was the strengthening of the Russian state through territorial expansion.[430] For obvious reasons, Poland, the Crimean Khanate, or Turkey viewed the "Pereyaslav deed" (in Zbigniew Wójcik's diction) unfavourably.[431] "The feudal Rzeczpospolita summoned all its powers to break the bond between Ukraine and Russia, which had put an end to the predatory policies of the Polish possessor classes."[432] The convergence of the interests of Moscow and Ukraine was quite

---

424 *Historia Polski. Makieta,* vol. 1, part 2, 561.
425 Baszkiewicz & Leśnodorski, *Materiały,* 113.
426 See Ivan L. Rudnytsky, "Pereiaslav: History and Myth," in: idem, *Essays in modern Ukrainian history*, Cambridge/Mass. 1987.
427 Baszkiewicz & Leśnodorski, *Materiały,* 112-113.
428 Ibidem, 567.
429 Zbigniew Wójcik, "Rywalizacja polsko-tatarska o Ukrainę na przełomie lat 1660-1661," *Przegląd Historyczny* 1954, 610.
430 *Historia Polski. Makieta,* vol. 1, part 2, 562.
431 See Wójcik, "Rywalizacja," 609.
432 Zbigniew Wójcik, "Feudalna Rzeczpospolita wobec umowy w Perejasławiu," *Kwartalnik Historyczny* 1954, 109.

clearly depicted in a work approved by the Central Committee of the Soviet Communist Party, *The Theses for the Tricentennial of the Unification of Ukraine and Russia*: "Bohdan Khmelnytsky's historical merit was that, by expressing the age-old longings and strivings of the Ukrainian nation for a close alliance with the Russian nation, and by guiding the formation process of Ukrainian statehood, he rightly perceived its tasks and perspectives, and he saw that the Ukrainian nation could not exist if not unified with the great Russian nation, which is why he relentlessly strove to unify Ukraine and Russia."[433]

For Poland, Khmelnytsky's uprising and Russia's annexation of a portion of Ukrainian territory were said to have been a blessing. The very fact of this territorial loss weakened the magnates.[434] Besides, the uprising in the Ukraine fostered anti-feudal movements in the Polish lands, sparking innumerable rebellions: "the metal-workers and miners' joining forces with Kostka-Napierski's revolt, the liberation of Warsaw in 1656, the anti-gentry townsfolk's movement in Lublin in 1656 under Wojciech Reklowski, gathered under the slogan 'Noblemen, your liberties are ceased,' and finally the few preserved positive appraisals of the English Revolution and the mass involvement of the townspeople, especially the petit-bourgeois and the poor, in the struggle against the Swedes."[435]

Although Khmelnytsky's Uprising played an important part in the works of Polish Marxists, it did not belong to native history, but was rather a fragment of the progressive traditions of Soviet Ukraine. For obvious reasons, it could not have been "Polonised," as had been the case with the Hussite movement in Ewa Maleczyńska's writings. One could, however, attempt to associate other events in Poland with the Cossack uprising, casting about for Khmelnytsky's Polish allies. In Marxist works, the little-known Kostka-Napierski's rebellion was viewed both as analogous to the Ukrainian movement and as influenced by it. The fact that Kostka-Napierski operated in the Podhale region reflected the similarity of the local peasantry's social situation to that of the Ukrainian peasantry.[436] Furthermore, Kostka-Napierski maintained close relations with Khmelnytsky. As Józef Leszczyński learned, "Kostka-Napierski, whose collaboration with Khmelnytsky is ultimately beside the point, waited in Czorsztyn for the arrival of troops conscripted in Silesia. It seems that the rebellion in Greater Poland, organised most likely by Khmelnytsky's agents,

---

433 Quoted in: Bohdan Baranowski, "Narodowo – wyzwoleńcza walka ludu ukraińskiego w XVII wieku," *Nowe Drogi* 1954, 37.
434 *Historia Polski. Makieta*, vol. 1, part 2, 113.
435 Zofia Libiszowska, "Ruchy plebejskie w Polsce w XVII w.," in: *Pierwsza Konferencja*, vol. 2, 83.
436 See Baszkiewicz & Leśnodorski, *Materiały*, 103.

enjoyed a certain resonance in Silesia."[437] The authors of the "Draft," on the other hand, wrote about the conspiracy of the Warsaw poor, "whose participants were expected to prepare an uprising which would explode when Khmelnytsky's army drew closer."[438] Given the broad influence the uprising enjoyed in Polish territories, Czapliński could hardly be said to have exaggerated when he stated that "in this period, the earth trembled under the feet of the gentry throughout Poland."[439]

Polish Marxist historians exploited only a fraction of Kostka-Napierski's "potential" in building up the history of their native progressive traditions. Among the obstacles they had to tackle was limited knowledge of the figure: "This peasant or bourgeois son was evidently filled with compassion for his injured and humiliated brethren, and must have viewed the brutal attempts at quelling the Ukrainian rebellion with undisguised aversion" – ventured Bohdan Baranowski, who admitted at the same time that he had no specific knowledge of Kostka-Napierski's supposed plans for spreading the rebellion throughout the country, nor of the particular means for communicating with the Ukrainian rebels.[440] The weak peasant movement, commanded by a man of unverified origin and unknown past, essentially could never compare with the anti-feudal revolts in neighbouring countries.

The tradition of the uprising of 1651 was nonetheless construed as the foundation for all later peasant political movements. According to Marxist historians, it was also one of Poland's most decidedly progressive national traditions.[441] Juliusz Bardach claimed that "During the popular movement of 1651, there was a clear coming together between the Polish peasants and the Ukrainian folk, representing the progressive forces of social and national liberation, in a united front against the main force of reaction – the Polish feudal nobles. ... The Ukrainian peasants were the armed avant-garde of the rest of the Rzeczpospolita's peasant masses, which, led by the Ukrainians' example, and maybe even working in tandem with them, joined the struggle against feudal

437 Józef Leszczyński, "Agenci Bohdana Chmielnickiego i Jerzego II Rakoczego na Morawach i na Śląsku," *Sobótka* 1955, 678.

438 *Historia Polski. Makieta*, vol. 1, part 2, 563.

439 Władysław Czapliński, "Ruchy ludowe w roku 1651 (Wyniki badań, poprawki i uzupełnienia)," *Przegląd Historyczny* 1953, 70.

440 Bohdan Baranowski, *Powstanie chłopskie Kostki Napierskiego. Odczyt*, Warszawa 1950, 27-28.

441 See Historia Polski. Makieta, vol. 1, part 2, 565; Baszkiewicz & Leśnodorski, *Materiały*, 115.

oppression and exploitation."[442] The most shocking part of the Marxist interpretation of Khmelnytsky's Uprising is precisely this attempt to construe a movement aimed against the Polish-Lithuanian Commonwealth as beneficial for the state. To corroborate this view, historians needed to identify a sufficiently broad section of Polish society that possessed a suitable comprehension of Khmelnytsky's progressiveness. Such a portion of society would then act as an ally of the Cossacks in their attempt to overthrow feudalism in Poland. Hence, the peasant anti-feudal movements, Kostka-Napierski's rebellion, and the presence of Khmelnytsky's and Rákóczi's agents were all acting to counterbalance the fact that Khmelnytsky's uprising was aimed against the Polish state.

Slovak historians writing on the anti-feudal movements of the 17th century could not name Khmelnytsky's uprising as a direct source of inspiration for their native revolutionaries. In their case, far more compelling, but also more troubling, were the ties that existed between class warfare in Slovakia and the Hungarian anti-Habsburg rebellions of István Bocskay, Imre Thököly and Francis II Rákóczi, as well as the involvement of Transylvania against Austria in the Thirty Years' War.

The attitude of Slovak historiography toward the Hungarian rebellions grew out of its appraisal of the Revolution of 1848 (which will be discussed in more detail later). Indeed, both in the popular understanding of Hungarian history and in the opinion of numerous Hungarian Marxists, the liberation movements formed a continuous lineage that culminated in the revolution of 1848-1849, both as the most glorious moment of national history and the deepest fall from grace which Hungary ever experienced. During the first years of the new methodology's implementation, one would be excused for assuming that Slovak scholars would follow Marx in his appreciation of Bocskay, Thököly and Rákóczi. Indeed, in the first yearbook of the *Historický Časopis SAV*, Ľudovít Holotík wrote of the alliance between Hungarian and Slovak common folk, who had joined in a struggle against foreign and local forces of reaction.[443] The theses on the history of Slovakia, formulated some two years later, proposed that Rákóczi's uprising began as a social struggle of Slovak and Ukrainian farmers. Only later was this vivid movement used to further the cause of an anti-Habsburg state revolt, losing its class character along the way.[444] After the suppression of the Hungarian Revolution of 1956, Czechoslovak

---

442   Juliusz Bardach, "W 300-ną rocznicę powstania chłopskiego pod wodzą Kostki-Napierskiego," *Nowe Drogi* 1951/3, 109.
443   Ľudovít Holotík, "Z výsledkov kongresu maďarských historikov," *Historický Časopis SAV* 1953, 317.
444   *Dejiny Slovenska (tézy)*, 68.

historiography's tune turned sour. In the 1958 draft of the university history textbook, the authors pointed out that most of the victims of the feuds between the Hungarians and the Habsburgs were Slovak civilians, that the uprisings only served the gentry, and that "one could never treat them as national liberation struggles, as the Hungarian bourgeois historiography did. ... The state rebellions ... from the vantage point of the history of the Slovak people, should be judged as a struggle of two ruling classes over the right to exploit Slovaks."[445] Furthermore, as Jozef Vlachovič observed, the rebellious Hungarians allied with the most reactionary power in Europe, the Ottoman Empire.[446] The increasingly critical appraisal of the anti-Habsburg rebellions eventually affected the appraisal of the Habsburgs themselves. This observation seeped into Vlachovič's article from 1960, quoted above; as he wrote, "We cannot accept the high appraisal Bethlen's revolt received from Hungarian historians. A revision is also in order when it comes to their unanimous damnation of the Habsburg monarchy in the same period."[447] A year later, the editors of *Historický Časopis SAV* criticised the participants in the congress of the CISH in Stockholm for idealising Transylvanian policies and demonising the Habsburgs.[448]

The events referred to above served more or less successfully as "early-bourgeois revolutions" in the histories of the countries discussed. At the same time, other revolutions affected national histories only partially – like Khmelnytsky's Uprising or the Hungarian struggles against the Habsburgs. Given that they were accorded comparable roles in compendia of national histories and in catalogues of progressive traditions, an analysis of the differences between them seems pertinent. We would be excused for supposing that the signifier "early-bourgeois revolution" finds its fullest representation in the German Reformation and the Great Peasants' Revolt (After all, this is how Friedrich Engels saw them.).[449] Still, a reading of Marxist analyses shows that it was not German history that served as the point of departure for progressive traditions of other countries in the area. The Reformation, and Luther in particular, received a great deal of criticism. All the admiration for Thomas Müntzer could not conceal the extremely unfavourable assessments of the

---

445 *Přehled československých dějin (maketa),* vol. 1, 456-460.

446 Jozef Vlachovič, "Stredoslovenské banské mestá a protihabsburské povstania v prvej tretine 17. stor. (Prispevok k problematike dejín pätnásťročnej a tridsaťročnej vojny na Slovensku)," *Historický Časopis SAV* 1960, 526.

447 Ibidem, 556.

448 "XI. Medzinárodný Kongres Historikov v Štokholme," *Historický Časopis SAV* 1961, 528-534.

449 See Foschepoth, *Reformation,* 33.

peasant rebels' capabilities. The most praised, least controversial and "most modern" early-bourgeois revolution, as it turned out, was the revolutionary Hussite movement. Czech Marxists completed an arduous task: they managed to depict a thoroughly religious movement as a powerful social and anticlerical revolution. Their triumph was all the more significant because of the fact that this same evaluation of the Hussite movement was also accepted by foreign Marxists, who engaged in broad research on the resonances of the Hussite movement in their native countries, sometimes even attempting to stake a claim to the movement. Compared with the Hussite movement, the partly progressive movements discussed by Polish historiography, such as the pagan revolt, Kostka-Napierski's rebellion, or banditry in the Carpathian Mountains, lacked some of the same flair, either due to an absence of sufficient ideological foundations, or because they never reached the grand scale of the Hussite movement. In truth, only the revolt of the miners in Banská Bystrica (though probably in large part because of Peter Ratkoš's efforts as its chronicler) claimed a similar status as an uncontested, progressive, national and internationalist revolutionary movement – though it still failed to reach as great a scale.

This "success" of the Hussite movement resulted from a particular virtue of Czech Marxist historiography, which claimed, for the most part, the national-liberal image of history, and infused it both with Marxist terminology and analogies to modern history. The Hussites were accorded a special place already in Palacký's works, and the historians of the 1950s by necessity cited him more often than Marx and Engels in their own analyses.[450] Neither Polish, nor German scholars could rely on such a self-explanatory, socially acceptable interpretation of national history.

The differences between particular early-bourgeois revolutions highlight the role which local historical traditions played in Marxist historiographies. In this respect (as in many others), the similarities deriving from a shared methodology and similar political commitments did not preclude the divergences that resulted from differences in the prior achievements in historiographies in East Central Europe. It was the relative weakness of the historiographic tradition in Slovakia that facilitated the formation of new interpretations, perfectly attuned to the current needs of the Marxist vision of history. In the case of Slovakia, the catalogue of "progressive traditions" was enriched not only with the miners' rebellion, but also with Jánošik who, according to Polish historians, did not merit serious scholarly study.

The interpretation of uprisings, rebellions and revolutions also provides particularly colourful examples of interactions between different Marxist

---

450   More on the subject in my *Między Marksem a Palackým*, passim.

historiographies. All popular movements were treated as one system infused with the "boiling" revolutionary *élan*. At times, an "enhancement" of a local "progressive tradition" resulted in the degradation of a tradition hailed by one's neighbours. Hence Slovak history became for Slovak historians more progressive as Hungarian history became less progressive. The emphasis placed by Czech historians on connections between Müntzer and the Prague townsfolk was also meant to "diminish" somewhat the image of the greatest German revolutionary until Marx. A particularly spectacular example of this course of action are the works of Ewa Maleczyńska, whose high appraisal of the Polish Hussite movement forced her into a critical relativisation of Hussitism in Bohemia. The only peerless progressive traditions belonged to the nations of the Soviet Union, and neither Polish, Czechoslovak, nor East German Marxist works ever attempted to belittle their legacy.

The unquestionable interactions between particular Marxist historiographies also prove that, to properly analyse their achievements, one cannot limit oneself to a model comparing only Soviet historiography with any one of the historiographies belonging to the people's democracies. This model works well so far as methodological considerations, general statements, or a few historical analogies are concerned. The history of East Central (and South Eastern) Europe, broadly understood, provides us with unlimited specific material for comparative analysis. As we have seen, the early-bourgeois revolution was made to conform with the model of the Czech Hussite movement, the ideas of interpretation provided by East German historians were critically evaluated by their Polish peers, and Slovak scholars constantly participated in an exchange of opinion with Hungarian historians. On the lookout for ways to describe events in local histories in a new, Marxist fashion, historians reached out for the experiences of their neighbours, read their analyses, assuming that many of the phenomena in question probably found proximate analogies in other countries of the region. Marxist historians seemed to have taken more note of those analogies than our contemporaries. Small wonder, given the schematic approach favoured by Marxism, which encouraged this search for analogies. If the laws of historical progress were replicated everywhere, regardless of the circumstances, the claims to national distinction, untranslatability, and exceptionality had to yield to a highly specific kind of comparative study.

Between the French Revolution and the Russian Tanks

Just like in numerous other versions of history, the French Revolution is also a unique event within the Marxist schema of history. It forms the frame of reference for every other revolution in multiple aspects, ranging from its particular vocabulary (for instance, use of the term "Jacobins" for revolutionaries such as Ignác Martinovics or Hugo Kołłątaj, or the numerous Robespierres and Saint-Justs of the many failed Central European revolts), through the division into left and right sides of the political stage it introduced, up until the creation of such useful catchphrases as "revolutionary terror," "counter-revolution," and "reactionary intervention." Within the "table of rank," this revolution had at first claimed a precious spot, earning the moniker of "the mother of all bourgeois revolutions," as well as being, in a way, the mother of the Great Socialist October Revolution. Lenin, for instance, compared Bolsheviks to Jacobins. In time, in the later 1930s, the French Revolution began to lose significance, particularly as it ceased to be mentioned as the forerunner to the October Revolution. However, despite yielding its status as the single proper context for the October Revolution in Russia, the French Revolution retained all its progressive glamour for East Central European states well into the 1950s.

It was said to have sparked unrest in rural areas of Bohemia and Slovakia; the peasants eagerly anticipated breaking of bonds of serfdom, erroneously perceiving Napoleon as their saviour.[451] For authors of the Marxist history textbook (particularly Josef Kočí), the pro-French tendencies among the Czech peasantry caused "an exacerbation of class warfare."[452] As Zdeněk Nejedlý wrote, "The news that the French forces were approaching the borders of Bohemia were reason enough for unrest among our peasants ... willingly offering their services to the revolutionary French army as their liberator."[453] The revolution sparked similarly vivid reactions in Germany. In 1790, peasants in Saxony erupted in revolt. Though their movement was brought about by social oppression and a bad harvest, events in France added fuel to its fire.[454] Still, the revolt was said to have been doomed to fail, with the peasants unable to enlist bourgeois support for their cause. The author of a dissertation describing the event mentioned only in passing that the rebel forces were limited to some 500 men, arguably an even more convincing cause of the movement's failure.[455]

---

451 Jan Novotný, "Příspěvek k otázce úlohy některých lidových buditelů v počátcích českého národního obrození," *Československý Časopis Historický* 1954, 627.

452 *Přehled československých dějin*, vol. 1, 639.

453 Zdeněk Nejedlý, *O smyslu českých dějin*, Praha 1953, 226.

454 Percy Stulz, "Der sächsische Bauernaufstand 1790", *Zeitschrift für Geschichtswissenschaft* 1953, 20-38.

455 Percy Stulz, "Der sächsische Bauernaufstand 1790 (II)," *Zeitschrift für Geschichtswissenschaft* 1953, 404-405.

In the early 1950s, this pioneering research by Percy Stulz was complemented by further analyses of the early 1790s unrest in rural Germany.[456]

German historians also pointed to the positive response the revolution enjoyed in literary and scientific circles. Joachim Streisand, author of the relevant volume of the university textbook on German history, stressed that, just like the peasants, the German intelligentsia constituted an oppressed class. They had had to serve the Evangelical Church or "make the princes' courts shine" just to make ends meet, but, in fact, the slogans of the French Revolution were very dear to their hearts. Furthermore, they also always affirmed that the very same slogans should serve as a call for the liberation and reunification of the German fatherland.[457] The revolution won the admiration of the most formidable of Germans, Goethe, as well as of Hegel, Lessing, Kant, Schiller – German classicism in general.[458] For the Romantics, on the other hand – the Schlegel brothers, Tieck, Novalis, Schelling and Schleiermacher – the initial awe was quickly replaced by a wariness of social progress and support for remnants of the feudal order.[459]

Though Marxist historians perceived the reaction to news from France as being similar across the entire East Central Europe, only Germany was blessed with a "sisterly" Republic of Mainz, formed on German territory and functioning under actual French occupation. This ephemeral state-like entity was described as "the first democratic republic on German lands" and consequently received positive evaluation. Its native character and relative independence from the French government or inspiration seemingly invited amicable treatment. Streisand wrote extensively on the various initiatives undertaken by the townsfolk of Mainz, who began spreading revolutionary [*sic* – M.G.] propaganda already in the 1750s.[460] Figures such as Andreas Joseph Hofmann, a professor of philosophy and history, or the writer, librarian and naturalist Georg Forster, as well as other, unnamed German Jacobins were said to have been even

---

456   See Heinz Kamnitzer, "Disposition des Hochschullehrbuches der Geschichte des deutschen Volkes (1789-1815)," *Zeitschrift für Geschichtswissenschaft* 1954, 258-260, as well as: Joachim Streisand, "Aus dem Entwurf zum Lehrbuch der Geschichte Deutschlands (1789-1805)", *Zeitschrift für Geschichtswissenschaft* 1956, 66; Joachim Streisand claimed that numerous peasant revolts in Germany proved the existence of the same class divergences that had existed in France. – Joachim Streisand, *Deutschland von 1789 bis 1815 (Von der Französischen Revolution bis zu den Befreiungskriegen und dem Wiener Kongreß)*, Berlin 1959, 12-14.

457   Streisand, *Deutschland*, 12-14.

458   Ibidem, 100-108.

459   Ibidem, 109.

460   Ibidem, 36.

more radical than the French military-men occupying Mainz.[461] Scholars also emphasised that, though the peasantry of the Rhineland were grateful to the French for repealing feudalism, this should not have been taken to mean that they perceived themselves as French. "The love of the people for their fatherland," wrote Streisand, "was so powerful that no political or military threats, nor material gains could obliterate the German character of the region."[462] The peasants of the Rhineland were to prove their German patriotism several years later, when Germany engaged in a war against France.

Precisely, if France could turn from a progressive force into a reactionary enemy of the German peasantry in such a short time, it became essential to locate the specific moment this change occurred, the point when the country took on its negative role. This task, however, proved rather difficult to complete. German historians recognised two competing answers: the first, offered by Heinrich Scheel, ascribed a progressive nature to France up until the collapse of the internal counter-revolution and the beating back of foreign intervention forces, in other words, until sometime between 1794 and 1795. Most of the participants in the international discussion (attended by Polish and Czechoslovak scholars as well), organised by the Institute of History at DAW in November 1956, leaned toward the claim that France remained progressive until it beat reactionary Austria at Austerlitz, and Prussia at Jena and Auerstedt. The Polish historians (e.g. Stefan Kieniewicz), who played quite a significant role in the proceedings, argued that the formation of the Duchy of Warsaw should receive a positive appraisal.[463] In accordance with this claim, the East German university history textbook established the date for the transformation of France into a reactionary power as 1807, when the French bourgeoisie achieved a dominant position in Europe and resistance began to germinate in Germany.[464] Several years later, Heinrich Scheel radically altered his views and decided that the French accelerated the advent of capitalism, and their progressive role in that regard had not ended even as late as 1807, as Streisand believed.[465] In the same way, Scheel also entered another dispute, initiated by Alfred Meusel and Ernst Engelberg, and conducted on the pages of *Sonntag*, a cultural weekly. Meusel fully agreed with Polish historians, while Engelberg asked, rhetorically, whether Napoleon should be named the benefactor of the German nation. As was the

---

461   Ibidem.
462   Ibidem, 72.
463   "Arbeitstagung des Instituts für Geschichte an der Deutschen Akademie der Wissenschaften zu Berlin," *Zeitschrift für Geschichtswissenschaft* 1957, 364.
464   Streisand, *Deutschland*, 132.
465   Heinrich Scheel, "Zur Problematik des deutschen Befreiungskrieges 1813", *Zeitschrift für Geschichtswissenschaft* 1963, 1281.

case with other debates between the two scholars, the disagreement culminated in a rather brutal mutual smearing by means of letters to the Central Committee of the SED.[466]

The appraisal of France's progressiveness was problematic to Polish historians as well. Just as in the GDR, the evaluation of the revolution was at odds with the appraisal of native progressive traditions, represented by the anti-Russian Kościuszko Uprising of 1794. The Uprising's greatest achievement was said to have been in aiding the first bourgeois revolution by engaging the forces of the states intervening in it. This is why, in spite of all the debates concerning the extent of the progressiveness of the entire movement as well as its particular participants, it was assumed that within Europe as a whole, it did play an eminently progressive role. The ties between the two movements in question were underscored already by the classics of Marxism.[467]

While Kościuszko aided France, there was hardly any reciprocity on the part of the Revolution's leaders because all Polish calls for help were patently ignored. The Polish Marxists were in disagreement as to the evaluation of this fact. Stanisław Herbst, author of the corresponding chapter in the Polish "Draft," stated that the Committee of Public Safety "proved to lack sufficient insight and failed to reckon with the fact that the fate of the revolution was, to an extent, decided over the banks of Vistula; and that, by aiding the rebels, it would not only weaken the feudal-absolutist states inimical to Poland, but also strengthen the Jacobin regime."[468] Witold Łukaszewicz offered a much more severe appraisal of the French policies: according to his interpretation, Polish émigré activists succumbed to the deceitful propaganda spread by the "matadors of the Gironde." "The Poles did not realise that the whole Convention, clamouring with decrees and bursting with calls to the oppressed and slogans of brotherhood of the revolutionary arms, was in reality merely a cunning political tactic, designed to ward off the anti-French coalition; that the appeals to the peoples of the land to engage in a war against the tyrant-kings resonated quite differently on the parliamentary tribune than in the secluded cabinets of the ministers of the almighty Committee of Public Safety ... The Poles did not realise that just when Kościuszko appeared in Paris, the ministry of foreign affairs was busily preparing a recognition of the second partition of Poland, treating it as a part of the perfidious plan to pacify European relations."[469] Łukaszewicz followed this dramatic account with an admission that, while he generally approved of the

---

466 Keßler, *Exilerfahrung*, 87-88.
467 *Historia Polski. Makieta*, vol. 2, 371.
468 Ibidem, 347.
469 Witold Łukaszewicz, *Targowica i powstanie kościuszkowskie. Ze studiów nad historią Polski XVIII wieku*, Warszawa 1952, 174.

French Revolution, "one has to admit that the uprising received no aid, not only because it was led by the gentry, but also, to a rather large extent, because ties to the uprising would have been unwelcome for the French who, by rejecting calls for help, furthered their peace talks with Prussia and consequently facilitated the dismantling of the coalition besieging France."[470]

An opposite argument, patently rejected by Łukaszewicz, was made in Celina Bobińska's work published two years later. Bobińska believed that the highly positive appraisal of the Uprising and the Constitution of May 3rd by the classics was greatly exaggerated. As far as non-existent French aid was concerned, Bobińska claimed that the Jacobins displayed "an unbending class line and revolutionary vigilance with respect to the uprising – a movement of the gentry, in class terms, politically tending toward a compromise with feudalism."[471] Furthermore, she believed that the "slandering of the Jacobins," accused of cold-hearted calculation, was characteristic of Polish bourgeois historiography of a nationalist bent.

Though Marxist historians treated the first bourgeois revolution as a generally positive phenomenon, their sympathy for the movement was evidently limited in a myriad of ways. In the case of both Poland and East Germany, the French Revolution collided more or less emphatically with national history, and, as a result, was often accorded a mixed evaluation, if only for that reason. Further on, we will learn that a similar judgement was meted out to the Hungarian revolution of 1848-1849. Still, the revolution's positive influence was placed in doubt not only because of the praise heaped on Kościuszko or the *Befreiungskriege*, but also as a result of the fact that one of the powers seeking to quash revolutionary, and later Napoleonic, France was Russia.

Zdeněk Nejedlý, whom we have quoted above, named in one breath two incidentally if not entirely mutually contradictory progressive events, of which the Czech folk both delightedly approved. The peasants did not only await impatiently for the eruption of the French Revolution in their own country – they also "understood" the Slavic idea at precisely the same time and welcomed with open arms the Suvorov-commanded Russian army, advancing to do battle with the French. "And with his fervent friendship for the newly-found Slavic brethren, [Suvorov – MG] infused our people with a new, Slavic consciousness, which later played such an important role in our renaissance."[472]

Nejedlý's idea of connecting the Russian presence in Moravia in 1799 to the national revival received a mixed response from Marxist historians. Josef Kočí

---

470 Ibidem, 195.
471 Celina Bobińska, *Marks i Engels a sprawy polskie do osiemdziesiątych lat XIX wieku*, Warszawa 1954, 41.
472 Ibidem.

assumed that the Russians were responsible for a significant strengthening of Slavic ideology, which played a seminal role at an early stage of the revival, thereby aiding Czechs in an indirect manner. Besides, "the Czech people saw in their own eyes the beautiful traits typical of the Russian soldiers, their humility ... self-assurance, cordiality, generosity and devotion. They were pleased by the hearty treatment their children received from the Russians, and admired the travelling soldiers' courage and strength. They enjoyed the songs of the Russians."[473] Čestmír Amort claimed that the passage of the Russian troops proved indispensable for the national revival, since they virtually raised the nation from the dead. The same author also discussed the passage of the Russians through Slovakia, which occurred during the retreat from Austerlitz. He stressed not only the moral virtues of the simple soldier folk, but also the genius and paternalistic care of Mikhail Kutuzov, their commander: "Contemporary accounts – those already known and those we have just recently discovered – pay due homage to Kutuzov, an exceptional commander, who was not only a brilliant strategist and a strict superior, but also a caring father to all of his soldiers. He was just; when one of his subordinates was at fault, the culprit received due punishment whether or not he was a 'blue blood.' Not only did he care for his soldiers, their provisions, quarters, clothes, etc., but also for the civilians whom they met on their routes. Many orders, directives and letters reveal these traits of his character."[474]

The works of Amort were vehemently criticised in the *Československý Časopis Historický*, first by Milan Švankmajer, then by Jan Novotný, as well as in the *Historický Časopis SAV* by Zdeňek Konečny. Švankmajer accused Amort primarily of grave exaggeration. It was not the passage of the Russian forces, but the development of capitalism that propelled the Slavic revival. This analysis led to Švankmajer's severest accusation: Amort's theories were not only non-Marxist, but actually anti-Marxist.[475] Novotný, on the other hand, charged Amort with an uncritical treatment of his sources. He singled out Amort's use of documents which originated in an urban environment as illustrative of the situation in the rural Moravia. At the same time, he agreed with Amort in his assessment of national activists who were critical of the Russians as instruments in the hands of the global forces of reaction. These activists were mistaken in undervaluing the influence which the Russians had on the development of the

---

473   Josef Kočí, *Naše národní obrození*, Praha 1960, 125.
474   Čestmír Amort, "Michail Kutuzov na Slovensku v rokoch 1805-1806," in: *Z dejín československo-slovanských vzťahov*, ed. Jozef Hrozienčik, Bratislava 1959, 437.
475   Milan Švankmajer, review of: Čestmír Amort, *Ruská vojska u nás v letech 1798-1800*, Praha 1954, *Československý Časopis Historický* 1953.

national life of the Czechs.[476] Konečný limited his input to a recognition of Amort's book's striking unreliability, listing the places where its author was at odds with the facts.[477]

The debate over Amort's dubious claims continued during a conference devoted to the role of the Soviet Union in Czech and Slovak history since the end of the 18th century. Jaroslav Vávra attempted to reconcile the French Revolution and Suvorov's influence through a precise distinction: while Russia and Austria were reactionary so long as they wanted to destroy revolutionary France and attacked Napoleon, they became progressive once forced to defend themselves against the French. Later, when Napoleon began to lose ground, both his opponents turned reactionary yet again.[478] For Vávra, the Russia of the late 18th century embraced the role of Europe's policeman, keeping all progressive currents in check. At the same time, he did not follow Amort's lead in claiming that the Czechs were happy about the situation when forced to provide for the Russian army wintering on their lands. Furthermore, Vávra believed that Russia's reactionary position did not antagonise Czech national revivalists – in truth, they were anxious that the ideas of the French Revolution might take root in their fatherland. There were no documents that could prove the thesis that Austrian authorities engaged in any sort of combat against Russophilia during the period.[479]

Švankmajer took a similar stance at the aforementioned conference. He faulted Amort for being mistaken in claiming that popular Russophilia dating from 1798-1799 formed a particularly important element of contemporaneous relations between Czechs, Slovaks and the Soviet Union. That feeling, he reasoned, had far more reasonable grounds in then present-day Czechoslovakia. Amort responded that, while the goals of the Russian soldiers might have been extremely reactionary, objectively they played a positive role, exerting a "progressive" influence on the Czech people. In response, Švankmajer accused Amort of idealisation and oversimplification. There was to be no compromise position on the matter.[480]

---

476 Jan Novotný, "Nová práce o bratrských stycích československého a ruského lidu v našem národním obrození," *Československý Časopis Historický* 1954.

477 Zdeněk Konečný, review of: Čestmír Amort, *Ruská vojska u nás 1798-1800*, Praha 1954, *Historický Časopis SAV* 1955, 245.

478 Jaroslav Vávra, "Česko-ruské vztahy v první etapě národního obrození (1775-1830)," in: *Z bojů za svobodu a socialismus. Úloha SSSR v osvobozeneckých bojích a budovatelském úsilí českého a slovenského lidu*, ed. Jaroslav Vávra, Praha 1961, 42.

479 Ibidem, 43-45.

480 „Z diskuse," in: *Z bojů za svobodu*, 128-131.

It seems that Amort's claims on the essential role the Russians played in the national revival were far more welcome in Slovak historiography. Karol Golán's 1964 volume of studies, published posthumously, stated that the sense of belonging to the Slavic community, which proved crucial for the revival of the Slovak nation, was born in 1805, when Kutuzov crossed Slovakia with his army, the greatest force in Europe.[481]

While even Čestmír Amort agreed that the time spent by the Russians in Moravia and Slovakia affected the Czech and Slovak national revival only indirectly, Russian involvement in the war against Napoleon undoubtedly mattered for Germany. The Russians took part in the campaign of 1806-1807, culminating in the crushing defeat of Prussia, as well as, the campaign of 1813, during which the French were cleared entirely from all German territories. Russia also offered solace to Prussian patriots who were developing plans for liberating their fatherland from French domination.

The defeat of Prussia sparked political and military reforms, bound up with the names of Baron Heinrich Friedrich Karl vom und zum Stein, General August Neithardt Gneisenau, Gerhard Johann von Scharnhorst, Karl von Grolman and Hermann von Boyen. The reforms, though enforced from the top down, received positive appraisal as a catalyst for the new capitalist formation. With the gentry compromised by the defeat to France, the key role in reforms was played by the bourgeoisie.[482] Although Stein himself hailed from the wealthy nobility, he adhered to an ideology so progressive that in the early 1950s he rose to rank as one of the seminal figures in the Marxist retelling of German history. It was not insignificant that, having been deposed as the King's minister, he travelled to Russia, where, as an advisor to tsar Alexander, he acted as an ambassador for Germany. Alexander Abusch compared Stein's activities to the role played by the Communist Nationalkomitee Freies Deutschland in Moscow.[483] Heinz Kamnitzer wrote emphatically of the achievements of Stein and other like-minded patriots: "How hard was it for these people! How different was their situation from the one we live in! The German patriots of 1812-1813 were forced to rely on a spontaneous popular movement. Their official ally, tsarist Russia, had just at that point become the rallying point for the forces of resistance against the French occupation, and yet, at the same time, it was bent on achieving its own dynastic goals. Today, every German patriot knows that the German people living in a section of our fatherland can depend on its parties, organisations and the government, which inscribed on the land's banners the slogan of freedom for our

---

481   Karol Goláň, *Štúrovské pokolenie (Výber z diela),* Bratislava 1964, 370.
482   Streisand, *Deutschland,* 143.
483   Abusch, *Der Irrweg,* 67.

entire country. Their powerful, infallible bedrock is Socialist Russia, which shields us from American aggression and aspires to ensure the unity and independence of every nation."[484] In the popular East German interpretation of the *Befreiungskriege*, every participant in the contemporary struggle had an historical counterpart: the United States were the France of the Napoleonic era; the countries of Western Europe, and West Germany in particular, were the Confederation of the Rhine; the *Freikorps* were described as "partisan troops," and the role of tsarist Russia, the liberator, was handed to the Soviet Union.[485]

The people inhabiting German territories were painfully tested by the French occupation while absorbing ever more patriotic propaganda. The first anti-French popular revolt broke out in Tyrol, but the townsfolk were isolated from the peasant movement, and the ruling classes of Austria betrayed the Tyroleans by striking a deal with Napoleon. These events created a rift between Austria and Germany.[486] Another wave of popular revolts swept through Germany in 1813, with German patriots returning to the fatherland along with Russian troops. The Russians were offered a welcome befitting liberators, the more so because of the presence of a German legion among their ranks. The way in which the Russian folk defeated Napoleon was to serve as an example for the Germans.[487] The heroism of the Russian soldiers and officers (and also the German patriots), however, contrasted with the cautious, greatly reserved conduct of the Prussian court, which was consumed by fears of a real popular uprising. After the Battle of Leipzig, when Russian and German officers of the "folk's kin" argued for a continued offensive to the West of the Elbe, "reactionary circles" in Prussia halted the coalition's victorious march.[488] In general, East German Marxists believed that the tsar's troops implemented German policies far more successfully than Prussian ruling circles.

Just as had been the case during their earlier passage through Moravia and Slovakia, Russians proved their exceptional goodwill, internationalism and

---

484 Heinz Kamnitzer, "Stein und das "Deutsche Comité" in Rußland 1812/13", *Zeitschrift für Geschichtswissenschaft* 1953, 92.

485 Georg von Rauch, "Das Geschichtsbild der Sowjetzone," in: *Gibt es ein deutsches Geschichtsbild? Konferenz der Ranke-Gesellschaft Vereinigung für Geschichte im öffentlichen Leben*, Frankfurt/Main-Berlin-Bonn 1955, 112.

486 Streisand, *Deutschland*, 170-173.

487 Heinz Kamnitzer, "Disposition des Hochschullehrbuches der Geschichte des deutschen Volkes (1789-1815)", *Zeitschrift für Geschichtswissenschaft* 1954, 279. See also A. L. Naročnickij, "Völker und Regierungen zu Beginn des Befreiungskrieges 1813," *Zeitschrift für Geschichtswissenschaft* 1964, 60.

488 Heinrich Gemkow & Gerhard Thiele, "Die Völkerschlacht bei Leipzig", *Zeitschrift für Geschichtswissenschaft* 1953, 867.

discipline to the Germans as well: "They were infused with the spirit of popular war, driving them to defeat Napoleon's armies. The entire nation offered generous support to their cause. And even though the Russian armies of 1812-1813, as earlier, were of a feudal nature in class terms, one could never perceive them as a blind tool of the tsar."[489] They were marked by a very high morale and even the unfavourable, pedantic Prussian authorities had nothing to complain about in relation to the passage of the allied troops.[490]

The role Marxist historians of the GDR and Czechoslovakia assigned to the Russian soldiers remained perennially obvious up until 1989. The highly positive appraisal of German reformers in works produced before and during the jubilee of 1953, on the other hand, proved far less durable. Already in 1950, Soviet scholars attacked the exceedingly positive depiction of Baron vom Stein in Heinz Kamnitzer's *Stein und das Deutsche Komitee in Rußland 1812/1813*. In the pages of *Voprosy Istorii*, they pointed out that the German baron was not only an aristocrat, but also an English sympathiser.[491] The Party's guidelines for historians, published in 1955 as *Die Verbesserung der Forschung und Lehre in der Geschichtswissenschaft der Deutschen Demokratischen Republik*, stressed, among other things, the necessity of providing appropriate definition to the role played by the masses in the *Befreiungskriege*.[492] The university textbook on German history emphasised the national-liberal movement's leaders' persistence in pursuing a liberal-bourgeois political program for fear of an anti-French revolt turning into a social revolution. Joachim Streisand even recalled that Gneisenau's plan for the rebellion put in place specific measures meant to hold back the "hotheads" who wanted to bring about a war against the gentry.[493] During the next jubilee in 1963, criticism was heaped on the publications of 10 years before, with claims that those publications had often overstated the role of the reformers at the expense of the aspirations and achievements of the German folk.[494]

---

489 Fritz Staube, "Russische Armee und deutsches Volk im Frühjahr 1813," *Zeitschrift für Geschichtswissenschaft* 1962, 1139.

490 Ibidem, 1129.

491 See von Rauch, *Das Geschichtsbild*, 112.

492 "Die Verbesserung der Forschung und Lehre in der Geschichtswissenschaft der Deutschen Demokratischen Republik", *Zeitschrift für Geschichtswissenschaft* 1955, 511.

493 Streisand, *Deutschland*, 194-195.

494 Heinrich Scheel, "Zur Problematik des deutschen Befreiungskrieges 1813", *Zeitschrift für Geschichtswissenschaft* 1963, 1287. A similar statement can be found already in the volume prepared in view of the CISH conference in Stockholm: Ernst Engelberg & Rolf Rudolph, "Zur Geschichtswissenschaft der DDR", in: *Historische Forschungen in der DDR. Analysen und Berichte. Zum XI. Internationalen Historikerkongreß in Stockholm, August 1960*, Berlin 1960, 8.

The role Napoleonic France, or indeed the Russian troops, played in Polish history simply could not be viewed in a manner analogous to the prevailing interpretations in historiographies of the GDR or Czechoslovakia. Even in the early 1950s, it was unthinkable to write of Suvorov's humaneness when his army was culpable for the slaughter of the populace on the eastern outskirts of Warsaw. One could never hope to prove the existence of a Polish-Russian brotherhood of arms, nor of any positive influence the Russians could have exerted on the development of Polish national culture; neither did Russians exert any recognizable influence on local radical social movements, which typically harboured an anti-Russian attitude. Works of the kind Čestmír Amort produced in Czechoslovakia never emerged in Poland. Still, the role played in Polish history by Napoleon, the Legions, or the Duchy of Warsaw, were re-evaluated.

Bonaparte ranked as one of the historical figures who grew steadily less and less progressive in the eyes of Marxist scholars with the passage of time. The young general of revolutionary France, successfully commanding the Army of Italy against one of the culprits of the partitions of Poland, was a pristine figure. The same could not be said of Napoleon the First Consul, and even less of Emperor Napoleon I, a reactionary ruler if there ever was one. The Napoleonic legend was just as reactionary, especially in the part involving Poland, "the legend of Napoleon as 'the father of all Poles' or 'the reviver of the Fatherland.'"[496] Adam Korta observed that "The Napoleonic legend ... was exploited by the Polish bourgeoisie ... as a means of spreading and deepening anti-Soviet sentiments within our society."[497] The lion's share of responsibility for popularising this legend went to Józef Piłsudski, who did all he could to transfer "onto the Soviet Union all the hatred the Poles harboured for the tsars."[498]

Just as Napoleon could represent the forces of progress as well as reaction, his subordinates served divergent causes, especially the Polish troops in the

---

495 Scheel, "Zur Problematik," 1284. The interpretation of the Galician slaughter of 1846 as a Polish national-liberation movement, described in the next subsection of this chapter, seems to be an obvious analogy to Heinrich Scheel's claim.
496 See Adam Korta, *O postępowych tradycjach i antynarodowych mitach*, Warszawa 1955, 140.
497 Ibidem, 141.
498 Ibidem, 132-133.

service of France, and the army of the Duchy of Warsaw. Some of these bore a certain resemblance to just wars, others were unquestionably unjust. The very fact that the dedication and courage of Polish soldiers remained the same regardless of the nature of the wars they were engaged in, inclined some scholars toward vehement criticism of their attitudes. For Adam Korta, it was precisely during the Napoleonic period that "the romance arises of glorious cavalry assaults or courageous bayonet charges, with standards aflutter to the sound of the drum, drowning out, in seeming willfulness, any consideration of the goals and meaning of the struggle at hand, any question regarding the actual value of the struggle for Poland."[499] However, Marxists did recognize some positive values in the democratic nature of the Polish Legions. Radical émigré leftists "were struck" by the contrast between the often reactionary role the legionnaires were largely made to play and the popular character of the formation in which they served. With the latter trait enjoying an undeniable supremacy, "many ... Polish radicals joined the Legions to fight for Poland hand in hand with the Polish soldier-peasant."[500] Cooperation between radicals and the peasant soldiers of the Legions spawned numerous plots against Bonaparte's dictatorial rule.[501] The fact that the Polish forces were formed for the most part from the peasantry had far-reaching consequences, as they were later transformed into "rural 'troublemakers' and peasant leaders in the class struggle."[502]

At the same time, as already mentioned, the Legions were sometimes tasked with fairly inglorious duties. They occupied an ambiguous position at the very beginning of their service, acting as gendarmerie, or perhaps the overseers of Napoleon's less reliable Italian allies.[503] The involvement of Polish soldiers in quelling the rebellion in San Domingo proved particularly vile and damaging. According to the authors of the "Draft," the Poles were sent into the Caribbean primarily because of the spread of anti-Napoleon plots among the soldiers. The fact that "people who fought for Polish freedom were ordered to subdue the Negroes fighting for their own freedom" was deemed the most disagreeable of

---

499 Ibidem, 133.
500 *Historia Polski. Makieta,* vol. 2, 457-458; Stefan Kieniewicz offered similar views on the matter, ascribing a progressive character to Legionnaire republicanism, while observing at the same time, "We evidently honour the fact that in Italy, the Legions served the French drive for acquisitions, that they were riddled with a Napoleonic legend inimical to Poland" – Stefan Kieniewicz, "Z postępowych tradycji polskich ruchów narodowo-wyzwoleńczych," *Kwartalnik Historyczny* 1953, 187.
501 *Historia Polski. Makieta,* vol. 2, 462.
502 Ibidem, 513.
503 Ibidem, 457.

all. The soldiers did not want to be involved in the expedition: "Polish soldiers, being of peasant stock, did not enjoy this combat, in their hearts siding with the Negro peasant."[504]

Yet, the involvement of Polish forces in the Napoleonic wars sometimes proved beneficial. In 1806, hearing news of the impending arrival of French forces into the lands Prussia claimed during the Partitions of Poland, "The richer section of landowners remained inactive, but the peasants, especially the farm retinue, gladly joined ranks with the enemies of the Prussians. ... In the Łęczyca voivodship, a peasant mob wilfully arrested a German squire as an enemy of the French."[505] The Poles played a particularly important role in the siege of Gdańsk.[506] Even later, in another "ever Polish" territory – Silesia – the local folk welcomed the soldiers of the Duchy with arms wide open.[507] The defensive war of 1809 also had a positive impact as a national liberation struggle. Of particular interest is the manner in which the tactical moves of the Polish commander-in-chief, prince Józef Poniatowski, were interpreted. His decision to distribute arms to the people of Warsaw right after the battle of Raszyn was read as a timid attempt at sparking resistance among the popular strata. The fact that the withdrawal of Polish forces from Warsaw and their relocation to Galicia, behind Austrian lines, prompted the archduke Ferdinand to engage in talks with Poniatowski was understood to have been occasioned by the fear of "a possible resistance in a town renowned for its traditions of revolt." At the same time, the move was also deemed to have been caused by Poniatowski's anxiety with regard to a vivid popular movement. By giving the town away to the Austrians, Poniatowski "from a political standpoint, freed himself from pressures exerted by the revolutionary capital and robbed the Jacobins of all power to mobilize the people of Warsaw. The people itself was outraged at the news of capitulation, and Warsaw's saleswomen slung mud at the withdrawing commander-in-chief."[508] In other words, Poniatowski handed Warsaw to the Austrians for fear of the revolutionary stirrings of the popular masses, and the Austrians engaged in negotiations with the Poles because of this very same revolutionary fervour.

Comparing the treatment accorded the French Revolution, Napoleon and his Russian adversaries in the historiographies in question, we witness another interesting methodological problem: how should one relate commonly approved progressive traditions to local national histories? In Stalinist incarnations of Marxist historiography both the French Revolution and, to an even greater

---

504   Ibidem, 464.
505   Ibidem, 473.
506   Ibidem, 477.
507   Ibidem, 527.
508   Ibidem, 519-520.

extent, the Russian army, were the bearers of historical progress. Evidently, scholars of Central and Eastern Europe tried to prove (if possible) that their nations, or at least the popular strata, viewed both the French Revolution and the courageous tsarist soldiers favourably. This was more easily said than done, when the two progressive phenomena in question stood on opposite sides of the barricade. The clash of these positive ideas was typically won by the eventually victorious Suvorov, while the French Revolution, having proven itself defective in ever-new ways, ultimately transformed into a reactionary Napoleonic regime. It is hard not to notice that East German works painted Napoleon in a much darker hue than Polish studies. Both Polish and German authors retained essential sections of their national traditions which maintained their positive resonance despite changes in the frame of reference. Thus, the Baron vom Stein, a Prussian reformer, was associated with the liberation struggles of the German folk rather than the reactionary monarchy (or monarchies) he served. The Legions, on the other hand, remained a progressive, popular force even while serving such unjust causes as the oppression of other nations. It seems that scholars of the GDR went farther than their Polish counterparts in this drive toward incorporating particular figures and events of the Napoleonic era into their "progressive traditions." The reactionary "Napoleonic legend" made its way into numerous Polish Marxist studies, while the analogous problem posed by the interpretation of the *Befreiungskriege* in 19th and 20th century Germany did not attract as much attention, despite the Prussian reformers' persistent presence as the most favoured historical protagonists of the "Prussian school," and despite Johann Gustav Droysen's belief that the Prussian reforms ranked among the most important revolutions in human history (on par with the American and French Revolutions).[509] Marxist scholars were also silent on the role the *Befreiungskriege* played in the Third Reich's propaganda around the end of the Second World War.

Of note is also another virtue of the historical plots discussed above. As Karl Heinz Schäfer noted, the Marxist interpretation of the *Befreiungskriege* elevated the people while pushing the ruling classes deep into obscurity.[510] This somewhat self-explanatory observation sidesteps a rather arresting aspect of the phenomenon in question. The fact that the popular masses are cast almost exclusively in progressive roles was used not only to further the critique of the ruling classes; at times, phenomena of note for national history were "redeemed"

---

509 Otto Hintze, *Soziologie und Geschichte. Gesammelte Abhandlungen zur Soziologie, Politik und Theorie der Geschichte*, ed. Gerhard Oestreich, Göttingen 1964, 466-467.

510 Karl Hainz Schäfer, "1813 – Die Freiheitskriege in der Sicht der marxistischen Geschichtsschreibung der DDR", *Geschichte in Wissenschaft und Unterricht* 1971/21, 19.

in the face of Marxist critique precisely because they engaged the popular masses. The *Befreiungskriege*, the Polish Legions in Italy, and even the positive views of the Russian army held by Czech and Slovak peoples serve as perfect examples of this phenomenon. Their popular nature sufficed as evidence of their progressiveness, in a way, even though the reins of power continued to be held by the privileged classes, and political programs often proved to be far from revolutionary.

The National Movements of the 19th Century

Czech and Slovak Marxist historians repeatedly stressed the unchallenged status of national revival movements as supreme achievements in the histories of their respective nations. The revival was said to have been designed and executed by the Czech and Slovak people. The author of the preface to the Polish edition of Arnošt Klíma's book on the events of 1848 commends Klíma precisely for debunking "the traditional belief that the revival was the fruit of the work of exceptional individuals of noble or bourgeois origin."[511] At the same time, Marxist historians never failed to reckon with the impact of particular national revivalists, quite a few of whom were born and raised among the people. Lenin's dictum to the effect that the intelligentsia does not constitute a social class, but merely a stratum, and thus can be of service to different classes, was invoked repeatedly. During the revival, the intelligentsia served the Czech and Slovak people.[512] Yet, the main protagonists of the revival, the priest-revivalists, would never attain the status of social reformers, being heavily implicated in the feudal system.[513]

Nevertheless, the assessment of the national revivalists was unquestionably positive. In Marxist studies, Josef Dobrovský became a tireless pioneer and champion of human progress; Jan Kollár, the creator of the theory of Slavic reciprocity, was imbued with progressive humanism and a democratic spirit. Their errors stemmed solely from a self-explanatory ignorance of Marxist thought. Dobrovský, for instance, a representative of the Enlightenment, "could not have fully understood the revolutionary underpinnings of the Hussite

---

511 B. O., "Przedmowa," in: Arnošt Klíma, *Rok 1848 w Czechach. Początki ruchu robotniczego w Czechach,* Warszawa 1951, 5.

512 Koči, *Naše*, 201.

513 Ibidem.

movement,"[514] while the arrival of Ľudovít Štúr's national activists rendered Kollár and his pan-Slavism objectively reactionary.[515]

The national revival also played a seminal role in shaping the common future of Czechs and Slovaks in a single state.[516] Ideas of Slavic cooperation were rooted in the period of national revival.[517] According to Koči "Hence it is not by chance that our socialist society, imbued with a vivid, loving interest, evaluates and appreciates the significance of our national revivalists. At the same time, it steers clear of an uncritical cult of these great people, accepting the historical conditions of their efforts and struggle."[518]

Independent Slovak research on the national revival was in many ways reminiscent of the work conducted by Czech Marxists. Slovak scholars also relied on a fixed set of assumptions about the significance for the national revival of the masses' involvement, the decomposition of feudal relations, and the emergence of a new, capitalist order.[519] Likewise, they appreciated the role played by exceptional individuals, the national revivalists. Historiography of the 1950s made great strides in this respect, recognising the achievements of Ľudovít Štúr as well as his predecessors, especially Anton Bernolák. This area was also the scene of several battles between Czech and Slovak scholars. The Czech Slavist, Frank Wollman, in his *Slovantství v jazykově literárním obrození u Slovanů* (Praha 1958), offered a critique of Bernolák's 1787 proposal for the codification of a Slovak literary language that was accepted by Catholic circles of the Slovak intelligentsia. Wollman, like other Czech scholars of the era, tended to promote an alternative current of late 18th century Slovak culture that advocated the assumption of Czech as the literary language for Slovaks. Slovak Marxists were far more supportive of Bernolák and his followers, recognising their involvement in the shaping of the national language, as well as their progressive political program.[520] This positive appraisal of Bernolák made its way into the university textbook on the history of Czechoslovakia.[521]

---

514   Ibidem, 86-87.
515   Ibidem, 169.
516   Jan Novotný, *O bratrské družbě Čechů a Slováků za národního obrození. Kapitoly z dějin vzájemných vztahů Čechů a Slováků v národním hnutí do roku 1848*, Praha 1959, 6.
517   Klíma, *Rok 1848*, 91.
518   Koči, *Naše*, 15.
519   Ján Tibenský, "Počiatky slovenského národného obrodenia," *Historický Časopis SAV* 1954, 526.
520   Ján Tibenský, "K problému hodnotenia bernoláčtiny a bernolákovského hnutia," *Historický Časopis SAV* 1959, 557-576.
521   *Přehled československých dějin (maketa)*, vol. 1, 634.

There was also room enough for a positive assessment of the Slovaks who had laid the groundwork for the Czech national revival. Pavol Jozef Šafárik, the author of a fantastical theory of the European indigenousness of the Slavs, "proved beyond all doubt that Slavs participated actively in the history of Europe from time immemorial, and besides, demonstrated that Slavs also took an active part in the shaping of European culture.... [T]he goal of his work was to abolish the superstitious belief in Slavic retardation, to illustrate the influence the Slavs exerted on ancient culture, and further, to prove that they played a major role in the formation of European culture in the first millennium A.D."[522] Jan Kollár, who "sympathised with the Russians since his childhood,"[523] was also named as a source of Slovak progressive traditions.[524]

Slovak publications often addressed the problem of Czech-Slovak relations during the period of national revival. The tone employed, however, differed from that found in the works of Czech scholars. Scholars researching the 19th century from a Slovak perspective often compared the two national movements, finding the Slovak one to be more progressive. This was supposedly most visible during the Springtime of the Peoples. Jarmila Tkadlečková pointed out that the Czech bourgeoisie attempted to dominate the young Slovak national movement in order to eventually lead it into reactionary positions.[525] Although in the end both Czech and Slovak national activists failed to join in with the Revolutions of 1848, Slovaks continued to embrace a progressive standing for a longer time, mostly because they initially considered resolving the Slovak national issue through becoming a part of a multi-national, democratic Hungary.[526]

The national revivalists were typically bound to the Slavic idea. In her comparative studies of the cultural consciousness of Western and Southern Slavs, Maria Bobrownicka counts Czechs and Slovaks among the nationalities particularly badly infested with the "Slavic myth." Embraced by national

---

522 Jozef Kudláček, "P. J. Šafárik a jeho koncepcia pôvodu Slovanov," *Historický Časopis SAV 1957*, 78; See also: N. A. Kondrašov, "Význam diela P. J. Šafárika pre ruský vedu," in: *Z dejín.*

523 *Přehled československých dějin (maketa)*, vol. 1, 749.

524 Ľudovít Bakoš, "Úvod," in: Ján Kollár, *Pamäti z mladších rokov života*, Bratislava 1950, 7.

525 Jarmila Tkadlečková, "Názory a činnosť Karla Havlíčka Borovského z hľadiska vývoja česko-slovenských vzťahov," *Historický Časopis SAV 1958*, 38-47. See also article of the Czech historian: Jan Novotný, "Otázky obrozenských vztahů Čechů a Slováků v dosavadní historiografii," *Historický Časopis SAV 1958*, 269.

526 Jan Novotný, "Příspěvek k vzájemným vztahům Čechů a Slováků v první etapě revoluce roku 1848," *Historický Časopis SAV 1963*, 366-387.

cultures, this myth inadvertently translated into a willing rejection of an original, existing tradition that bound the respective nations to the European West. Instead of pursuing a more comprehensive realisation of a culture of the West (which, for Bobrownicka, would be the "natural" course of development), the Slavic revivalists turned away from it.[527] It is debatable whether the Czech and Slovak national revivals did indeed represent as singularly an anti-European drive as Maria Bobrownicka claims, but one can hardly overlook the fact that her interpretation bears a number of similarities to the popular reading of the "Slavic myth" disseminated across Bohemia and Slovakia in the latter half of the 19th century – the difference being that the pan-Slavist nationalist activists tended to ascribe a diametrically opposite value to the phenomenon than did Bobrownicka.

The "anti-Occidentalism" of the national revival was also a crucial subplot of Marxist analysis of the phenomenon, and was typically approved of by Marxist historians. Given that the revival was bound up with the emergence of the idea of cooperation between Slavic states and nations under the aegis of the Russians, the political implications of the Slavic myth seem to have played a crucial role in this respect. It was clear for Marxist historians that true Slavic reciprocity could only take place in collaboration with the Soviet Union.[528] In January 1948, Zdeněk Nejedlý offered a telling parallel with 19th century pan-Slavism: "We are fighting in the name of a Slavic orientation represented by Stalin. This is how we understand Slavic politics today. But we can see that the bourgeoisie fully comprehends the implications of this. And it looks to history, too, hoping to prove that we have always been a Western nation and never had anything to do with the East."[529]

The Slavic idea underpinned the drive toward independence for Slavic nations. Polish scholars who did not accept this view found themselves under fire from Czechoslovak Marxists.[530] For the Czechs, the idea was undoubtedly progressive, although not without important reservations. While Russophiles of the early 19th century were seldom criticised, their later counterparts received less favorable assessments. Capitalist society produced two forms of Russophilia: the first, a regressive, bourgeois attachment to the tsarist order; the second, a progressive and revolutionary workers' movement.[531] Nonetheless,

---

527 Bobrownicka, *Narkotyk*, 39.
528 Kočí, *Naše*, 252.
529 Nejedlý, *O smyslu*, 207.
530 Milan Kudělka, "Význam slovanské myšlenky pro národní obrození ve Slezsku," *Slezský Sborník* 1960.
531 See Zdeněk Konečný, *Revoluční hnutí v Československu a jeho vztahy k SSSR. Morava a Slezsko-dokumenty 1879-1938*, Praha 1960, 11.

any variant of pan-Slavism ranked higher than Austro-Slavism. The Slavic idea diminished in time, as a result of tsarist policies: the quelling of both Polish uprisings, in 1830 and 1863, seriously affected the image of Russia in Czechoslovak Marxist historiography. In both cases, the most progressive currents within Czech and Slovak societies sided with the revolutions and against the tsar.[532] At the same time, scholars repeatedly stressed that "the Russian folk had nothing to do with this eruption of tsarist despotism."[533] After the collapse of the January Uprising of 1863 in Poland, Czech Russophilia became an unequivocally progressive cultural movement, devised to salvage progressive and lasting values from the wealth of Russian culture.[534]

Similarities between the Marxist interpretation of Slovak and Czech national revivals go far beyond the parallels we have drawn here. In truth, the only significant difference was the fact that Czech historians looked to the German revolution of 1848 as a point of departure for their national movement, while their evaluation of the Hungarian revolution of the same year played an important, but hardly crucial role.

The events of 1848 were often joyfully recounted in Marxist historiography, with the radical wing of the revolution and the aborted Prague uprising receiving the highest accolades. Marx and Engels' praise of the uprising was eagerly recollected. Marxist scholars also directed attention to the fact that different groups involved in the uprising took divergent stances toward it, resulting in clear-cut divisions between the reactionaries (opposing the movement) and progressives (taking part in it).[535] In scholarship devoted to the events of 1848, the leading role was invariably ascribed to Josef Václav Frič, an insurgent leader. Espousing a supposedly correct view of the situation, Frič advocated a revolutionary outbreak; the moderate Palacký, on the other hand, was invariably cast as his misguided counterpart.[536] At the same time, Czech scholars did not fail to add that Czech liberals were hardly isolated in their embrace of a reactionary position in 1848 – Hungarian and German liberals did likewise. The Germans of Prague were even said to have sabotaged the initiatives of Czech democrats from the outset.[537] Even the German democrats failed to comprehend the nature of events and did not support "the Czech national interest in a

532   Ibidem, 14-15.
533   *Přehled československých dějin*, vol. 2, part. 1, 89.
534   Oldřich Říha, "Úloha SSSR v osvobozenských bojích českého a slovenského lidu," in: *Z bojů*, 15.
535   *Přehled československých dějin*, vol. 2, part 1, 62.
536   Klíma, *Rok 1848*, 131.
537   *Přehled československých dějin*, vol. 2, part 1, 37.

common, revolutionary struggle against the feudal, imperial Vienna."[538] This misjudgment allowed the Czech bourgeoisie to introduce appeals for a fight for national equality, a position which swayed the popular vote. The proletariat was alone in rejecting the nationalists' propaganda.[539] Czech Marxist historians also often stressed that the uprising was quelled by units formed from Germans and Hungarians.[540]

The Slavic Congress was another historical event which received divergent appraisals from Czech historians and their Soviet colleagues. For Ivan Udaltsov, the sole progressive aspect of the Congress stemmed from the involvement of Polish delegates,[541] but the authors of the university textbook on the history of Czechoslovakia had a much more positive opinion of the event.[542] According to Czech historians, the year 1848 also reinforced a rising sense of community between Czechs and Slovaks, with both nations forced into strict cooperation because of German and Hungarian nationalisms.[543]

The attitudes Marx and Engels espoused toward the Czech national movement became a stinging matter for Czech historians – so much so that the subject was rarely even broached. Typically, historians limited their input to passing remarks about the positive response of the classics to the eruption of the Prague uprising.[544] Engels' view of the Czechs as a people with no history, condemned to dissolution in the German sea, was never quoted in any Czechoslovak publication. Udaltsov favored a different approach, arguing in the preface to his book that, "[i]n a number of works, Marx and Engels vehemently condemned the Czech nationalist movement of the year 1848-1849 for its counterrevolutionary stance toward the European revolution."[545] In conclusion, he concurred with the opinion of the classics: "In this light, it becomes apparent that the role played in 1848-1849 by the Czech national movement should be deemed counterrevolutionary, and the positions taken by the Czech nation in the second stage of the movement—in the decisive period for the revolution raging throughout Austria—cannot be taken as anything other than reactionary."[546]

---

538 Ibidem, 42.
539 Ibidem, 44.
540 See Klíma, *Rok 1848*, 112 & 129-130.
541 Iwan I. Udalcow, *Studia z dziejów walk narodowych w Czechach w r. 1848*, transl. A. Szklarska, Warszawa 1953, 54-60.
542 *Přehled československých dějin*, vol. 2, part 1, 54-55.
543 Novotný, *O bratrské*, 247.
544 See *Přehled československých dějin*, vol. 2, part 1, 59 and Klíma, *Rok 1848*, 129.
545 Udalcow, *Studia*, 3.
546 Ibidem, 155. Józef Chlebowczyk called Udaltsov's work a glorious example of a "superficial, uncritical exegesis" of the classics. Udaltsov did not attempt to account for

The Hungarian revolution of 1848-1849 was a crucial component of Udaltsov's "European revolution." According to Udaltsov, in this European conflict, the Czech national movement opted to side with the monarchs, proving itself "reactionary." As already evident, Czech Marxist historians attempted to defend their national tradition from such a slanderous opinion. However, they never went as far as their Slovak colleagues, who denied the progressive nature of the revolution, because that would have set them in conflict not only with the opinions of Marx and Engels, but also (and more importantly) with those of Soviet historiography, represented by Udaltsov. They preferred laying stress on the notion that the Czech bourgeoisie was isolated in its aversion to the Hungarian revolution, which meant that Udaltsov was right in deeming its position reactionary. The lower classes, however, took a different course of action, often exhibiting sympathy with the Hungarians.[547]

This was not the only means employed by Czech historians to rehabilitate the Czech national movement. They also tried to indirectly defend the position of the national leadership, so vehemently criticised by Udaltsov. The strategy they used was borrowed from their Slovak colleagues. As Arnošt Klíma noted, "Undoubtedly, the Hungarians, much like the Germans, were themselves partially responsible for the Slavs' rejection of their revolutionary cause in 1848."[548] In the university textbook on the history of Czechoslovakia, one can also find a passage comparing the two Hungarian revolutions – of 1848 and 1956 – and highlighting the reactionary aspects of both.[549]

The task set before Polish and German Marxists was never as demanding as the aforementioned reinterpretation of the classics. Marx and Engels viewed the Polish national movement in a decidedly more positive light than they did its Czech or Slovak counterparts; they supported the Polish uprisings, and were themselves actors in the events of the Springtime of the Peoples in Germany. I already discussed the problem the Kościuszko Uprising posed for Polish Marxist historiography. The same doubts – whether the limitations of the Polish liberation movements outweighed their progressiveness – were raised with respect to each of the later revolts. Only the folk was deemed to have played an indisputably positive role throughout – it was solely due to its support and inspiration that the November Uprising ever broke out. In studies from the 1950s, Marxist historians highlighted the role of the Warsaw townsfolk in keeping the movement

---

Engels' dramatically harsh review of the Czech national movement. – Józef Chlebowczyk, *O prawie do bytu małych i młodych narodów*, Warszawa – Kraków 1973 (2nd ed.), 170.

547   Ibidem, 76.
548   Klíma, *Rok 1848*, 142.
549   *Přehled československých dějin*, vol. 2, part 1, 127.

(established by young members of the intelligentsia) alive. Participants in the original plot – "adolescent members of the gentry and intelligentsia, a potential reservoir for the left, were easily manipulated by aristocratic circles that sought to employ them as an advance guard for the counterrevolution." This may have been inevitable had it not been for the commotion among the Warsaw folk, and particularly the seizure of the Warsaw Arsenal. It was "[t]he peasants and the plebeians [who] single-handedly transformed a minor military disorder into a major movement, an almost year-long battle against the might of the tsarist regime," and, since the outbreak of the uprising on that November Night, "the victory of the uprising lay in the hands ... of the people of Warsaw."[550]

With the urban popular masses claiming initiative, "cautious milieus" grew uneasy. They (successfully) attempted to gain control over the uprising in order to strip it of its revolutionary aspect. It may seem a paradox, but Marxist studies of the uprising tended to depict members of extremely reactionary circles as having been supportive of the idea of incorporating Ukrainian and Belorussian territories into the Kingdom of Poland – which indirectly meant they were supportive of an energetic spread of the uprising to the East. Obviously, they were guided by the desire to reconstitute their rule over the Belorussian and Ukrainian peasantry.[551]

Of the political currents represented in the uprising, only the far left consistently, though clumsily, opposed the counterrevolution. The left was isolated in its struggles to improve the peasants' lot, but "it failed to formulate a revolutionary call for peasant enfranchisement, this being the foremost reason why it could not attain victory."[552] The fact that the left wing of the uprising was specifically involved in seeking a total break with Russia was largely omitted in studies published in the 1950s.

The Marxist assessment of Joachim Lelewel, one of the leaders of the insurgents' left wing, was very typical of his political camp. This exceptional historian proved a wobbly politician, seeking "to use his political club as a sort of conduit between the people and the parliament, a conduit which would neutralize and blunt the vehemence of the plebeians' assaults on the government."[553] Żanna Kormanowa stressed the difficulties faced by the leader of the only revolutionary club and a member of a procrastinating insurgent government, as well as the irreconcilable paradox of his position: "He should have preferred leaving the compromise-seeking government," she reasoned, "to

---

550 *Historia Polski. Makieta*, vol 2, part 2, 170 & 177. See also Tadeusz Łepkowski, *Początki klasy robotniczej Warszawy,* Warszawa 1956, 341.
551 *Historia Polski. Makieta*, vol. 2, part 2, 203.
552 Ibidem, 230.
553 Ibidem, 58.

contend for power in the name of the left wing of the movement under the banner of agrarian reform. It would have been wiser to prepare the grounds for a resolution by force, or for a coup d'état." But – as the historian duly noted – "[Lelewel] was not a man of action – he was a scholar."[554]

The erroneous, wobbly, undecided, and sometimes even reactionary politics of the insurgent leadership were poignantly illustrated in its diplomacy. Prince Adam Jerzy Czartoryski, tasked with maintaining foreign relations, persistently failed to reckon both with the enmity of Western European elites toward the Poles, and with the sympathy of their countries' popular strata. Even in Bohemia, despite the dominance of pan-Slavic ideology, "The popular masses ... and a significant proportion of the townsfolk supported the Polish cause against the tsar." In addition, Russian soldiers sometimes switched sides to join the Poles.[555]

Given the impotence (or treason) of the upper classes, the better part of responsibility for conducting military operations rested with the people. A sense of "treason by the elites" spread wildly, finding expression, e.g., in popular songs and a growing "revolutionary turmoil" in rural areas.[556] Successive counterrevolutionary measures by the government finally led to an eruption of the disaffected people of Warsaw. On August 15th, 1831, a mob lynched prisoners and demanded a more energetic prosecution of the military campaign. Though these events were brought about by the leftist Patriotic Society, none of its leaders commanded the mob. While the events of August 15th did not result in a leftist coup, the fact that they presented the possibility of this kind of a development had a bearing on the period after the demise of the uprising: "It is extremely telling," Tadeusz Łepkowski stated, "that the tsarist regime ruthlessly pursued and punished the 'perpetrators' of the events of the night of August 15th, while showing so much compassion to several members of the uprising's 'top."[557]

Taking into account the various factors affecting the critique of particular political groupings and politicians of the November Uprising, one would be excused for assuming that the assessment of the event by Marxist historiographers could not be positive. However, the fact that the uprising sparked some radical activism swayed historians to accept the notion that the uprising was – at least to an extent – a bourgeois-democratic revolution. Though Engels saw it for a "conservative revolution," Józef Dutkiewicz observed that

---

554 Żanna Kormanowa, *Joachim Lelewel*, Warszawa 1946, 42-43.
555 *Historia Polski. Makieta*, vol. 2, part 2, 207-208.
556 See Ibidem, 201 & 211.
557 Łepkowski, *Początki*, 361.

"In the term 'conservative revolution,' one should not put too much stress on the adjective 'conservative,' but conversely, underline clearly and firmly that the uprising was, in the particular conditions of the era and contemporary understanding of its significance, a revolution."[558] From a broader perspective, the collapse of the uprising compromised the aristocracy and, hence, hastened the advance of a future revolution.[559] For Marxists, the movement's primary gain was the crystallisation of the Polish political scene: a clear-cut division into the popular progressive camp and the noble-aristocratic reactionary camp. In studies I gained access to, the necessity of an all-national movement and a bloody Polish-Russian war for the representation of the progressive and regressive camps in Polish society was never presented as a possible question for scholarly examination. Though an inquiry into the merits of the uprising would seem pertinent in the wake of the war, it did not occur to historians to pursue this problem until later on.

With the collapse of the uprising, its active participants sought refuge abroad. The émigré political factions that emerged from these events served as a subject of particular interest to Marxist scholars, if only for the rich ties binding the refugees to the creators of Marxist philosophy. However, this interest did not translate into an unequivocally positive representation of the Great Emigration in studies from the 1950s. The characteristic critical edge of the Marxist interpretation of Polish history manifested itself in the description of the nature and achievements of the Hotel Lambert's conservative-liberal camp. In works published toward the end of 1940s, Stefan Kieniewicz characterised the politics of Prince Adam Jerzy Czartoryski as approximating other, more radical émigré societies. Each of those "were staked nearly single-mindedly on the revolutionary card," always in pursuit of the goal of peasant enfranchisement.[560] On the other hand, Żanna Kormanova's booklet on Lelewel, published in 1946, identified Czartoryski as a member of the aristocratic reactionary camp.[561] The "methodological breakthrough" in Polish historiography pushed Polish historians into embracing Kormanowa's views in this regard. In studies published during the next few years, one could find passages on the so-called "Czartorism" (czartoryszczyzna), a reactionary political program of rightist

---

558 Józef Dutkiewicz, "Ewolucja lewicy w powstaniu listopadowym," in: *Z epoki Mickiewicza. Zeszyt specjalny „Przeglądu Historycznego" w rocznicę śmierci Adama Mickiewicza 1855-1955*, eds. Stefan Kieniewicz, Izabela Bieżuńska-Małowist & Antoni Mączak, Wrocław 1956, 89.

559 *Historia Polski. Makieta*, vol 2, part 2, 385.

560 See Stefan Kieniewicz, *Oblicze ideowe Wiosny Ludów*, Warszawa 1948, 55; idem, *Czyn polski w dobie Wiosny Ludów*, Warszawa 1948, 7-9 & 149.

561 See Kormanowa, *Joachim Lelewel*, 92-93.

circles of the Great Emigration. The programmatic goals of Czartorism affected the camp's politics: "Czartoryski's aristocratic camp sought to resolve the Polish question via a reactionary, 'top-down' approach – desiring an adjustment to necessary capitalist shifts, it also wanted to smuggle them through in a similar manner. The goal was to betray the revolutionary, patriotic strivings of the masses: to subordinate the future of Poland exclusively to international haggles and intrigues conducted in the anterooms of distinguished diplomats, avoiding the engagement of revolutionary classes at home and the forces of European revolution. This faction wanted most of all to avoid binding the cause of liberation to dangerous social aspirations."[562]

This final aspect of the internal politics of the Hotel Lambert faction drew particular focus in studies published in the 1950s. "Czartorism perpetually talks about independence," wrote Bronisław Baczko, "but the cause of national liberation is always treated as separate from the struggles of the popular masses for anti-feudal transformation." The reactionary camp was consumed with a fear of the masses. For this reason, liberal émigré circles proved even more hostile to the cause of liberating the oppressed classes than openly reactionary politicians. Baczko compared Hotel Lambert to national renegades like Henryk Rzewuski (who declared that the demise of the Polish state led first to a degeneration, and then to an obliteration of the Polish nation).[563] The "aristocratic-feudal camp" of the Emigration propagated an Occidentalism that was pernicious to the Polish cause.[564] It also circulated anti-Russian propaganda, seeking to prevent all cooperation between Polish and Russian revolutionaries.[565]

Czartoryski's reactionary camp was contrasted with the leftist émigré societies – the Polish Democratic Society (Towarzystwo Demokratyczne Polskie, TDP) and the Communes of the Polish People (Gromady Ludu Polskiego, GLP). Potentially, these organisations constituted highly "efficient" elements of a progressive heritage for the Polish nation. The stated goal of both was a reconstruction of social relations, but each bound the transformations to a nationalist agenda. Foremost among the Polish Democratic Society's virtues was a widely shared distaste of Czartoryski's camp. The Polish Democratic Society

562 Bobińska, *Marks*, 49.
563 Bronisław Baczko, "Wstęp," in: *Towarzystwo Demokratyczne Polskie. Dokumenty i pisma,* ed. Bronisław Baczko, Warszawa 1954, IX-XI.
564 Gryzelda Missalowa, "Francuski socjalizm utopijny i jego wpływ na polską myśl ewolucyjną w latach 1830-1848," in: *W stulecie Wiosny Ludów 1848-1949,* ed. Natalia Gąsiorowska-Grabowska, part 2: *Wiosna Ludów w Europie. Zagadnienia ideologiczne,* Warszawa 1951, 173.
565 Irena Koberdowa, "Walka czartoryszczyzny przeciwko sojuszowi polskich i rosyjskich rewolucjonistów w czasie powstania styczniowego," in: *Z epoki,* 222.

contradicted the clerical bent of Hotel Lambert by embracing a decidedly more advanced position: "The left of the Society railed against mysticism and messianism, vindicating the tradition of the Polish Enlightenment, with its materialist and rationalist achievements. The Society was particularly vehement in its assaults on *towiańszczyzna*[566], which spread like a fungus in the 1840s, feasting on the dearth of ideological development and the collapse of numerous progressive thinkers and activists of that period."[567] Still, neither anti-clericalism nor rationalism were enough to treat this element of the Polish Democratic Society's ideology as undeniably progressive. Bronisław Baczko observed that "The Enlightened taunts of TDP's publications sometimes overshadowed its limited outlook – a lack of a decidedly materialist position."[568] The Society's insufficiently radical social program resulted from the organisation's class composition – most of its members hailed from the gentry.[569]

A number of members of the Polish Democratic Society were clearly conscious of the class limitations of its political program. These members promptly left the Society, dominated by "compromisers" and "liberals," to fight for a revolutionary transformation of their fatherland. According to Baczko, it fell to the founders of the Communes of the Polish People to finally overcome the barrier created by the revolution's identification with the gentry, in order to become true revolutionaries.[570] Witold Łukaszewicz wrote biographies of the two leaders of this political group, a fact which in itself illustrates Marxist historiography's esteem for their achievements. Łukaszewicz – a scholar noted for his criticism of the country's history – even found himself capable of awe at Tadeusz Krępowiecki's ideological maturity. He contended that Krępowiecki's writings were "strikingly rich in the ability to apply dialectical thinking to problems as complex as the genesis and role of absolutism, feudal exploitation, nationalist and religious oppression; [his work] reveals a baffling array of beliefs with respect to peasant revolts in the Ukraine, the role of masses in the formation of nation-states, the popular dictatorship, property and work."[571]

The contributions of the other leader of the Communes centred around a problem of key importance to Marxist scholars. "As we all know," wrote Celina Bobińska, "the main contribution of [Stanisław Gabriel] Worcell was a glorious rapprochement and engagement in cooperative work with Herzen ..., a policy of

---

566 Towiańszczyzna – a section of Polish émigrés in France grouped around the charismatic Andrzej Towiański (1799-1878).
567 Baczko, "Wstęp," XXXVII.
568 Ibidem, XXXVIII.
569 Witold Łukaszewicz, *Stanisław Gabriel Worcell*, Warszawa 1951, 29.
570 Baczko, "Wstęp," XV; see also: Missalowa, "Francuski socjalizm," 279.
571 Łukaszewicz, *Tadeusz Krępowiecki*, 92.

alliance with the Russian revolution, the emergence and development of which
were registered and acknowledged by Worcell, albeit in a thoroughly naïve,
Utopian Slavic phraseology."[572] Władysław Bortnowski stressed that Stanisław
Worcell overcame nationalist prejudice and fully comprehended the
fundamental discord between the reactionary tsarist regime and the progressive
Russian folk.[573] That an alliance with Russia was an element of the Humań
(Uman, today's Ukraine) Commune's program was a fact noted even by
Bolesław Bierut.[574] The fact that this cooperation was initiated by the left spread
terror among reactionary circles, particularly the Czartorist camp.[575]

The Polish-Russian alliance, however, was not an alliance of equal partners.
In terms of ideology, Russian émigré circles far outpaced even the most radical
Poles. Alexander Herzen was unrivalled in the extreme as a model of a true
revolutionary: his revolutionary democratic political program was decidedly
more radical than anything the Polish revolutionaries would concoct, whether
abroad or at home.[576] Already before 1863, he unconsciously shared Marx's line
of thinking, despite not having contacted him yet by that point. "We should be
impressed even more," stressed Bobińska, "by the proximity of their ideas ... on
the uprising [of 1863] – Marx and Engels on one side, and the Herzen-Ogarev
camp on the other."[577] Comparisons between members of the Communes of the
Polish People and the Russian revolutionaries stripped the former of some of
their virtues, which were conversely highlighted when related to the outlook of
Polish Democratic Society representatives. While the Communes were
comprised of revolutionary democrats, the Society was supposedly a gathering
of revolutionary nobles. However, when compared to Herzen, members of the
GLP seemed more akin to revolutionary nobles, with the Russian meriting the
title of a "revolutionary democrat."[578]

In spite of their unquestionable – in the Polish context – progressiveness, the
Communes of the Polish People and specific political leaders were criticised in
Marxist studies, not only for not holding their own with regard to the Russian

572 Bobińska, *Marks*, 129.
573 See Władysław Bortnowski, "Przedmowa," in: Łukaszewicz, *Stanisław Gabriel Worcell*, 5; see also: *Historia Polski. Makieta*, vol 2, part 2, 339.
574 Bolesław Bierut, *O Konstytucji Polskiej Rzeczypospolitej Ludowej. Konstytucja Polskiej Rzeczypospolitej Ludowej*, Warszawa 1954, 41.
575 See Irena Koberdowa, "Walka czartoryszczyzny przeciwko sojuszowi polskich i rosyjskich rewolucjonistów w czasie powstania styczniowego," in: *Z epoki*, 215 & 225.
576 See Łukaszewicz, *Stanisław Gabriel Worcell*, 47.
577 Bobińska, *Marks*, 157.
578 See *Historia Polski. Makieta*, vol 2, part 2, 551.

revolutionaries, but also for their so-called objective faults. For instance, according to Łukaszewicz, Stanisław Worcell failed to surmount the burdening relics of feudalism in his thinking, which inevitably limited the revolutionary impact of his ideology.[579] An even more significant error of the Polish radicals was that, while they undoubtedly espoused socialism, they tended toward its Utopian incarnation rather than its scientific one represented by Marxism. As Władysław Bortnowski lamented, "Until the very end of his active life, Worcell proved incapable of choosing the right field of combat – he could not turn away from utopianism, and draw closer to the scientific socialism of Marx and Engels."[580] To make matters even worse, the ideological evolution of the Communes tended toward socialist messianism.

The "methodological breakthrough" in Polish historiography coincided with the centennial anniversary of the revolution of 1848. Just as during the preparations to the Year of Renaissance or Year of Enlightenment in later years, historians were expected to play a very significant role in the celebrations. The year 1948 saw the publication of a whole series of historical works devoted to questions related to the anniversary, spearheaded by a volume edited by Natalia Gąsiorowska-Grabowska, *W stulecie Wiosny Ludów 1848-1849* (The 100th Anniversary of the Springtime of the Peoples 1848-1849). In the first volume of the publication, its editor declared that "The People's Republic of Poland looks for its roots in a period removed from our times by a hundred years, dating its emergence to the period of the Springtime of the Peoples as a source for its current constitution."[581] Given such an outlook, the evaluation of the revolution could not have been other than positive; hence the tone of the majority of publications from 1948. In the edited volume mentioned above, Stefan Kieniewicz wrote about the heroism of the scytheman from Miłosław who washed the Polish people clean of the disgrace of the Galician Slaughter. He stressed the unity of the nation in the struggle for independence.[582] The image of a national, class-indifferent solidarity was drawn even more compellingly in *Oblicze*

579 See Łukaszewicz, *Stanisław Gabriel Worcell*, 30.
580 Bortnowski, "Przedmowa," 6.
581 Natalia Gąsiorowska-Grabowska, "Sytuacja gospodarczo-społeczna na zachodzie i wschodzie Europy w połowie XIX stulecia," in: *W stulecie Wiosny Ludów 1848-1948*, ed. Natalia Gąsiorowska-Grabowska, vol. 1: *Wiosna Ludów na ziemiach polskich*, eds. Natalia Gąsiorowska-Grabowska, Stefan Kieniewicz, Anna Minkowska, Irena Pietrzak-Pawłowska, Leon Przemyski & Mieczysław Tobiasz, Warszawa 1948, 42; other publications of the anniversary year were listed in articles by Stefan Kieniewicz, "Polski dorobek naukowy stulecia Wiosny Ludów," Marian Tyrowicz, "Tematyka dziejów 1848/9 r. w jubileuszowej historiografii obcej" and Henryk Batowski, "Z pokłosia Wiosny Ludów w dziejopisarstwie słowiańskim" (all included in *Kwartalnik Historyczny* 1949).
582 Stefan Kieniewicz, *Czyn polski w dobie Wiosny Ludów*, Warszawa 1948, 149.

ideowe Wiosny Ludów (The Ideological Countenance of the Springtime of the Peoples). There, Kieniewicz wrote that "the programs and social slogans promulgated at home and abroad – enfranchisement, government of the people by the people – for most patriots are means toward a national end.... In the upper strata of the nation, one would be hard-pressed to name more than a few individuals willing to renounce statehood, even if its price was cultural dependence."[583] It seemed only right, then, that "for later generations, 1848 became the year of the last armed effort in the [Prussian] partition, a memory of a reconciliation of all social strata in the struggle for a sacred cause, yet another proof of the vitality of the Polish nation."[584]

Another characteristic feature of the images of the events of 1848 drawn by Polish scholars in anniversary publications was criticism of all symptoms of pan-Slavism, particularly visible in depictions of the Slavic Congress in Prague. Henryk Batowski viewed the organisers of the Congress in a highly critical manner, though conceding that their pan-Slavism had not yet become as degenerate as it would be in the 1860s and 1870s. Still, even in this relatively benign shape, the ideology was inadmissible, primarily because of "operating solely according to nationalist criteria ... in total disregard of universal human values." As Batowski added "Revolution, the rights of the working masses, the class movement of the proletariat – all of this was foreign, perhaps even hostile, to pan-Slavists and Austro-Slavists."[585] A detailed description of the Congress, presented by Kieniewicz, criticised Czechs who "were game to remove Poles from the proceedings for fear of having a revolution on their hands in their native Prague. Powerless to avoid inviting them, they demanded that active participation in the Congress be restricted solely to Austrian subjects. Nevertheless, the Polish name commanded so much respect that no one cared much for the rule."[586]

The claims presented by Stefan Kieniewicz were an extension of his beliefs dating from before the war. Kieniewicz saw the Polish cause of the 1848 period as equivalent to the cause of revolution, a belief disseminated by Marxist classics as well. Nonetheless, the "methodological breakthrough" deeply transformed the manner in which the events of the period were assessed. Looking through Kieniewicz's texts from 1948, one could, for instance, find the

583 Stefan Kieniewicz, *Oblicze ideowe Wiosny Ludów*, Warszawa 1948, 17.
584 Stefan Kieniewicz, "Wielkopolska i Prusy Zachodnie w latach 1846-1848," in: *W stulecie*, vol. 1, 164.
585 Henryk Batowski, "Zagadnienia roku 1848 w Słowiańszczyźnie (Fakty, literatura, uwagi metodyczne, materiał dyskusyjny)," *Przegląd Historyczny* 1948, 50-51.
586 Kieniewicz, *Czyn*, 107.

claim that the tsarist regime served the cause of Russian national expansion.[587] Later publications typically included a disclaimer stating that the tsar and the nation – the Russian folk – had no common agenda (and would never have one). However, for Kieniewicz, even the most reactionary policies of tsarist Russia did not affect the assessment of "national expansion." Furthermore, after 1948, a vehement critique of Czech pan-Slavism, and particularly the Slavic Congress, would contradict the accepted interpretation of history and stand in conflict with Czechoslovak historiographic foundations.

Publications dating from after 1949, outlining the progress of the Springtime of the Peoples in Polish territories as well as its international ramifications, passed an entirely different judgment. Just as in 1794 and 1830, the people were said to have joined the national liberation struggle en masse. Attitudes toward the uprising in Greater Poland, however, were dependent on social status: "In the early days, the rural poor showed more initiative than the landowners."[588] Members of privileged classes and even democratic conspirators faced much sterner judgment. In chapters of the "Draft" authored by Stefan Kieniewicz, the idea of a national solidarity of all Poles was patently rejected.[589]

Polish Marxist historians stressed the ambiguous role Russia and the Russians had played in the Springtime of the Peoples. "News of the revolution in the West coincided with a rising tide of peasant unrest throughout Russia," Kieniewicz observed. Furthermore, "Among the volunteers from the Kingdom joining ranks with Poles, there were also some Russians – soldiers of the tsar's army."[590] Celina Bobińska, on the other hand, underlined the commonality of interests between Polish and German democrats, claiming that "in the Poznań area, Prussian reactionaries trumped not only the local folk, but also the German revolution."[591] Publications dating from before 1948 maintained that "the radicalism of the Polish social agenda in the Greater Poland revolution stands in glaring opposition to the social program of the province's German population, overwhelmed by a love of the old order, adhering to a bureaucratic and military despotism, enamored of tyranny and slavish subjection."[592] Especially in the

---

587 See Kieniewicz, *Oblicze*, 18.

588 *Historia Polski. Makieta*, vol. 2, 469.

589 Ibidem, 470–471, 475 & 478 as well as Natalia Gąsiorowska-Grabowska, "Proces formowania się narodu burżuazyjnego w ramach kształtowania się stosunków kapitalistycznych w Polsce," in: *Pierwsza Konferencja*, vol 2, 38.

590 *Historia Polski. Makieta*, vol. 2, 473.

591 Bobińska, *Marks*, 81.

592 Tadeusz Cieślak, "Program społeczny wielkopolskiego ruchu rewolucyjnego 1848 r.," *Przegląd Zachodni* 1948, 270.

pages of the *Western Review*, events in Greater Poland were treated as yet another chapter in the perennial struggle between Poles and Germans.[593]

According to Marxist authors, the progress of the Springtime of the Peoples in Polish lands proved that "Polish revolutionaries had not yet forged strong enough ties with the people." A section of the Polish possessor classes was scared by the realistic prospect of an agrarian reform, leading them to consider cooperation with occupying governments. The revolutionaries were expected to know that the future of Poland depended solely on the people, who – though unenlightened – remained the only class to have passed the exam of 1848.[594]

The last of the great national uprisings, in 1863, was framed in a similar interpretive scheme. Beginning with the top rungs of the social ladder, "major landowners and the grand bourgeoisie, consumed with a fear of an agrarian revolution, were both opposed to the idea of an armed struggle for independence insofar as its success hinged solely upon the involvement of broad national masses, primarily peasants."[595] The middle gentry and bourgeoisie were not as openly hostile to an armed struggle for independence, but erroneously bound their hopes to the involvement of Western powers. Besides, "landowners and bourgeois wanted to create a Poland that would include the lands of the Kingdom as well as the Stolen Lands, i.e., territories of Lithuania, Belarus and right-bank Ukraine within 1772 boundaries. The native Polish lands of the Prussian and Austrian partition, however, were not considered."[596]

Marxists placed the rightist socio-political camps in opposition to the "plebeian-popular" radicals, among them students, a section of the intelligentsia, artisans and plebeian masses, especially in Warsaw.[597] Members of this group were positively affected by contacts with Russian revolutionaries. Ties with Russians, on the other hand, also forced Poles to accept radical solutions to the peasant question.[598] They could rely on ranks of Russian regulars for performing the complex task of reaching distrustful social strata. Consequently, the left attempted to claim and radicalize the patriotic movement. To limit the possibility of a settlement with the tsar, they imposed upon the demonstrators slogans that positioned them in support of the restoration of the Stolen Lands. In studies from the 1950s, this was treated as a hindrance: "Unitary manifestations were a

593 See Bożena Osmólska-Piskorska, "'Wiosna Ludów' na Pomorzu," *Przegląd Zachodni* 1948; Tadeusz Grygier, "Powstanie wielkopolskie a plany wyzwolenia reszty ziem zachodniej Polski," *Przegląd Zachodni* 1948.
594 *Historia Polski. Makieta*, vol. 2, 540-541.
595 Ibidem, 159.
596 Ibidem, 160-161.
597 See Korta, *O postępowych*, 158.
598 *Historia Polski. Makieta*, vol. 2, 635-636.

political error of the reds. Instead of acknowledging the national struggles for liberation of the Lithuanian, Belorussian, and Ukrainian peasants, they evoked the meanest tradition of the Polish nobility, claiming Polish dominion of these countries."[599] The fact that the problem of the Stolen Lands was addressed by some of the reds automatically threw them into the movement's right wing, in accordance with the rule set out by Andrzej Ślisz, who stated that "All those who demanded the inclusion of the Eastern territories of the ancient, feudal Commonwealth were concurrently engaged in upholding a superior role for the nobility in the country."[600] An important judgment with bearing for the whites as well as the reds stipulated that the uprising was brought about not by manifestations of patriotism, but by peasant resistance to serfdom.[601]

The outbreak of the uprising, like the months of national agitation that preceded it, moved different groups within Polish society to take divergent positions with respect to it. Having assessed the insurgents' military efficacy, Adam Korta claimed that "parties" consisting of peasants or poor artisans and proletarians enjoyed the most success. The very fact that the uprising lasted so long was a result of the popular masses' active support.[602] Emanuel Halicz wrote that the increased revolutionary commotion in rural areas of Poland even suggested a kinship with a bourgeois-democratic revolution.[603] The peasants involved in the insurrection "sought to mold it into a mass, truly popular movement."[604] Sadly, in the end, the inclusion of the popular masses in the uprising failed to spark a revolution, the reason being the lack of a working class – a hegemon capable of rousing the whole nation. Still, the uprising played a crucial role in accelerating the formation process of the Polish nation.[605]

The people greeted the National Government's 1863 program of enfranchisement with mild approbation. During the Otwock conference, Emanuel Halicz assigned the program the key role in forcing the tsar to approve peasant enfranchisement, in 1864, on terms beneficial to the peasants. (Halicz's opinion did not affect the generally approved Marxist timeline, in which 1864

---

599   Ibidem, 657.
600   Andrzej Ślisz, "Współpraca polskich i rosyjskich sił postępowych w polskiej prasie emigracyjnej i konspiracyjnej lat 1859-1864," in: *Z dziejów współpracy rewolucyjnej Polaków i Rosjan w drugiej połowie XIX wieku*, eds. Ludwik Bazylow, Helena Brodowska & Krzysztof Dunin-Wąsowicz, Wrocław 1956, 10.
601   See *Historia Polski. Makieta*, vol. 2, 692.
602   Ibidem, 177-178.
603   Emanuel Halicz, "Ruchy chłopskie a powstanie styczniowe," in: *Pierwsza Konferencja*, vol. 2, 155.
604   *Historia Polski. Makieta*, vol. 2, 705.
605   Ibidem, 736.

continued to carry greater significance than 1863.) The involvement of the peasantry in the uprising amounted to not only a direct engagement in combat against the tsar's army, but also – perhaps even, most importantly – it represented "the involvement in an anti-feudal struggle against the manors."[606] The fact that the peasants generally did not support the insurgents resulted primarily from the actions of the possessor classes who attempted to isolate the radical agitators from the peasantry.[607] Representatives of a reactionary direction in the insurgent government, the whites, strove to gain control over the entire movement. With respect to the Russian people, they introduced a "decidedly nationalist line."[608] Marxists interpreted the gentry's casting about for international support as the recruitment of allies for combat against the indigenous progressive camp. Even the members of the lower sections of the clergy were seen to have played an ambiguous part in the uprising, joining the ranks of the insurgency not for reasons of patriotism, but to prevent an excessive radicalisation of the movement.[609] A major error of the red left was the pursuit of a compromise with the right-wing members of the movement because "the concept of a national front, of unity and cooperation with the landowners" would have never appealed to the peasant masses.[610]

In addition to covert internal enemies, the uprising had powerful external foes (as well as equally deadly false friends) more perfidious than the tsar himself. "Pius IX offered his blessings to the ruling powers in the pursuit of a conservative, Catholic Poland. But ... he refused Poles the right to liberate themselves, by means of a revolution."[611] In the "camp of enemies of the uprising," Adam Korta counted Pius IX, Napoleon III and Władysław Czartoryski, next to Alexander III, Bismarck and Aleksander Wielopolski. Policies of countries such as England or France, though seemingly sympathetic, "hid a decidedly anti-Polish position behind platitudes about friendship with the Polish nation."[612] Indeed, Poles could only depend on the support of the popular masses and the revolutionary milieux of Western Europe.[613] Finally, the uprising was also sabotaged by the tsar's propaganda, which played up "a perfidious argument that its aristocratic, regressive nature was supportive of the privileges of the nobility and the Church."[614]

---

606   See Halicz, "Ruchy," 157.
607   Korta, *O postępowych*, 155.
608   Ibidem, 176.
609   *Historia Polski. Makieta*, vol 2, 674.
610   Gąsiorowska-Grabowska, "Proces," 42.
611   *Historia Polski. Makieta*, vol. 2, 717.
612   Korta, *O postępowych*, 181. *Historia Polski. Makieta*, vol. 2, 718.
613   Ibidem, 721.
614   Ibidem, 735.

Still, the uprising could depend on the most reliable of allies: the Russian folk and Marx and Engels, "two people who, with their genius minds, mapped out new pathways for all humanity to follow."[615] In studies on the January Uprising, it was customary to refer to both as "the tested friends of the Polish people." In numerous works, one could find reproductions of the same photograph, depicting Karl Marx with his daughter who wore a stylised cross from the uprising on her neck. Celina Bobińska, who devoted a separate book to the attitudes of the classics toward Poland, stressed that both Marx and Engels assessed the situation of the Polish with uncommon sobriety: "Both friends felt particular unease concerning the Bonapartist influences and dealings in the camp of the reds," while "the whites for them were already branded direct agents for Palmerston and Bonaparte."[616] After the fall of the uprising, Engels made a comment which was commonly reproduced in Polish Marxist studies (with or without a citation): "Polish independence and Russian revolution are mutually dependent." "This ingenious guideline," wrote Andrzej Ślisz, "for the Polish liberation movement signified another, far more fundamental realisation of a shift of the center of the revolution's international forces from the West toward the East."[617]

For Marxist historians, it was abundantly clear that Russian revolutionaries deeply sympathised with the Poles, a view at times confirmed by the Russians' personal involvement in the uprising. The Russians saw a connection between the Russian revolution they craved and the Polish national liberation movement. They also tried to educate Poles concerning the true nature of the liberation struggle: "Only an agrarian revolution could ensure the masses' broad involvement in the Polish independence movement. The red left, commanded for the most part by men raised under the influence of the great Russian revolutionary democrats, understood this, and, thus, formed the closest of ties with the anti-tsarist movement in Russia, with its program of peasant revolution. The Polish landowning reaction, on the other hand, constantly pestered by peasant revolts, was scared of the Russian revolutionary spirit due to its radicalising influence on Poland.... The threat of an alliance with Russian revolutionaries also bode ill for the reds' liberal-bourgeois right who willingly compromised with the feudal squire, the forerunner of the capitalist landlord."[618] As already mentioned, Russian soldiers were deeply concerned with the fate of the Polish peasantry. Furthermore, "Even among officers who did not switch

---

615 Korta, *O postępowych*, 156; see also Celina Bobińska, "Marks i Engels wobec powstania styczniowego," *Kwartalnik Historyczny* 1953.
616 Bobińska, *Marks*, 169-170.
617 Ślisz, "Współpraca," 19.
618 Ibidem, 10.

sides for the insurgents, the uprising found some sympathisers, who covertly worked to its advantage. Among others, this group included the father of Nadezhda Krupskaya."[619]

Despite numerous reservations, Polish Marxist historiography assessed the uprising positively. In fact, one should perhaps rephrase this last sentence because the typically positive evaluation of the uprising in general was usually qualified by a series of reservations as to particular dictators, the leaders of specific units, politicians (whether whites, reds, or émigrés), and entire sections of Polish society. The January Uprising received a more positive reading than the November Uprising, primarily due to its National Government's decision to enfranchise the peasants. Another reason for the positive response was the involvement of Russians on the Polish side, a precious ornament in the annals of Polish-Russian friendship. The November Uprising did not provide as many opportunities for celebration. Studies from the 1950s added a corollary of sorts to descriptions of the progressiveness of the January Uprising – a reminder that several decades after the executions of captured insurgents in Warsaw, in the very same locations, on the banks of the Warsaw citadel, activists of the first Polish socialist party were also hung.[620]

The January Uprising concluded the period of national liberation struggles begun with the Kościuszko revolt. It seems instructive to consider attempts to develop a Marxist interpretation of the history of Polish struggles for independence, as well as an interpretation of the Polish national movement's program. All revolts were summarily subjected to a unitary criterion of progressiveness and, at the same time, effectiveness: to win independence, the movements had to treat social issues as a part of the national liberation struggle and instigate the agrarian revolution. Some declared that these conditions were in fact met; Such was the case, for example, with Józef Cyrankiewicz, in his address at the Unification Congress of PPS and PPR, or with Witold Kula during the Otwock conference.[621] Typically, though, authors pointed to the fact that the

---

619 *Historia Polski. Makieta*, vol. 2, 719.

620 Ibidem, 183; An almost identical statement can be found in Żanna Kormanowa, "Gospodarczo – społeczne przesłanki ukształtowania się pierwszej partii polskiej klasy robotniczej (w 70-lecie powstania partii "Proletariat")," *Przegląd Historyczny* 1952, 417.

621 See *Podstawy ideologiczne PZPR. Referat tow. Bolesława Bieruta wygłoszony w dniu 15 XII 1948 r. Koreferat tow. Józefa Cyrankiewicza wygłoszony w dn. 16 XII 1948 r. na Kongresie Polskiej Zjednoczonej Partii Robotniczej. Deklaracja ideowa PZPR*, Warszawa 1952, 84; Witold Kula, "Narastanie elementów kapitalizmu w Polsce XVIII w. Splatanie się walki klasowej z narodowo-wyzwoleńczą. Stosunek historiografii polskiej do procesu tworzenia się narodu burżuazyjnego," in: *Pierwsza Konferencja*, vol. 2, 126-127.

class aspect of the Polish struggles for independence was far more visible from a general European perspective than from within Poland. While Celina Bobińska admitted that in the West, "Suspicious and distrustful of silver-tongued liberal-bourgeois politicians, the masses tested their faithfulness to revolutionary principles by looking at their attitude toward the Polish question," she nevertheless repeatedly stated that, beyond just the Kościuszko Uprising, all other Polish revolts played a far more progressive role outside rather than within Polish lands. For this reason, it was easy to effect a kind of "closing" of history. Just as the stated point of the constitution of 1952 was to correct the shortcomings of the Constitution of May 3rd, so "The agrarian revolution was completed only under the government of the People's Republic of Poland, in 1944 and 1945, when the working peasant gained a hegemonic ally in the industrial proletariat."[622]

Marxist scholars rued the Polish uprising's missed opportunity – for engaging in cooperation with Russians. This notion infiltrated the analyses of nearly all patriotic outbursts, and was applied to all uprisings as parts of a single process. Generally, though, Polish national insurrections had a moderately progressive character. Pavel Tretiakov, the Russian historian, persuaded the participants at the Otwock conference to accept this belief on the very first day of the event, stating that "No one can question the progressive nature of the Polish national liberation movement of the 19th and early 20th century.... The movements directed against the Russian tsardom in the 19th century, though, such as the one in Kazakhstan, led by local feudal lords, should be treated in a completely different manner."[623]

Still, none of the Polish uprisings met each of the conditions of progressive national traditions. None enjoyed the kind of praise heaped on the national awakenings in Czechoslovakia by local historians. The success of these national movements – whose aim was to form cultures, literatures and political representations for the oppressed Slavs – was evident enough in the fact that, a hundred years later, people discussed them in Czech and Slovak. Meanwhile, the Polish uprisings failed. But even if they had succeeded, it is doubtful whether the Marxist assessment of their achievement would improve. How can one praise a successful war against Russia, even if it was ruled by a tsar? A conservative pan-Slavist, such as Palacký, Kollár or Štúr, seemed less controversial in that regard than an anti-Russian democrat like Kościuszko or Lelewel.

---

622 Korta, *O postępowych*, 95-96.
623 Pavel Tretiakov, "Znaczenie prac Józefa Stalina o zagadnieniach językoznawstwa dla nauki historii," in: *Pierwsza Konferencja*, vol. 1, 75-76.

The problematic nature of assessments of the Polish uprisings according to their progressiveness becomes even more evident when compared with Marxist interpretations of a phenomenon which one would appropriately call a national counterrevolution. There were few events in Polish history which garnered as many unequivocally negative responses from later generations as the Galician Slaughter – an armed movement of Galician peasants in "good emperor's" defense who had murdered insurgent noblemen or handed them over to the Austrian authorities. Karl Marx offered a different interpretation of the events of 1846, claiming that the Kraków uprising constituted a revolution, an ultimately failed, but commendable attempt at combining a struggle for national independence with the fight for social liberation: "The Kraków revolution," he wrote, "was neither reactionary nor conservative. On the contrary, it was more inimical to Poland than to its foreign oppressors, because it undermined the old, barbarian, feudal, aristocratic Poland that had been based on the bondage of the majority of the nation. Far from attempting to revive the old Poland, the Kraków revolution sought its complete devastation, so that, working hand in hand with a completely different class, it could raise from the old order's ruins a new, modern, civilised, democratic Poland."[624] The revolutionary classic's assessment served as a point of departure for the Marxist reinterpretation of the Kraków uprising and the Galician Slaughter.

In the 1950s, scholars stressed that the Kraków revolution began a period of revolutionary commotion across Europe. In a way, events in Galicia heralded the Springtime of the Peoples.[625] Though the efforts of Polish revolutionaries eventually proved futile, this fact did nothing to change their interpretation. As Celina Bobińska asked rhetorically, "So what if the uprising was a local affair, if … the broad peasant masses failed to comprehend it? … what mattered was that the peasant was counted upon, that he was promised agrarian revolution, while the landlords were threatened with it."[626] Despite historians' high esteem for it, nothing could alter the fact that the Kraków uprising failed. This failure must have had causes; some of them, in a way, had to have displayed an objective character. Marxists stressed that, in economic terms, Galicia was particularly backward, while the local "landowning gentry" did everything in their power to prevent radical propaganda from seeping through to the country. A part of the responsibility for the failure of the revolution has been laid at the door of the

---

624   Karl Marx & Friedrich Engels, *Dzieła wybrane*, Warszawa 1949, vol. 1, 61, quoted in: Henryk Jabłoński, *Międzynarodowe znaczenie polskich walk narodowo-wyzwoleńczych XVIII i XIX w.*, Warszawa 1955, 43.
625   See Bobińska, *Marks*, 72; Stefan Kieniewicz, *Legion Mickiewicza 1848-1849*, Warszawa 1955, 31.
626   Bobińska, *Marks*, 67.

revolutionaries themselves. Roman Werfel accused them of an excess of moderation and inability to grasp the moment's consequence.[627] According to the authors of the "Draft," the right wing of the revolutionary party bore the brunt of responsibility for the failure, since it "engaged in compromises with the possessor classes."[628]

Yet, the assessment of the Galician Slaughter proved a far greater challenge for Polish Marxist historiography. The anniversary publications, which also addressed the Springtime of the Peoples, typically offered criticisms of the peasant movement. In 1948, Stefan Kieniewicz wrote of an uprising "drowned in the blood shed by the hands of Polish peasants," while claiming that the uprising in Greater Poland, two years later, cleansed the people of the taint of the Slaughter.[629] His description of the course of events of February 1846, for the most part, followed the traditional narrative: "The peasants read the propaganda of the emissaries mistakenly: called upon to fight for liberty, they turned upon their lords and the insurgents. Ever perfidious, and at that point shaken with fear, the Austrian bureaucracy asked the peasants to quell the rebellion by themselves, leading to a catastrophe. A 'popular leader' emerged in the guise of Jakub Szela, who led the peasants on the manors, blindly avenging old wrongs committed against the people."[630]

The at times dramatic efforts to reinterpret national history are illustrated in the sections of the "Draft" authored by Stefan Kieniewicz. The attitudes of this particular historian to his subject of inquiry changed radically over a short span of time. The shifts introduced in his *Ruch chłopski w Galicji w 1846 roku* (The peasant movement in Galicia in 1846), a work honored with a national prize in 1952, were still deemed insufficient by Natalia Gąsiorowska-Grabowska. As she observed, "One still finds the main chapter bearing the title 'Slaughter,' the case of Jakub Szela is not explained in view of historical truth, there is insufficient connection between social and national struggles and between the Kraków revolution and the peasant uprising, the subversive role of the Austrian authorities is assessed wrongly."[631] In the volume of the "Draft" published in 1956, Kieniewicz already argued that neither the ignorance of the peasants, nor the machinations of the Austrian bureaucracy were responsible for the Slaughter. In

---

627 Stefan Kieniewicz, "Walka klasowa chłopów polskich w XIX i XX wieku w oświetleniu historiografii polskiej," *Kwartalnik Historyczny* 1951, 53.
628 *Historia Polski. Makieta*, vol. 2, part 2, 438.
629 See Kieniewicz, *Oblicze*, 56; idem, "Wielkopolska i Prusy Zachodnie w latach 1846-1848," in: *W stulecie*, vol. 1, 164.
630 Kieniewicz, *Czyn*, 22-23.
631 Archiwum PAN, sygn. III – 152, Materiały Natalii Gąsiorowskiej-Grabowskiej, j. 68 Opinie o dorobku naukowym pracowników nauki.

fact, "opinion-makers of noble stock sought to denigrate this movement and distort its character," and then "The enemies of the Polish people for decades pointed the finger at the peasant, blaming him for the sin of 'fratricide' in 1846."[632]

In the new, Marxist-Leninist interpretation, the Slaughter became a progressive peasant movement. "The peasant uprising of the time," wrote Kieniewicz, "struck a severe blow against the feudal social order, … it sought to reverse the Prussian direction of capitalist development and reinstate the revolutionary way, and … it opened a road to liberation for the country through an agrarian revolution. The anti-feudal movement of the peasant masses was in essence, despite the errors it committed, a national liberation movement, which, though failed, deeply shook the system of bondage."[633] The peasants were not governed by a desire for financial gain, though the Austrian bureaucracy paid for every Polish noble's head. The interpretation of the role played by Jakub Szela was also subjected to revision: the ironic designation "popular leader" was no longer printed in quotation marks. The "Draft" included the claim that "In his struggle with the nobility, Szela did not assume the mask of a servant to the emperor, but rather openly voiced peasant demands," though sadly, "He did not control the peasant element to the extent that he could effectively command the resistance movement."[634]

Marxist scholars went even further in underlining the similarities between the political role of the Kraków Uprising and the Slaughter. Not only did both movements supposedly threaten Austrian rule in Galicia to a similar extent. Studies from the 1950s basically equated the insurgents to the peasants.[635] The two liberation movements did not join forces, but, in a way, they did engage in cooperative action: "As we all know, the coming eruption of peasant fury became for the plotters of Tarnów an incentive to hasten the uprising. The insurgents' assault on Tarnów, on the other hand, gave the peasant masses a chance to engage in combat."[636] During the Otwock conference, Natalia Gąsiorowska-Grabowska spoke of the commonality of goals between the insurgents and the peasants, stressing the progressive nature of the Slaughter.[637]

The Galician Slaughter's inclusion among the progressive traditions of the Polish nation stands in stark contrast with the approach of Czechoslovak historians to their native history. Polish scholars did not care to prove, as did

---

632   *Historia Polski. Makieta,* vol. 2, part 2, 438 i 447.

633   Ibidem, 447.

634   *Historia Polski. Makieta,* vol. 2, part 2, 444-445.

635   Ibidem, 428; see also Stefan Kieniewicz, "Problem rewolucji agrarnej w Polsce w okresie kształtowania się układu kapitalistycznego," in: *Z epoki,* 11.

636   Ibidem, 439.

637   See Gąsiorowska-Grabowska, "Proces," 37.

Slovaks or Czechs, that the national movement was a popular movement as such, even if peasants were not involved. Perhaps it was indicative of the belief that the history of Poland was in itself reactionary, anti-Russian, and focused on the nobles and not the masses. The same belief could lead to a search for connections between the revolutionary Hussite movement and the uprising of Spytko of Melsztyn, or between the Khmelnytsky Uprising and Kostka-Napierski. Hence the uprisings were not picked up for their immanent progressiveness, but rather for their examples of cooperation with Russian revolutionaries, and the assessment of the insurgents proved far less compelling than that of the Polish peasants, who murdered Polish nobles at the behest of the Austrian administration.

The search for an event in German history that would play a role similar to that of the Czech and Slovak national awakenings or the Polish uprisings should probably begin with a description of the *Befreiungskriege*. However, this topic was already sufficiently addressed in the previous subsection. Here, I will only discuss events which, for Marxist-Leninist historiography of the GDR, seemed a continuation of the progressive struggles for the unification of Germany. Marxist interpretations of *Vormärz* and the events of Springtime of the Peoples in Germany included elements bearing an uncanny similarity to the descriptions of the Polish uprisings. The 100th anniversary of the revolution became an opportunity for state-sponsored celebrations throughout the Soviet German occupation zone.[638] At least until the 1960s, in the period when German history focussed on unification efforts, historical studies concentrated on workers and peasants who fought for a single Germany. (The absolute dominance of the working class among the actors of the Springtime of the Peoples did not necessarily mean that it received much attention from the writers.) Karl Obermann wrote that "the search for a solution to this question of national importance uncovered differences of approach among particular classes and strata with regard to common national interests. From the very beginning, the bourgeoisie's treatment of the nation was burdened by its interests as an oppressing class.... It preferred for changes to occur not via a revolution, but through reforms, compromises with the feudal and militarist reaction. Already at that point, the bourgeoisie opposed the forces of democracy and prevented the unification of the country on a democratic platform. It raised its class interest above the interest of the German folk, thereby objectively taking the path of

---

638 Günther Heydemann, "Die deutsche Revolution von 1848/49 als Forschungsgegenstand der Geschichtswissenschaft in der SBZ/DDR", in: *Krise – Umbruch – Neubeginn. Eine kritische und selbstkritische Dokumentation der DDR-Geschichtswissenschaft 1989/90*, eds. Rainer Eckert, Wolfgang Küttler & Gustav Seeber, Stuttgart 1992, 310.

treason."[639] This assessment of the bourgeoisie failed to account for the divergences within the unitary bourgeois camp, but Marxist historians cared little whether they were writing about liberals or conservatives (just as their Polish colleagues found it pointless to recognize the camp of Prince Adam Czartoryski for being more progressive than the conservative "national turncoats" like Henryk Rzewuski).[640] The petite bourgeoisie occupied a more privileged position. Its actions, however, were marked by an inability to grasp the moment's consequence and a fear of decisive action.[641]

Though the bourgeoisie in its entirety was not determined to pursue unification, particular representatives of the social group sometimes received positive evaluations from Marxist scholars. The choice of figures for elevation could often be quite puzzling. While discussing "the struggle of the industrial bourgeoisie for German unity," Obermann lauded Friedrich List's attempts at eliminating tolls and creating a common German market. The fact that the very same List fathered the idea of a German *Mitteleuropa* did not deserve Obermann's mention.[642] Another protagonist in the struggles for unification was the liberal politician and physician, Rudolf Virchow, whom "bourgeois studies sought to depict as a Prussian patriot and nationalist."[643] Among the positive figures one often also found Hegel, whose idealism did not preclude or diminish the progressive nature of his philosophy – after all, he did introduce the dialectical method. At this stage of development, Hegel's philosophy suited the needs of the liberal bourgeoisie who were striving to form an all-German constitutional monarchy.[644]

The drive toward the unification of Germany was, then, progressive in itself (up to a point) and merited plaudits even when it did not come with a democratic ideology.[645] The scholars' attitude toward the movement began to change as soon as an organised working class entered the stage. From that point on, the

---

639 Karl Obermann, *Deutschland von 1815 bis 1849 (Von der Gründung des Deutschen Bundes bis zur bürgerlich-demokratischen Revolution),* Berlin 1963, XIII.

640 See Heydemann, "Die deutsche Revolution," 315.

641 Ibidem. See also Walter Ulbricht, Horst Bartel, Lothar Berthold, Ernst Diehl, Friedrich Ebert, Ernst Engelberg, Dieter Fricke, Fritz Globig, Kurt Hager, Werner Horn, Bernard Koenen, Wilhelm Koenen, Albert Schreiner & Hanna Wolf, *Geschichte der deutschen Arbeiterbewegung, vol. 1: Von den Anfängen der deutschen Arbeiterbewegung bis zum Ausgang des 19. Jahrhundert,* Berlin 1966, 91.

642 Karl Obermann, "Disposition des Hochschullehrbuches der Geschichte des deutschen Volkes (1815-1849)," *Zeitschrift für Geschichtswissenschaft* 1954, 114.

643 Kurt Winter, "Rudolf Virchow und die Revolution von 1848", *Zeitschrift für Geschichtswissenschaft* 1954, 844.

644 Obermann, *Deutschland,* 128.

645 Ibidem, 189.

bourgeoisie's struggles with the remnants of feudalism paled in comparison to the struggles of the proletariat with capitalism.[646] This interpretation of the events of 1848 appeared already in *Der Irrweg einer Nation...* and continued unchanged from that point on.[647] The first workers' unions, such as Bund der Gerechten, and the first appearances of an organised working class, such as the Silesian weavers' revolt, opened a new chapter in the history of progressive traditions. No longer were they national traditions, but the traditions of the German Communist party.[648]

During the Springtime of the Peoples, the working class was not yet sufficiently organised to stand at the helm of the revolution. The petit bourgeois intelligentsia, on the other hand, was perfectly capable of taking up the task. According to Karl Obermann, two antagonistic classes – the workers and the bourgeoisie – vied for the attention of the petite bourgeoisie. The fact that the intelligentsia assumed the leadership of the revolution resulted in a dearth of resolve among German activists, who were multiplying "handsome resolutions" rather than actions.[649] The Frankfurt Parliament's demand that worker meetings taking place across the city be forcibly dispersed came to have a symbolic significance.[650]

Evidently, this characteristic of 1848 revolutionary participants did not yield much optimism. The bourgeoisie betrayed the national movement by openly assuming reactionary positions. The petite bourgeoisie and the intelligentsia lingered awhile before taking the same step. Therefore, the only group remaining on the battlefield was the working class, which was, nevertheless, robbed of its "hegemony," that is, its own political party. It was impossible to decide whether this hegemony was indispensable to the success of a revolution. East German historians tended to offer conflicting views on the matter, as the masses were often credited with a consciousness sufficient for independent revolutionary action even without an organised leadership.[651] Still, the Marxists managed to note a number of shortcomings in the conduct of the German working class – primarily, the absence of a worker-peasant alliance: "The German proletariat stood at the forefront of all battles of 1848-1849 and

---

646 Ibidem, 145.
647 See Abusch, *Der Irrweg*, 96.
648 Ulbricht, Bartel, Berthold, Diehl, Ebert, Engelberg, Fricke, Globig, Hager, Horn, Koenen, Koenen, Schreiner & Wolf, *Geschichte*, 36.
649 Karl Obermann, *Die deutschen Arbeiter in der Revolution von 1848*, Berlin 1953, 121 & 134.
650 Ibidem, 260-262.
651 Helmut Rumpler, "Revolutionsgeschichtsforschung in der DDR," *Geschichte in Wissenschaft und Unterricht* 1980/31, 183.

consistently fought for democracy. Yet, it was not strong enough to lead the peasants and the petite bourgeoisie, and, hence, the German bourgeoisie was allowed to sell the revolution off to reaction."[652]

As with Luther and the Reformation, the image of the German bourgeoisie during the Springtime of the Peoples grew more and more positive with time. In 1962, in Jena, a research group devoted to the history of the bourgeois parties was formed under the leadership of Dieter Fricke. Its goal was to scientifically verify theories of "two lines" of historical development in Germany. At the same time, the group was also expected to specifically describe the "class enemy" responsible for the failure of a progressive unification of Germany in 1848, as well as, to locate those among the bourgeois politicians who could merit inclusion in the catalog of East German progressive traditions.[653] In this last case, any spectacular success was unlikely to occur. No one could rival Marx and Engels, who were not only commentators upon, but actors in the events of 1848. The treatment of the actors of the Springtime of the Peoples in Germany was determined by the fact that the failed revolution, to an extent, led to the top-down imposed unification of the country. This phenomenon was approached with much criticism until the turn of the 1980s, when a new, positive assessment of Bismarck and of Prussian heritage changed the way German bourgeois politicians of 1848 were looked at, as well.

There are many analogies between the attitudes of East German and Polish Marxist historiographies toward 19th century national movements. Both the Polish uprisings and the German grassroots movements for unification were interpreted as narrowly progressive phenomena. They lacked an understanding of social questions and the support of the peasant masses and the working class. As Andrzej Walicki points out, the postulate of agrarian revolution, which for Polish Marxists constituted the sole condition of success for the Polish national liberation movement, was picked up and adopted from Lenin's writings, where it was treated as a political postulate for his own party. The application of such a measure to the analysis of the Polish political movements of the 19th century can hardly be justified in Marxist terms and inevitably led to profound criticism. The Polish Marxists expected the national movement to espouse far more radicalism than the classics of Marxism themselves (and the classics of

652 Obermann, *Die deutschen*, 332.
653 Johannes Schradi, *Die DDR-Geschichtswissenschaft und das bürgerliche Erbe. Das deutsche Bürgertum und die Revolution von 1848 im sozialistischen Geschichtsverständnis*, Frankfurt am Main 1997, 130-154.

Marxism-Leninism as well).[654] From a Marxist standpoint, Walicki continued, the accusations leveled against the democrats, charging them with a lack of understanding for the national aspirations of Lithuanians, Ukrainians and Belorussians, were just as unfounded. By refusing these nations a right for self-determination, activists of the Polish national movement were closely approximating the position supported by Marx and Engels at that time.[655] Analogous practices of Marxist scholars can be observed in the GDR. It remained forever unclear how and for what reason representatives of the German working class of yore should have become conscious of the necessity of establishing a peasant-worker alliance as a condition for the revolution's success (rendering them more advanced than Marx and Engels). Even if it was possible, could this alliance (or, in the Polish context, the agrarian revolution) really have led to the victory of the revolution?

This warrants the question: were Czech and Slovak national movements not riddled with the same faults, being additionally accused by Marxism's classics of collaboration with the European forces of reaction? It seems they were. Yet still, the image of the national awakening painted by Czechoslovak historiography was far more positive than the interpretation of Polish and German national movements' struggles with European reaction. It is hard to tell which of the potential reasons for this state of affairs played the key role. Was it because 19th century movements of "historical" nations were aimed against the bedrock of the Holy Alliance: Russia, while the Slavic national awakenings typically relied on a Slavophile, and sometimes even a pan-Slavic backdrop? Did it matter that there was a powerful defender of the national-liberal interpretation of history in Czechoslovakia, in the guise of Zdeněk Nejedlý, since neither Poland, nor the GDR produced a like-minded individual who could draw binding rules for the interpretation of the national past? Or was it because the compensatory role which history plays in the life of a nation was more relevant to Czechs and Slovaks than to Poles or Germans? Doubtless, it mattered that Polish or German Marxists who invoked national traditions were dealing with a much richer collection of political movements and a wealth of historical interpretations concerning them. A wealth of national historiographical traditions and a far richer tradition of national and radical movements in the 19th century was, in the case of Poland, but especially East Germany, more of a hindrance than a facilitator to interpretation. As a whole, the Czech or Slovak

---

654 Andrzej Walicki, "Marks i Engels o sprawie polskiej. Uwagi metodologiczne," in: *Powstanie listopadowe 1830-1831. Geneza – uwarunkowania – bilans – porównania*, eds. Jerzy Skowronek & Maria Żmigrodzka, Wrocław 1983, 314.
655 Ibidem, 310.

national movement, which served as a basis for national cultures, proved resistant to a critique from the standpoint of historical materialism – the more so since, in its Stalinist guise, historical materialism no longer adhered to Marx's belief in the existence of "historical" and "non-historical" nations. Since it was impossible to simply deem the Czech or Slovak nation reactionary, one had to include their respective national movements among the "progressive traditions."

Comparing the attitude of Marxist historiographies to the national movements of the 19th century, one should also take into account the fact that a commonality of critique of the indigenous traditions in the Polish and German context on the one hand, and the Czech and Slovak on the other, would yield divergent results with respect to the Marxist vision of history. Questioning the role of the Polish uprisings or the skeptical attitude of East German Marxists toward the achievements of the liberal bourgeoisie and the workers' movements during the Springtime of the Peoples did nothing to challenge the fundamentals of national consciousness. Had the same brand of criticism been employed toward figures of importance to Slovak national culture, such as Ľudovít Štúr, it would have forced Slovak historians to reinterpret their national history anew, as the operation would result in casting away a man who framed the modern Slovak nation's course of development – a man who, in a way, shaped the nation itself. In the final analysis, the role played by individuals such as Štúr or Palacký is incomparable to that of any insurgent commander or leader of the Great Emigration. In the Czech and Slovak case, a harsh, Marxist criticism of the national revivalists could have produced the effects which Rafał Stobiecki (in my view, erroneously) ascribed to Polish Stalinist historiography – a "rupture in the elementary rules of social life, expressed in the demand for a historical continuity of state and nation."[656]

The Impact of the Great Socialist October Revolution on the History of East Central Europe

The Great Socialist October Revolution served as the key event for Marxist interpretations of the history of popular democracies. In every case, the claim that the revolution decisively affected the most significant socio-political processes became axiomatic. In Poland, the Great Socialist October Revolution was named as (to quote the title of a chapter from a schoolbook for 11th graders) "the decisive precondition in the reconstitution of the Polish state." This relationship was explained by a Soviet historian: "The victory of the socialist

---

656 Stobiecki, *Historia*, 182.

revolution and the constitution of the dictatorship of the proletariat in Russia enabled the rebirth of the Polish state and the unification of all Polish lands, including the Western territories. However, the ruling classes of bourgeois-aristocratic Poland betrayed the interests of the Polish people. The majority of Polish lands in the West – a significant portion of Silesia, Pomerania, Warmia and Mazurias [sic], the delta of the Vistula including Gdańsk – remained in German hands. With the support of English, French and American imperialists, the Piłsudski faction and the National Democrats instigated a criminal war against the Soviet Union, seeking to claim the territories of Ukraine and Belarus."[657]

Marxist scholars paid particular attention to the activities of Józef Piłsudski, the leading Polish enemy of the revolution. "Piłsudski and his followers," asserted Tadeusz Daniszewski, "were always characterised by extreme chauvinism and a deeply nationalist hatred of the Russian revolutionaries."[658] The Polish-Bolshevik war was the crowning achievement of his anti-Soviet activities. Adam Korta devoted a sizable article to the subject, giving it the telling title "The Brawl that Became a Legend." In the article, he recounted the already cited findings of Soviet scholars, who claimed that the war in the East shattered all Polish hopes of claiming the territories in the West. The Soviet state conducted a policy of peace, and "The working class of capitalist countries gazed at the first state of free workers and peasants in the world with a growing affection," but the "bourgeoisie and landlords, dreaming of long-lost manors in the Ukraine and the factories of the Donbas, ... were pushing for an aggressive war from the very beginning."[659] Semen Petlura, Piłsudski's ally in Ukraine, was, in Korta's words, "a half-criminal figure, a black reactionary, a Ukrainian chauvinist, a die-hard Polish-hater."[660]

Marxist scholars went out of their way to stress the superficial character of political differences between Piłsudski's federal camp and Dmowski's nationalists because of their common enmity to Soviet Russia.[661] This

---

657 J. Rubinsztein, "Polityka kolonizacyjna wilhelmowskich Niemiec na zachodnich ziemiach polskich (1900-1914)," in: *Historycy radzieccy*, 218-219; see also Walentyna Najdus, "Lenin o prawie narodu polskiego do niepodległości," *Kwartalnik Historyczny* 1953; M. Wągrowski, "Rewolucja Październikowa a Polska," *Nowe Drogi* 1952/11; M. Wągrowski, "Rewolucja Październikowa a Polska (cz. II)," Nowe Drogi 1953/1.

658 *Historia Polski 1864-1945. Materiały do nauczania w klasie XI*, ed. Żanna Kormanowa, Warszawa 1952, 175.

659 Korta, *O postępowych*, 187-189.

660 Ibidem, 195.

661 "Thus, neither of these orientations embraced national guidelines or demands. Both were an expression of the interests, needs and aspirations of the Polish bourgeoisie ...

partnership was considered a continuation of a factual alliance between the PPS and National Democracy, dating back as far as the revolution of 1905.

Adam Korta also engaged in an attempt at the "demythologisation" of the course of the Polish-Soviet war. He claimed that the debates over actual authorship of the Polish victory at Warsaw were of secondary importance, and the ascription of this "achievement" to Piłsudski was meant to "exemplify the supposed 'genius' of a Führer, a crucial aspect of every fascist ideology."[662] The significance of the debate was, in itself, quite questionable – elsewhere, Korta observed that the "Miracle at the Vistula" was only an "alleged" Polish victory. In fact, the whole image of the war was turned upside down: Poland was represented as the dominant, aggressive side, pursuing total obliteration of the enemy while Russia merely conducted defensive actions. The key role was no longer assigned to the Battle of Warsaw, instead having been ascribed to the Soviet counter-offensive "which became a great national war against the Polish landlords and ended in the banishment of the Polish armies from the Ukraine."[663] Meanwhile, behind the Polish lines, a fervent class war was brewing, with the people realising that – as Korta put it – "The Soviet army set out toward Poland as a liberator, an ally to the Polish working masses."[664]

Not all Poles, however, displayed as negative an attitude toward the Russian revolution as Dmowski or Piłsudski. Marxist scholars often stressed that members of the Social Democrats in the Kingdom of Poland and Lithuania wholly supported the October Revolution.[665] Feliks Dzierżyński, who performed enormous services to the security apparatus of the revolution, took center stage: "The amount of hatred that the bourgeois of the world exhibited – and continue to exhibit – toward him is a just measure of this man's dedication to the cause …. Dzierżyński was always typified by an affectionate care for the people, a revolutionary blaze, limitless dedication to the party, a deep patriotism and proletarian internationalism that always goes hand in hand with it."[666] Side by side with Dzierżyński stood other

and hoped to ensure the best possible conditions for the development and expansion of the Polish imperialism, even at the cost of true independence." – Leon Grosfeld, "„Prawidłowość i specyfika polskiego imperializmu," in: *Pierwsza Konferencja*, vol. 2, 282.

662 Korta, *O postępowych*, 186.
663 Ibidem, 196-197.
664 Ibidem, 197; see also Franciszek Ryszka, "Radykalizm społeczny ludności Górnego Śląska na przełomie lat 1918/19," *Przegląd Zachodni* 1950.
665 Walentyna Najdus, "Polacy w Rewolucji Październikowej (w XXXV rocznicę Rewolucji Październikowej)," *Przegląd Historyczny* 1952, 437.
666 Bronisław Baczko, "Wstęp," in: Korta, *O postępowych*, 21-22; see also: Edward Ochab, "Największy polski rewolucjonista," *Nowe Drogi* 1951/3; J. Kole, "Feliks Dzierżyński Budowniczy Gospodarki Socjalistycznej," *Nowe Drogi* 1951/3.

supporters of the revolution – Julian Marchlewski, Bronisław Wesołowski, as well as numerous nameless heroes, because "Nearly all fronts of the civil war saw Polish revolutionary units engaged in heroic combat."[667]

Czechoslovak Marxist historiography similarly ascribed the collapse of the Habsburg monarchy to the October Revolution. This claim was staked out primarily in Jurij Křížek and Oldřich Říha's work bearing the candid title *Bez Velké říjnové socialistické revoluce by nebylo Československa* (Without the Great October Revolution there would be no Czechoslovakia) (Praha 1951). The Czech and Slovak peoples' struggle for independence and socialism had already begun with the arrival of news about the February Revolution. The later revolution only fueled that fire: "Though the working class, as we shall see further, tried to imitate the victorious progress of the Russian workers, it did not yet possess a complete understanding of all the fundamental conditions for their victory – first of all, it was unfamiliar with Leninism."[668] For this reason the working class would only enjoy limited success – it managed to break the monarchy apart, but it failed to erect a socialist Bohemia.[669] Like Polish Marxists, their Czech counterparts did not pay heed to the essential divergences between different bourgeois organisations – in this case between the proponents and opponents of the monarchy. Furthermore, the bourgeoisie, in the guise of Masaryk, worked objectively against Czechoslovak independence. Since independence was gained through the Great Socialist October Revolution, and the Czechoslovak Legions, of which Masaryk was the political commander, were opposed to the revolution, Masaryk inadvertently acted as a stumbling block in the struggle for independence.[670] The formation of Czechoslovakia was said to have incited "nationalist illusions" among the workers, leading them to abandon the struggle for social liberation.[671]

In Czechoslovak historiography, the role played in Polish studies by Piłsudski's Legions and the "brawl become legend" was ascribed to the Czechoslovak Legions in Russia, formed of prisoners of war and deserters from the Austro-Hungarian army. These units fought against Germans; similar units were also formed in Italy, France, and Serbia. Later on, the Legions in Russia fought against the Bolsheviks, and even managed to claim control of the Trans-Siberian Railroad and significant portions of Siberia. During the interwar period,

---

667 *Historia Polski 1864-1945*, 299; see also: Zygmunt Modzelewski, "Julian Marchlewski (1866-1925)," *Nowe Drogi* 1950/1.

668 *Přehled československých. dějin*, vol. 2, part 2, 1222.

669 See Oldřich Říha, "O národním hnutí a národnostní otázce 1848-1918," *Československý Časopis Historický* 1954, 68.

670 Karel Herman, "Hlavní rysy česko-ruských vztahů v letech 1870-1917," in: *Z bojů*, 95.

671 Ibidem.

the Czechoslovak legionnaires became a privileged group, like their Polish counterparts. This situation was completely upturned in the 1950s. The Legions' Eastern escapade was recounted in a manner reminiscent of the treatment of the Polish-Bolshevik war: "The anti-Soviet intervention of the Czechoslovak Legions in 1918-1920 is a painful memory for every honorable member of our nations, a stain on the Czechoslovak-Soviet friendship, which nevertheless is today firm as rock and immutable."[672] The soldiers were not responsible for the conflict, instigated by the international forces of reaction, who craved the destruction of the Soviet Union. The Slovak author, Ján Kvasnička, added that within particular military units, subjectively progressive Czech and Slovak privates were influenced by tsarist and Czech officers "who, significantly aided by rightist social-democratic leaders, isolated the soldiers from the Russian revolutionary milieu."[673] Masaryk was said to have relished the international reaction, becoming a toady for his "superiors" by sacrificing the lives of Czechs and Slovaks.[674] Despite accounts of personal bravery, the legionnaires were merely a tool. As Vlastimil Vávra put it, "Logic suggests that those who died sacrificed their lives for an alien cause."[675]

Czech and Slovak prisoners of war were easy to recruit because they lacked political experience. The social-democratic leadership was to blame for that, having fed them "toothless revisionist theories." Because of this influence, only a few, "led primarily by a class instinct," joined the Red Army.[676] Numbering around 10,000, according to Vlastimil Vávra, Czech soldiers of the Red Army "salvaged the honor of the Czech and Slovak proletarian."[677] They were particularly exposed to the brutality of their countrymen.[678] The Soviet government, on the other hand, as Marxist historians stressed, treated the legionnaires in a friendly manner.[679]

Slovak historians copied in many points the historical framework elaborated by their Czech colleagues. They wrote of the people's vivid reaction to news of the October Revolution, of a wave of strikes and calls for an immediate ceasefire. Much attention was devoted to the Russian revolutionaries' slogan of

---

672   Vlastimil Vávra, *Klamná cesta. Příprava a vznik protisovětského vystoupení československých legií*, Praha 1958, 5.
673   Ján Kvasnička, *Československé légie v Rusku 1917-1920*, Bratislava 1963, 323.
674   Vávra, *Klamná*, 5 & 23. See also Václav Král, *O Masarykově a Benešově kontrarevoluci proti sovětské politice*, Praha 1953.
675   Vávra, *Klamná*, 28.
676   Ibidem, 50.
677   Ibidem, 130.
678   *Přehled československých. dějin*, vol. 2, part 2, 1265.
679   Ibidem, 1265.

self-determination for all nations.[680] The Slovak (and Hungarian) bourgeoisie, on the other hand, were unwelcoming toward the Russian proletariat.[681] The emergence of a Czechoslovak state was an (unintended) effect of the people's liberation struggle, inspired by the Great Socialist October Revolution.[682] This lack of intention was apparent in the fact that the key participant in the events, the working class, had not actively sought to form a state. Sadly, in a decisive moment, national liberation efforts were taken over by the bourgeoisie, which led to the creation of an independent Czechoslovakia. The bourgeois-democratic revolution thereby failed to transform into a proletarian revolution.[683]

This should not be taken to mean that there was no attempt in Slovakia to introduce a government of the Soviets. The invasion of Hungarian Bolshevik forces received a surprisingly positive assessment. As a rule, the progressive potential of the resulting Slovak Soviet Republic was never belittled – so much so that Ľudovít Holotík's 1959 article, despite his accusation that the Czechoslovak bourgeoisie acted as agents for the French government during the suppression of the Hungarian revolution, was received as an assault on tradition. Holotík offered a very positive assessment of the revolution itself, lauding Slovak participants for their noble internationalism.[684] Though highly positive, this assessment proved insufficient and became a hindrance to Holotík's career.[685] Readers of Slovak historical publications and later yearbooks of the *Historický Časopis SAV* will note, however, that the Slovak Soviet Republic was rarely mentioned, typically only during major anniversaries.

680 Ľudovít Holotík, *Októbrová revolúcia a národooslobodzovacie hnutie na Slovensku v rokoch 1917-1918,* Bratislava 1958, 121.

681 *Dejiny Slovenska (tézy),* 187-189.

682 See *Slovenská republika rád. Výsledky bádania a spomienky súčasníkov prednesené na vedeckej konferencii v Prešove 8. a 9. Júna 1959,* ed. Michal Dzvoník, Žilina 1959; Michal Dzvoník, *Ohlas Veľkej októbrovej socialistickej revolucie na Slovensku (1918-1919),* Bratislava 1957, passim. Ján Mlynárik holds this last work, and Dzvoník's publications in general, in high esteem, deeming them exceptionally pointed and free of falsifications – Mlynárik, *Diaspora,* 90.

683 Ľudovít Holotík, "Ohlas Veľkej Otóbrovej Socialistickej Revolucie na Slovensku od konca roku 1917 do vzniku ČSR," Historický Časopis SAV 1957, 448. See also: Ľudovít Holotík, *Októbrová revolucia a národnooslobodzovacie hnutie na Slovesku v rokoch 1917-1918,* Bratislava 1958; Ľudovít Holotík, "Vznik Československa a jeho význam pre slovenský národ," *Historický Časopis SAV* 1958, 495.

684 Ľudovít Holotík, "O Slovenskej republike rád roku 1919," *Historický Časopis SAV* 1959, 174. See also Martin Vietor, "K tridsiatemu piatemu výročiu Slovenskej Republiky Rád," *Historický Časopis SAV* 1954.

685 Mlynárik, *Diaspora,* 20.

In Slovakia, the reactionary legend of Piłsudski and the Czech Legions had a counterpart in the legend of one of the founding fathers of the country, Milan Rostislav Štefánik. This tragically departed plane pilot became an iconic figure for Czechoslovakia, serving as proof of the state's rootedness in the actions of the Czech and Slovak bourgeoisie. By referencing Štefánik, the ruling circles of Czechoslovakia attempted to disavow the impact which the Great Socialist October Revolution had on the emergence of the state. The right-wing "Ľudacy," on the other hand, sought to prove that Štefánik pursued independence for Slovakia.[686] Holotík intervened in this debate, contending that Štefánik played an anti-national role, like Masaryk and Beneš. This time, the focus of the debate was not on the person's so-called objective role, but simply on an uncompromising recognition that Czechoslovakia's founding fathers were in fact agents of France.[687]

German historians found that the October Revolution's impact on Germany was far harder to trace. Any attempt to describe the Weimar Republic as a product of the events of 1917 in Petrograd would have been ridiculed. Besides, the German state enjoyed a sizable presence even before that time. There was another problem, too: the Russian revolution had a direct counterpart in German history, the November Revolution of 1918, an unsuccessful, but nonetheless ideologically related event. Alexander Abusch named the *Novemberrevolution* the first stage in a process that culminated in April 1946, when the Communist Party and the social-democratic left joined ranks as the SED. Had such a united party of the working class existed in 1918, the revolution would have succeeded – he asserted.[688]

In spite of several differences with other states within the Communist bloc, the historiography of the GDR also stressed the decisive influence of the Great Socialist October Revolution on the German working class. As Albert Schreiner noted in his anniversary speech, "The impact the Great Socialist October Revolution had on Germany before and after the November Revolution cannot be exhaustively described in a two-hour presentation."[689] In the first issue of the *Zeitschrift für Geschichtswissenschaft*, Heinz Kamnitzer mentioned the October Revolution's influence as one of two discoveries made on the basis of documents studied by Marxists (the other being the contention that, during the

---

686   Ľudovít Holotík, *Štefánikovská legenda a vznik ČSR*, Bratislava 1958, 6, 9 & 326-327.
687   The Marxist assessment of Štefánik was subjected to a scrupulous analysis by Mlynárik, *Diaspora*, 220-243.
688   Abusch, *Der Irrweg*, 282.
689   Albert Schreiner, "Auswirkungen der Großen Sozialistischen Oktoberrevolution auf Deutschland vor und während der Novemberrevolution," *Zeitschrift für Geschichtswissenschaft* 1958, 7.

war, the German ruling classes had no fear but for the German workers.).[690]
News from Russia had sparked a movement that ultimately established the
Bavarian Soviet Republic. Officers on the Eastern Front were powerless to
prevent simple soldiers from fraternising with Russians.[691] Though bourgeois
historiography fabricated a different explanation, it was, in fact, the Russian
revolution that made the workers abandon stations and organize mass strikes.[692]
The involvement of German prisoners of war in the revolution, on the Bolshevik
side, was also of considerable importance.[693]

The November Revolution, however, drew much more focus. Though
Marxist scholars unanimously praised figures such as Karl Liebknecht or Rosa
Luxemburg, the very task of defining the revolution proved highly problematic.
In the first postwar publications, it was considered a proletarian revolution.[694]
Albert Schreiner told the audience of his aforementioned speech that he was
himself led astray as to the nature of the revolution. It was only after he read the
History of the All-Union Communist Party (Bolsheviks): Short Course that he
developed the conviction that the revolution was indeed of bourgeois making.[695]
Yet, when Schreiner shared this personal story with his audience in 1958, the
Short Course was no longer the single, undisputed source of knowledge about
the world. So, already in 1957, right after the thaw, the *Zeitschrift für
Geschichtswissenschaft* initiated a debate on the November Revolution, focusing
on two problems: the class character of the revolution and the assessment of the

---

690   Heinz Kamnitzer & Klaus Mammach, "Aus Dokumenten zur Vorgeschichte der
       deutschen Novemberrevolution," *Zeitschrift für Geschichtswissenschaft* 1953, 810. See
       also: Karl Obermann, "Bemerkungen über die Entwicklung der Arbeiterbewegung in
       Berlin 1916/1917 und ihr Verhältnis zur russischen Februarrevolution und zur Großen
       Sozialistischen Oktoberrevolution," *Zeitschrift für Geschichtswissenschaft* 1957;
       Wolfgang Ruge, "Zur Taktik der deutschen Monopolburgeoisie im Frühjahr und
       Sommer 1919," *Zeitschrift für Geschichtswissenschaft* 1963, 1088.

691   Walter Bartel, "Die Wirkungen der russischen Revolution," *Zeitschrift für
       Geschichtswissenschaft* 1957, 923.

692   Klaus Mammach, "Das erste Echo der Großen Sozialistischen Oktoberrevolution in der
       deutschen Arbeiterklasse im November 1917," *Zeitschrift für Geschichtswissenschaft*
       1957, 1033.

693   See Sonja Striegnitz, "Die aktive Teilnahme ehemaliger deutscher Kriegsgefangener an
       der Oktoberrevolution 1917 und an den Kämpfen des Bürgerkrieges 1918-1922,"
       Zeitschrift für Geschichtswissenschaft 1960.

694   See Lutz Winckler, "Die Novemberrevolution in der Geschichtsschreibung der DDR,"
       Geschichte in Wissenschaft und Unterricht 1970/21, 218.

695   Albert Schreiner, "Auswirkungen der Großen Sozialistischen Oktoberrevolution auf
       Deutschland   vor   und   während   der   Novemberrevolution," *Zeitschrift   für
       Geschichtswissenschaft* 1958, 29.

workers' and peasants' councils' progressive impact (the circumstances of that debate was described in some detail in chapter two). Historians gradually abandoned a radically positive assessment of the revolution, finding it more and more deficient. Peter Hintze stated that the councils had already lost their revolutionary character in December 1918.[696] Roland Bauer claimed that the revolution, though proletarian in its beginnings, was not properly concluded and hence swiftly transformed into a bourgeois movement.[697] Walter Mimtz offered a slightly altered interpretation, acknowledging that a proletarian revolution could not arrive in Germany until the bourgeois revolution was concluded (as we already know, this deficiency was an effect of the events of 1848). The November Revolution was therefore, in a way, doomed to certain limitations, though, of course, the fact that neither the Spartacus League nor the budding Communist Party of Germany was capable of leading working classes to victory was noted as well.[698] Walter Ulbricht closed the debate by condensing the ruminations of the historians into a compromise formula: "In conclusion, we are forced to concede that the November Revolution had a bourgeois-democratic character, yet in some cases it was conducted by proletarian ways and means."[699]

A comparison of Marxist studies on the events of 1917-1920 in Poland, Germany, Bohemia and Slovakia, illustrates the ways in which bits of local history were placed in the context of the superior, revolutionary tradition of the Great Socialist October Revolution. Historians writing in the 1950s had no doubt that the Russian revolution was a special event, progressive in the utmost. Not only was its "superiority" over the founding fathers of the postwar states obvious – its impact on all events, not only in their region of the world, became indisputable. The scheme recurring in the outlines of the history of Poland, Bohemia, and Slovakia (the impact of the Great Socialist October Revolution on the struggle for independence, the reactionary intervention in Russia, the dominance of regressive possessor classes, the glorious engagement of Poles, Czechs and Slovaks on the side of the Red Army) becomes disputed however, if

---

696 Peter Hintze, "Zur Frage des Charakters der Arbeiter und Soldatenräte in der Novemberrevolution 1918, dargestellt am Beispiel der Räte in Mecklenburg," *Zeitschrift für Geschichtswissenschaft* 1957, 264.

697 Roland Bauer, "Zur Einschätzung des Charakters der deutschen Novemberrevolution 1918-1919," *Zeitschrift für Geschichtswissenschaft* 1958, 162-163.

698 Walter Mimtz, "Über den Charakter der Novemberrevolution von 1918/1919 in Deutschland," *Zeitschrift für Geschichtswissenschaft* 1958, 706 i 712.

699 Walter Ulbricht, "Über den Charakter der Novemberrevolution. Rede in der Kommission zur Vorbereitung der Thesen über die Novemberrevolution," *Zeitschrift für Geschichtswissenschaft* 1958, 729.

we consider some of the problems presented by recent German history. The German November Revolution could well be an indigenous reference point and a standard of progressiveness. It had its own mythos, its own martyrs, and its own heirs – this final heritage claimed, as was often repeated, by the GDR.

It seems that it was precisely this potential competition between the November Revolution and the October Revolution that convinced East German historiography to accept, in agreement with the *Short Course*, that the former was not of proletarian, but of bourgeois-democratic character. Interestingly, this amounted to equating it with events such as the formation of the Czechoslovak Republic in 1918, or the revolution of 1848 in Germany and Hungary. Rosa Luxemburg and Karl Liebknecht's revolution was thereby resignified as a link between the early bourgeois revolution (the Hussite movement, the Great Peasants' Revolt, the uprising of the Slovak miners, Khmelnytsky's Uprising) and the "real" October Revolution. It is unlikely that the members of the Spartacus League saw themselves in these terms. That they were thrust into it perfectly illustrates the fact that Marxist-Leninist interpretations of the histories of Germany, Poland, Bohemia, and Slovakia were not a simple continuation of some new current of Marxism, but rather an attempt to read the traditions of national historiographies anew.

Chapter IV
The Marxist History of Historiography

Historians can show varying degrees of deference, honesty, and care toward national histories. Witold Kula accused Polish historiography of the 1950s of lacking respect toward national traditions: "The never-ending collections," he wrote in the allusive *Gusła*, "comprised of Egyptian, Greek, Germanic, or Persian temples, weaponry of different nations, living quarters from all over the globe... That is their attitude toward history. A lumber room for minutiae acquired on the cheap, used for the most part only as ornaments. If plebeians or their chaplains dislike them – as the profane dislike the plebes – the minutiae can be replaced at all times. This lumber room is huge and wealthy."[700]

For the excavation of exhibits from this treasure-trove (or lumber room) to make sense, it has to be subjected to a set of rules. It is these rules, Lucian Boia writes, "[that] bring into history a principle of order, attuned to the necessities and ideals of a particular society."[701] The Czech and Slovak national revival was particularly marked by this sense of self-consciousness, by this need to provide assurance of the necessity of one's existence. This sensation can also be traced in the idea of the reconstitution of an independent Poland or in the idea of German unification (as well as, for example, in pan-Slavist ideology). As Leszek Kołakowski observed, "factual history requires myth."[702] To make sense of history, we need to go beyond it, into the realm of myth. This claim applies not only to national ideas of the 19th century or historiography of the Stalinist period, but also to the achievements of well-known and revered founders of scientific historiography. It also applies to the following introduction to the traditions of historiography – German, Polish, Slovak, and Czech –, as well as to any other attempt at cataloguing the various research approaches, methodological choices, writing styles and positions particular to historians. Sadly, by reducing the creative work of historians to a set of beliefs on subjects of particular interest to posterity, we often lose sight of the most arresting aspect

---

700 Kula, *Wokół*, 386.
701 Lucian Boia, *History and Myth in Romanian Consciousness*, Budapest 2001, 29.
702 Leszek Kołakowski, *The Presence of Myth*, trans. Adam Czerniawski, Chicago: University of Chicago Press, 2001, 32.

of history: the individual historian. In the introductory sub-chapters below, I will for the most part follow the most commonly accepted interpretations of national historiographies' output. I will also pay attention to those elements of 19th and 20th century historians' outlook which, in my opinion, were of particular significance to Marxist historiographies in East Central Europe.

Historiography and the Concept of the State – German Historical Sciences

German historiography is typically represented in two mutually contradictory manners. The first tendency characterizes Marxist studies and, even more, works published in countries which went through a period of German occupation during the war. In this case, authors repeatedly raise accusations of nationalism, racism, or *Großdeutch* arrogance, against German historians (going as far back as Thietmar of Merseburg, the Medieval chronicler of the Slavic-German borderlands), drawing abundantly from an arsenal of arguments and motives formed during the early postwar years. In the GDR, this manner of writing was tinged with a class critique of the bourgeois classics (discussed in more detail in a later section of this chapter). This brand of reflection on German culture persists even now, though nowadays one would be hard-pressed to find examples of it in scientific publications.[703] Representatives of the other approach to German historiography assume that they are dealing with a leading European historiography, a host of exceptional scholars, whose theoretical ruminations inspired the entire continent. In effect, this tendency shifts the burden of analysis from the content and ideas about history to the methodological reflections of German historians. Though the latter tendency seems to promote a far deeper and wiser examination of the conduct of historians, in some cases the division between politics and research is not only hard to achieve, but also pointless. The shape of the German national concept in the 19th century unquestionably affected historiography no less than it did in other countries that will be our focus later. Broadly conceived, politics also explain some of the differences between German historians and their colleagues from other countries in East Central Europe, quite often graduates of the same German universities.

---

703 Among the exceptions are, for example, the activities of several employees of the Masaryk Institute (Masarykův ústav AV ČR), who condemned the supposed nationalism of contemporary German historians and the lack of patriotism in a section of the Czech intelligentsia. Cf. Miloslav Bednář, "Filosofie a historiografie – obtížné zvládání česko-německých dějin," in: *Spory o dějiny I. Sborník kritických textů*, ed. Miloslav Bednář, Praha 1999, 70-80.

These differences were comparatively less pronounced during Enlightenment. At the same time, though, Germans were distinguished by the institutionalisation of historiography to an incomparable degree. While in Poland or Bohemia historical syntheses were produced within closed circles of enlightened favourites at royal and aristocratic courts, often in works resulting from a private or public commission, in Germany science had already become institutionalised in the 18th century. Enlightenment-era historians simply became university professors – they lectured and published course-books. They also enjoyed a numerical superiority over their Eastern counterparts – so much so, that the first commonly acclaimed works of the Enlightenment-era German historiography more often than not focused on countries other than Germany itself. Among other endeavours, August Ludwig Schlözer, a member of the Academy of Sciences and Arts founded by Peter the Great, and the author of *Geschichte von Russland* (History of Russia, 1769), conducted research into the controversial issue of the beginnings of the Kievan Rus', and succeeded in locating sources that supported the claim of the state's Norman origins. His contribution to the development of Russian historiography did not consist solely in setting the standards for the practice of history, but also in sparking the critical reaction of scholars such as Lomonosov, and opening the debate over the so-called Norman theory, a subject prevalent years after East Central Europe became dominated by Marxist methodology.[704] Of note is the fact that the critical edition of the chronicle of Nestor, prepared by Schlözer, preceded analogous editions of source materials on the history of Germany.[705] The first works on lands Germans had inhabited for centuries, such as Livonia, were also written in German.[706]

Another result of this institutionalisation was the preponderance of topics researched by professors from different German universities, spearheaded by the University of Göttingen. Historians such as Schlözer or Johann Christoph Gatterer made attempts at creating syntheses of general history. Other scholars focused on regional history, the history of law, of trade, of art, and so forth. Many of them shared Voltaire's disdain for the *Mordgeschichte*, believing instead that history deserved subjects other than kings and commanders, and objects other than wars.[707] Schlözer's subject of choice was society organised in a state, conceived – typically of historians of the 18th century – entirely in the

---

704 Macůrek, *Dějepisectví*, 216-217.
705 Herbert Butterfield, *Man on his Past*, 56.
706 Hubertus Neuschäffer, "Deutsch-baltische Geschichtsschreibung im 18. Jahrhundert," *Journal of Baltic Studies* 1980/1, 71-77.
707 Grabski, *Dzieje*, 299-300.

abstract, as the perfect safeguard of freedoms of individuals and as the sum of all individuals – a peculiar machine in the service of the people.[708]

Historians of historiography typically associate this shift in perspective, and most of all, the completely new concept of the state, with the Napoleonic Wars. Prussia's humiliating defeat and the French occupation paved the way to ascribe a national character to the philosophy of Herder, to Wilhelm von Humboldt's ruminations on national grammar, or to the collections of songs and legends created by the brothers Grimm. With the *Befreiungskriege* demonstrating German military might, the national past was expected to become a force just as indomitable.[709] Critical editions of sources for the history of Germany began to emerge promptly (the first volume of the *Monumenta Germaniae Historica* was published in 1826). Conceptions of national history of the time often reference the figure of the state as a goal all Germans should have been seeking to attain. The way to this ideal was blocked by the military and spiritual domination of foreigners, who – as Ernst Moritz Arndt noted – first usurped dominion over the country, and then, when finally expelled from it, they ascribed the main roles in European conflict to themselves, completely ignoring the achievements of the Germans.[710] Interestingly, Arndt, a poet and historical writer, believed Germans to be an exception on a European scale: a racially pure nation untainted by alien blood, simply deserving an eminent position in the world (his racial theory was also recalled in later times in the Third Reich).[711] The postulated united German state ceased to be a purely philosophical entity when inspired by the "spirit of the nation."[712]

Ideas developed in Germany throughout the Napoleonic Wars did not immediately dominate local historiography. They were hindered not only by the restoration period's conservative political order, but also by the influence of one of the most distinguished historians, Leopold von Ranke. After the war, this theoretician of the methodology of German historicism was accused of being a "precursor" to Nazism. In a way, the denunciation was paradoxical: the stipulation was that his theological vision of the state, implying its impeccability, was used to justify the Nazi state. For Ranke, history is "God's playground," presided over by Providence, and thus historians should abstain from passing judgment. Indeed, Pieter Geyl observed that Ranke's works are

---

708   Heinrich Ritter von Srbik, *Geist und Geschichte vom deutschen Humanismus bis zur Gegenwart*, vol. 1, Salzburg 1964, 170.

709   G. P. Gooch, *History and Historians in the Nineteenth Century*, London 1952, 60.

710   Ernst Moritz Arndt, *Schriften für und an seine lieben Deutschen*, Leipzig 1845, 409.

711   Ernst Moritz Arndt, *Volk und Staat. Seine Schriften in Auswahl*, ed. Paul Requadt, Stuttgart 1940, passim.

712   von Srbik, *Geist*, 171.

full of understanding for even the most drastic of events.[713] Ranke did not perceive world history as a linear route of development; instead, he assumed that every epoch of humanity is characterised by its own spiritual tendency that it tries to fulfil.[714] As he wrote, "every epoch stands immediately before God, and its worth is measured not according to that which it has left behind, but rather the very fact of its existence."[715]

With all its reverence toward the past, such an approach to history demanded the establishment of a periodisation. Ranke rejected Hegel's philosophy as the epitome of determinism, leaving no room for man's free will, but he did not propose an equally far-reaching conception to match Hegel's theory of the successive stages of human development. He believed that each epoch had its own ideals which we may try to grasp, but without ever managing to organize them in an immutable sequence of successive stages. History is the realm of God: "From the perspective of God's idea," Ranke wrote, "I cannot imagine it in any other way than that humanity carries in itself an inexhaustible multiplicity of possibilities, which surface interchangeably according to a rule we cannot know, more mysterious and elevated than we are accustomed to think it is."[716] The epochal divisions he employed were practically limited to the region of which he believed himself to possess sufficient knowledge to propose a periodisation. As boundary dates, he used events from the history of ancient Greece, Rome, the Holy Roman Empire and France (e.g., the Reformation). In his view, each epoch was marked by a conflict of opposing powers, for example, the German idea of secular rule and the Roman Catholic idea of spiritual rule. It was not the historian's prerogative to side with any of the competing ideas, as their competition and mutual complement to each other provided a necessary stability. There was generally only one event in human history which did not fit into that system because Christianity emerged through God's direct intervention.[717]

Ranke's understanding of history was characterised by a partial return to the broad, general perspective typical of the Enlightenment. The historian would not place the history of his own people at the centre of general history. In accordance with the principle of stability, political events contemporary to the historian were also viewed as if from a distance. Ranke did not perceive the unification of Germany under the aegis of Prussians as the desired "end of

713 Pieter Geyl, *From Ranke to Toynbee. Five Lectures on Historians and Historiographical Problems,* Northampton 1952, 9.
714 Leopold von Ranke, *Historische Meisterwerke,* ed. Horst Michael, Hamburg 1929, 133.
715 Ibidem, 133-134.
716 Ibidem, 135.
717 Ibidem, 142.

history." For him, all of the numerous German states were useful institutions, and he perceived the dominant Austro-Prussian dualism as Germany's strength, not weakness.[718] As a faithful servant of the Prussian king, Ranke was far removed from the idea of any particular European power's continental domination. His moderate views were based on a certain assumption pertaining to foreign policy, a sphere of action which he held in particular esteem. He believed that equilibrium between European powers was historically the key element of stability.[719] In broad syntheses of the history of England and France, which he wrote on the basis of research conducted in foreign archives (he also visited archives in Belgium, Italy, Germany and Spain), he maintained an objective focus, writing – as G.P. Gooch observes – as a European more than a German.[720] Attempting to describe the role Ranke played in German and international historiography, Gooch calls him "the Goethe of history."[721] I find the comparison to a later historian, Fernand Braudel, far more attractive, given that Braudel – in an even broader territorial focus than Ranke – was capable of writing impressive books of true general history, though using economy rather than politics as his frame of reference.

Ranke's objectivity did not consist in withholding the expression of any aspect of the author's convictions, nor in providing a dry list of established facts.[722] His objectivity resulted more probably from the ground rules he set for himself as a historian: the rejection of the idea of a linear narrative of progress and – consequently – a reluctance to express opinion on historical figures and events.

Ranke's influence on German historiography stemmed not solely from his methodological innovations, but also his pedagogical successes. The historian developed new methods for the critical analysis of sources, and the seminar he conducted became a widely replicated model. The success of his students might

---

718 Wilhelm Mommsen, *Stein, Ranke, Bismarck. Ein Beitrag zur politischen und sozialen Bewegung des 19. Jahrhunderts*, München 1954, 89-92.

719 Geyl, *From Ranke*, 8.

720 Gooch, *History*, 87.

721 Ibidem, 97.

722 The fact that this brand of objectivity is sometimes tied to Ranke's name prompted Herbert Butterfield's general observation: "Great historians, indeed, have to be rescued from the cages into which their immediate successors try to confine them; and this is another service that can be performed by the history of historiography. It may even happen that initial misunderstandings about an historian will be greatly magnified through insistent reiteration and careless transmission. A paradoxical example of this is the prolonged currency in this country of the view that Ranke was a historian who had no ideas – and even disapproved of them – desiring to reproduce only 'facts,' only events as they actually happened." – Butterfield, *Man*, 100.

serve as a measure of his achievement: they dominated German historiography even before their teacher's demise.[723]

Nevertheless, Ranke and his pupils faced competition in the guise of liberal-minded historians with diametrically opposed views on objectivity. Karl von Rotteck and Friedrich Christoph Schlosser, as well as Georg Gottfried Gervinus, treated history primarily as a means of character formation. The task of the historian was to point the readers (as well as nations, that is, collective readers) to the proper manners of conduct. The assignment of grades, historical depictions as dictated by the concept of freedom, and a faith in progress found numerous analogies in Romantic historiography outside Germany (among others, in the works of Joachim Lelewel). In the preface to *Weltgeschichte für das deutsche Volk*, Schlosser wrote that "the main task of the author was to represent content, rather than expressing the tone of given period's literature; to excite every free soul through contact with the work, rather than encouraging literary criticism. The author assumed that the free spirit of an unconstrained man can understand this better than the captive mind of the scholar, desirous of glory, and entangled in low pursuits."[724] Gervinus believed that the historian should primarily judge his own times.[725] In history, on the other hand, he saw a combat between the democratic ideas inspired by the spirit of the Reformation and the aristocratic structures, rooted in the Middle Ages and monarchic absolutism.[726]

The youngest of the liberal historians, Georg Gottfried Gervinus, went so far as to define the rightful place of this school in the academic world of Germany in the later 1800s. In his view, Ranke was not political enough, which, in fact, meant that he was a conservative because a lack of bias in historiography inexorably led to the consolidation of the status quo. Another reference point for Gervinus was the so-called Prussian school. Its representatives in the period directly preceding the Springtime of the Peoples, the liberals Friedrich Christoph Dahlmann and Johann Gustav Droysen (who edited the liberal-patriotic *Deutsche Zeitung* together with Gervinus) were in his opinion too political, having been constrained by the Prussian-German authorities whom he himself deemed a military dictatorship.[727]

---

723 Gooch, *History*, 117-120; see also Rudolf Vierhaus, "Ranke und die Anfänge der deutschen Geschichtswissenschaft", in: *Geschichtswissenschaft in Deutschland. Traditionelle Positionen und gegenwärtige Aufgaben*, ed. Bernd Faulenbach, München 1974, 20-25.

724 Friedrich Christoph Schlosser, *Weltgeschichte für das deutsche Volk*, vol. 1, Frankfurt am Main 1844, XXII.

725 Gondolf Hübinger, *Georg Gottfried Gervinus. Historisches Urteil und politische Kritik*, Göttingen 1984, 221.

726 Gooch, *History*, 104.

727 Ibidem, 9 & 220.

The development of the Prussian school, as well as the evolution of some of Ranke's pupils, were strictly related to the program for German unification. The liberals were hoping for a strong state that would safeguard individual freedoms. Many of them pinned their hopes for unification on a Prussia increasing in strength. However, these hopes were very far removed from a liberal program (a fact painfully experienced by delegates to the parliament of 1848). The dilemma faced by liberals pertained to the hierarchy of values – to simplify, one could say that despite persistent support, liberal positions were soundly defeated in 1848, when it transpired that there was no real force capable of enacting the national program. A repository of this necessary force, the conservative Prussia, on the other hand, was (according to numerous liberals) capable of unifying the country. A sizable group of the revolutionary period's nationalist activists decided in the latter 1800s to pin their hopes on the Prussian state, pushing the liberal program to the side. Chief among them were historians. Otto Hinze named this phenomenon "a spiritual process by which the nation of poets and philosophers created for itself a state."[728]

Heinrich von Treitschke, Heinrich von Sybel, Hermann Baumgartner and Wilhelm Dilthey also espoused views different from those of Ranke. While he was more of a moderate conservative from the restoration period, who was attached to the idea of an efficient, enlightened absolutism and the concept of the European balance of power, they opted for national liberalism and criticised his objectivity. Historians of the Prussian school openly expressed a commitment to support the policies of their state. In their view, then, historical objectivity could only mean not falsifying facts. It was perhaps Ranke's successor both at the university and in the role of Prussian state historiographer, Heinrich von Treitschke, and also Sybel (one of Ranke's pupils), who most vehemently rejected Ranke's views in this regard.[729] The latter commented on his tutor: "A historian who endeavours to retreat into an elevated neutrality will irrevocably become soulless and pretentious, and even if he conducts his research in the most thorough manner and expresses his thoughts in the most apt and decorative way, he will never attain the heights of real nature, with its depth, warmth, freedom."[730] The goal of the historian was not objectivity at all, but

---

728 Otto Hintze, *Soziologie und Geschichte. Gesammelte Abhandlungen zur Soziologie, Politik und Theorie der Geschichte*, ed. Gerhard Oestreich, Göttingen 1964, 453.

729 Walter Bußmann, *Treitschke. Sein Welt –und Geschichtsbild*, Göttingen 1952, 201.

730 Heinrich von Sybel, "Über den Stand der neueren deutschen Geschichtsschreibung," in: idem, *Kleine historische Schriften*, vol. 1, 349, quoted in: Jerzy Kałążny, *Opowiadanie historii w niemieckiej refleksji teoretycznohistorycznej i literaturoznawczej od późnego oświecenia do współczesności*, in: *Opowiadanie historii w niemieckiej refleksji*

rather the pursuit of truth. As Johann Gustav Droysen declared, "I do not seek to give more, or less, than a relative truth from *my own* point of view, the one I owe to my fatherland, my religious and political beliefs, and my times. A historian needs to possess the courage to admit his own limitations, as that which is limited is greater and richer that that which is limitless. An objective impartiality ... is inhuman. It is far more human to side with a party."[731]

The difference of opinion between Ranke and the new school of history found perfect illustration in the dispute over German unity, which raged in the 1850s. In *Geschichte der deutschen Kaiserzeit* (1855), Wilhelm Giesebrecht depicted the empire as an oasis of culture in Medieval Europe. He identified the Hohenstaufens' reign as the apogee of German history, stressing the universalist, "European" content of their politics. Giesebrecht was critical of the Saxon dynasty's rule, just as he was of Northern and Eastern Germany's impact on national culture and history. Responding to Giesebrecht's book, Heinrich von Sybel stated that Germany's progress was distorted by expansion into Italy, which wasted the country's potential. The idea was far from new – similar statements were made, for instance, by Johann Gottfried Herder, who wrote that "the finest ... and least important of all jewels for the Germans was the Roman imperial crown; alone, it brought more misery upon the country than all the Tartar, Hungarian and Turkish invasions together. ... The German was cheated by the Italian; in Rome, German emperors and empresses were insulted, while German tyranny defiled Italy."[732] According to Sybel, the only true and proper direction of expansion was the East. Soon, the Austrian professor Julius Ficker joined the dispute, criticising Sybel's political engagement on the side of Prussia. Sybel responded in kind, pointing an accusatory finger at Ficker's pro-Austrian sympathies.[733]

Indeed, the historical practice of representatives of the Prussian school depended on elements of liberal historiography, which were endowed with highly patriotic overtones. Droysen noted that the tendency toward the unification of the state had already existed among the early Hohenzollerns. Through the Reformation, they infused the German national idea with the spirit of Protestantism, which from then on became the determinant of true

---

teoretycznohistorycznej i literaturoznawczej od oświecenia do współczesności, ed. Jerzy Kałążny, Poznań 2003, 24.

731 Quoted in Eberhard Straub, "Vorwort zur Neuauflage", in: Johann Gustav Droysen, *Friedrich I. König von Preußen,* Berlin 2001, V.

732 Johann Gottfried Herder, "Myśli o filozofii dziejów," transl. Jerzy Gałecki, in: *Państwo a społeczeństwo,* 291.

733 Grabski, *Dzieje,* 481-484.

Germanness. Austria, on the other hand, lost its German roots in Catholicism and cosmopolitanism.[734]

In the Prussian state and the German empire, Treitschke saw primarily beauty and might typical of every great country, and particularly of the talented German nation. "The unprejudiced beholder," he wrote, "of the majesty of history will see in the growth of our nation an even progress, so systematic, so certain, that our hearts brim with pride and hope."[735] In the history of Germany, Treitschke saw the transformation process of spiritual powers, which at first found expression in the realm of culture, but then morphed into political, national, Protestant unity under the aegis of the Prussians.[736]

However, the differences between Ranke and the Prussian school did not consist solely in the rejection of Ranke's idea of objectivity. A lack of objectivity was more likely an expression of a far more deep-seated dissimilarity in the understanding of history. One of the major "neo-Rankists," Max Lenz (incidentally, Josef Pekař's teacher), pointed to the idea of German unification as the perfect illustration of these differences. He observed that the national-liberals did not connect their hopes for unification with Prussia out of a desire for any personal gain, but with German interests in mind. After unification, Prussia was expected to melt into the newly-formed national state, losing its distinction. By offering the Hohenzollerns the German crown in 1848, the liberals were therefore seeking to deprive them of the Prussian crown. They operated according to a unanimously accepted national-liberal dogma. For Lenz, this was the understanding of history which Ranke abhorred. In the days when liberalism shaped historical thought, Ranke sided not with the Whigs, but with the Tories.[737]

The fundamental methodological difference between the two perspectives on history lay in an entirely different approach to the idea of historical progress. In his *Historik*, Droysen defined precisely these two mutually contradictory manners of describing the past. The first, where the scholar focuses on the ethical horizon of every epoch and culture, enables the ordering and translation of events and human actions in terms of a particular epoch and culture. The second, toward which Droysen himself was predisposed was based in a search for the moments in the past which anticipated the coming of a new, more

---

734 Droysen, *Friedrich I.*, 169, see also Gooch, *History*, 129.
735 Heinrich Treitschke, *Briefe*, ed. Max Cornicelius 1913-1920, vol. 2, quoted in Bußmann, *Treitschke*, 99.
736 Ulrich Langer, *Heinrich von Treitschke. Politische Biographie eines deutschen Nationalisten*, Düsseldorf 1998, 358.
737 Max Lenz, *Kleine historische Schriften*, München, Berlin 1910, 394-395.

progressive order. Such a perspective allowed for the description of human struggles, victories and failures, on the road toward progress.[738]

Questioning Ranke's methodological assumptions had serious consequences for the historians of the Prussian school. A German-centric vision of history, culminating in the formation of the Reich, did not leave much room for further development toward progress. Generally speaking, the goal was already achieved. At the end of the road stood a German state that was neither the aggregation of individual citizens nor the realisation of their will. This state was the embodiment of freedom – the stronger it got, the more freedom it offered.[739] Hence, national-liberals leaned more and more toward conservatism. The youngest exponent of this approach, Heinrich von Treitschke, once an ardent proponent of English Whig historiography, soon ceased to perceive England as the realisation of his political ideals. "The old Treitschke condemned parliamentary reforms with the same vehemence he had applied in his youth to damning the Tories. Since the British had succumbed to the tyranny of 'public opinion,' the German state evidently offered much more freedom."[740] In a way, the fulfilment of the political objectives of the German national liberals deprived them of their rationale for existence. With the death of Treitschke in 1896, the Prussian school ceased to exist.[741]

From that point on, German historiography came to be dominated by historians who invoked Leopold von Ranke's works and accepted his principle of objectivity.[742] After the unification of Germany, however, his views came to be interpreted in a very peculiar manner. Lenz wrote of Ranke's "objective realism," analogising it to Bismarck's *Realpolitik*.[743] The concept of balanced European empires no longer attracted much interest as an interpretative tool, with Germany tightening its grip on the continent. "Neo-Rankists" apparently borrowed not only from Ranke, but also from the members of the Prussian school.[744] The most significant methodological battle of the late 19th century did

---

738 Johann Gustav Droysen, *Historik. Vorlesungen über Enzyklopädie und Methodologie der Geschichte,* ed. Rudolf Hübner, München 1960, 343.

739 Ibidem, 353.

740 Charles E. McClelland, *The German Historians and England. A Study in Nineteenth-Century Views,* Cambridge 1971, 186.

741 Gooch, *History,* 145.

742 Fritz Hartung, "Otto Hintzes Lebenswerk," in: Otto Hintze, *Staat und Verfassung. Gesammelte Abhandlungen zur allgemeinen Verfassungsgeschichte,* ed. Gerhard Oestreich, Göttingen 1962, 9.

743 Elisabeth Fehrenbach, "Rankerenaissance und Imperialismus in der wilhelminischen Zeit", in: *Geschichtswissenschaft in Deutschland,* 55-56.

744 Ibidem, 65.

not focus on objectivity, however, but on the philosophical basis of historical research: the theory of cognition. Within German historiographic tradition, the commonly accepted view on cognition within the humanities, perhaps most fully expressed in the philosophy of Wilhelm Dilthey, was that it did not proceed in the same way as in the natural sciences. In the humanities, the hermeneut reconstructs the cultural context and interprets the object of his study anew each and every time, thereby approaching its truth. The search for a sense of history or faith in the progress of history belong to the metaphysical sphere, hence both are out of place in the work of the historian.[745] This approach to the humanities ran counter to the philosophical assumptions of positivism, whose impact on the work of German historians grew in significance toward the end of the 19th century.

The *Methodenstreit* between Karl Lamprecht and the "neo-Rankists" to this day remains a sort of model, a reference point for participants in all later historical debates. Lamprecht criticised what he perceived as the basic guidelines of historicism, proposing in its stead a *Kulturgeschichte* – a historical endeavour spreading across all spheres of social and individual life, a total history.[746] In his opinion, the state was not the most fitting (nor actually, the only) object of interest for the historian. Neither did exceptional individuals captivate him: there was no room for the great national heroes in his works, as his exposition was all about materialism. Finally, Lamprecht questioned the possibility of hermeneutic cognition.[747]

Lamprecht aimed his critique straight at Ranke. He asserted that "The time of descriptive historiography is reaching its end, its dominion claimed by evolutionist historiography. Our work is no longer about describing, but about progress: we are facing the transformation of one fundamental rule of research into another."[748] Though he renounced positivism, his theory and statements obviously displayed their positivist inspiration. Characteristic comparisons of historical and biological sciences led him to conclude that the ideal object of

---

745 See Andrzej Miś, *Filozofia współczesna. Główne nurty*, Warszawa 1995, 135-150.

746 The question whether this particular principle of Lamprecht's differed as significantly from Ranke's thought remains unanswered. As Hans Cymorek notes, Ranke would likely offer his support to the concept of *Kulturgeschichte*, while at least a section of neo-Rankists were hardly as methodologically conservative as Lamprecht believed. Hans Cymorek, *Georg von Below und die deutsche Geschichtswissenschaft um 1900*, Stuttgart 1998, 215-219.

747 Roger Chickering, "The Lamprecht Controversy," in: *Historikerkontroversen*, ed. Hartmut Lehmann, Göttingen 2000, 18.

748 Karl Lamprecht, *Alternative zu Ranke. Schriften zur Geschichtstheorie*, ed. Hans Schleier, Leipzig 1988, 137.

study for both is an organism (human or state) in all its spheres of activity. In his view, economic and social history were indelibly tied to the history of art – his source of inspiration for the periodisation of general history. Lamprecht was convinced that all historical events belonged to a causal chain: any suggestion that history might be irrational was soundly rejected.[749]

As I already mentioned, Lamprecht's theses were opposed by the "neo-Rankists," primarily young historians who, in later years, played significant roles in German historiography (Felix Rachfahl, Hermann Oncken, Georg von Below, Friedrich Meinecke). They vehemently criticised both Lamprecht's claims concerning the philosophy of history (rejecting primarily his Western positivism), as well as examples of the unreliability and arbitrariness peppering his works. His divisions of history into eras raised significant doubts because they were unrelated either to the periodisation approved by legal or political historians, but rather rooted in analogies between the history of art and economic history. For instance, Lamprecht wrote of the "intensity" of particular styles of art, which he found comparable to the level of economic development in particular eras. At the same time, he acerbically criticised idealism, dubbing it an "easy" interpretative scheme susceptible to the omission of myriad details shaping the life of societies.[750]

On the face of it, the result of this dispute seemed unequivocal: German academic historiography disowned Lamprecht, proved his reliability lacking in terms of research, and did not exhibit significant interest in his methodological concepts. Still, the reception of Lamprecht's positions abroad was far more positive.[751] Even in Germany, Lamprecht enjoyed a significant impact on the development of regional historiography. His ideas, laying stress on the ethnic community rather than the state and its institutions, were widely referenced in the interwar period. He was cited by representatives of the *Ostforschung*, writing of the cultural achievements of Germans in the East, as well as proponents of the *Westforschung*, raising analogous issues in relation to German-French relations. His concepts were also referenced in the so-called *Volksgeschichte*.[752]

---

749 Ibidem, passim.
750 Ibidem, 258 & 189.
751 Grabski, *Dzieje*, 584-591.
752 Chickering, "The Lamprecht," 26-28. The fact that Lamprecht's works were cited also during the Nazi period obviously cannot be held against him: a historian should not be held accountable for the way posterity makes use of his work. The connection to *Volksgeschichte* is of considerable interest, however, as Lamprecht himself approached pan-Germanic nationalism politically. In these terms, then, one could hardly speak of any "perversion" of the essence of his thought.

There are several issues within German historiographic traditions which could potentially play a significant part in Marxist studies, both in terms of methodology and politics. Marxists could relate to the liberal and patriotic historiography of the early 19th century, Though idealist, this brand of historiography was also dialectical and accepting of the laws of historical progress. The stumbling block in this regard was Leopold von Ranke. On the one hand, his political conservatism – the rejection of linear progress (outside of technical thought), or the assignment of a primary role to foreign policies – were unacceptable in Marxist historiography. On the other hand, the intellectual formation which followed Ranke in German historiography – the Prussian school – rejected Ranke not only in terms of methodological ideas, but also because of their German chauvinism, which Marxists would not assess in favourable terms. Finally, Lamprecht, whose positivist methodology approximated historical materialism to a certain degree, also held extremely right-wing political views. The wealth of German historiographic traditions thus proved to be a huge problem for Marxist-Leninists of the GDR.

Dilemmas of Polish Historiography since the Late 18th Century

German historiography of the 19th and early 20th century was an obvious reference point and inspiration for historians in countries of East Central Europe. Other sources were also in use, of course, such as Romantic historiography – often of French origin – or positivism from France and England, but for the most part, Czech, Slovak and Polish historians (not to mention their numerous peers in the West) looked to Germany as a reference point. Of historiographies that are discussed in this text, only the German fails to conform to the formula devised by Josef Macůrek in relation to Central and Eastern European historical sciences, according to which the only feature distinguishing Eastern European historiographies from their Western counterparts was their backwardness.[753] German historiography was always among the finest of Europe. It was a source for guidelines concerning historical work and criticism, as well as the origin of the idea of the historical seminar. Part of the reason for its success lay with personal connections: many historians from East Central Europe studied in Germany.[754] For numerous writers, German historiography also became an

---

753   Josef Macůrek, *Úvahy o mé vědecké činnosti a vědeckých pracích*, Brno 1998, 91.
754   This subject demands separate treatment. Maciej Janowski writes of the impact Georg Waitz or Robert Mohl had on Michał Bobrzyński, and Waitz alone on Josef Pekař – see Maciej Janowski, "Three historians," *CEU History Department Yearbook* 2001-2002,

adversary in journalistic and scientific debates. Tracing the methodological concepts inspired by German examples (or drawn from the same sources as their German counterparts), one has to keep in mind that the reception of historiography is neither straightforward nor unequivocal. Even if one ignores the obvious fact that every reading may be understood in a myriad of different ways, one cannot (and should not) construe straightforward connections between a Western methodological source and its East Central European counterpart. A difference in political, social and historical relations in each case colours common scientific concepts in a different way. Few historians look to a singular methodological influence – to call someone a "positivist" hardly makes for an exhaustive description. Typically, scholars summon a number of sources, borrowing from, for example, Ranke's concept of progress (or rather, lack thereof), but also from some of the claims made by Lamprecht (this mixture seems prevalent in East Central Europe). Below, I will reflect on different visions of national history as well as detail the context of Polish, Czech and Slovak historiography to a larger extent than previously, while putting methodological concepts (that relate mainly to references from German historiography) in the background.

Polish historians of the Enlightenment era – particularly the most celebrated of them, Adam Naruszewicz – supported a powerful and enlightened centralised government, and wrote their works from the point of view of the state rather than the gentry. Consequently, Naruszewicz found the "absolutist" reign of the Piasts, who held the country in a tight grip, especially arresting and valuable, while the liberties of the gentry and the magnates appeared to him for the most part as a reason for the Commonwealth's demise and as a serious threat to the state's future. In Naruszewicz's opus, the six volumes of the *Historia narodu polskiego* (History of the Polish Nation), published between 1780 and 1786, aside from a professional approach to the issue, rooted in a thorough familiarity with the sources, readers found a political, monarchic program designed as a contingency plan for saving the Commonwealth from total collapse. Naruszewicz, alongside a host of Enlightenment-era thinkers and politicians, abandoned the idea of the nation as limited to the gentry and considered the term

---

222-224. Writing about Palacký, Pekař underlined that the high school in Bratislava Palacký attended was associated with a German Protestant university – cf. Richard Georg Plaschka, *Von Palacký bis Pekař. Geschichtswissenschaft und Nationalbewußtsein bei den Tschechen,* Graz 1955, 11. Czech and Slovak national revivalists (Ján Kollár, Pavol Jozef Šafařík) graduated from the University of Jena; there are numerous similar examples. Mapping of the scientific influence of various German schools of history on Central and Eastern Europe, beyond state borders and national boundaries, seems a fascinating task.

in its political sense, as the totality of landowners. This redefinition of the term "nation" could hardly be called daring; some 18th-century authors suggested far more modern applications. "Nation – is a conglomerate of people sharing a common language, customs and mores, ensconced in a single code of law for all citizens,"[755] wrote Franciszek Salezy Jezierski, who also believed that the Commonwealth would not prosper without returning the once revoked freedom to the people.[756] The remaining portion of the definition quoted above refers to another previously mentioned trait of Enlightenment consciousness: "Nation and the reign of the nation are two separate things, even though it would seem that a nation cannot exist without a country, that is, its habitat, and then, that a country cannot exist without a government."[757] Though in a later section of his work Jezierski drew from the example of the Italians to eventually concede that a nation can persist without a singular state, state and nation remained the main subject of the historical imagination of the creators of the Polish Enlightenment.

Toward the end of the 18th century, historians raised calls for a break with a strictly political history limited to a catalogue of rulers and the wars they conducted. This pushed interest in the meaning of the "nation" and the redefinition of that term to the forefront of historical thought. Naruszewicz included lawmaking, economy, and the development of the sciences among his interests – elements which decisively broadened the field of historical reflection. This new perspective served to highlight Poland's backwardness as well as the potential (including the dormant force of the "nation," regardless of the definition applied) which its rusty state apparatus was unable to fulfil. Only reform, a return to the road of progress, already followed by countries across Europe, could have saved the Polish state. This claim stood in stark contrast with past popular perspectives on the history of the Commonwealth, which saw Poland's exceptional position as a virtue, not a vice – as Stanisław Staszic or Naruszewicz described it.

The brash, Cassandra-like claims championed by Naruszewicz soon proved to have been timely. His prophecies of the Commonwealth's demise under the weight of its own impotence were proven to be true with a painful precision. Even though after the Second Partition, a group of authors promptly produced *O ustanowieniu i upadku Konstytucji polskiej 3 maja 1791* (Of the establishment and collapse of the Polish Constitution of May 3rd 1791), opposing the theory of a self-inflicted fall from grace with unequivocal condemnations of the rapaciousness of the partitioning states (and also a scathing critique of king

---

755   Franciszek Salezy Jezierski, *Wybór pism*, Warszawa 1952, 217.
756   Serejski, *Naród*, 54.
757   Jezierski, *Wybór*, 217.

Stanislaus August's conduct), Naruszewicz's clearly stated question of responsibility for Poland's failure remained for years the basic problem of Polish historiography.

This penchant for assigning responsibility for the demise of the Commonwealth suited the general character of Enlightenment-era works, which viewed history primarily as a material for character formation and education, for depicting the good and bad routes of historical development. The Royal Society of the Friends of Learning (Towarzystwo Królewskie Przyjaciół Nauk), formed in the Duchy of Warsaw (established in 1807), assumed the task of producing a forthcoming history of the Polish nation: "The book of history, whose publication is planned by the Society, will not only contain the most detailed collection of facts, but also a genuine picture of the national character, considered as a source of the nation's rise, consolidation, and decline. National character is understood as the virtues and vices, or rather the good and bad habits, which, like winds pushing a ship, thrust it upon the boundless canvas of the ages, and either raise it to the heights of supreme glory, or plunge it deep into the abyss."[758] Stanisław Staszic perceived the tasks of national history in a similar manner. He saw history as marked by "firm deeds" that had a bearing upon the prospects of a nation, and the task of identifying those deeds was assigned to historiography. Writing in the same year in which the Royal Society of the Friends of Learning published its address, the thinker attempted to trace the events that shaped Polish history. Characteristically, Staszic focused on the demise of Poland rather than the causes of its revival under Napoleonic patronage: "The enfeeblement and impending collapse of monarchic power (while the magnates gained in might), the extension of privileges for the gentry, the repulsion of the people's claims to citizenship and the land, were all an evil growing steadily since Louis of Hungary until the death of Sigismund Augustus. It will be made apparent that even the glory of the reign of the Sigismunds was merely a persisting surface glimmer, reflecting off of past fame and the greatness of the nation. Inside, the political body was ill to the bone."[759]

Of course, the search for the causes of the Commonwealth's demise was not Enlightenment-era historians' only activity. Whether Poland enjoyed limited independence, or even none at all, historians continued to couple their ruminations with efforts to collect national memorabilia, reinforcing the traditions of a country which would reemerge again sometime in the future. A

---

758 "Odezwa Towarzystwa Królewskiego Przyjaciół Nauk w sprawie prospektu historii narodu polskiego" (1809), quoted in *Historycy o historii*, vol. 1, 62.
759 Stanisław Staszic, "Jak powinna być pisana historia Polski" (1809), quoted in *Historycy o historii*, vol. 1, 75.

serious debate over Naruszewicz's claims began only when Joachim Lelewel presented his democratic, Romantic vision of Polish history. The notion of history as a means of character formation was retained, but the consensus of opinions on the causes of Poland's collapse and the prospects for its restitution had changed. One of the most striking differences between Lelewel's interpretation and the convictions of his predecessors was evident in the approach to the state: "At the root of Lelewel's concept of Polish history lay the belief that the republican form of government was the necessary, and also the 'natural' paradigm for unhindered progress."[760] Lelewel, politically a staunch republican, considered rule by the communes as the Slavs' primary and native form of rule (this belief was also shared by the exceptional Czech Romantic historian, František Palacký). Furthermore, according to the historian, not only did this form of government predominate in primordial Slavic communities, but it also served as a basis for the democracy of the gentry. Again, this contention highlights the disparity between Lelewel's and Naruszewicz's claims: instead of serving as proof of the region's backwardness with respect to other countries on the continent, the democracy native to Poland and other Slavic countries signified that "in terms of government, Poland was further ahead than the rest of Europe."[761] This politically backward Europe, however, affected the Commonwealth, causing deviations from the correct course of progress and imposing faulty, or even criminal, feudal rules upon the progressive state.

Lelewel's concept of national history often stood in stark contrast to the conceptions favoured by Enlightenment-era historians. For Lelewel, the reign of the despotic Piasts was a rejection of the ideals of rule by the communes – the Republic ought to have looked to its own past rather than apply experiences of the West. The collapse of the state was caused primarily by the countries that participated in the Partitions, with Poles cast in secondary roles. Lelewel's interpretation of national history had a fundamental political significance both for Polish internal disputes and in the European context. It collected arguments for the democratic outlook of Polish Romanticism, and it nurtured the patriotism of Poles who had been robbed of their own state. It was also a product of an unusual time, when Polish exiles tended to think of themselves as Europe's teachers and guides – whether because they belonged to a nation which experienced a suffering that made them more mature politically, or, as in Mickiewicz's works, because Poland constituted a mystical redeemer for the entirety of humanity, suffering for the sins of all. Lelewel's output also belongs to a period when Poles enjoyed a reputation for heroism in Europe's democratic

---

760   Andrzej Wierzbicki, *Historiografia polska doby romantyzmu*, Wrocław 1999, 310.
761   Ibidem, 313.

circles, an opinion which, by and large, the historian shared, "All nations are bound in one indivisible family; in that family, no one is foreign, all are brothers."[762]

The defeat of the anti-Russian uprising of 1863-1864 marked a breakthrough in Polish intellectual life, opening a new literary era (positivism), and inspiring new readings of national history. Furthermore, the uprising's aftershock was soon compounded by the unparalleled collapse of France, the empire Poles had hoped would aid Poland's political reconstitution as an independent state. Defeated France, forced to defer toward Russia as a necessary safeguard against a possible assault by Bismarck's Germany, ceased to act as an attentive host to Polish political exiles. At the same time, the introduction of a constitutional monarchy in Austria, and especially the granting of autonomy to Galicia, with its two Polish universities, meant that, even before Sedan, moderate Polish émigrés in France were considering siding with the Habsburgs in hopes of attaining at least a partial independence. In Galicia itself, a new current of historical thought, known as the Kraków school, emerged, taking an oppositional stance toward Lelewel (though not unequivocally).

Rev. Walerian Kalinka and Józef Szujski, two historians most frequently named as the founders of the new school (next to Stanisław Smolka and Michał Bobrzyński), embraced the output of the Polish Enlightenment, stressing the firm ties between Polish and general history. Their attitude toward historians of the Romantic era, on the other hand, was far more critical. According to Szujski, the historiographic efforts of Lelewel and his followers were simultaneously unprofessional and overly tendentious: "Nothing is as common as the use of history, especially among us. ... It is used as a weapon – quotidian, commonplace, stitched through with oversize platitudes and supposedly faultless dogmas. According to a fairly widespread belief, national history is completely removed from the currents of general history, a tool that only serves our current aspirations, a humble servant to political views and a boundless source of bombastic dictums."[763]

Historians associated with the Kraków school saw the causes of the demise of the Commonwealth in a similar light as did Naruszewicz or Staszic. In the preface to the book *Ostatnie lata panowania Stanisława Augusta. Dokumenta do historii drugiego i trzeciego podziału* (The final years of the reign of Stanisław August: Documents to the history of the Second and Third Partition, 1868)

---

762   Joachim Lelewel, *Polska; dzieje i rzeczy jej*, vol. 20, Poznań 1864, 421; quoted in Andrzej Wierzbicki, "Lelewel i Ojczyzna," in: *W kręgu historii*, 48.
763   Józef Szujski, "Wstępna prelekcja otwierająca kurs historii polskiej" (1869), quoted in *Historycy o historii*, vol. 1, 143.

Walerian Kalinka wrote: "The source of our political impotence, and therefore, the main, if not the only cause of the collapse, were ... those countless deficiencies of the national character, displayed by and large by the entire ruling class of the time, which found their ultimate embodiment in notorious insolents, from Zborowski and Zebrzydowski down to the last hetmans of the Commonwealth."[764]

The critique which Szujski or Kalinka levelled at Lelewel and his successors only marginally touched upon the problem of methodological principles – or at least, in a manner quite distant from our contemporary perception of it. Though they accused their predecessors of manipulations leading to the exploitation of history for political or philosophical arguments, the works of the earliest exponents of the Kraków school were not entirely devoid of personal opinion. In their critique, the members of the school did not construct a general opposition between an ideological history and an objective history, but rather they condemned a false ideology, demanding that a different philosophical construct take its place. For Szujski, to a far larger extent than for Leopold von Ranke, the emergence of Christianity shaped all other historical processes. It was Christianity that moulded the concept of humanity and the national idea (which is why, Szujski wrote, Greeks and Romans had not constituted distinct nationalities in their time). The rule of history stated that nations transform into states. Poland abandoned this natural route of progress: "In the West, nations die out, leaving states in their wake, but in Poland, the state organism dies in the face of a increasingly self-sufficient nation."[765] Still, with the idea of history rooted in Christianity, one could share the Romantics' hope for independence. Though Szujski thought of the state as a significant factor and desirable entity, he did not profess that its absence must necessarily precipitate the disappearance of a nation: "Only Christian nations share in unending progress and immortality," he wrote, "only Christian nations possess the privilege of constant rebirth, as it is guaranteed to them through the idea, not contained in them, but standing beneath them, an idea that does not age, that always returns with renewed energy: the idea of the reunification of humanity."[766]

Slavs, and Poles in particular, became active participants in world history only when converted to Christianity. Szujski named the Baptism of Poland a "Piast revolution," meaning a reconfiguration of loosely tied lands of the

---

764   Walerian Kalinka, "Ostatnie lata panowania Stanisława Augusta. Dokumenta do historii drugiego i trzeciego podziału [Przedmowa]" (1868), quoted in *Historycy o historii*, vol. 1, 339.
765   Józef Szujski, *O fałszywej historii jako mistrzyni fałszywej polityki. Rozprawy i artykuły*, Warszawa 1991, 43.
766   Ibidem, 25.

Norman Lechites into a Slavic state.[767] In European terms, the Piast state made the right choice in bonding with the Papacy against the barbaric German empire, as well as against the Byzantine civilisation (whose impact Szujski traced also in the Medieval history of Germany). Since the first elective kings, the history of Poland became "a veritable deluge, a muddle of forces and drives consuming one another, a storm of elements which never achieved harmony."[768]

Poland, born with the assumption of Christianity and unhappily torn apart from the proper route of progress, instinctively grasped for some means of renewal. Szujski acknowledged the efforts of the reformers of the Great Diet, and even noted Polish involvement in the Napoleonic epic: "Napoleon seemed destined to replace all the Medieval rubble with the rule of the nation whose greatness elevated him and made him a potentate. Such was the root of inspiration that made Poles join the Legions and die in the ices of Berezina. But every great idea has to mature before it can turn into a reality. Napoleon fell and understood it only in seclusion, on a lonely isle in the Atlantic."[769] According to Szujski, the situation changed only with the failed January Uprising: "Today, with enfranchisement complete, it transpires that conspirators are thoroughly in the wrong, while those who favour normal, organic work are absolutely right!"[770] Szujski stressed the historical analogy between the perversions of the democracy of the gentry and the unceasing irredentism of the post-January Uprising period, between *liberum veto* and *liberum conspiro*: "Just as *liberum veto* turned into Targowica after the Constitution of May 3rd, so *liberum conspiro* after the emancipation of the folk would bring about another [national calamity like Targowica - MG], only in a far scarier form. It is not freedom – it is socialism; it is not independence – it is being devoured by Moscow!"[771]

Neither political conservatism, nor methodological positivism are terms which could exhaustively describe the Kraków school in all of its guises. To a far larger extent, the positivist approach to writing history – whether in the sense of employing modern methods of historical research and an objective analysis of collected material, or in the sense of an acceptance of positivism's philosophical dogmas – applies to the youngest exponent of the school, Michał Bobrzyński. In his interpretation of Polish history, Bobrzyński did not rely solely on a conservative, Catholic worldview, but also on sociological and political analogies between the West and Poland. He believed that "Historians who endeavour to reconstruct an image of the historical progress of humanity from

---

767 Ibidem, 27.
768 Ibidem, 48.
769 Ibidem, 66.
770 Ibidem, 200.
771 Ibidem.

isolated facts, or manifestations of life, must assess and analyse these phenomena by depending on sound scientific bases (i.e., social and political sciences), analysing the social life of man and deciphering the conditions and laws on which it relies."[772] Bobrzyński considered the adjustment of facts to suit worthless philosophical beliefs just as pernicious as the principled rejection of any philosophy of history in order to shape views of the past exclusively on the basis of established facts. In the spirit of his time, just like Karl Lamprecht, Bobrzyński explained his beliefs with resort to natural sciences: "Every historian can be compared to a paleontologist, who dug up some remnants of several prehistoric animals somewhere. He found bones – not a complete skeleton, of course – and also traces of skin and hair. From the remnants, the paleontologist should reconstruct the prehistoric animals and reproduce an image of each of them. If he applies to this work an arbitrary conviction, for example, that the animals of that period were half-fish and half-bird, he will use the excavated remnants of fish and birds to construct bird-fish creatures that never existed. If he should seek to prove that all animals walked in an upright position, he will place all leg pieces at the bottom, beneath the spinal column, like the historian, who claims that Slavic peoples were originally ruled by love and virtue alone with no need for law or punishment, and who reconstructs some contrived, incredible oddities out of the historical traces of those peoples of yore. However, if the learned naturalist endeavours to place those remnants in their original order solely on the basis of a detailed analysis, without any predetermining forethought, he will promptly give up his work. After all, no bone cleaves to another bone so strongly that it always remains stuck there. There were once sinews and flesh between them that have decomposed, and sometimes even bones dissolve. Hence, there is nothing left for him to do but clean every single bone, describe it, put in separate boxes, and fill a whole cabinet with them. What lesson does such science teach?"[773]

Bobrzyński favoured the use of the rules which social sciences had applied to the study of homogeneous entities, primarily nations and states. Analogies to Lamprecht's methodological ideas lead us to believe that in his positive postulates, particularly with relation to the periodisation of history, Bobrzyński operated on a far more solid basis, dividing historical eras according to their forms of government.[774] It seems that the difference between Polish and German positivists (because, in the eyes of their contemporaries, and also later

---

772 Michał Bobrzyński, "W imię prawdy dziejowej" (1879), quoted in Michał Bobrzyński, *Dzieje Polski w zarysie,* ed. Marian Serejski & Andrzej Feliks Grabski, Warszawa 1977, 416.
773 Ibidem, 415.
774 See Janowski, "Three Historians," 203-206.

commentators, both Lamprecht and Bobrzyński, and Josef Pekař also, belong in this group) stems in part from the different recipients of their critiques. Lamprecht tussled with Ranke; and, attempting to create a philosophy of history that could rival historicism, he emphasised the role of all-encompassing theories, enabling the placement of history in a framework of (progressively) successive epochs. Bobrzyński, fighting against the successors of Polish Romanticism, criticised their idealism, their detachment of Poland from historical processes taking place in the West, and their excessive reliance on creating philosophical frameworks for history. Some of his beliefs would perfectly suit Ranke and his followers, rather than Lamprecht. Hence, Bobrzyński belongs among the historians from East Central Europe who responded in a highly creative manner to the various methodological concepts coming from the West, transforming them and enriching them in new contexts.

The application of Bobrzyński's methodological concepts in his magnum opus, *Dzieje Polski w zarysie* (An Outline of the History of Poland), produced an interpretation of history that completely abandoned Romantic ideas, but also differed from the historical interpretations shaped by the Kraków school's elder exponents. Even Bobrzyński's chapter titles betrayed the historian's disposition toward the events described: "The weak and shortsighted policies of Sigismund I forfeit the historical mission of the nation and cause anarchy," "The Reformation: Gentry fails in its battle against anarchy and its pursuit of reform in the Commonwealth," "Return to Catholicism: Sigismund III wastes the fruits of Stephen Batory's hard labour." It was anarchy among the magnates, along with the weakness of the government, that led to the collapse of the Commonwealth. Bobrzyński rejected the idea of Slavic primacy in forming democracy, but lauded all phenomena which tied Poland to Western culture. Even when moralising, the historian did not adopt the overly religious tone typical of the elder representatives of the Kraków school.[775]

The theory of a self-inflicted collapse (authoritatively supported by a positivist science striving for critical objectivity), along with the conservatism and overt Catholicism of the Kraków school historians (with each of those traits present in varying degrees in the outlook of particular exponents) sparked a vehement reaction from those who were incapable of cherishing the liberties available in autonomous Galicia, as well as from those with a strong affinity for a different, less self-critical view of national history. The outrage at Kraków historians' critical analyses of the national past was distinctly palpable in the so-called Warsaw school, formed in the 1870s and 1880s. Its members – such as Tadeusz Korzon and Władysław Smoleński – shared Michał Bobrzyński's belief

---

775 Ibidem, 206-207.

that history is governed by laws which can be unearthed with the use of social sciences, yet, at the same time, they negated Bobrzyński's objectivity in his pursuit of historical truth. Smoleński wrote: "Bobrzyński, like Szujski, is a doctrinaire, merely of a different kind. Szujski desires to bind Catholicism with Medieval scholastics and asceticism in the framework of an absolute monarchy. Bobrzyński, on the other hand, excludes moral and religious rules from politics, and approves of all methods, so long as they curb the people's self-sufficiency and enable a strong government fashioned after the Byzantine model."[776]

The Warsaw historians rejected claims of Poland's self-inflicted demise, proposing in its stead the thesis that Poland engaged in a modernising effort just before the final defeat, undergoing a period of revitalisation, which would have resulted in a new prosperity, were it not for the brutal violence of the states engaged in the Partitions: Russia, Austria, and Prussia. Still, since the Enlightenment, Poland was again on the right track of history and, sooner or later, it would have reclaimed its rightful place among the countries of Europe (this last claim was seldom expressed openly due to limitations instated by Russian censorship).[777] It seems that the conflict between the Warsaw school and the Kraków historians (Bobrzyński in particular) resulted from differences in worldview rather than in methodological approaches. Historians on both sides of the barricade used the same methods of analysis and offered similar critiques of their sources, and they shared similar philosophical beliefs. Criticising Bobrzyński, Smoleński seemed not to notice these similarities, or at least, he considered them less important than the fact that Bobrzyński was a conservative, a Catholic and a high-ranking Austrian official.

At the turn of the century, exchanges between the conservative historians from Kraków and the liberals from Warsaw were replaced by a far more volatile conflict of belief, and the ties between historiography and politics became even more pronounced than before, judging by the categories applied to these disputes. Historians of Polish historiography without hesitation referred to "national-democratic," "conservative," and "socialist" currents in the debate.[778] In more recent studies, divisions among Polish historians are often categorised according to three currents of thought: the traditional and conservative continuation of the Kraków school's historiography; the liberationist current, best represented by Szymon Askenazy; and the nationalist current, with representatives such as Wacław Sobieski and Władysław Konopczyński, among

---

776 Władysław Smoleński, *Szkoły historyczne w Polsce (Główne kierunki poglądów na przeszłość)*, Wrocław 1952, 128.

777 See Grabski, *Zarys*, 139.

778 See Jerzy Maternicki, *Historiografia polska XX wieku, część I lata 1900-1918*, Wrocław 1982, 59.

others.[779] The fact that these divisions relate only marginally to the scientific outlook of the scholars involved highlights a certain deficit at the heart of the Polish history of historiography. It is useful to remember that, at least until the 1970s, Marxist scholars were also unable (or unwilling) to apply any viewpoint to their descriptions of "bourgeois" historiography other than the one rooted in a consideration of their particular worldview.

Wacław Sobieski, one of the outstanding representatives of the nationalist current, described two opposing tendencies in Polish historiography: the optimistic and the pessimistic. The latter was, in his view, represented by Kalinka, Szujski and Bobrzyński, though it found its perfect embodiment in the works of the youngest of the Kraków school historians. "Professor Bobrzyński's stern judgment of our past," wrote Sobieski, "though painful, would never have provoked such a spirited response if it was not for the Russian historians who borrowed from him eagerly and explained his claims in their own way."[780] Władysław Konopczyński offered an even more brutal assessment of the attitudes of the young generation of historians toward Bobrzyński: "I recall how we pored over his audacious arguments on the beneficial role of the great despots – the Louises and Henrys, the Ferdinands and Ivans, on the wisdom of the aristocratic hierarchy which ruled Poland at the time of the Battle of Grunwald, on the ineptitude of the kindly kings and the do-nothing kings.... His schoolbook was a tad too big for us – and too foreign. Thanks to this, some of its lessons were missed. We did not grow to detest Polish history as much as we could have if we had soaked in all the bitterness and loathing toward traditional national sanctities expressed in *The History of Poland*, a text which we took as a confirmation of the poisonous teachings being served to us from the pulpit by the official educator."[781]

Historians criticising Bobrzyński and other exponents of the Kraków school expressed the conviction that history should not only strive toward truth, but also provide the nation with documented reasons for taking pride in one's own past. Critical works by Galician professors became unwitting instruments for the hated Russification, whereas, as Konopczyński asserted in the text cited above, "Nations must defend themselves from others' loathing and self-inflicted dejection."[782] Therefore, in 1890, at the 2nd Convention of Polish Historians, Tadeusz Korzon demanded that Polish historians condemn the Kraków school.

---

779 Grabski, *Zarys*, 147-150; Maternicki, *Historiografia*, 59-59.

780 Wacław Sobieski, "Optymizm i pesymizm w historiografii polskiej" (1908), quoted in *Historycy o historii*, vol. 1, 572.

781 Władysław Konopczyński, "O wartości naszej spuścizny dziejowej" (1918), quoted in: ibidem, 596-597.

782 Ibidem, 597.

Though the Convention ultimately fell short of a complete excommunication of conservative historiography, the first decades of the 20th century brought about an emphatic return to an "optimistic" vision of history. This wave of "conversions" culminated during World War I, when studies of the Polish past were often geared toward justifying the country's existence. As Andrzej F. Grabski asserts, though, nearly all European historiographies of the period exhibit similar tendencies.[783]

Works produced by historians who, unlike Sobieski, were unrelated to the nationalist camp, were also often politically charged. New ideological boundaries between Polish historians replicated the general, national conflict between the biggest political camps – the Piłsudski camp and the National Democrats. Each camp was, in itself, quite heterogeneous, not only in scientific terms, but also in terms of ideology (a proponent of Piłsudski could have had any political background, as the Marshal was the decisive connector). The level of engagement in public service, understood in a highly particular way, also tended to vary: Marceli Handelsman, linked to the Piłsudski camp, accused Szymon Askenazy of fabricating national hagiography.[784] It is a crucial task for the history of Polish historiography to emphasize perspectives other than those of this dichotomous political division. Works of Polish historians of the 20th century also reflect the methodological dilemmas raised by German historians. Early into the century, Stanisław Zakrzewski transferred the Prussian school's concept of the historical significance of "great men" into Polish history, criticising "Lamprechtian" novelties in economic history and associated historical sciences.[785] Polish historians often mentioned cultural history as the most likely future focus of historiography. Marceli Handelsman wrote of the problem of possibility and inescapability in history, which had come to the attention of German historians as well.[786] Stefan Czarnowski, on the other hand, expressed the belief that "to satisfy the task of the historian, it is essential for him to become a sociologist."[787] Conflicts of belief and a given scholar's political orientations were overlaid with various methodological inspirations whose diversity equalled the variety found in other 20th century European countries.

---

783   Grabski, *Zarys*, 153.
784   Józef Dutkiewicz & Krystyna Śreniowska, *Zarys historii historiografii polskiej*, vol. 3., Łódź 1959, 134.
785   Stanisław Zakrzewski, "Kultura historyczna" (1906), quoted in *Historycy o historii*, vol. 1, 526-531.
786   See Marceli Handelsman, "Możliwości i konieczności w procesie historycznym" (1931), quoted in *Historycy o historii*, vol. 2.
787   Stefan Czarnowski, "Metoda socjologiczna a historyczna" (1939), quoted in ibidem, 193.

In other words, the traditional conflict of belief among Polish historians gained a new meaning in the 20th century. The subject of the debate changed as well: scholars no longer focused solely on the causes of the Commonwealth's demise. Andrzej F. Grabski singled out two competing historical orientations in the interwar Polish state: Western and Eastern, or the Piast and Jagiellon camps. The former Western-Piast orientation was dominated by proponents of a nationalist ideology. Aside from elder scholars, whose careers began in the previous century, this camp was represented by younger historians such as Zygmunt Wojciechowski (incidentally an outstanding expert in the history of Medieval law). Proponents of this orientation eagerly addressed subjects such as the beginnings of the Polish state or struggles against the Germans, and were particularly opposed to specific beliefs shared by their German counterparts (e.g. beliefs concerning the German cultural mission in the East). Zygmunt Wojciechowski formulated the concept of "indigenously Polish territories," which were said to match the territories of Poland during the early Piasts. Ideas shared by historians adhering to this camp, in particular the principle of a return to the "natural" borders in the West, dominated the political imagination of Polish politicians during the Nazi occupation.[788] They also played a significant part in the historiography and political propaganda of prewar Poland.

In the interwar period, the "Piastist" doctrine faced opposition in the guise of a strong "Jagiellonian" current represented by historians such as Oskar Halecki or Ludwik Kolankowski. These historians developed different strands within the same historical school. While Halecki's concepts were rooted in the idea of voluntary cooperation between Poland and Lithuania in a federated state, Kolankowski sided with historians who emphasised the Polish role as "Kulturträgers" in relation to Lithuanians, Ukrainians and Belorussians. Hence, the conflict boiling at the heart of this current of Polish historiography was rooted in a discord between scholars who interpreted the Commonwealth as a manifestation of cooperation between independent nations, and those who believed it to have been the product of the political expansion of the Polish state and nation. This was a discord between the historical programs of federation and incorporation.[789]

The interwar period not only shifted the focus of Polish historical debates, but it also sparked a thorough reconstruction of the conditions of scholarly work in history. No longer did historians need to tackle restrictions imposed by occupying governments or evade the grasp of Russian censorship. However, one

---

788 Włodzimierz Borodziej, "Wstęp" in: *Niemcy w Polsce 1945-1950. Wybór dokumentów,* eds. Włodzimierz Borodziej & Hans Lemberg, vol. 1, Warszawa 2000, 46-49.

789 Grabski, *Zarys,* 177-179.

could still be fired for espousing beliefs contradictory to the ideology of the ruling party (which is what happened to Wacław Sobieski, among others). Working conditions undoubtedly improved, primarily in the territories of the Russian partition. Autonomous universities were crowded with students drawn not to corresponding worldviews so much as to historical methodology. These schools were able to offer steady work to exceptional scholars. New schools were formed by Marceli Handelsman, Wacław Tokarz, and Franciszek Bujak; Władysław Konopczyński and Wacław Sobieski were likewise surrounded by pupils. The two former scholars educated a whole string of historians who shaped the image of Polish historiography in the postwar era, for example, such historians as Tadeusz Manteuffel, Marian Henryk Serejski, Stanisław Arnold, Marian Małowist, Wanda Moszczeńska, Aleksander Gieysztor, or Henryk Jabłoński. The interwar decades also witnessed developments in the research of economic history (conducted by Bujak, Jan Rutkowski, Arnold, and Natalia Gąsiorowska-Grabowska). Polish historians could finally enjoy working conditions similar to those which had been available in other more fortunate countries for over a century before, and they promptly began narrowing the methodological distance that had developed under foreign rule. In this respect, the congress of the Comité International des Sciences Historiques which took place in Warsaw in 1933, achieved a symbolic status.

Czech Historiography in the Shadow of the National Revival

The historiography of the Enlightenment period played no less a significant part in meditations on the status of state and nation in Bohemia than the works of Naruszewicz, Kołłątaj, or Staszic did in Poland. Nevertheless, conditions faced by Czech scholars affected the political resonance of their works in a manner different than that traced in the works of Polish historians. During the reform efforts under the reign of Joseph II, historians sided with the gentry of Bohemia in a defence of its class privileges, implicitly opposing a strong, centralised government. The centralisation of power in Vienna would have inevitably led to a restriction of the historical rights of the Kingdom of Bohemia. At the same time, as evident in Mikuláš Adaukt Voigt's *Über den Geist der böhmischen Gesetze* (1788), a defence of these rights paved the way for the formation of a history of the Czech nation as an entity distinct from the other constituent nations of the Habsburg monarchy.[790] In describing any of the currents of the

---

790 Kutnar & Marek, *Přehledné*, 152-155.

19th century's national revivalism, one should remember that the scholar's gaze is inevitably ahistorical. Indeed, it was never a certain or established fact that books devoted to the history of the lands of Bohemia would affect the formation of the nation in the shape it took during the 19th century. The alliance between the aristocrats indifferent to the Czech national idea almost by default and the scientists engaged in furthering the revival lasted almost until the end of the 19th century.[791] Yet, Czech historians had addressed the issue of the Hussite movement already during the Enlightenment, at first depicting it mainly as a protest against the corruption of the Church. František Kutnar and Jaroslav Marek pointed out that Enlightenment thinkers, such as Josef Dobrovský, had not yet embraced the political role that was ascribed to historians during the Romantic period. Dobrovský himself, for instance, did not hesitate before publicising a "patriot's opinion," judging in 1825 that the Manuscript of Zelená Hora was a forgery intended to further the political goals of Czech national movement activists. His personal (highly pessimistic) beliefs on the future of Czech nationality and the Czech language were also unsuited to the program of the burgeoning national movement. The new generation of historians, spearheaded by František Palacký, treated history as a science tied fairly closely to the national cause, and often even subservient to it.[792]

The significance of František Palacký extends well beyond his work as a historian. The "father of the nation" was also a political – at first a moderately liberal, then conservative – leader of the Czech national movement. At the dawn of his political and scientific career, in the 1820s, the movement had barely developed; at his deathbed in 1876, the Czech nation was universally admired (at least in East Central Europe) for achieving a position equal to that of other respected European nations. His funeral established the pattern for Czech national ceremonies of mourning, even though no Czech state yet existed.[793] As a scholar, he shaped a coherent concept of Czech history, which in many aspects retains validity to this day. For later historians, Palacký became a reference point.

The creator of modern Czech historiography did not avoid critically evaluating the Czech national character and consistently strove to identify the

---

791 Jiří Štaif, "Czech Historiography in the 30s to 60s of the 19th Century," in: *Jan Evangelista Purkyně in Science and Culture. Scientific Conference, Prague, August 26, - 30, 1987*, ed. Jaroslav Purš, Praha 1988, 123-126; Miroslav Hroch, *Na prahu národní existence. Touha a skutečnost*, Praha 1999, 75-78.

792 Kutnar & Marek, *Přehledné*, 165.

793 Vladimír Macura, "Poslední slova Františka Palackého," in: *František Palacký 1798/1998. Dějiny a dnešek. Sborník z jubilejní konference*, eds. František Šmahel & Eva Doležalová Praha 1999, 529-530.

deeper significance of Czech history, the historical destiny of Czechs and the human virtues peculiar to the nation. Much like Lelewel's work, his research produced a thesis on the possibilities and necessities of nationhood. In accordance with contemporaneous Romantic historiography, Palacký searched national history for traces of the spirit of freedom. It manifested itself with particular poignancy in two historical moments: the primary Slavic democracy (in this case, Palacký referred to works by Polish historians, Lelewel and Maciejowski),[794] and the Hussite revolution. Palacký devoted far more attention to the Hussite period than to any other period in the history of Bohemia, editing an enormous collection of sources for the history of the 15th century. For him, the Hussite period constituted the only moment in history when Bohemia outpaced Europe in terms of ideological development – when its name came to represent historical progress. Still, Palacký staunchly opposed all religious fanaticism and viewed the cruelties of the Hussite wars as an abomination. In time, his views on the period altered somewhat (in the 1860s, he stressed the Slavic tropes of the Hussite ideology much more emphatically), but his fundamental premises remained basically unchanged.[795]

Palacký was the first Czech historian to attempt to answer the question of the meaning of the history of Bohemia. From his perspective, it lay with Bohemia's confrontation with Germany, a view reflecting his general outlook on history, perceived dialectically as a conflict between opposing terms (body and spirit, democracy and feudalism, etc.).[796] This confrontation developed into an open struggle only very rarely, typically remaining confined to the spiritual sphere, with the peaceful coexistence of both nations unhindered; yet, for Palacký, it remained permanent and indelible.[797] In politics, Palacký, the author of a famous letter to the Frankfurt parliament, established the fundamental distinction between Czechs and Germans with uncommon clarity. The Czech historian was also set apart from numerous idealist and liberal German authors by his interpretation of the German idealists' philosophy of history. While he agreed that the logic of history was defined by the pursuit of freedom, he did not

---

794 Josef Pekař, "Ke sporu o zádruhu staroslovanskou," *Český Časopis Historický* 1900, 243-265.

795 See Petr Čornej, "Ke genezi Palackého pojetí husitství," in: *František Palacký*, 123-135.

796 Karel Štefek stresses that the dialectic put forward by Palacký was not a restatement of the Hegelian concept, and the historian himself was by no means a Hegelian. Characteristically, the disparities between the two thinkers centred on the concept of free will and the capability for action among individuals who, in Palacký's opinion, were not subject to the universal laws of history. In this, Palacký accepted the perspective of Ranke. Karel Štefek, "Palacký a Hegel," in: *František Palacký*, 43-52.

797 Plaschka, *Von Palacký*, 17.

believe this pursuit to have reached its apex in the history of Prussia, nor did he accept that it should end with the realisation of the objectives of the German national movement. Since Germans continued to observe the feudal idea, true freedom should rather be sought in the history and destiny of the Czech Slavs.[798] In the key moment of the history of Bohemia, the Hussite period, Palacký discerned a struggle for freedom of conscience, as well as an iteration of the everlasting Czech-German (and democratic-feudal) conflict.

Palacký's role in shaping Czech national culture is even more impressive for the fact that at the time when he set out to write his works, the existence of a Czech nation was less easily accepted than was the case with the Polish nation. His most significant work appeared first in German (entitled *Geschichte von Böhmen, grösstentheils nach Urkunden und Handschriften*). He only got around to publishing a Czech edition some 12 years later. As a result, the binding of the "Czech cause" to universal values seemed natural and necessary not only to Palacký, but also to many subsequent Czech thinkers.[799]

Palacký's domination of Czech historiography and the popular imagination of the past had already faced challenges in the 19th century – from both political and methodological perspectives. The year 1854 saw the publication of *O synchronické methodě při dějepise rakouském*, written by Václav Vladivoj Tomek Tomek Václav Vladivoj, a former democrat and admirer of Palacký, who became a political conservative following the Springtime of the Peoples. Tomek (incidentally a student of Johann Gustav Droysen) proposed the creation of a history of the Austrian monarchy that would incorporate the national histories of its constituent parts. He defined the task of Austrian (and, by extension, also Czech) historians to be a research project that sought to understand the means by which the state they lived in was formed. Such a supranational perspective allowed Tomek to, for example, consider Ottokar II as the first ruler to ever attempt the unification of the lands of the later monarchy, and, by that same token, he could even include elements unrelated to the traditions of the ruling dynasty among the historical traditions of the state.[800] With regard to the role of the Catholic Church, an issue of particular significance to the Czech national consciousness, Tomek expressed quite a different opinion from that of the national-liberal majority, because he appreciated the role the Church played in integrating Czech society. Furthermore, he saw the Hussite movement as an historical anomaly of fatal

---

798   Štefek, "Palacký," 49.
799   See Piotr Wandycz, "Odrodzenie narodowe i nacjonalizm (XIX-XX wiek)," in: *Historia Europy Środkowo-Wschodniej*, ed. Jerzy Kłoczowski, vol. 2, Lublin 2000, 158.
800   Plaschka, *Von Palacký*, 30-31.

implications, claiming that "Hus ... had abandoned the path of progress which we had followed before his time."[801] Tomek believed that the Hussite movement had caused the decline of the king's power, which had been increasing in the period before the Hussites. Antonín Rezek also favoured strong, centralised governments, while criticising the oligarchic rule of the gentry.[802] Palacký's views were placed under scrutiny from another angle as well, by Josef Kalousek, a devout Catholic of national-liberal persuasion, who defended claims concerning the authenticity of the manuscripts of Zelená Hora and Dvůr Králové. Kalousek considered Hus a Catholic and vehemently opposed all claims that he played a primary role in the Reformation (including those put forward by Palacký).[803]

Czech historiography of the Romantic period faced a different challenge from Jaroslav Goll (who earned his habilitation from the University of Prague in 1875, a year before Palacký's demise). Goll did not seek to frame the entirety of national history with a particular philosophy of history. Neither did he share the conviction that a historian's main task was to shape the tone of public debate. Goll unambiguously supported the legal government, siding with Austro-Hungarian authorities during the First World War (a fact which, after 1918, became a reason for the boycott of Goll by his fellow scientists). He introduced new, German rules for the analysis of sources, laying stress on the precision of their work, which prevented him also from forming his own synthesis of national history. This task was assumed by his students, of which Goll had scores, many of whom dominated Czech historiography up until 1945.[804]

Goll is usually typecast as a positivist, as is his school. In this context, however, "positivism" does not connote a philosophical perspective, but rather the so-called positivist, critical research attitude, with which Goll familiarised himself as a student in Göttingen. As far as his research perspective is concerned, he relied on German historicism, and particularly on Ranke, whose views on the task of the historian he shared.[805] The Czech historian rejected the idea of linear progress (incidentally a crucial aspect of positivist philosophy), opting against the inclusion of elements of sociology into history and

801 Wáclav Wladivoj Tomek, "O stavovských nepokojích v zemích mocnářství rakouského za panování Rudolfa II. a Matyáše (mezi léta 1594 až 1614)," *Časopis Českého Musea* 1854, 240, quoted in Zdeněk Kalista, Josef Pekař, Praha 1994, 174.
802 Plaschka, *Von Palacký*, 51-55.
803 Ibidem, 46-50.
804 Kutnar & Marek, *Přehledné*, 384-399. Among Goll's students were Josef Pekař, Václav Novotný, Josef Šusta, Jaroslav Bidlo, Gustav Friedrich, Kamil Krofta, Julius Glücklich, Rudolf Urbánek and also Zdeněk Nejedlý.
805 Kalista, *Josef Pekař*, 139.

approaching with utmost scepticism the idea of subjecting history to any kind of an overarching philosophy.[806] Like Michał Bobrzyński, among others, he believed that "Ethical values and historical events often go separate ways. Those who find this appalling should not seek solace in history. It teaches us that oftentimes the best plan is the one which is not chosen, that virtue is seldom rewarded. We find the idea of a world that does not improve unedifying, and this is what makes history worthless *ad usum delphini*. By itself, history does not promote optimism, though neither is it pessimistic. Nonetheless, ethics, as far as it is binding to everyone, apply likewise to historians and their work."[807]

Goll's belief in the ethical responsibilities of the historian compelled him to partake in the debate over the authenticity of the falsified manuscripts of Zelená Hora and Dvůr Králové, supposedly discovered in 1816-1818 by Josef Linda and Václav Hanka. In reality, the works were fabricated, most likely by Hanka (in fact, their authenticity had been placed in doubt already by Josef Dobrovský).[808] The contribution of Goll and several other Czech humanists lent the debate a certain gravity, as both manuscripts had already become fundamental readings for the history of literature in Bohemia, and proof of the early existence of a highly developed Czech poetry, as well as of its precedence over German poetry in the use of numerous literary motifs. In his articles on the state of Czech historiography, published in the *Revue Historique*, Goll himself described the situation of those criticising the manuscripts in these words: "Public opinion treats them as heathens. ... Political journals cast them out of the country and call upon the nation to rise in numbers to bear witness to an *auto da fé*."[809] In the end, though, the critics of the manuscripts emerged victorious from this debate.

Jaroslav Goll's favourite student, Josef Pekař, was a historian of very firm views, eager to reinterpret Palacký's canonical theses. Pekař also excelled in economic history, proving his skills by capturing in a single panorama the political events, changes in laws, and accounts of peasant life in the 17th century, combined in a "Lamprechtian" comprehensive picture of the history of the Czech estate of Kost.[810] Finally, he was the staunchest defender of the "purity"

---

806   Ibidem, 140.

807   Jaroslav Goll, "Historický rozbor básní rukopisu Královedvorského" (1886), quoted in Plaschka, *Von Palacký*, 61.

808   Macura, *Znamení*, 151-160.

809   Jaroslav Goll, *Posledních padesát let české práce dějepisné*, Praha 1926, 50.

810   Jaroslav Čechura, "Josef Pekař a Karl Lamprecht," in: *K poctě Jaroslava Marka. Sborník prací k 70. narozeninám prof. dr. Jaroslava Marka,* eds. Lubomír Slezák & Radomír Vlček, Praha 1996, 82.

of Goll's teachings from the concepts propagated by Tomáš Garrigue Masaryk in his new philosophy of history.

Yet Pekař himself proved a none-too-faithful apprentice to his master. As the Czech commentator on the conflict between the neo-Rankists and Lamprecht, while far from repudiating the latter's concepts, he did not recognize historical laws or necessities. Both in his stated views and in his works, however, he included elements of economic history and sociology.[811] Zdeněk Kalista, who compared Lamprecht's views to those of Pekař, concluded that the latter did not treat the "laws of history" as determinative, but explicatory. Things did not have to proceed the way they did, and yet, the aggregation of cultural and developmental phenomena characteristic of a given epoch eventually prevailed and gave a new shape to the world. One could say that in his periodisation, rooted in the distinctions between the periods of the history of art, Pekař borrowed as much from Lamprecht and the positivists, as from Ranke. The latter's role was underlined by the Czech historian's claim that particular epochs should be approached as distinct cultures that were governed by different (or rather, differently apprehended) values and that breathed a different air. These epochs align, as in Lamprecht's works, as links in a chain of stages following one after another in a strictly defined order.[812] In Pekař's dispute with Tomáš Garrigue Masaryk, this distinction between each successive epoch became the bone of contention between the philosopher and the historian.

Masaryk's *Česká otázka*, published in 1895, initiated a debate that lasted many decades, commonly referred to as the dispute over the meaning of Czech history.[813] Thanks to his involvement in the debate over the authenticity of the Zelená Hora and Dvůr Králové manuscripts (on Goll's side – the young Pekař also published a critical analysis of the manuscripts, pointing out anachronistic details concerning his native North Bohemia), Masaryk opened the dispute as a well-known person. He believed that "the history of nations is not the work of coincidence, but the manifestation of a certain plan of Providence, and hence the task of historians and philosophers, the task of every nation, is to fulfil that plan, recognize their place in it and act accordingly … in every line of work, including politics."[814] Masaryk's vision of the history of Bohemia was rooted in Palacký's claims. He contended that, while the Hussite period constituted the seminal moment in the history of Bohemia, the failure of the uprising of the Bohemian estates in 1620 was the result of the decline of Hussite ideals. During

811 Kalista, *Josef Pekař*, 151.
812 Ibidem, 150-153.
813 See *Spor o smysl českých dějin 1895-1938*, ed. Miloš Havelka, Praha 1995.
814 Foreword to the first edition in Tomáš Garrigue Masaryk, *Česká otázka*, Praha 1990.

the dispute, Masaryk pointed to religion as the defining factor in Czech history. The great universal human values once upheld by the Hussites returned to Czech history with the national revivalists of the 19th century.[815]

In his argument, Masaryk committed factual errors, which, together with logical inconsistencies, became the main object of criticism for Jaroslav Goll's followers, and Pekař most of all. The latter pointed out the lack of a direct connection between the Hussite movement of the 15th century and the national revival of the 19th century, indicating that the Czech national revivalists were influenced by German philosophy rather than by the thought of the Bohemian Brethren. In Pekař's eyes, Masaryk's theories were rich in such contentious claims, where facts were subjected to an overarching philosophical concept.[816]

Pekař himself saw nationality as a "leitmotif" of Czech history. As he himself stressed, it was an idea picked up from the thought of Palacký, who perceived the history of Bohemia as the field of struggle between Slavic and German principles. Pekař believed in the continuity of national consciousness in the lands of Bohemia. His nationalism, however, of which he spoke openly, was peculiar in nature. The historian based his political ideas on the concept of historical rights granted to the crown of Bohemia, not on any particular ethnic basis. Hence, he showed no interest whatsoever with respect to Slovakia, and sought to improve relations between the Germans and the Czechs.[817] Up until 1918, he advanced a program for the transformation of the Habsburg monarchy into a federation of states. He hoped that the First World War would bring about the fulfilment of the Czechs' political objectives in the same way that the Austro-Prussian War had resulted in the acceptance of the demands of the Hungarians.[818] Masaryk, on the other hand, derived Bohemia's right to independence from the innate rights of all nations. Kalista writes of Pekař's "creative conservatism"[819] – "creative" because, in political beliefs as much as in historical works, Pekař sought to join rather than divide, to do justice to every component of the national tradition rather than eliminate any of them in the name of "true patriotism." In fact, Pekař defended himself against accusations of nationalism by drawing attention to the way in which Masaryk's concept, supposedly developing national elements from religious ones, lay the foundations for nationalism in the interwar Bohemia.[820] Pekař's adversaries, on

---

815 See Jarosław Kilias, *Naród a idea narodowa. Nacjonalizm T. G. Masaryka*, Warszawa 1998, chapter "Filozofia dziejów."
816 Miloš Havelka: "Spor o smysl českých dějin 1895–1938," in: *Spor o smysl*, 25-26.
817 Kalista, *Josef Pekař*, 71.
818 Josef Pekař, *Na cestě k samostatnosti*, Praha 1993.
819 Ibidem, 74.
820 Havelka, "Spor o smysl," 57.

the other hand, resented not so much his supposed nationalism, as the work he conducted to rehabilitate the period which followed from the Battle of White Mountain, the Baroque period. While Masaryk and his proponents saw that period as an intermission in national history, Pekař recognised the value not only of Baroque art, but also of Czech folk culture of the 17th and 18th centuries. Furthermore, he identified the latter as a source for the 19th century's national revival.

Czech historiography provides us with a particularly striking illustration of a phenomenon most likely relevant, to a greater or smaller extent, to every other country. While, in Bohemia of the early 20th century, history was almost totally dominated by the pupils of Jaroslav Goll and Josef Pekař, the popular imagination of history was shaped more profoundly by the inheritors of the Romantic vision of national history, whether in its original shape defined by Palacký, or in an "ahistorical" version produced by Masaryk. Because of this divergence between academic and popular audiences, the Marxist redefinition of historiographic traditions could take place, so to speak, on two levels. The new historiography could challenge Romantic clichés, thereby siding with critiques from Goll's school (or from the Polish Kraków School). Or, it could approve the vision of history promoted by the Romantics, who, after all, shared many similarities with Marx and Engels in generational and philosophical terms (for example, with respect to the idea of historical progress). Finally, it could also strive to create a new entity, opposed to the entire historiographic edifice inherited from the past.

A History Struggling for the Right to Exist – Slovak Historiography

In the comments on Czech historiography above, a certain crucial aspect of its development, as well as of the development of all Czech culture, was omitted. That aspect is the Slavic idea, defined in the works of two Slovaks who bound their lives and careers to Bohemia: Pavol Jozef Šafarík (or, Pavel Josef Šafařík, in Czech) and Ján Kollár (Jan Kollár). At the same time, both belong to Slovak culture, espousing beliefs which warrant their inclusion in the lineage of Slavophile and pan-Slavic thinkers. At the root of their historiosophical ideas lay the conviction that Slavs were a single nation speaking a single tongue (merely divided into local variants, according to Šafarík). Within the confines of the great Slavic family (both the Czecho-Slovak authors and a plethora of later proponents of the "Slavic idea" repeatedly stressed the numerical strength of this family, totalling about 80 million members in the early 19th century), Czechs and

Slovaks formed a common branch. As Robert Pynsent observed, both the aforementioned graduates of the University of Jena not only developed marginal concepts from Herder's *Ideen zur Philosophie der Geschichte der Menschheit*, but also applied the principles of the German national movement, formulated in the wake of the wars of liberation from Napoleonic oppression, to Slavic realities.[821] The characteristic equation of culturally and linguistically singular Germany with "artificially" divided Slavic peoples counted among the most common observations in the works of the Slavic national revivalists.[822]

In their historiosophy, Šafařík and Kollár attributed the greatest achievements in furthering the progress of humanity to the Slavs. The Slavs' exceptional virtues – their gentleness, as well as the ability to create cultural artefacts – set them apart from violent, primitive German tribes. Kollár went so far as to find Slavs among the inhabitants of ancient Rome, surmising that Latin was merely an ancient Slavic dialect.[823] Meanwhile, Slovaks became something akin to "Slavs in miniature," Upper Hungary being a territory endowed with an immeasurable wealth of Slavic dialects. Just as Slavs in general always fell victim to assaults from their aggressive neighbours, so did the Slovaks suffer from Hungarian oppression. The sense of belonging to a caste of people numbering in the millions fed hopes for retaining one's own nationality, and for figures as poetic as Kollár, it also bred confidence. Besides, Slovak prophets of the Slavic idea kept their spirits high also by remembering Herder's famous sentence on the dearth of opportunities for the Hungarian nation's progress.[824]

Pavol Jozef Šafařík and Ján Kollár occupy a very special place in the history of the Slovak historiography. Their predecessors, a few trained amateurs, typically engaged in disputes over regional issues, writing local histories in Latin, defences of the Slavic language spoken by the inhabitants of Upper Hungary, or tales of the past glory of Great Moravia. The creators of the idea of Slavic reciprocity placed Slovaks in the very broad context of an idealised Slavic land, at the same time picking them out from a specific, real local context. History, however, was not central to Slovak culture because the key problem was language. Historiographic theses became, in a way, subjected to linguistic considerations, while the latter turned into political programs in the context of the Slovak national revival. Kollár and Šafařík were Slovak Protestants, members of a group which treated Czech as a literary language appropriate for liturgical use among Slovaks. There was also a separate cultural

---

821   Robert B. Pynsent, *Pátrání po identitě*, Praha 1996, 76-80.
822   See Josef Jungmann, *Zápisky*, Praha 1998, 78-79.
823   Kutnar & Marek, *Přehledné*, 251-252.
824   Pynsent, *Pátrání*, 85-90.

movement of Slovak Catholics who usually referred to the Slovak language codified by Anton Bernolák. This division was only overcome with the arrival of the Protestant Ľudovít Štúr in the early 1840s.

Though Štúr was not a historian (incidentally, neither were Kollár and Šafarík), his impact on Slovak historiography cannot be exaggerated. On the one hand, he rejected the claim framed by his predecessors who endorsed Slovak-Czech unity, invoking in its stead the idea of Slovak national independence on the basis of a separate language. In time, the success of his attempt at nation-formation transformed him into a "father of the nation," not only in the sense applied to the figure of Palacký, but also as someone who actually "invented" Slovaks (further on, we will discuss numerous examples of this aspect of Štúr's historical significance).

Štúr outlined his beliefs on Slovak history in his book *Starý a nový vek Slovákov* (The Old and New Era of the Slovaks) (manuscript dated 1841), which was written in a conversational tone. He wholeheartedly agreed with his predecessors, who wrote of the might and cultural power of Great Moravia. Nevertheless, it was constantly menaced by the invasive Franks, who insidiously murdered successive Moravian rulers. Štúr even attributed the arrival of the Hungarians to a Frankish plot. The Magyars initially exploited the peace-loving Slovaks, who tried to share some of the spirit of their Christian civilisation with their untamed neighbours. Finally, with the help of Saint Adalbert and missionaries from Bohemia, they succeeded in convincing the Magyars to accept Christianity. According to Štúr, "From that point on, Magyars and Slovaks lived side by side in peace, faithful to a common fatherland. They elected separate kings to administer their lands, treated them with deference and showed unbreakable faith. They led joyous lives, for their country gained in power through the harmony among its citizens."[825] Slovaks continued to excel in their abilities, lawfulness and intelligence; and Štúr devoted a portion of his work to the argument that nearly all Hungarian subjects who had achieved anything of note up until the 19th century had actually been Slovaks. This primacy of Slovaks in all walks of life inevitably incited envy: "The supremacy of Slovaks over the Magyars and the wealth they acquired through diligence sowed envy among the Magyars, who were enraged by their inability to match the Slovaks either in mind, or in riches."[826] This anger – wrote Štúr – lay at the foundation of the plan to rob Slovaks of their former laws and refuse them the right to their own language: to oppress them.

---

825 Ľudovít Štúr, *Wybór pism*, Wrocław 1983, 34.
826 Ibidem, 35.

Starý a nový vek Slovákov, however, was not merely the historiosophic statement of a Slovak revivalist. Štúr's magnum opus, *Das Slawentum und die Welt der Zukunft* (written after the failure of the Springtime of the Peoples and published posthumously in Russian in 1867) pushed to the extreme ideas which Štúr appropriated from Kollár. Maria Bobrownicka, who analysed Štúr's claims very meticulously (and with a healthy dose of criticism) pointed out that his pan-Slavic ideas were bound up with the rejection of culture outside of folklore: "Folklore is ahistorical," writes Bobrownicka, " ... [H]ence, the promotion and entrenchment of Štúr's cultural model in Slovakia resulted in the elimination from native cultural traditions of the ancient literature of the Renaissance, the Baroque and Classical Periods, which had been shaped – due to envelopment in the Latin Kingdom of Hungary – by the philosophy and aesthetics of the European *universum*. Even if the erasure was not definitive, these literary traditions were underappreciated and decidedly impoverished, as if the culture's only role was the conservation of age-old forms of local folklore and the imitation of its elements."[827] This work of the national revivalist was also a manifesto of pan-Slavism. Perhaps dismayed by the defeat of the Slovak political movement of 1848-1849, he transferred his hopes onto Russia, in the expectation of peasant enfranchisement and the extension of the *mir* into aspects of economic life other than agriculture. The Russia he longed for was a state desired by every Slav; hence, he should promptly abandon his independence, embrace Russian as his native tongue and convert to the Orthodox faith.[828] Štúr struck a prophetic note, proclaiming: "One revolution will follow another, and each shall wreak more and more misery upon the Western nations. Successive generations seemingly plunge ever deeper into madness and feebleness."[829] This rather typical pan-Slavic manifest, written from a conservative Russian standpoint rather than from a Slovak perspective, also included a critique of the Poles who "through their light-minded and ineffectual uprisings, through their incessant ties to maleficent foreigners, betrayed the trust of their own native folk. All their history clearly proves that they are unfit for the leadership of all Slavic nations."[830] This leadership was reserved for the noble and modest Russian tsars.[831]

Though Štúr's "final word" was far more pan-Slavic than the ideas of Šafařík or Kollár, he remained a patron for Slovak national and cultural independence. As a historiographer, he enjoyed undisputed primacy for many

827 Bobrownicka, *Narkotyk*, 79.
828 Ibidem, 40.
829 Štúr, *Wybór*, 110.
830 Ibidem, 107.
831 Ibidem, 113.

years, the more so since, faced with oppression from the ruling Hungarian nation, the Slovak national revival continued to focus on the struggle for the preservation of language and culture. The development of historiography was also hindered by the absence of native universities and academic associations (the scientific-cultural Matica slovenská was dissolved in 1875 by Kálmán Tisza's government). Administrative decisions were reinforced by Hungarian "scientific imperialism," manifested in historical publications that wholeheartedly denied Slovaks the status of a nation.[832] They were merely an ethnic conglomerate, primarily formed from the offspring of Czech colonists, Hussite *bratríci* and other minor Slavic groupings. The problem of identifying the primary inhabitants of Slovakia became a fundamental issue for Slovak historiography of the day. Hungarian theories were vehemently opposed by the most accomplished historian of the "matičny period," Franko Víťazoslav Sasinek, who instead offered his own theory claiming that Slovaks inhabited Slovakia since time immemorial, and the seizure of their country by Hungarians was not a conquest, but a voluntary acceptance of the newcomers by the civilised Slovaks: "Since ancient times, Slovaks inhabited the territory they live in now. They lived here as Sarmatians or Quadi, before and after the Vandals, before and after the Goths. They were here before the Huns came, and stayed on after Attila's death. The orphaned Slavic cohorts of the Rugians dominated, but could not eliminate, the Slovak population. After their departure, the Langobards, so to speak, passed the night in Slovakia, but after they were gone, the Slovaks were no longer troubled by anyone else in the shade of the Carpathian Mountains, up until the 9th century."[833]

Scholars who shaped modern Slovak historiography (and decisively affected the social imagination of the past) increased their activities only in the 20th century. The same period saw the development of dominant trends in Slovak politics and national life. An inquisitive analyst of Slovak relations during the interwar period, Henryk Batowski, distinguished four factions (one of them consisting of one person only) in Slovak politics on the eve of the assassination in Sarajevo. Milan Hodža, up until 1914 a close associate of Archduke Franz Ferdinand and a proponent of the transformation of the Habsburg monarchy into a federation of states, after the war joined ranks with the "Hlasist" camp (consisting of activists tied to *Hlas* magazine). They supported the notion of a Czechoslovak state. In 1920, Hodža published *Československý rozkol*, a

---

832   Ján Hučko, "Problematika národnoobranného boja v dielach významných slovenských historikov v rokoch 1895-1918," in: *Slovensko na zčiatku 20. storočia (Spoločnosť, štát a národ v súradnicach doby),* eds. Milan Podrimavsky & Dušan Kováč, Bratislava 1999, 233.
833   Franko Víťazoslav Sasinek, "Slovensko v pradobe," *Slovenský letopis* 1882, 129, quoted in Hučko, „Problematika," 236.

reinterpretation of the Slovak national revival. In his view, the success of Štúr's linguistic endeavour was not the culmination of an organic process that roused a slumbering consciousness, but, rather, it was a political act. He saw it as an attempt at protecting the nation from Magyarisation at the cost of relinquishing Czechoslovak unity and creating a separate nation loyal to the Hungarian state.[834] The "Hlasist" ideology was opposed by the pan-Slavists, such as Svetozár Hurban Vajanský, who, perhaps unwittingly invoking the jargon of Ukrainian nationalist activists, claimed that he would rather see Slovaks "drown in the Russian sea than in the Czech swamp."[835] Finally, Batowski identified a national camp, which in Czechoslovakia was dominated by the clergy of both denominations. Among the antecedents of this particular movement, one could name the prodigious historians, Július Botto and Josef Škultéty, authors of all-encompassing interpretations of Slovak national development.[836] Debates among historians tied to particular political camps inevitably took place in newspaper articles rather than in mass-produced books.

The year 1918 was a turning point for Slovak culture. As Ľubomír Lipták observes, at the moment of Czechoslovakia's formation, the last Slovaks who may have had the opportunity of attending a Slovak high school would have been around 60 years old. Common ignorance concerning the rules of orthography became a serious challenge.[837] "Slovakness" experienced a painful birth. Hungarian monuments were torn down more often at the behest of visitors from Prague than of the locals; the newly-established state holiday commemorating Jan Hus was not appreciated by the Catholic section of the Slovak folk, who saw him merely as a heretic.[838] Paradoxically, this tremendous political upheaval yielded only a minor shift in the views of the most revered elderly Slovak historians.

In his works (primarily *Slováci, vývin ich národného povedomia* from 1906-1910), Botto (1848-1926) depicted the struggle of the national movement against a setting of Magyarisation and the oppression of a people devoid of all support from the intelligentsia. The vision of history he promoted was anti-Hungarian, but also anti-German and anti-Jewish, since Botto accused all those nations of exploiting the Slovak peasant. It was the peasant that bore the brunt of

834 Kutnar & Marek, *Přehledné*, 936-937.
835 Rudolf Chmel, "Kwestia słowacka w XX wieku," in: *Kwestia słowacka*, 12.
836 Henryk Batowski, "Zarys dziejów Słowacji w ostatnim dwudziestoleciu (1918-1937)," in: *Słowacja i Słowacy. Praca zbiorowa*, ed. Władysław Semkowicz, Kraków 1938, 122-124.
837 Ľubomír Lipták, *Changes of Changes. Society and Politics in Slovakia in the 20th Century*, Bratislava 2002, 35.
838 Ibidem, 32.

anti-Habsburg Hungarian uprisings; it was the Slovaks who paid the price for the aggressive politics of Matthias Corvinus. Finally, Botto reinterpreted the Hungarian revolution of 1848 as just another assault on the Slovak people.[839] This history of their nation seen through the lens of its torments left a lasting mark on Slovak historiography, evident even after 1989.[840] Botto authored the popular thesis of a several centuries long interruption in Slovak history. He believed that the "true" history of the Slovaks took place in the 10th century, and then was cut off until reemerging at the dawn of the national revival. The intervening period did not yield anything befitting the name of Slovak history. Paradoxically, this thesis did not suggest a pessimistic interpretation of national history – Botto identified similar discontinuities in the histories of Hungarians and other European nations: "Hungarians have no history between the year 1000 and 1848, just like Slovaks. Ever since the formation of the feudal state, the political nation of Hungary became limited to the landowners."[841]

Škultéty (1853-1948) shared most of Botto's beliefs. Before 1918, he engaged in disputes with his Hungarian peers, invoking the philosophy of Herder as well as the theses and achievements of Štúr.[842] After the formation of Czechoslovakia, he debated the Czechoslovakists, such as Hodža, and a group of Czech professors at the newly-formed University of Jan Ámos Komenský in Bratislava. He pointed out to his rival colleagues that the claim that Slovaks and Czechs were bound by common ethnic origins was a simple restatement of ideas spread by Hungarian propaganda. Before 1918, the claim was used in support of statements denying Slovaks any sedition rights in Upper Hungary; after the formation of Czechoslovakia, it was reinstated in support of the fiction of a "Czechoslovak nation."[843] Škultéty also sought to prove the ethnically Slovak character of Great Moravia. In his opinion, Slovaks and Czechs were divided by too many differences for the nations to be capable of merging. Contrary to Václav Chaloupecký, the Czech lecturer at the university in Bratislava, he believed that the Slovak revival was in no way tied to the Protestant tradition that had cultivated a cultural bond with Bohemia, stating rather that it had arisen due to the personal efforts of the first generations of revivalists, such as Anton Bernolák.[844]

---

839   Hučko, "Problematika," 237-239.
840   Kutnar & Marek, *Přehledné*, 647-648.
841   Július Botto, *Slováci. Vývin ich národného povedomia*, Bratislava 1971, 26.
842   Hučko, "Problematika," 240. See Jozef Škultéty, *Slovanská vzájomnosť v publicistike Jozefa Škultétyho (výber)*, Martin 1998, 22-23.
843   Jozef Škultéty, *Za slovenský život*, Martin 1998, 22.
844   Hučko, „Problematika," 652-654.

Chaloupecký represented official state ideology, providing it with arguments drawn from history and linguistics. In *Staré Slovensko* (published in Bratislava in Czech), he wrote that ancient Slovakia was inhabited by Czechs. In later periods, the language spoken by the locals was influenced by other languages and cultures, without substantially changing the Czech character of Slovakia: "In those olden times, Slovakia belonged geographically to the Czech people and formed a political entity in tandem with Moravia, while also maintaining unity with Western Czech territories in national and linguistic terms. This should not be taken to mean that the language used in the Western parts of Slovakia was devoid of its own unique colouring, yet throughout the Medieval period, as well as later on, for all its nuance, it was still considered a form of Czech, and the people who spoke it were thought of as Czech folk."[845]

In his typology of the political attitudes in Slovakia, Henryk Batowski failed to mention any intellectual current that supported the idea of tying Slovakia's national future to the Hungarian state. In fact, after 1918, such attitudes virtually disappeared from the national discourse. Activists pursuing an autonomous status for Slovakia within a reestablished Hungary simply moved to Hungary and became engaged in revisionist propaganda efforts there.[846] Foremost among the supporters of this current before 1914 was Samuel Czambel. He called upon Hungarian authorities to undermine Czech influence in Slovakia by supporting the development of Slovak nationhood. According to his philological theory, Slovaks belonged to the ranks of the Southern Slavs, having emerged from the South to claim territories heretofore inhabited by Polish tribes. While there was no room for any talk of a Czecho-Slovak kinship within this concept, the national policy of pre-Trianon Hungary rendered the formation of any Slovak sense of authentic belonging to the Crown of St. Stephen virtually impossible.[847]

The troubling conditions of Slovak historiography's development played a crucial role in delaying the impact of modern methodology (which was observable in Bohemia since the beginnings of Jaroslav Goll's activity) until after 1918. It was precisely the interwar period that saw the beginning of the scholarly work of Daniel Rapant, a figure whose prominence in Slovak historical sciences did not diminish even during the 1950s, when, after having declined subjection to Marxist methodology and Communist politics, the historian was pushed to the margins. Rapant rejected the idea of a Czechoslovak nation, claiming that Czechs and Slovaks had formed separate nationalities "since always." The historian's magnum opus was the monumental *Slovenské*

845   Václav Chaloupecký, *Staré Slovensko*, Bratislava 1923, 273.
846   Batowski, „Zarys," 162.
847   Kutnar & Marek, *Přehledné*, 650-651.

povstanie roku 1848-1849. Dejiny a dokumenty (1935-1972), supplemented by numerous shorter monographs and academic and popular articles. Relying on a rich and well-developed collection of sources (a starkly distinguishing feature vis-à-vis most of his predecessors), Rapant painted the Slovak uprising of 1848 as an eminently just struggle for liberty, even though it had been conducted hand in hand with the Habsburg army. This high esteem regarding the uprising resulted, in part, from his interpretation of the Hungarian revolution as a movement geared toward the maintenance of feudal relations and nationalist oppression rather than an upheaval meant to bring democracy to the Slovaks.[848] At the same time, the scholar rejected the tearful vision of national history put forward by Botto. He believed that Slovaks had been proven to be capable of forming their own state not only through the part they played in shaping Great Moravia, but also through their contribution to the formation of the Medieval Kingdom of Hungary.[849] One should add that Rapant's scholarly qualifications were also evident in his 1952 book on the peasant uprising of 1831.[850] Though the author found himself under fire from Marxists because he did not discuss the social significance of the uprising sufficiently, he did not come close to claiming that the peasant revolts had national significance for the Slovaks, despite the fact that such an argument would have supported his own argument about the strength of the national spirit in Slovakia.[851] Rapant sought above all to conduct himself in a professional manner, which was not a characteristic which his predecessors would have pursued as essential for themselves.

***

One of the most urgent problems for Polish, Czech, Slovak, and East German historiographies of the 1950s was the critical evaluation of modern national historical science from its beginnings in the Enlightenment to the final years of the interwar period. Researchers were supposed to find their way between two extremes: a total rejection of the older historiography and a 'positive' search for a progressive historiographical tradition. One of the few Polish interwar Marxists, Wanda Moszczeńska (1896–1974), called it a "dialectical negation" of

---

848 See Daniel Rapant, "Madziaryzacja, Trianon, rewizja i demokracja" (1930), in: *Kwestia słowacka*, 98-103.

849 Daniel Rapant, "Słowacy w historii. Retrospektywa i perspektywy (Przyczynek do filozofii i sensu słowackiej historii)" (1967), ibidem, 407-408.

850 Daniel Rapant, *Sedliacke povstanie na východnom Slovensku r. 1831*, 2 vols., Bratislava 1952.

851 Ladislav Tajták, "Prínos D. Rapanta vo výskume vychodoslovenského sedliackeho povstania v roku 1831," in: *Historik Daniel Rapant – život a dielo (1897-1988-1997)*, eds. Richard Marsina et al., Martin 1998, 171.

the pre-Communist heritage.[852] As a matter of fact, what Marxists were expected to do was simply to build up a new school in national history through suitably selected predecessors. The following remarks refer to the Marxist-Leninist history of historiography in the so-called Stalinist period.

While describing the various attitudes towards pre-Marxist historiographical traditions, one should not overlook some differences between the respective national and political contexts. First of all, the frequency and sharpness of historical debates were more pronounced in the Polish and East German cases than in the Czech or Slovak Marxist-Leninist historical sciences (although the period under scrutiny was much shorter in Poland than in other countries). Czech and Slovak Marxist interpretations of the national past, in contrast, borrowed a great deal from the traditional stock of liberal-nationalist ideas; this influence was present in Czech culture since the first edition of František Palacký's magisterial historical work, while the origins of the Slovak heritage had been linked to Ľudovít Štúr's national movement program. One should not assume, however, that Czech and Slovak attitudes towards the history of historiography were 'national' in the same way.[853] Meanwhile, neither the German, nor the Polish Marxists, followed their own liberal-nationalist tradition so explicitly. In these two cases one can observe a hesitation over recognition of various historical traditions, which led to more frequent and sharper ideological confrontations among Marxist historians. It should also be mentioned that interest in the history of historiography in the 1950s seems to have been more evident in the Polish case than in any other of the four previously mentioned historiographies. The number of Polish Marxist publications devoted to this issue was substantially higher than in the GDR or in Czechoslovakia.

Marxists dealing with the history of historiography faced several important problems of a methodological, cultural, and political nature. The first set of problems related to the translation of historiographical traditions into the language of Marxism-Leninism. In this regard, 19th century historians were transferred from their original cultural and scientific context and transposed onto a different theoretical frame. They were interrogated with ahistorical questions from the point of view of Soviet Marxism, not from the point of view of their own times or the history of historiography.

---

852 Wanda Moszczeńska, "Stosunek do dorobku dawnej historiografii polskiej," in: *Pierwsza Konferencja*, vol. 1, 91.

853 I analysed similarities between Czech liberal-nationalist traditions and the Marxist interpretation of national history in the article: "Past in the Future. National Tradition and Czechoslovak Marxist Historiography," *European Review of History-Revue européenne d'Histoire* no. 1 (2003).

The second group of problems may be described as geopolitical, as has been illustrated in the previous chapter. This is probably the easiest to understand and, in many cases, clearly leads to an obvious conclusion: Marxist historiographies in East Central Europe often praised those historical phenomena that were pro-Russian without paying much attention to their social or political context. Thus the conservative pan-Slavists were less problematic than the anti-tsarist democrats. Even Marx and Engels could be wrong in those moments when they criticised or neglected the historical role of Russia.

Finally, the third set of problems refers to the role of 19th century nationalism. Since Marxist-Leninist historiographies in East Central Europe never adopted a radical Pokrovski-type 'Bolshevik' historiography with all its anational and anti-national features, they remained deeply indebted to the national traditions shaped by such personalities as Palacký, Lelewel, Štúr, the Prussian school, or the Warsaw and Kraków positivists. In fact, it would have been drastic to sever the ties that had bound Marxist historians with the tradition of national movements, and none of the examined historiographies seriously dared to undertake such extreme measures. Gradually they became more and more 'nationalist,' but even in their beginnings, in the 1950s, one could find many traces of continuity between the older historiographical tradition and the new methodological trend.

In the following considerations, I will present some sample problems illustrating the interferences of different methodological traditions, political affiliations, and interpersonal relations in the Polish, East German, Czech, and Slovak history of historiography. I concentrate on two main problems: different attitudes towards each nation's tradition of national historiography, as well as the main methodological problems of Marxism in the debates on East Central European historiographies. Finally, I will try to select and describe several elements that were present in every Marxist history of historiography and that shaped the academic landscape of the 1950s and early 1960s.

Poland: Criteria of Progressiveness and Pan-Slavism

Assessing historiographical traditions was not only a difficult task, but proved to be a very complex topic and thus probably the only one that would occasion a broader discussion in Polish historiography of the 1950s. Marxists were supposed to look upon 19th century historians from at least three different angles. The first issue was the evaluation of the political sympathies of the historians, and their attitudes towards progressive ideologies of their time. Second came the evaluation of their work in both methodological and factual contexts. Finally, it was deemed necessary to characterize not only particular individuals, but also the ideologies they had subscribed to, and to locate them in the established theoretical framework of socio-economic formations. This attitude towards history seemed quite natural for the representatives of Marxist ideology. As the Soviet Medievalist Evgenii A. Kosminskii put it, "from the Marxist point of view, historiography is just one of the disciplines of the history of social thought, and it is therefore always clearly and closely connected with politics. By various alternating visible and invisible means, bourgeois ideology is able to infiltrate historiography together with those achievements of bourgeois historiography which we both appreciate and make use of."[854]

To characterize the effects of new interpretative efforts, we shall focus upon a few crucial questions. Starting from the Polish example, we will see the way Marxist historians characterised one of the most important Polish scholars of the 19th century, Joachim Lelewel, and another Romantic historian, the far less known Polish Slavist and pan-Slavist, Zorian Dołęga Chodakowski. Later we will focus on Marxist interpretations of the forerunner of positivist historiography, Karol Boromeusz Hoffman, and of the two historical 'liberal' schools of the second half of 19th century: the so called Kraków and Warsaw schools. What is important to note is that all the scholars under discussion belonged to a small group of Marxist historians from the 1950s who did not belong with the majority of Polish scholars. Thus, the controversies surrounding their work reflect—so to speak—the internal debates of certain scientific collectives and not a hegemonic act of dominance over the non-Marxist milieu.[855]

Joachim Lelewel, perceived as the first Polish professional historian and author of the Romantic interpretation of Polish history, was also a democratic politician. The first postwar Marxist opinions on this friend of Marx and Engels were positive. A leading Stalinist historian and author of the first Communist guidelines for schools, Żanna Kormanowa, characterised him in 1946 as an exemplary progressive democrat.[856] The same opinion was officially accepted by representatives of Polish scholars in the humanities gathered at the First Congress of Polish Science (I Kongres Nauki Polskiej) in Warsaw in 1949. The

---

854 Evgenii A. Kosminskii, *Istoriografiia srednykh vekov (V v. – seredina XIX v.)*, Moscow 1963, 7; quoted after: Rafał Stobiecki, "Between Continuity and Discontinuity: A Few Comments on the Post-war Development of Polish Historical Research," *Zeitschrift für Ostmitteleuropa-Forschung* 2 (2001), 128.

855 I refer to the phenomenon of "Denkkollektiv" as described by Ludwik Fleck in his *Entstehung und Entwicklung einer wissenschaftlichen Tatsache. Einführung in die Lehre vom Denkstil*, Basel 1935.

856 Kormanowa, *Joachim Lelewel*, 6.

1950s brought several editions of Lelewel's writings, which constantly manipulated his texts to achieve the picture of a relentless fighter for social progress. His theory of ancient Slavic democracy as well as his internationalism and sympathy for the peasantry were highly appreciated.

However, as Marxist researchers analysed Lelewel's opinions more deeply, they identified more limitations to his 'progressivism'. For example, praising the democratic heritage of the Slavic past, Lelewel came to the conclusion that the democracy of the Polish gentry was a progressive phenomenon. Thus Marxist historians could rightly accuse him of ignoring the exploitation of the peasants that characterised the period. Even more important, Lelewel was not ready to recognize the rights of Ukrainians and Belorussians to foster national development (we should also mention that Polish democrats shared this erroneous position also with Marx and Engels). But the most problematic aspects of his biography were his critical attitudes towards Russia and his supposedly insufficient political radicalism. The most ill-fitting criticism of Lelewel can be found in a book by Celina Bobińska, *Marks i Engels a sprawy polskie do osiemdziesiątych lat XIX wieku* (Marx, Engels, and the Polish question until the 1880s), published in 1954. The historian, closely linked to the Party leadership, described Lelewel as a man "unable to decide," a "liberal-opportunist" if not clearly a reactionary politician. Disregarding the Polish national tradition and even Marx and Engels, she had attempted to prove that the Romantic historian's "two great friends" had made a mistake in their appreciation of him, and did not realize that he was not "worthy of their friendship." Only Marxist historiography was able to judge historians properly.[857] Other critical remarks of Polish Marxist historians targeted the fact that Lelewel was not a Marxist.

Relatively little attention was paid to other historians of the Polish Romantic tradition, more or less influenced by Lelewel. Perhaps the only exception is the particularly interesting case of Zorian Dołęga Chodakowski, who became the object of an article published in 1955 in *Kwartalnik Historyczny* by Andrzej Poppe.[858] The author stressed Chodakowski's democratic and pro-Russian opinions, incorporated him into the group of progressive heirs to the Polish Enlightenment and described him as a forerunner of revolutionary democratic historiography. Poppe pointed to Lelewel's unparalleled influence on Chodakowski, which seems unlikely, especially if we take into consideration the fact that Chodakowski was older than Lelewel and died before the publication of

---

857 Bobińska, *Marks*, 32.
858 Andrzej Poppe, "U źródeł postępowej historiografii szlacheckiego rewolucjonizmu: Zorian Dołęga Chodakowski (1784-1825)," *Kwartalnik Historyczny* 1955, 27–40.

the most important and popular works of the Romantic historian. Nonetheless, Poppe claimed that almost every progressive feature of Chodakowski's ideology was borrowed from Lelewel. Furthermore, all limitations in the works of the Polish Slavist were also attributed to Lelewel's influence. An attentive reader of the article might have had the impression that Poppe was trying to prove that while Chodakowski's virtues were his own achievement, it was Lelewel who was responsible for all his ideological shortcomings.

A comparison of the official attitude towards these two historians allows one to conclude that, in the case of the almost forgotten Chodakowski, it was easier to include him in the category of "progressive traditions" than had been the case with the popular writer and influential politician Joachim Lelewel. The fact that Lelewel was a democrat, and Chodakowski a conservative Slavophile, was no obstacle. On the contrary, sometimes it was possible to be a reactionary thinker who in some aspects "objectively" represented progress; in fact, it could be preferable to being a "progressive" ideologist who made inexcusable mistakes. At the same time, this comparison shows how one's attitude towards Russia became the basic criterion of Marxist evaluation. Both of these observations on Marxist research in the field of historiography will prove useful in further discussion.

In 1953, the leader of a group of Marxist historians from Łódź, Marian Serejski, published a study on the liberal historian Karol Boromeusz Hoffman, who had been a representative of the 19th century liberal-conservative wing of the Polish Great Emigration and a forerunner of positivist historical research.[859] According to Serejski, Hoffman was not only a better, more professional historian than Lelewel, but also a representative of another stage of social progress (from the period of late feudalism to early capitalism). At the same time Serejski openly admitted Hoffman's political liberalism and social conservatism and acknowledged that his ideology became reactionary in the late 19th century. Nevertheless, at this particular stage Hoffman played a progressive role as a follower, and also as a critic, of Lelewel's philosophy of history.

Serejski's book was strongly criticised by the Warsaw sociologist Nina Assorodobraj for having judged Lelewel unfairly. She accused Serejski of 'sociologism'—a serious methodological error. According to Assorodobraj, Hoffman could not be progressive and reactionary at the same time. He was actually always hostile towards the idea of agrarian revolution, the only progressive Polish ideology of his times. These conclusions led Assorodobraj to raise the theoretical problem of 'objective' and 'subjective' criteria of progress. In short, Assorodobraj stated that not every change brings progress. If a liberal

859   Marian H. Serejski, *Studia nad historiografią Polski, Cz. I, K. B. Hoffman*, Łódź 1953.

thinker lays foundations for the development of capitalism, he remains a liberal and capitalist despite the fact that what follows capitalism in its late phase is socialist revolution. In fact, his activity may be interpreted as an attempt to repair and preserve an existing social order; thus his activities might have been more dangerous than open feudal reaction. Finally Assorodobraj compared Serejski's picture of Hoffman to a hypothetical monument to a landowner who had introduced new capitalist methods, improving the productivity of his estate. Her article ends with the following statement: "People's Poland draws from the progressive traditions of the Polish nation. It will not draw from Hoffman."[860]

The methodological discussion begun by Nina Assorodobraj soon continued far beyond the biography of Karol Boromeusz Hoffman. The next point of contention was the Marxist-Leninist reassessment of the so-called Warsaw school of history: liberal historians from the Russian part of Poland who opposed the conservative Kraków school which had become influential after the fall of the January Uprising (1863–1864). Serejski described the leading Warsaw positivist scholar Władysław Smoleński as an anti-clerical and highly 'progressive' follower of Lelewel. According to Serejski, both Smoleński and the entire Warsaw school should have been incorporated into progressive national traditions, despite various limitations.[861] Rather than Nina Assorodobraj, it was Celina Bobińska who criticised Serejski's "attempts to fabricate a progressive political biography of Smoleński."[862] In her view, positivism belonged to the ideologies of reaction, along with positivist historiography and the positivist Smoleński.

Marian Henryk Serejski decided to express his disagreement with Bobińska's critical remarks openly and published a polemical article in *Kwartalnik Historyczny*.[863] He questioned the very idea whether there was, after the fall of the January Uprising, any possibility of an agrarian revolution in Polish lands. This fact—Serejski claimed—placed limitations on the possible progressiveness of the liberal bourgeoisie. To reinforce his arguments, the historian built an analogy between the Warsaw school and a group of liberal Russian historians from the same period. According to Serejski, the Poles were

---

860 Nina Assorodobraj, "W sprawie kryterium postępowości w historii historiografii (z powodu książki M. Serejskiego o K. Hoffmanie)," *Kwartalnik Historyczny* 1953, 186.
861 Marian H. Serejski, in Władysław Smoleński, *Szkoły historyczne w Polsce (Główne kierunki poglądów na przeszłość)*, Wrocław 1952.
862 Celina Bobińska, "Spór o ujęcie pozytywizmu i historyków pozytywistów. W związku ze wstępem do reedycji W. Smoleńskiego *Szkół historycznych*," *Kwartalnik Historyczny* 1954, 187.
863 Marian H. Serejski, "Miejsce pozytywistycznej szkoły warszawskiej w historiografii polskiej XIX stulecia,," *Kwartalnik Historyczny* 1955.

as progressive as their Russian contemporaries. In turn, Serejski criticised Bobińska's attitude towards the youngest representative of the conservative Kraków school, Michał Bobrzyński. Bobińska praised the former governor of Galicia for his methodological achievements, especially his usage of sociological research in an attempt to establish universal principles of social development, which—according to her—was very close to Marxist methodology. During the First Congress of Polish Science, Bobińska even went so far as to assert that openly conservative historiography—above all the Kraków school—was in a way much less problematic for Marxist researchers since they did not need to unmask it, whereas liberal historiography required a new critical Marxist examination.[864]

The debate possessed an interpersonal dimension as well. In 1956, several days before the massacre of the Poznań workers, a meeting of the scientific board of Institute of History of the Polish Academy of Sciences took place. Marian Henryk Serejski claimed that Nina Assorodobraj and Celina Bobińska had conducted a political campaign against him.[865] Bobińska answered that her polemic with Serejski was a "normal" scientific discussion (a rarity under Stalinism), and had nothing to do with politics.[866] The continuation of the personal conflict between Serejski and Assorodobraj was even more embarrassing. In 1958, Serejski published a book on Joachim Lelewel for which he was accused of plagiarism by Assorodobraj. This personal conflict did not reach any final conclusion. The deterioration of the quality of scientific debate to this level of personal animus did not stimulate the growth of a new, homogenous interpretation of Polish 19th century historiography.

Describing these controversies helps us to draw a schema of Marxist attitudes towards Polish historiographical traditions. Despite the scarcity of historical debates in the Stalinist period, in general, historiography inspired broad controversies. None of the Polish Marxists managed to create a general vision of the shortcomings and achievements of past historians. Different, often contradictory, interpretations divided the already numerically small group of Polish Marxists. Serejski, Bobińska, Assorodobraj, and Żanna Kormanowa were all representatives of largely the same methodological tendency among leftist scholars, but the conflicts and controversies between them made it impossible to create a 'common front' against non-Marxist historians. The effect was discouraging from the point of view of Communist authorities. Neither Lelewel,

864 See: Celina Bobińska on the 1st Congress of Polish Science, *Kwartalnik Historyczny* 1951, 404.
865 Archiwum Instytutu Historii PAN, 5/26 Protokoły Rady Naukowej 1956-1959 – Protokół z posiedzenia Rady Naukowej IH PAN, 25 VI 1956.
866 Ibidem, Protokół nr 15 z posiedzenia Rady Naukowej IH PAN, 15 XII 1956.

Hoffman, Smoleński, nor Bobrzyński could be seen as a part of a Polish progressive tradition. Instead of a clear vision of the Polish history of historiography, Marxist historians contributed another chapter to the traditional debates shaped by their 'bourgeois' colleagues.

Czechoslovakia: Defence of the Founding Fathers

In many respects the founding father of Czech historiography, František Palacký, can be seen as a Czech counterpart to Lelewel. Like the Pole, he was a national political leader. His vision of national history is generally perceived as Romantic. They both shared the belief in an ancient Slavic democracy, the "German" character of feudalism, and the bright future of their nations. The most striking differences between Palacký and Lelewel were of a political nature and reflect the differences between Polish and Czech nationalism in the 19th century. Lelewel belonged with democratic radicals, whereas Palacký shifted from liberalism to a social conservatism with pan-Slavic undertones. His reception among Marxists was, interestingly enough, quite positive. Josef Macek deemed Palacký's interpretation of Czech history progressive since Palacký had appreciated the importance of the Hussite movement. Palacký did not distinguish between the more progressive radical Hussite movement of Tábor and the moderate Hussites, but this detail did not change the positive reception of his work. According to Macek, Palacký as a historian and politician allegedly represented the most progressive part of the bourgeoisie in its glory days, especially before the revolution of 1848. As a liberal, and later a conservative politician, Palacký however could not always count on appreciation. The Soviet scholar Ivan I. Udaltsov accused Palacký of being not only conservative but also nationalist (chauvinist), and found Palacký's idea of Austro-Slavism reactionary. Udaltsov also called the Czech national movement as a whole reactionary, as it had supported the Habsburg monarchy in its struggle against the 1848 revolution in Vienna and Hungary. This opinion presented by not only a Soviet historian but also a prominent Soviet diplomat in Prague could not be rejected openly by Czech historians. It was furthermore historically 'justified' by Friedrich Engels' severe judgment of the Czech national movement. As far as research shows, only two Czech historians dared challenge Udaltsov in order to defend Palacký from Marxist criticism. In 1948, when the nascent Marxist-Leninist "methodological revolution" was not yet fully defined, Josef Macůrek, the brilliant "bourgeois" historian from Brno, confronted Soviet researchers during his stay at the congress of Polish historians in Wrocław. Macůrek debated Udaltsov, pointing to the international context of the Czech national movement.[867] Several years later the first president of the Czechoslovak Academy of Sciences and the main codifier of the Czech Marxist vision of history, Zdeněk Nejedlý, firmly (and successfully) rejected Udaltsov's attempt to erase Palacký from the Museum of National Literature (Památník národního písemnictví) in Prague.[868] Nevertheless, the only promising way to defend national values permanently was to try to "reconcile" Udaltsov with Palacký. In the university handbook on Czech history, Udaltsov was referred to as "the best expert on the revolution of 1848."[869] Josef Kočí, the reviewer of Udaltsov's book in *Československý Časopis Historický*, shared this laudatory evaluation but added that Udaltsov did not pay attention to some positive aspects of the Czech national movement, especially to the role of Palacký as a historian.[870] Bedřich Šindelář formulated the same idea in a different way when he wrote, "We must distinguish between Palacký the historian, and Palacký the politician."[871]

The Marxist assessment of František Palacký was more positive than the Polish Marxist assessment of Lelewel, despite Palacký's political beliefs and the harsh criticism which Marx and Engels leveled against the Czech national movement as a whole. The Czech émigré Joseph F. Žáček wrote in the late 1960s that Palacký's work was "still regarded as classic, valuable not only for much of its factual content but especially for the philosophy of history which permeates it (It is, of course, the only comprehensive philosophy of Czech history besides the Marxist one)."[872]

The Slovak Marxist interpretation of Ľudovít Štúr, the leader of the 19th century Slovak national movement, demonstrates striking analogies to the picture of Palacký. The Communist literary theoretician Vladimír Mináč described him as a creator of the Slovak nation: "In the beginning was the Word. And the Word was with Štúr. ... So, Štúr was the beginning."[873] Historian Karol Goláň described Štúr as a combatant for social and political progress, for Slovak national identity and Slovak culture, as well as for universal values.[874] Although

---

867 Macůrek, *Úvahy*, 79.

868 Hanzal, "Čeští historici," 283.

869 See *Přehled československých dějin*, vol. 2, part 1, 10–11.

870 Josef Kočí, "Revoluce v Čechách roku 1848," *Československý Časopis Historický* 1954, 511.

871 Bedřich Šindelář, "František Palacký a dělnická třída," *Časopis Matice Moravské* 1952, 35.

872 Joseph. F. Žáček, "Palacký: A Marxist Portrait," in *Czechoslovakia Past and Present*, vol. 1, *Political, International, Social and Economic Aspects*, ed. Miloslav Rechcigl, The Hague–Paris 1968, 603.

873 Vladimír Mináč, "Tu żyje naród," in: *Kwestia słowacka*, 376.

874 Karol Goláň, *Štúrovské pokolenie (Výber z diela)*, ed. František Bokes, Bratislava 1964, 367.

critical of the idea of Czecho-Slovak national unity, Štúr always expressed sympathy towards Czechs.[875] Július Mésároš called him an internationalist and political moralist on the way to becoming a revolutionary.[876] He was said to have been the best student, economist, linguist, educator, publicist, poet, politician, and—last but not least—the best Slovak historian of his times.[877] Karol Goláň stated that he possessed some prophetic abilities, for he was supposed to have foreseen the decline of capitalism in Slovakia.[878] In his later years Štúr became a pan-Slavist, dreaming of the assimilation of all Slavic nations into Russian language and culture, but this conservative turn did not fundamentally alter the positive assessments which Marxists made of Štúr.[879]

    In fact, if anything could tarnish this image of a national hero, it was his attitude towards the Hungarian revolution of 1848–1849. Not only did the Revolution belong to the 'progressive traditions' of socialist Hungary, it was also one of the democratic movements passionately supported by Marx and Engels. At the same time, their opinion of the Slovak national movement was as critical as it had been in the case of Czech liberals. In 1954, the young Slovak historian and ethnographer Vladimír Matula highlighted this conflict. According to Matula, the commonly used interpretation of the Slovak national movement was highly subjective and idealising. The truth was that Štúr and other Slovak politicians had supported the reactionary Austrian state against the spirit of European revolution, embodied in Lajos Kossuth. Only a few marginal radical democratic Slovak groups that supported Hungarians were truly progressive. The mainstream of the Slovak national movement had not come close to embracing any kind of democratic ideology. From 1848 on, Matula found no traces of social progressiveness in the Slovak national camp.[880]

    This reevaluation of Štúr radiated out like a local earthquake, eliciting an almost immediate response to some of Matula's theses. Karol Goláň admitted that the Slovak national movement cooperated with Vienna, but it simply had no other choice: "The national chauvinism of the Hungarian movement ... had

875 Goláň, Štúrovské, 371.
876 Július Mésároš, "Štúrov boj za oslobodenie slovenského roľníctva spod jarma feudalizmu," in Ľudovít Štúr – život a dielo 1815-1856. Sborník materiálov z konference Historického ústavu Sloveskej akadémie vied, ed. Vladimír Matula, Bratislava 1956, 152–153.
877 Almost every aspect of his rich personality was analysed by the authors of the volume: Ľudovít Štúr – život a dielo.
878 Goláň, Štúrovské, 376.
879 "Veľke jubileum," Historický Časopis SAV 1956, 4.
880 Vladimír Matula, "K niektorým otázkam slovenského národného hnutia štyridsiatych rokov XIX stor.," Historický Časopis SAV 1954, 375–405.

excluded any other option."[881] In January 1955, Matula faced his opponents during a conference at the Historical Institute of SAV. This time Karol Goláň was supported by a curious coalition, composed of the Stalinist literary historian Andrej Mráz and the young, bright and 'apolitical' sociologist and historian, Július Mésároš.[882] The first phase of the debate was closed in 1955, when the Slovak Academy of Sciences published the so-called "theses" for the Marxist university handbook for history students. According to the collective authors, Štúr was partly wrong because the agenda of the Hungarian revolution could have had a clearly progressive impact on all nationalities. On the other hand, they stated that he was correct in noting that the Hungarian liberal opposition had decided to accept historical-feudal rights and ignore national rights (and accordingly, they disregarded the objectives of the Slovak national movement).[883]

In 1956, the Slovak scientific community celebrated the centennial of Štúr's death. His portrait graced the cover of the central historical journal, *Historický časopis SAV*, and the foreword to the volume described the latest debates over the Slovak national movement of the 19th century. Its author criticised equally two extreme options: bourgeois nationalism and national nihilism.[884] One of the studies by Július Mésároš was entitled "Boj Ľudovíta Štúra proti feudalizmu" (Ľudovít Štúr's struggle against feudalism). Mésároš highlighted important social differences between Hungarian revolutionaries and members of the Slovak national movement. In his view, Slovaks were common people, whereas Hungarian liberals were of noble origin. Thus their social radicalism was seriously limited. For Štúr and his fellow fighters—as Mésároš claimed—the Hungarian revolution was simply not progressive enough: "Bourgeois reform, as shaped by the liberal gentry in March 1848, was only a shadow of the ideas for which Štúr had fought. The abolition of serfdom, and the radical transformation of the feudal means of production and of the gentry's privileges were accomplished only in part. It was not enough."[885] These opinions were supported by Soviet researchers during the Štúr conference in Moscow in 1956.[886] Several

---

881   Karol Goláň, "Ľudovít Štúr a slovenské národné hnutie v štyridsiatych rokoch XIX.
         Storočia," *Historický Časopis SAV* 1955, 91.
882   (JT) [Ján Tibenský] "Konferencia slovenských historikov o tézach slovenských dejín,"
         Historický Časopis SAV 1955, 300–301.
883   *Dejiny Slovenska (tézy)*, 115.
884   "Veľke jubileum," 4.
885   Július Mésároš, "Boj Ľudovíta Štúra proti feudalizmu," *Historický Časopis SAV* 1956,
         6–19.
886   "Vedecké zasednutie v Moskve venované stému výročiu smrti Ľudovíta Štúra,"
         Historický Časopis SAV 1956, 43.

weeks before, a conference in Bratislava had taken place. Its participants simply ignored any critical remarks concerning the national hero. Vladimír Matula himself gave a speech on Štúr's Slavic idea, stressing its "healthy features" and by no means recapitulating his previous critical remarks.[887]

In the meantime, Matula's critical positions were completely abandoned. One should point to the Hungarian revolution in 1956 as one of the reasons for the posthumous victory of Štúr over Kossuth. In 1959, the Czechoslovak university handbook described Štúr as an unquestionable source of progressive traditions and national values. The Hungarian revolution was then compared to the contemporaneous Hungarian "counterrevolution" and thus excluded from progressive traditions.[888] The rhetorical perfection of this construction warrants an extensive quote: "The aversion toward the Hungarian revolution ... coupled with an apologetic attitude toward the Slovak interventions of 1848-1849 became an ideologically important source for Slovak bourgeois nationalism. On the other hand, as the grievous events of 1956 in Hungary prove, they still exert a detrimental influence and lead to nationalist exaggerations and the blind cult of the Hungarian revolution. In truth, the Hungarian revolution of 1848-1849 was marked by even more pronounced limitations and indecisiveness than other 'true' bourgeois revolutions. The particular merit of the Hungarian nation in 1848-1849 was that it acted not only in its own name, but also in the name of international progress. Within the counterrevolutionary putsch of 1956, the wilful replication and manipulation of the revolutionary-democratic traditions of 1848-1849 was a weapon used by reactionary instigators and false petit-bourgeois democrats for the purpose of effecting the restoration of former exploitative classes, and by international imperialists, the greatest enemies of popular and national freedom."[889] Finally, Matula tried to defend the remnants of his theory by claiming that the old Štúr, while politically conservative and pan-Slavist, bore striking similarities to 1848's radical democrats, "'Kráľ and Francisci, of course without their revolutionary strategy."[890] Matula's attempt to connect the "conservative revolution" with the democratic one did not open any wider debate.

The more progressive Štúr and the Slovak national movement looked, the more reactionary the Hungarian revolution became. In the mid-1960s, Vladimír Mináč wrote: "This revolution we fought against was odd from its very

---

887 Vladimír Matula, "Štúr a slovanstvo," in Ľudovít Štúr-život a dielo, 386–387.

888 Přehled československých dějin (Maketa), vol. 1, 769.

889 Přehled československých dějin, vol. 2, part 1, 127.

890 Vladimír Matula, "Vyvrcholenie štúrovskej koncepcie myšlienky slovanskej vzájomnosti v štúrovom diele Slovanstvo a svet budúcnosti," Historický Časopis SAV 1960, 376.

beginnings: *drôle de revolution*. The figures were changing: the casino in Pest instead of the Viennese court; five Hungarian aristocratic families instead of the emperor. It was characteristic of this strange revolution, that no other reaction, restoration, or counterrevolution was needed to stop it. This revolution had an inborn protest, reaction, and restoration—revolution bearing a victorious reactionary seed."[891]

In turn, Matula's article had been extensively quoted after 1954 as a negative example, especially during the political liberalism of the so-called Slovak Spring period in the 1960s. His attempt to reinterpret Štúr and the Slovak national movement was labelled as the "Stalinisation of historiography." Moreover, it became the main example for all the anti-national and ungainly ugly features of the Stalinist period. Ľudovít Holotík, director of the Institute of History at the Academy, wrote in 1963 that "the ideological campaign against nationalism was one-sided; it was restricted to Slovakia and accompanied by a system of distrust and terror. In those conditions the necessity of searching for Slovak progressive traditions was wrongly understood, it was labelled as nationalism (for example when it came to the characteristics of Ľudovít Štúr, etc.)."[892] The allusion to Matula was quite clear, but it was still not the last assault on his claims. The idea of an anti-national Stalinist historiography that attempted to "destroy" Štúr is still present in Slovak public and scientific life. In 1991, during the congress of the Slovak Historical Society, Richard Marsina claimed that in the Communist period only the small nations were accused of nationalism, whereas it should be clear, that whatever they do, they do it to defend their existence from suppression by the large nations.[893] Interestingly, a similar position is defended by Adam Hudek in a book which, by all accounts, is a work of undeniable quality. Accepting without reservation all manifestations of sympathy among Slovak Marxists for Štúr and national traditions, Hudek argues that up until the 1960s, historical discourse was in that regard dominated by the self-critical position of Ladislav Novomeský, who harked back to the 1930s.[894]

Neither the Štúr controversy, nor any other element of the Slovak Marxist interpretation of history justifies such theses. It appears rather that the 'purges' at Slovak universities and historical societies did not produce a rapid reinterpretation of the national narrative. Daniel Rapant, probably the most outstanding Slovak historian of the 20th century and a symbolical figure, was

---

891 Mináč, "Kwestia słowacka," 383.
892 Ľudovít Holotík, "Desať rokov Historického ústavu Slovenskej akadémie vied," *Historický Časopis SAV* 1963, 601.
893 Richard Marsina, "Slovenská historiografia 1945-1990," *Historický Časopis SAV* 1991, 372.
894 Hudek, *Najpolitickejšia*, 50.

relieved from his duties as a historian, but his interpretation of the Slovak national movement remained widely accepted.[895] In 1966, this traditional interpretation was challenged again by a Hungarian Marxist, Erzsébet Andics. The Slovak responses demonstrated already a good deal of distance from the national 'nihilism' of Matula. Július Mésároš quoted both Vladimír Mináč and Daniel Rapant to prove that—whatever Marx and Engels might have said about the Hungarian revolution—Kossuth was simply fighting for power. His victory would not have positively advanced the prospects of the Slovaks.[896]

GDR: Rather Treitschke than Ranke

Czech and Slovak Marxist historiographies do not offer many examples of bitter clashes between adherents of various "bourgeois" methodological directions. To find an equivalent to the vivid Polish debates on Hoffman, Lelewel, or the Kraków and Warsaw historical schools, one should search in the historiography that inherited the most sophisticated (but also the most problematic) tradition: East German Marxist historiography. I will focus on two problems of crucial importance: the reevaluation of Leopold von Ranke, and the so-called Prussian historical school consisting of Johann Gustav Droysen, Heinrich von Sybel, Heinrich von Treitschke, and Theodor Mommsen (considered as a member of this group by the East Germans). As in the Polish case, all the historians taking part in the East German debates were Marxists, though some of them did not necessarily belong to the mainstream.

East German historians only started to elaborate on their pre-Marxist scientific traditions rather late. In the 1950s, one of the leading Marxist scholars, a professor at the university in Halle (and veteran of the Soviet Army), Leo Stern, addressed the issue in his work *Gegenwartsaufgaben der deutschen Geschichtsforschung* (published separately, as well as in the newly created *Zeitschrift für Geschichtswissenschaft*). The chapter devoted to Ranke was entitled simply "Ranke and the fall of German historiography." Stern criticised Ranke's notion of objectivity, which led to social and political conservatism,

---

895 On the 'purges' in Slovakia see: Vladimír Michalička and Daniela Vaněková, "Die Entwicklung des Hochschulwesens in den Jahren 1945-1989," in *Die Bildungs-, Wissenschafts- und Kulturpolitik in der Slowakei 1945-2004*, eds. Beata Blehova & Peter Bachmaier, Frankfurt am Main 2004, 81–90.

896 Július Mésároš, "Treba revidovať názory Marxa a Engelsa o revolúcii rokov 1848-1849?," *Predvoj*, 1966, 10–11; I use the new edition in: idem, *Zložité hľadanie pravdy o slovenských dejinách. Výber štúdií, odborných polemík a článkov z polstoročnej výskumnej a publikačnej činnosti*, Bratislava 2004, 259–267.

and moreover, paved the way to German nationalism.[897] He faulted the "moral indifferentism" of this form of objectivity, which could make every past crime justifiable. Surprisingly, Stern did not accuse Ranke of being a reactionary political thinker – he considered his striving for an objective picture of the past as serious and sincere. Still, he noted that, by resort to objectivity, Ranke weakened the moral strength of German historiography, leaving it unprepared to face the historical outcomes of 1918 and 1945.[898]

In 1956, the prominent economic historian Jürgen Kuczynski (1904–1997) presented a completely different evaluation of Ranke's impact on German historiography. Kuczynski wrote that Ranke was a brilliant historian who raised the professional level of historiography: "As a matter of fact Ranke used those new scientific tools to strengthen the ruling classes .... But how much closer we are to the uncovering of the real past thanks to his efforts! ... All means that help us better describe reality are important for social progress and therefore objectively help the new win its battle against the old in society."[899] Jürgen Kuczynski's assessment of Ranke was one of the main arguments in an official campaign against "revisionism" that, thanks to his good political relations with the German and foreign Communist elite, did not have any serious personal effects.[900]

The official GDR narrative of German historicism was created throughout the 1960s. It was much more simplified than any passage from Stern or Kuczynski. The young German sociologist, historian, and director of the Historical Institute at Humboldt University in Berlin, Joachim Streisand (1920–1980), simply described Ranke as a part of the feudal reaction against the progressive intellectual current(s) of Enlightenment.[901] Gerhard Schilfert noticed that Ranke's reactionary character was evident even in his youth, when he remained unmoved by the flourishing radical movement of the *Burschenschaften* and thus supported European reaction during every single 19th century revolutionary attempt.[902] He was set against such progressive Romantic

---

897 Stern, *Gegenwartsaufgaben*, 20.
898 Stern, *Gegenwartsaufgaben*, 24-25.
899 Jürgen Kuczynski, "Parteilichkeit und Objektivität in Geschichte und Geschichtsschreibung," *Zeitschrift für Geschichtswissenschaft* 1956, 887.
900 Kuczynski described these events in his book *Frost nach dem Tauwetter. Mein Historikerstreit*, Berlin 1993.
901 Joachim Streisand, "Progressive Traditionen und reaktionäre Anachronismen in der deutschen Geschichtswissenschaft," *Zeitschrift für Geschichtswissenschaft* 1961, 1783.
902 Gerhard Schilfert, "Leopold von Ranke," in *Die deutsche Geschichtswissenschaft vom Beginn des 19. Jahrhunderts bis zur Reichseinigung von oben*, ed. Joachim Streisand, Berlin, 1963, 242-243.

historians as Schlosser, Gervinus, Rotteck, and Zimmermann.[903] When in the early 1960s the Marxist evaluation of Hegel began to change rapidly,[904] and the philosopher was at least partly adapted to the progressive heritage, Ranke lost another point, for he had criticised Hegel's philosophy of history.[905] Ranke was unfairly accused of "worshiping the Prussian regime," and, on the other hand, quite "fairly" faulted for negating historical progress and stressing the role of foreign policy and social conservatism. Ernst Engelberg, the leader of the GDR historical association, wrote, "shortly, Ranke was useful to justify imperialist aggression abroad as well as for fighting against the German workers' movement."[906]

The Marxist appreciation of Ranke had gradually deteriorated, becoming more and more one-sided. The Prussian historical school had a similar trajectory, albeit in the opposite direction. In the late 1940s, when the Marxist vision of the German past was still under the influence of postwar criticism (with Alexander Abusch as the most prominent representative of the new historical direction), the role of Sybel, Treitschke, and Droysen seemed to be quite clear: through their works they had prepared the way for Hitler.[907] As Gottfried Koch stated, "their works reflected a compromise between the great bourgeoisie and the Prussian feudal-absolutist reaction."[908] The young Marxist historian of historiography, Hans Schleier (born in 1931), characterised the Prussian school as antidemocratic and counterrevolutionary. Its members were Prussian chauvinists and militarists. They were afraid of social democracy and did their best to destroy its influence on German society. They supported Bismarck's aggressive policies, and some of them (namely Treitschke) were also anti-Semitic.[909] In methodological matters Droysen, Treitschke, and Sybel were said to combine the old liberal agenda with all the reactionary features of

---

903 Schilfert, "Leopold von Ranke," 253.

904 For the turn of the former interpretation of Hegel see: *Skizze zur Geschichte der Hegel-Literatur in der SBZ und der DDR* (www.hegel-institut.de/Diskussion/DDR).

905 Schilfert, "Leopold von Ranke," 256.

906 Ernst Engelberg, "Politik und Geschichtsschreibung. Die historische Stellung und Aufgabe der Geschichtswissenschaft in der DDR," *Zeitschrift für Geschichtswissenschaft* 1958, 482.

907 Stern, *Gegenwartsaufgaben*, 29; Hans Schleier, *Sybel und Treitschke. Antidemokratismus und Militarismus im historisch-politischen Denken großbourgeoiser Geschichtsideologen* Berlin 1965, 161.

908 Gottfried Koch, "Die mittelalterliche Kaiserpolitik im Spiegel der bürgerlichen deutschen Historiographie des 19. und 20. Jahrhunderts," *Zeitschrift für Geschichtswissenschaft* 1962, 1842.

909 Hans Schleier, "Die kleindeutsche Schule (Droysen, Sybel, Treitschke)," *Die deutsche Geschichtswissenschaft*, 271–301.

German Romanticism (first of all its fondness for feudalism).[910] They were hostile towards the Enlightenment, the French Revolution, and—despite formal declarations—towards the progressive heritage of German Classicism.[911]

Despite all this, East German Marxists saw some of the positive aspects of the Prussian school, and—interestingly enough—observed them mostly in those aspects where it differed from Ranke and his followers. Gottfried Koch stated that the conflict between Sybel and Giesebrecht had a clear political meaning: Prussian historians were correct in stating that the Medieval German empire spent its vital power in Italy instead of strengthening its internal coherence and expanding to the Slavic East. Figures such as Sybel or Treitschke wanted a united Germany, and thus they were more progressive than conservatives who supported existing political relations.[912] Had they not supported the *Ostexpansion* as well, their assessment by Marxists could have been even more positive.[913]

It is thus very interesting to compare the Marxist attitude towards Ranke and his younger colleagues. Interestingly enough, the Prussian school came to be perceived more favourably than the most influential German historian. Hans Schleier explained this problem in a similar way to what Marian Henryk Serejski had done with the historians Karol Boromeusz Hoffman and Joachim Lelewel: "Political historians, representatives of an alliance between the great bourgeoisie and the Junkers, adherents of the national and political unification of Germany, represented a new school of historiography, more progressive than the conservative, Romantic Ranke."[914] Surprisingly, even such features of the Prussian school as its German nationalism were interpreted as having been inherited from Ranke, and thus were not seen as a difference between Ranke and national-liberals. Schleier noted that "there were many more methodological and political similarities between Ranke and the Prussian-German historians than they, or the later bourgeois history of historiography, were willing to admit."[915]

Of course, it was Sybel's, Treitschke's, and Droysen's attitude towards the unification of Germany that played the main role in this Marxist interpretation. In the mid-1950s, the conflict between two leading personalities in German Marxist historiography, Alfred Meusel and Ernst Engelberg, also concerned this phenomenon. Meusel supported a more "national" interpretation and described 1871 as a victorious moment for the German national movement and the

---

910   Koch, "Die mittelalterliche Kaiserpolitik," 1841.
911   Schleier, "Die kleindeutsche Schule (Droysen, Sybel, Treitschke)," 304.
912   Koch, "Die mittelalterliche Kaiserpolitik," 1842.
913   Streisand, "Progressive Traditionen," 1785.
914   Schleier, *Sybel und Treitschke*, 228.
915   Ibidem, 230.

German working class. Engelberg (later known as the GDR biographer of Bismarck)[916] claimed more 'Bolshevik' positions, declaring his hostility towards Bismarck and the idea of unification "from above." Nevertheless in the 1960s, when Meusel died, and Engelberg was at the peak of his political and scientific career, he adopted the ideas of his former enemy. Odd as it may seem, this was bound to happen. Since the Marxist interpretation of German history in the 1950s saw national unity as the main objective of all progressive movements, starting with Thomas Müntzer, the fulfilment of this task had to be finally interpreted as a progressive phenomenon. And thus, the Prussian school that avidly supported unification was finally labelled as more progressive than Ranke, who was rather sceptical towards every attempt to change the political map of Europe.

***

We can now draw some conclusions from samples of Marxist historiographies in East Central Europe. We started with the Polish problem: how to define the criteria of progressiveness in the history of historiography. Then we examined the successful Czech attempt to 'defend' František Palacký from Marxist critiques, and the Slovak analogy—an unsuccessful 'attack' on Ľudovít Štúr. Finally, we demonstrated that the comparison of East German representations of Ranke and the Prussian school illustrate the same problem as Polish debates, namely the problem of recognising the criteria of progressiveness. At the same time, East German debates touched upon the question of the 'defence' of national tradition (in this particular example of the *Reichsgründung* in 1871) from a supposedly 'Bolshevik', 'anti-national' reinterpretation, addressed also in the Czechoslovak context. Now finally, we can summarize and re-consider the methodological parallels in this broad comparison.

For Marxist historians, the crucial problem of the criteria of progressiveness remained unsolved. On the one hand, it was quite natural to search for progressive values in Romantic historiography. Lelewel and Palacký, as well as Štúr (the latter two in their early works), described the Slavs' pre-historic freedom and equality, condemned German feudalism, and looked to the future with the optimism of liberal *Vormärz* democrats. They stressed the 'democratic' phenomena of national history: the Hussite revolution, previous Slavic freedom, and even the progressive elements of the democracy of the gentry. In many ways Marxists simply shared their conclusions. Still, on the other hand, it was clear to them that Romantic historiography was idealist, and methodologically less developed than later positivist or historicist schools. Thus some Marxists

---

916   Ernst Engelberg, *Bismarck* Berlin 1985.

identified with the latter, describing Karol Boromeusz Hoffman and Michał Bobrzyński as more progressive than Lelewel. Both options— 'Romantic' and 'Historicist-Positivist'—were equally likely to be represented in any given Marxist historian's position, both could be described as truly Marxist, and in fact both were introduced as the Marxist response to previous 'misinterpretations.' A highly interesting appendix to the Polish, Czech, and Slovak cases was provided by the East German interpretations of the Prussian school, which was treated as more 'national' and less conservative than Ranke, but it was, as had been the case with Lelewel, Palacký, and Štúr, neither an 'objective,' apolitical, nor a strictly 'scientific' group. Droysen, Sybel, and Treitschke were at the centre of the German national movement in their times and thus, functionally could play a role similar to that of the Romantic historians in Poland, the Czech lands, or Slovakia. Even if their political stance had been officially labelled as reactionary, their nationalism proved to be closer to the Marxist interpretation of history than any disinterested art of 'objectivity.'

The debate over the criteria of progressiveness saw the formation of a separate intellectual milieu, namely, that of socially and politically conservative scholars with strong pan-Slavic sympathies. In contrast to other Polish Marxist researchers, so reserved in their attitudes towards historiographical traditions, Andrzej Poppe tried to include Zorian Dołęga Chodakowski in the 'progressive' catalogue, and by so doing, he neglected the evident ideological shortcomings of pan-Slavism, not only in comparison to Marxism, but also in comparison to the democratic ideology of the first half of the 19th century. His attempt illustrates that in the eyes of the Marxist canonisers, a historian's attitude towards Russia was a crucial feature, offering redemption for ideological or methodological 'backwardness.' Unfortunately, neither the history of Poland in general, nor the history of historiography could supply many examples of pro-Russian sympathies. This was much easier to come by in the case of Czech or Slovak historiography, and in fact, according to Marxist researchers, a progressive pan-Slavism characterised both Štúr and the late Palacký, as well as the Czech and Slovak national movements in general.

Another aspect of the progressiveness debate was the adoption of the idea of historical progress. Marxist reassessments of different historical groupings rarely avoided this pitfall. Romantic historians, although idealist (and in fact simply because they were idealists), believed in historical progress, which to some degree made them similar to Marx and Engels. Adherents to a positivist philosophy, although in many ways different, also shared a belief in a linear and constant progressive evolution. This made them at least partly relevant to the Marxist vision of history. On the other hand, Ranke, with his critique of the Hegelian philosophy of history and with his division of history into separate epochs meant to be judged according to their own rules, was unacceptable. In comparison to Ranke's historicism, the nationalist tendency of the Prussian school was much easier to justify as a predecessor to German Marxist historiography.

The differences between Polish criticism of Lelewel, on the one hand, and Czech and Slovak admiration for Palacký and Štúr, on the other, is not at all a unique phenomenon. Many historians of historiography see the immanent difference between more or less 'nationalist' Marxist historiographies, with more or less national groupings contained within each of them. The division between more and less 'national' models of Marxist historiography can be subsumed in the conflict of 'right' and 'left' interpretations described by Lutz Raphael. Those on the 'left' always focus on the class struggle and ascribe progressiveness only to the lower classes. The more moderate 'right' interpretation sees a continuity of progressive development culminating in the climax of national history: an independent, "people's democratic" state. In this latter model, particular knights, kings and burghers are also included in progressive traditions.[917] The Czech and Slovak cases are an example of the more 'national' model, the Polish case seems to represent a different pattern altogether, and the East German case is the most dependent on political conjunctions and also the most dynamic, shifting from radical postwar 'pessimism' to the nationalist and Prussian 'renaissance' just before the collapse of the state.

On the whole, of the cases analysed here, one can consider the 'Czechoslovak model' as the most centralised. It is difficult to find any important historical controversies in the Czechoslovak context of the 1950s. If such a controversy emerged, it was almost immediately silenced (as happened to Vladimír Matula's theses). The interpretation of national history was dependent on the liberal-nationalist historiographical tradition inasmuch as it did not confront Marxist dogmas too openly. Critical comments concerning the Czech and Slovak national movements by the founding fathers of Communism were simply ignored. The Marxist vision of the past drew on the liberal-nationalist conviction in general (it described the history of the nation, not of the class struggle or economic development), as well as on some of its specific details (such as interpretations of the Hussite movement, 'national revival,' and František Palacký or Ľudovít Štúr). Paradoxically, such a development meant that any other Marxist (but non-orthodox) interpretation was barely possible.

---

917 Lutz Raphael, *Geschichtswissenschaft im Zeitalter der Extreme. Theorien, Methoden, Tendenzen von 1900 bis zur Gegenwart*, München 2003, 58-9.

The dominant collective of Marxist scholars was reproducing a pre-Marxist, eclectic vision of the national past.

The less 'national' models of Polish and East German historiography of the Stalinist period were much more open to certain types of historical discussion – which was quite different from the model of debates in 'normal sciences' because it stressed the need for achieving a single true interpretation for every single topic. The debates between Polish or German historians on the progressiveness of Lelewel, Hoffman, Ranke, or the Prussian school were supposed to lead (and in some cases really led) to the canonisation of one chosen solution. Once the canonisation was achieved, no other interpretation would be accepted, as there could not be two parallel Marxist interpretations of the same phenomenon. In practice, traces of 'pessimism' appeared mostly in places where Polish or German history interfered with the privileged Soviet vision of the national past. Polish democrats of the 19th century (such as Lelewel) unfortunately had been doing their best to fight Russian autocracy. Similarly, the anti-Slavic features of German history were summarily condemned (at least until the late 1960s) by GDR historiography.

In addition, one should also highlight the relatively broad German and Polish non-Marxist historiographical traditions as a catalyst for the multiplicity of opinions within the Marxist historical community. The decisions concerning which part of the ideological domain to draw from, and which traditions to condemn to oblivion, often proved to be too difficult. Whether one should praise the democrat Lelewel, or point to positivist historians as representatives of a new social-economic formation, remained an open question. Paradoxically, it could be said that German and Polish Marxists of the Stalinist period prolonged and revived the main historiographical debates of 19th century scholars. In the 1950s, though in a rather simplified way, the classic controversies between Romanticism and Positivism or Conservatism and Liberalism found their equivalent in the polemics of Bobińska, Serejski or Assorodobraj; Kuczynski, Engelberg or Stern. In contrast, in the Czech, and most clearly in the Slovak case, the exclusion of such an important figure as Ľudovít Štúr from the historical tradition was rightly perceived as a threat to the national identity; his role in his national culture cannot be compared to any Polish or German national hero.

However, it should be stated very clearly that neither a 'right' nor 'left' Marxist interpretation of national history can be perceived as better than the other in any sense. Both were only variations within the frame of Soviet-type Marxism. Both 'right' and 'left' could be equally destructive to the quality of scientific discourse, excluding the possible multiplicity of interpretations. Interpretations of both types aspired to a monopoly in nearly every topic (as in those described in this text). This monopolistic nature of historiography led to the application of a mythic structure of Stalinist science. If the interpretation of history (philosophy, biology, linguistics, or any other science) is understood as something similar to religious belief, and not as an *ipso facto* problematic and multi-faceted phenomenon, it transcends reality and begins to belong to the sphere of myth.[918] Within this mythic structure, interpretations, whether more or less national, played the same destructive role.

---

918 I refer to the broad understanding of "myth" as described by Leszek Kołakowski, *The Presence of Myth*, transl. Adam Czerniawski, Chicago: University of Chicago Press, 2001, passim.

Chapter V
Four Historiographies
in the Context of the Region

Every characteristic discussed above with respect to select Marxist historiographies also applies, to different degrees, to other countries in the region which I did not discuss in this work. The most obvious similarities pertain to structural and organisational aspects, as pointed out by Rafał Stobiecki.[919] After the war, the Party's educational institutions were established in every East Central European Communist country. Their goal was to prepare future Marxist teaching staffs. Some of the older institutions were universally dismantled and replaced with new entities, Marxist from the ground up. The same methodological grounds often led to analogous conclusions. Finally, Stalinist history-writing everywhere "treated as its main goal the elimination of all other, competing methods of writing history."[920] All of these traits perfectly illustrate the theoretical similarities among various Stalinist historiographies. If anything, the idea of blaming the Stalinist system for the drive toward centralisation seems less compelling – not because there was no such connection, but more for the fact that, in the postwar world, similar phenomena transgressed the boundaries of political blocs. After the war, centralisation was accepted as the proper course of scientific development by non-Communist scientists as well.[921]

Next to general characteristics shared more or less widely across Communist countries, one could name a few more specific traits, pertaining not only to the structures, but also to the content of historical analyses. The onset of Stalinism sparked the typically short-lived domination of Marxist interpretations of national histories that were strident in their criticism of the traditional perspectives. Mihail Roller's history of Romania, first published in 1947, rejected the idea of the nation as a subject of historical research and focused on the history of the territories of postwar Romania. Instead of tracing the achievements of rulers of Moldavia, Wallachia and Transylvania, it concentrated

---

919 Rafał Stobiecki, "Stalinizm w historiografii. Między radzieckim oryginałem a narodowymi kopiami," *Zeszyty Wiejskie* 2002.
920 Ibidem, 238.
921 Ibidem, 243.

on uncovering the history of peasant involvement in class warfare, with scant regard for nationality, while also underlining the ties between the people of Romania and Slavic folk and culture. The unification of the nation, writes Lucian Boia, is no longer perceived as a natural outcome of history and an unquestionable right of the Romanian nation, instead being framed as an imperial type of expansionism.[922] Roller completely ignored the formation of "Greater Romania" in 1918.

In no other case of which I am aware did the relapse of interwar "internationalism" in historiography reach as far as it did in Romania of the 1950s. Fairly early on, Bulgarian Marxists began to include the national revival among their progressive traditions, a fact Roumen Daskalov links with the shifting of perspective from class to state.[923] Hungary was also quick to produce a list of supposedly progressive historical figures. The dominant 'national-Communist' interpretation of Hungarian history was in many respects similar to that of Czech and Slovak history. The place of the 'progressive' anti-feudal revolutionary movement of the Czech Hussites or of the Slovak miners was occupied in early modern Hungary by the 16th century's György Dózsa uprising. The reproduction of the kuruc[924] narrative influenced the Marxist-Leninist picture of Habsburg rule over Hungary and of the Hungarian gentry who had opposed it. The anti-Habsburg uprisings of Imre Thököly (1672–1685) and Ferenc Rákóczi (1703–1711) were labelled as part of the 'progressive heritage' even though their 'class character' was ambiguous. Moreover, the 'Jacobin' conspiracy of Ignác Martinovics in the late 18th century attracted similar assessments. The peak of the continuous struggle for national and social liberation was the 1848–1849 revolution, with its undisputed leaders Lajos Kossuth and the Romantic poet Sándor Petőfi. Finally, after hundreds of years of misery and exploitation from time immemorial to the end of the First World War, the chain of Hungarian progressive traditions found its culmination in the 1919 Soviet Republic. Interestingly enough, this state was associated with the postwar 'Hungarian Stalin,' Mátyás Rákosi, rather than with its factual leader Béla Kun (who had been executed at Stalin's behest in the 1930s).

The attainment of an agreement between the new, Marxist interpretation and the national tradition was crucial not only for society at large, but also for the elites. For Gyula Szekfű, a conservative historian who "converted" to Marxism and, between 1945 and 1948, even became the Hungarian ambassador in

---

922 Boia, *History and Myth*, 71-2.
923 Roumen Daskalov, *The Making of a Nation in the Balkans. Historiography of the Bulgarian Revival*, Budapest 2004, 245-246.
924 The Hungarian term *Kuruc* refers to the denomination of anti-Habsburg Hungarian rebels in the seventeenth and eighteenth centuries.

Moscow, ideological transformation was rooted in the belief that Communism did not actually stand in opposition to the nationalist convictions he professed.[925] Though some changes to the dominant interpretations of Hungarian–Slavic coexistence in the Carpathian basin appeared, the hegemonic Communist narrative was largely shaped by the interpretations of two historians, József Révai and Aladár Mód. Both authors "presented an unholy mixture of superpatriotic *kuruc* and proletarian-internationalist historical analyses."[926] Thus the jump from the postwar vision of history to the Stalinist one proved less dramatic in Hungary than in Poland and Czechoslovakia. The postwar period had seen an attempt at uniting the 'revolutionary' with the 'national' even at the cost of reproducing explicitly nationalistic interpretations.

Outside of Romania, the national "nihilism" of Marxist historiography (which the Romanian scholars of today tend to downplay)[927] was exhibited only briefly and/or unconvincingly. Still, Roller's interpretation possessed another trait which we can easily ascribe to most Communist historiographies – an emphasis on the role which Slavs, especially from the East, played in the histories of particular countries. Mihail Roller belittled the linguistic influence of Latin, which had been so obvious to earlier (and later) Romanian historians, and he did not set it against Dacian traditions (which would characterize his contributions to the traditional Romanian historical debates). Instead, he underlined the role of the Kievan Rus' that had been responsible for laying the foundations for Romanian-Russian friendship.[928] Bulgarian Marxists concentrated on the Russian theme when criticising their "bourgeois" predecessors, accusing them of shrugging off Bulgarian-Russian ties, and even of negating the Slavic character of the Bulgarian nation and culture.[929]

All Marxist historiographies suffered from similar organisational issues that had resulted from objective problems posed by collective work on a mass scale. For this reason, delays in publication of Marxist syntheses of national histories were hardly exceptional. The achievement of significant scholarly output, both in numbers and in quality, demanded the cooperation of non-Marxist historians. This point is vividly illustrated by representative Communist addresses to their

925 Irene Raab Epstein, *Gyula Szekfű. A Study in the Political Basis of Hungarian Historiography*, New York 1987, 305.
926 István Deák, "Hungary," *The American Historical Review*, 97 (1992), 1054.
927 As did Cristina Petrescu, for instance, during the conference *Die Historische Nationalismusforschung im geteilten Europa, 1945-1989: Politische Kontexte, institutionelle Bedingungen, intellektuelle Transfers*, March 28th, 2008 in Prague.
928 Boia, *History and Myth*, 108.
929 Marin Pundeff, "Bulgarian Historiography 1942-1958," *American Historical Review* 1961/3, 683.

"bourgeois" colleagues. In 1949, the Hungarian Marxist, Erzsébet Andics, made an undisguised appeal for help by observing that, without the aid of non-Marxist scholars, victory in the "battle for the 5-year plan" would prove impossible.[930] Members of the Bulgarian Communist Party drew similar conclusions when the first "draft" of the university history textbook proved so inadequate that the aid of non-Party historians appeared indispensable.[931]

Romanian historiography differed also in this regard, as Mihail Roller not only questioned the traditional historical interpretations of the state and the nation, but also seemingly monopolised the 1950s book market. This was an isolated example of a "Bolshevik" historiography which actually rejected "national" values for the sake of class consciousness and internationalism, coupling ideological shifts with an unprecedented (outside the Soviet Union) postwar purge of historians.[932] In other cases of which I am aware, Marxist historians based their interpretations on older elements, harking back to the traditions of national historiography, including Marxism-Leninism and pro-Russian pronouncements only to a varying degree.

For many Marxist historiographies, the end of Stalinism marked the return of nationalism. As Ulf Brunnbauer claims, this process was particularly intense in Bulgaria and Romania, or, in states where the Stalinist interpretation was comparatively the most distant from previous traditions. The publication of Marx's works, which included positive assessments of the Romanian national movement and harsh criticisms of Russia, sparked a decisive paradigm shift, leading to the rehabilitation of the prewar historiography. After a relatively short period of liberalisation, the increasingly oppressive Ceaușescu regime suppressed a reinterpretation of the Marxist doctrine that had been inspired by the *Annales* school: "While only the devoted party historians would go to nationalist extremes, and most historians worked on ideologically less charged topics, almost all Romanian historians dealt exclusively with Romanian history, and stressed the role of the Romanian state which contributed to the party's historical vision."[933] Romanian and Bulgarian historiography of the 1970s

930 Balázs Németh, *Nationalism and Socialist Patriotism in the Hungarian Historiography between 1948 and 1956, and Its Influence on the Post-1956 Era*, MA thesis defended at the Institute of History of the CEU in Budapest, 1995 (holdings of the CEU Library), 8.

931 Pundeff, "Bulgarian," 683.

932 Alexandru Zub, "Romanian historiography under communism," in: *Culture and the Politics of Identity in Modern Romania, May 27-30 1998 Bucharest* (manuscripts of the presentations found in the CEU Library in Budapest), 2-3.

933 Ulf Brunnbauer, "Historical Writing in the Balkans," in: *The Oxford History of Historical Writing, vol. 5: Historical Writing since 1945*, eds. Axel Schneider, Daniel Woolf & Ian Hesketh, Oxford 2011, 361.

exhibited a symptomatic interest in dubious theories concerning the ethnogenesis of the respective nations within dynamically developed and politically supported studies on ancient Dacians and Thracians.

At the risk of oversimplification, one could claim that the political changes caused by Stalin's demise had a lasting and positive effect on the development of historiography in only two countries of the Eastern Bloc – Poland and Hungary. In the changed climate, the path was cleared for a reconnection with the international historical community. And this time 'international' did not necessarily mean Western, since Stalinism had not only eliminated professional communication with Western historical scholarship but also had handicapped cooperation between countries within the Soviet bloc. It is telling that the first significant multilateral meeting of East Central European Marxist historians took place as late as 1953 during the congress of Hungarian historians in Budapest. In 1955 delegations from Eastern Europe, including the biggest Soviet delegation, took part in the congress of the International Committee of Historical Sciences (CISH) in Rome. It was only in the 1960s and 1970s that Polish and Hungarian scholars 'caught up' with the most influential and promising Western current of historical thought, the *Annales* school. Through unofficial, personal ties, such Polish authors as Witold Kula, Tadeusz Manteuffel, Aleksander Gieysztor, Andrzej Wyczański, Bronisław Geremek, and Marian Małowist were not only inspired by Fernand Braudel and his colleagues and students, but also started to honour this intellectual debt by delivering a comprehensive analysis of the development of capitalism in East Central Europe. This applied to Kula above all, whose theses concerning Eastern Europe were included in Braudel's panoramic history of capitalism. Similar research agendas were realised in the works of György Ránki, Iván Berend, Péter Hanák, and Jenő Szücs. Along with these developments, a generation of researchers born in the late 1920s and early 1930s arrived on the scene, bringing with them new topics and interpretations. Under the influence of Kula, a research centre for Polish social history was formed at the Institute of History in the Polish Academy of Sciences. Impulses coming from economic history stimulated the growth of further research fields such as the history of ideas, mentalities, and cultural history. Later on, this intellectual ferment sparked the formation of the so-called Warsaw school of the history of ideas (with Jerzy Jedlicki, Andrzej Walicki, Jerzy Szacki, Bronisław Baczko, and Leszek Kołakowski). Both in Poland and in Hungary, the liberal directors of the historical institutes of the national academies (Zsigmond Pál Pach and Tadeusz Manteuffel) supported new, ambitious research programmes. The main research topic of the period has both a symbolic and ironic meaning: in East Central Europe, the Stalinist narrative of progress was replaced by a focus on the backwardness of the region. Both Marxist historiographies

cooperated in a number of bilateral joint conferences and meetings, debating the
backwardness of the region in historical perspective (with the notion of
'backwardness' masked by euphemistic descriptions, such as the 'Prussian
course of agricultural development').[934]

The period that witnessed the most dynamic development in Polish and
Hungarian historiography, the 1960s, lies beyond the chronological boundaries
of this volume. It also does not consider the stable and fully controlled situation
of East German historiography or the fleeting liberalisation and re-Stalinisation
of historiography that followed the invasion by the Warsaw Pact states
(including the GDR and Poland) – of Czechoslovakia in August 1968. Still, the
fact that Marxist historiographies in some countries of the Eastern Bloc
managed to exploit the favourable political situation and create works of real
value is significant. After all, it shows that Marxism had the potential for
liberating historical discourse from the dichotomy of national and revolutionary
values ubiquitous in the 1950s.

***

In spite of a declared breakthrough and innovative intentions, the Marxist
concepts of national history, whether "optimistic" or "pessimistic," remained
tied to existing traditions of historical thinking. The new paradigm did not take
root. No "Bolshevisation" of historiography occurred – instead, in some cases, it
was trivialised. Still, disadvantageous changes resulted from the manner of
scientific conduct, the pursuit of a single, canonical perspective on every
problem, rather than from any antipathies toward various elements of the history
of Poland, Germany, Slovakia or Bohemia. In other words, it had been an
attempt to force historians into active participation in a myth, or into partaking
in the formation of a myth. Time showed that Marxist historiographies quite
often "conserved" traditional interpretations, deeming them Marxist and
defending their "purity" from any kind of criticism.

The comparison of several Marxist historiographies in terms of their attitude
toward national traditions compels us to modify or reject some of the claims
raised toward each of them. Starting with Poland, it seems that the thesis about the
anti-nationalist nature of Stalinist historiography cannot be supported. While
several more or less "national" interpretations competed within Marxist
historiography, there was no established "anti-national" pattern (barring the
elements of Polish native traditions which collided with Russian traditions, of
course). The schematicism of Marxist historiography did not consist in the

---

934 Emil Niederhauser, *Eastern Europe in Recent Hungarian Historiography* (Budapest,
     1975).

imposition of a previously framed interpretation, but rather in the acceptance of a singular perspective as unquestionably binding in every particular case. Whether that perspective was "national" or "anti-national" was of secondary importance, never a point of view established beforehand. One could, of course, always claim that science done in this way was antithetical to the Polish historiographic tradition (and the claim would largely prove to be true), but the same model was applied in every other people's democracy, even in countries where "national" values were seemingly treated with more reverence than in Poland. Similar statements about Marxism's anti-national intentions in historiography are currently made also by Slovak historians, though the supposed anti-Slovak tendency of Marxist historiography in question is frankly untraceable. At the same time, I believe that schematicism was far more detrimental to the historiographies discussed here than the potential "anti-national" reinterpretation of the history of Poland or Slovakia would have been, since it limited the freedom to form any – national or anti-national – competing interpretations.

I counter claims about a breakthrough and rupture in the continuity of Polish and Slovak historiography with the model discussed herein, where the theory of formations, alliance with the Soviet Union, and aversion toward the Church acted as a scaffolding upon which historians could raise new Marxist visions of national history. The gaps in this scaffolding were filled for the most part with older, traditional interpretations, which thereby became, in a way, Marxist. This content, the evaluation of particular elements of national histories, remained somewhat shaky. That is, guidelines for deciding what was and was not "progressive" were missing.

Several Czech historians are inclined to note the virtues of past, Marxist historiography, in its relatively positive attitude toward national traditions. One can find statements extolling the merits of particular Marxists (Zdeněk Nejedlý being the most prominent example) in "defending" Palacký, Havlíček-Borovský, or other remnants of national traditions supposedly threatened with "Stalinisation." I cannot fathom any virtue in such a schematic, petrified historiography, which stifles all attempts at producing an alternative – "rightist" or "leftist" – reading of historical traditions. As was the case in Poland and Slovakia, the growing "nationalisation" or "Bolshevisation" of Czech Marxist historiography was merely a byproduct (and not necessarily final, at that) of a specific model of science. Assessments of particular national heroes, uprisings, national movements, and so forth, could change without shifting the foundations and mechanisms of Marxist historiography, fitting squarely within its logic. Comparing these few examples, I am led to believe that no national values, however defined, were endangered, but the quality of thinking about history, which, I am quite certain, does not count as a national value.

I believe that a comparison of several Marxist historiographies of Central and Eastern Europe also raises doubts concerning the German research model quite commonly applied to the study of historiography in the GDR, which repeatedly connects it with West German historiography and politics. It is clear as day that the East German vision of history contains many aspects which become intelligible only in comparison with other countries of the Eastern bloc. Meanwhile it relates to West German historiography only very superficially. Structural connections, evident in comparison to Polish, Czech or Slovak historiography, derive from the fact that East Central European historiographies (and histories) plainly represent the best mutual context. After all, they are tied together by shared traditions of writing about history (with an enormous role played by German historical sciences as the originator and transmitter of methodological ideas), post-1945 geopolitics, and obligations to submit to identical political pressures. This comparison does not exhaust all the virtues of setting the GDR against its Eastern neighbours; one should also take into account the vivid interactions between historians from East Germany and Poland, Bohemia or Slovakia, often tasked separately with fashioning Marxist interpretations of the same events and historical figures. Through their works, historians from the GDR engaged in a dialogue with their colleagues from Poland, the Soviet Union or Czechoslovakia, while their connections to West Germany went through prolonged dry periods, when one side or the other had little to say to the other side.

To summarize, we should re-emphasize the most general conclusion of my work – the claim that there was a multithreaded continuity of content and form before and after the so-called methodological breakthrough, regardless of institutional changes, and a particularly catastrophic change in the manner of conducting scientific debates. Earlier, pre-Marxist concepts did not curl up and die, but were rather absorbed into Marxist historiography. They were then revived bit by bit – usually incognito – in Marxist interpretations. Marxist historiographies of the Stalinist period owed great debts to preceding schools of thought far more thoroughly than might appear from reading the manifestos of the "methodological breakthrough."

Bibliography

Archival documents, sources, and memoirs

Archiwum Akt Nowych (Warszawa)
- KC PZPR
    Wydział Nauki i Szkolnictwa Wyższego
    Komisja Oświaty i Nauki
    Wydział Nauki
- Ministerstwo Oświaty

Gabinet Ministra
- Zygmunt Modzelewski. Archiwum Osobiste
- Tadeusz Daniszewski. Spuścizna

Universitätsarchiv Leipzig
- Rektorat
- Arbeiter und Beuern Fakultät
- Nachlass Max Steinmetz

Archiwum Polskiej Akademii Nauk (Warszawa)
- Materiały Tadeusza Manteuffla
- Polskie Towarzystwo Historyczne
- Materiały Bogusława Leśnodorskiego
- Wydział I PAN
- Materiały Natalii Gąsiorowskiej-Grabowskiej

Archiwum Instytutu Historii PAN (Warszawa)
- Zakład Historii Historiografii. Łódź
- Zebrania ogólne pracowników
- Nagrody naukowe – wnioski, korespondencja 1953-70
- Protokoły Rady Naukowej
- Samodzielna Sekcja d/s Osobowych
- Podręcznik Historii Polski
- Komisja wydawnictw źródłowych do historii klasy robotniczej
- Protokoły z posiedzeń Kolegium IHPAN
- Popularyzacja wiedzy historycznej
- *Kwartalnik Historyczny*
- Organizacja IHPAN

Private Archive Jerzy Jedlicki (Warszawa)
- Przeciw fałszerstwom Wydziału Historii Partii (materiały z lat 1955-56)

Dział Rękopisów BUW (Warszawa)
- Nina Assorodobraj
- Witold Kula

Karlheinz Blaschke, "Als bürgerlicher Historiker am Rande der DDR. Erlebnisse, Beobachtungen und Überlegungen eines Nonkonformisten," in, *Historiker in der DDR*, ed. Karl Heinrich Pohl, Göttingen 1997
Helena Brodowska-Kubicz, *Z chłopskiej łąki. Wspomnienia*, Łódź 1994
Maria Dąbrowska, *Dzienniki powojenne 1950-1954*, vol. 2, Warszawa 1996
Karol Górski, *Autobiografia naukowa*, ed. Wiesław Sieradzan, Toruń 2003
Kurt Hager, *Erinnerungen*, Leipzig 1996
"Anders werden." Die Anfänge der politischen Erwachsenenbildung in der DDR. Gespräche mit Hans Mahle, Paul Wandel, Kurt Hager, Alice Zadek, Wolfgang Harich, Heinrich Scheel, Helmut Bock, Erwin Hinz, Rosemarie Walther, Werner Hecht, Heinz Fleischer und Norbert Podewin, eds. Sabine Hering & Hans-Georg Lützenkirschen, Berlin 1995
Paweł Jasienica, *Pamiętnik*, Kraków 1990
"Kartki z historii (historyków)," *Newsletter IH UW*, March-April 2002
František Kavka, *Ohlédnutí za padesáti lety ve službě českému dějepisectví*, Praha 2002
Fritz Klein, *Drinnen und draussen. Ein Historiker in der DDR. Erinnerungen*, Frankfurt/Main 2000
Polska w dokumentach z archiwów rosyjskich 1949-1953, eds. Aleksander Kochański, Galina P. Muraszko, Albina F. Noskowa, Andrzej Paczkowski & Krzysztof Persak, Warszawa 2000
Żanna Kormanowa, *Ludzie i życie*, Warszawa 1982
Jürgen Kuczynski, *Memoiren. Die Erziehung des J. K. zum Kommunisten und Wissenschaftler*, Berlin-Weimar 1975
Jürgen Kuczynski, *Ein Leben in der Wissenschaft der DDR*, Münster 1994
Jürgen Kuczynski, *Frost nach dem Tauwetter. Mein Historikerstreit*, Berlin 1993
Jürgen Kuczynski, *Dialog mit meinen Urenkel. Neunzehn Briefe uns ein Tagebuch*, Berlin-Weimar 1983
Marcin Kula, "Śpij spokojnie – rząd myśli, partia czuwa... A co robią jej członkowie? Kilka dokumentów z historii życia naukowego w czasach PRL," *Przegląd Humanistyczny* 2005
Witold Kula, *Wokół historii*, Warszawa 1988

Witold Kula, *Rozdziałki*, ed. Marcin Kula, Warszawa 1996
Antonín J. Liehm, *Generace*, Praha 1990
Josef Macůrek, *Úvahy o mé vědecké činnosti a vědeckých pracích*, Brno 1998
Antoni Mączak & Wojciech Tygielski, *Latem w Tocznabieli*, Warszawa 2000
Joachim Petzold, "'Meinungsstreit' im Herrschaftsdiskurs", in: *Geschichte als Herrschaftdiskurs. Der Umgang mit der Vergangenheit in der DDR*, Köln 2000
Joachim Petzold, "Politischer Auftrag und wissenschaftliche Verantwortung von Historikern in der DDR," in: *Historiker in der DDR*, ed. Karl Heinrich Pohl, Göttingen 1997
Josef Polišenský, *Historik v měnícím se světě*, Praha 2001
"Pozbawienie profesora Władysława Tatarkiewicza prawa nauczania," *Przegląd Filozoficzny* 1995
Adam Schaff, *Notatki Kłopotnika*, Warszawa 1995
Adam Schaff, *Moje spotkania z nauką polską*, Warszawa 1997
Stefan Żółkiewski, *Przepowiednie i wspomnienia*, Warszawa 1963

Journals

Časopis Matice Moravské, 1948-1963 (ex. 1949)
Československý časopis historický, 1953-1967
Český Časopis Historický, 1946
Einheit, selected issues
Historia Slovaca, selected issues
Historický Časopis Slovenskej Akadémie Vied, 1953-1965
Historie a vojenství, selected issues
Jantar, 1946
Kwartalnik Historii Kultury Materialnej, 1953-1956
Kwartalnik Historyczny, 1939/45-1958
Nowe Drogi, 1947-1956
Przegląd Historyczny, 1946-1956
Przegląd Zachodni, 1948-1953
Slezský sborník, 1948-1963
Sobótka, 1949-1956
Věstník ČSAV, selected issues
Wissenschaftliche Zeitschrift der Martin-Luther-Universität Halle-Wittenberg, selected issues
Zeitschrift für Geschichtswissenschaft, 1953-1968

Primary sources

Alexander Abusch, *Der Irrweg einer Nation. Ein Beitrag zum Verständnis deutscher Geschichte*, Berlin 1951

Jan Adamus, *O monarchii Gallowej*, Warszawa 1952

Robert Alt, *Pokrokový charakter Komenského pedagogiky*, Praha 1955

Čestmír Amort, *Ruská vojská u nás v letech 1798-1800*, Praha 1954

Towarzystwo Demokratyczne Polskie. Dokumenty i pisma, ed. Bronisław Baczko, Warszawa 1954

Bohdan Baranowski, *Powstanie Kostki Napierskiego w 1651 r.*, Warszawa 1951

Bohdan Baranowski, *Powstanie chłopskie Kostki Napierskiego. Odczyt*, Warszawa 1950

Juliusz Bardach, Aleksander Gieysztor, Henryk Łowmiański & Ewa Maleczyńska, *Historia Polski do r. 1466*, Warszawa 1953

František Michálek Bartoš, *Dvě studie o husitských postilách*, Praha 1955

Jan Baszkiewicz, *Powstanie zjednoczonego państwa polskiego na przełomie XIII i XIV wieku*, Warszawa 1954

Jan Baszkiewicz & Bogusław Leśnodorski, *Materiały do nauki historii Polski. Historia Polski od wspólnoty pierwotnej do drugiej połowy XVIII wieku*, Warszawa 1953

Z dziejów współpracy rewolucyjnej Polaków i Rosjan w drugiej połowie XIX wieku, eds. Ludwik Bazylow, Helena Brodowska & Krzysztof Dunin-Wąsowicz, Wrocław 1956

Rudolf Beckmann, *K diplomatickému pozadí Mnichova. Kapitoly o britské mnichovské politice*, Praha 1954

Jan Beránek, *Rakouský militarismus a boj proti němu v Čechách*, Praha 1955

Bolesław Bierut, *O konstytucji Polskiej Rzecypospolitej Ludowej*, Warszawa 1954

Celina Bobińska, *Historyk, fakt, metoda*, Warszawa 1964

Celina Bobińska, *Marks i Engels a sprawy polskie do osiemdziesiątych lat XIX wieku*, Warszawa 1954

Celina Bobińska, *Marx und Engels über polnische Probleme*, Berlin 1958

František Bokes, *Dejiny Slovenska a Slovákov od najstarších čias po oslobodenie*, Bratislava 1946

Viktor Borodovčák, *Ohlas poľského povstania roku 1863 na Slovensku. Slovenskí polonofili a spolupráca demokratických síl Rakúska v boji proti petrohradskému a viedenskému absolutizmu*, Bratislava 1960

Július Botto, *Slováci. Vývin ich národného povedomia*, Bratislava 1971

Jiří Brabenec, *Po stopách starých pověstí českých*, Praha 1959

Jozef Butvin, *Slovenské národno-zjednocovacie hnutie (1780-1848)*. *K otázke formovania novodobého slovenského buržoázneho národa*, Bratislava 1965

Die bürgerliche deutsche Geschichtsschreibung von der Reichseinigung von oben bis zur Befreiung Deutschlands vom Faschismus, ed. Joachim Streisand, Berlin 1965

Václav Chaloupecký, *Staré Slovensko*, Bratislava 1923

Pavel Choc, *Boje o Prahu za feudalismu*, Praha 1957

Dejiny Slovenska II. Od roku 1848 do roku 1900, ed. Július Mésároš, Bratislava 1968

Dejiny Slovenska (tézy). Príloha Historického časopisu, ed. Ľudovít Holotík, Bratislava 1955

Die deutsche Geschichtswissenschaft vom Beginn des 19. Jahrhunderts bis zum Reichseinigung von oben, ed. Joachim Streisand, Berlin 1963

Josef Dobiáš, *Z dějin sociálních bojů v Čechách v 16. a 17. století*, Praha 1953

Julius Dolanský, *Masaryk a Rusko předrevoluční*, Praha 1959

Zoroslava Drobná & Jan Durdík, *Kroje, zbroj a zbraně doby předhusitské a husitské*, Praha 1956

Johann Gustav Droysen, *Friedrich I. König von Preußen*, Berlin 2001

Johann Gustav Droysen, *Historik. Vorlesungen über Enzyklopädie und Methodologie der Geschichte*, ed. Rudolf Hübner, München 1960

Krzysztof Dunin-Wąsowicz, *Dzieje Stronnictwa Ludowego w Galicji*, Warszawa 1956

Jan Durdík, *Husitské vojenství*, Praha 1954

Michal Dzvoník, *Ohlas Veľkej októbrovej socialistickej revolucie na Slovensku (1918-1919)*, Bratislava 1957

Ernst Engelberg, *Deutschland von 1871 bis 1897 (Deutschland in der Übergangsperiode zum Imperialismus)*, Berlin 1965

Jan Fajkus, *Husitské revoluční hnutí*, Praha 1956

Franku Wollmanovi k sedmdesátinám. Sborník prací, ed. Artur Závodský, Praha 1958,

Natalia Gąsiorowska-Grabowska, *Kapitalizm w rozwoju dziejowym*, Warszawa 1946

Georg Gottfried Gervinus, *Kleine historische Schriften*, Karlsruhe 1838

Geschichte der deutschen Arbeiterbewegung. Von den Anfängen der deutschen Arbeiterbewegung bis zum Ausgang des 19. Jahrhunderts, eds. Walter Ulbricht et al., Berlin 1966

Karol Goláň, *Štúrovské pokolenie (Výber z diela)*, Bratislava 1964

Jaroslav Goll, *Posledních padesát let české práce dějepisné*, Praha 1926

Miloš Gosiorovský, *Dejiny slovenského robotníckeho hnutia (1848-1918)*, Bratislava 1958

Klement Gottwald, *Kupředu, zpátky ni krok! (únor 1948)*, Praha 1951
Gottwald je s námi. Náš první dělnický president v zrcadle české a slovenské poesie a prózy, ed. Alexej Kusák, Praha 1953
František Graus, *Městská chudina v době předhusitské*, Praha 1948
František Graus, *Dějiny venkovského lidu v Čechách v době předhusitské*, 2 vols., Praha 1951-1957
Krzysztof Groniowski, *Problem rewolucji agrarnej w ideologii obozów politycznych w latach 1846-1870*, Warszawa 1957
Leon Grosfeld, *Polskie reakcyjne formacje wojskowe w Rosji (1917-1919)*, Warszawa 1955
Hipolit Grynwaser, *Sprawa włościańska w Królestwie Polskim w latach 1861-62 w świetle źródeł archiwalnych*, Wrocław 1951
Hipolit Grynwaser, *Kwestia agrarna i ruch włościan w Królestwie Polskim w pierwszej połowie XIX wieku (1807-1860). Studium archiwalne. Przywódcy i "burzyciele" włościan*, Wrocław 1951
Marceli Handelsmann , *Adam Czartoryski*, 3 vols., Warszawa 1948-1950
Historia Polski (Makieta), part 1 in 2 vols., ed. Henryk Łowmiański, Warszawa 1955
Historia Polski, part 1 in 2 vols., ed. Henryk Łowmiański, Warszawa 1957
Historia Polski (Makieta), part 2 in 2 vols., eds. Stefan Kieniewicz & Witold Kula, Warszawa 1956
Historia Polski, part 2 in 2 vols., eds. Stefan Kieniewicz & Witold Kula, Warszawa 1958
Historia Polski, part 3 in 2 vols., eds. Żanna Kormanowa & Walentyna Najdus, Warszawa 1968
Historia Polski 1864-1945. Materiały do nauczania w klasie XI, ed. Żanna Kormanowa, Warszawa 1952
Historia Polski (Makieta), part 3 in 2 vols., eds. Żanna Kormanowa & Irena Pietrzak-Pawłowska, Warszawa 1960
Historische Forschungen in der DDR. Analysen und Berichte. Zum XI. Internationalen Historikerkongreß in Stockholm, August 1960, Berlin 1960
Historiografia polska wobec problemu polsko-niemieckiego. Referaty i dyskusja na konferencji międzyśrodowiskowej we Wrocławiu 6 lipca 1950, Wrocław 1951
Historycy o historii 1918-1939, ed. Marian Henryk Serejski, 2 vols., Warszawa 1963-1966
Historycy radzieccy o Polsce. Wybór prac, ed. Stefan Gwich, Warszawa 1953
Ladislav Hoffmann, *Bratříci – slavní protifeudální bojovníci 15. století*, Praha 1959
Ľudovít Holotík, *Štefánikovská legenda a vznik ČSR*, Bratislava 1958

Ľudovít Holotík, *Októbrová revolúcia a národnooslobodzovacie hnutie na Slovensku v rokoch 1917-1918*, Bratislava 1958

Ján Horárik, *Boj s hierarchiou a cirkvou v rokoch 1841-45*, Bratislava 1953

Ladislav Hosák, *Nové československé dějiny*, Praha 1947

Thomas Höhle, *Franz Mehring. Sein Weg zum Marxismus 1869-1891*, Berlin 1956

Václav Husa, *Historia Czechosłowacji*, Praga 1967

Václav Husa, *Tomáš Müntzer a Čechy*, Praha 1957

Humanizmus a renesancia na Slovensku v 15.-16. storočí, eds. Ľudovít Holotík & Anton Vantuch, Bratislava 1967

Instytut Bałtycki – szkic informacyjny, Gdańsk-Bydgoszcz-Szczecin 1947

История Польши vol. 1, eds. В. Д. Королюк И. С. Миллер П. Н. Третьяков, Москва 1954

Henryk Jabłoński, *Międzynarodowe znaczenie polskich walk narodowowyzwoleńczych XVIII i XIX w.*, Warszawa 1955

Stanisław Kalabiński, *Antynarodowa polityka endecji w rewolucji 1905-1907*, Warszawa 1955

Stanisław Kalabiński, *Carat i klasy posiadające w walce z rewolucją 1905-1907 w Królestwie Polskim*, Warszawa 1956

Robert Kalivoda, *Husitská ideologie*, Praha 1961

Heinz Kamnitzer, *Zur Vorgeschichte des Deutschen Bauernkrieges*, Berlin 1953

František Kavka, *Z dějin českého národa, vol. 1. Staré pověstí české*, Praha 1955

Stefan Kieniewicz, *Ruch chłopski w Galicji w 1846 roku*, Wrocław 1951

Stefan Kieniewicz, *Konspiracje galicyjskie (1831-1845)*, Warszawa 1950

Stefan Kieniewicz, *Oblicze ideowe Wiosny Ludów*, Warszawa 1948

Stefan Kieniewicz, *Legion Mickiewicza 1848-1849*, Warszawa 1955

Stefan Kieniewicz, *Czyn polski w dobie Wiosny Ludów*, Warszawa 1948

Arnošt Klíma, *Čechy v období temna*, Praha 1958

Arnošt Klíma, *Rok 1848 w Czechach. Początki ruchu robotniczego w Czechach*, Warszawa 1951

Josef Kočí, *Naše národní obrození*, Praha 1960

Josef Kočí, *Boje venkovského lidu v období temna*, Praha 1953

Josef Kočí, *Selské bouře a české národní obrození*, Praha 1963

Ján Kollár, *Pamäti z mladších rokov života*, Bratislava 1950

Ján Kollár, *Wybór pism*, Wrocław 1954

Hugo Kołłątaj, *Wybór pism politycznych*, Wrocław 1952

Hugo Kołłątaj, *Listy anonima i prawo polityczne narodu polskiego*, Kraków 1954

Zdeněk Konečný, *Revoluční hnutí v Československu a jeho vztahy k SSSR. Morava a Slezsko-dokumenty 1879-1938*, Praha 1960

Konferencja pomorska 1954, eds. Bogusław Leśnodorski, Stefan Kieniewicz, Łukasz Kurdybacha, Bronisław Krauze, Gerard Labuda & Maria Bogucka, Warszawa 1956

Václav Kopecký, *Osvětu a kulturu do služeb socialismu! Výklad ministra informací a osvěty Václava Kopeckého v kulturním výboru Národního shromáždění dne 20. března 1950*, Praha 1950

Václav Kopecký, *ČSR a KSČ. Pamětní výpisy k historii Československé republiky a k boji KSČ za socialistické Československo*, Praha 1960

Żanna Kormanowa, *Joachim Lelewel*, Warszawa 1946

Adam Korta, *O postępowych tradycjach i antynarodowych mitach*, Warszawa 1955

Paweł Korzec, *Walki rewolucyjne w Łodzi i okręgu łódzkim w latach 1905-1907*, Warszawa 1956

Józef Kozłowski, *"Międzynarodówka" – wielka pieśń rewolucji*, Warszawa 1952

Václav Král, *O Masarykově a Benešově kontrarevoluci proti sovětské politice*, Praha 1953

Zdeněk Konečný, *Revoluční hnutí v Československu a jeho vztahy k SSSR*, Praha 1960

Jewgienij Kosminski, *Historia wieków średnich*, Warszawa 1953

Krótki słownik filozoficzny, eds. Mark M. Rozental & Pavel F. Judin, Warszawa 1955

Łukasz Kurdybacha, *Kuria rzymska wobec Komisji Edukacji Narodowej w latach 1773-1783*, Kraków 1949

Kuźnica Kołłątajowska, ed. Bogusław Leśnodorski, Wrocław 1949

Ján Kvasnička, *Československé légie v Rusku 1917-1920*, Bratislava 1963

Karl Lamprecht, *Alternative zu Ranke. Schriften zur Geschichtstheorie*, Leipzig 1988

Karl Lamprecht, *Ausgewählte Schriften zur Wirtschafts- und Kulturgeschichte und zur Theorie der Geschichtswissenschaft*, Aalen 1974

Joachim Lelewel, *Wybór pism politycznych*, Warszawa 1954

Max Lenz, *Kleine historische Schriften*, München – Berlin 1910

Kazimierz Lepszy, *Andrzej Frycz Modrzewski*, Warszawa 1953

Bogusław Leśnodorski, *Dzieło Sejmu Czteroletniego (1788-1792). Studium historyczno-prawne*, Wrocław 1951

Bogusław Leśnodorski & Kazimierz Opałek, *Nauka polskiego Oświecenia w walce o postęp*, Warszawa 1951

Tadeusz Łepkowski, *Początki klasy robotniczej Warszawy*, Warszawa 1956

Róża Luksemburg, *Rok 1905 (wybór artykułów)*, Warszawa 1951

Henryk Łowmiański, *Zagadnienie roli Normanów w genezie państw słowiańskich*, Warszawa 1957

Witold Łukaszewicz, *Szymon Konarski (1808-1839)*, Warszawa 1948

Witold Łukaszewicz, *Targowica i powstanie kościuszkowskie. Ze studiów nad historią Polski XVIII wieku*, Warszawa 1952

Witold Łukaszewicz, *Barykady paryskie (1827-1848)*, Łódź 1949

Witold Łukaszewicz, *Tadeusz Krępowiecki. Żołnierz rewolucjonista*, Warszawa 1954

Witold Łukaszewicz, *Stanisław Gabriel Worcell*, Warszawa 1951

Josef Macek, *Husité na Baltu a ve Velkopolsku*, Praha 1952

Josef Macek, *Husitské revoluční hnutí*, Praha 1952

Josef Macek, *Ktož jsú boží bojovníci*, Praha 1951

Josef Macek, *Jan Hus*, Praha 1963

Josef Macek, *Husyci na Pomorzu i w Wielkopolsce*, Warszawa 1955

Josef Macek, *Husitství – živý zdroj národních tradic*, Praha 1952

Josef Macek, *Tábor v husitském revolučním hnutí*, Praha 1956

Josef Macek, *Z dějin českého národa. Mezi proudy*, vol. 2, Praha 1955

Josef Macek, *Z dějin českého národa. Proti všem*, Praha 1955

Josef Macek, *Die Hussitenbewegung in Böhmen*, Praha 1958

Josef Macek, *The Hussite Movement in Bohemia*, Praha 1958

Přehled československých dějin (Maketa), eds. Josef Macek, František Graus & Ján Tibenský, 2 vols., Praha 1958-1960

Milan Machovec, *Husovo učení a význam v tradici*, Praha 1953

Josef Macůrek & Miloš Rejnuš, *České země a Slovensko ve století před Bílou horou*, Praha 1958

Ewa Maleczyńska, *Ruch husycki w Czechach i w Polsce*, Warszawa 1959

Materiały do powstania Kostki Napierskiego, ed. Adam Przyboś, Wrocław 1951

Matica slovenská v našich dejinách. Sborník statí, eds. Július Mésároš & Miroslav Kropilák, Bratislava 1963

Милослав Матоушек, *Зденек Неедлы-великий деятель чехословацкой культуры*, Прага 1953

Vladimír Matula, *Ľudovít Štúr (1815-1856)*, Bratislava 1956

Władimir W. Mawrodin, *Walka z "teorią normańską" w rosyjskiej nauce historycznej*, Warszawa 1951

Květa Mejdřická, *Z dějin českého národa*, vol. 7, *F. L. Věk*, Praha 1955

Andrej Melicherčík, *Juraj Jánošík. Hrdina protifeudálního odboje slovenského lidu*, Praha 1956

Andrej Melicherčík, *Jánošíkovská tradícia na Slovensku*, Bratislava 1953

Maksymilian Meloch, *Studia historyczne*, Warszawa 1958

Maksymilian Meloch, *Sprawa włościańska w powstaniu listopadowym*, Warszawa 1953

Alfred Meusel, *Thomas Müntzer und seine Zeit*, Berlin 1952

Karel Michl, *Husitství na Hradecku*, Hradec Kralové 1955

Andrej Mráz, *Zo slovenskej literárnej minulosti*, Bratislava 1953

Zdeněk Nejedlý, *O smyslu českých dějin*, Praha 1953

Zdeněk Nejedlý, *T. G. Masaryk, kniha první, Masarykovo mládí, 1850-1876*, Praha 1949

Zdeněk Nejedlý, *Staré pověsti české jako historický pramen*, Praha 1953

Zdeněk Nejedlý, *Dějiny husitského zpěvu*, Praha 1954

Zdeněk Nejedlý, *Dějiny národa českého II. Raný středověk*, Praha 1955

Zdeněk Nejedlý, *Alois Jirásek Studie historická*, Praha 1949

Zdeněk Nejedlý, *Z české kultury*, Praha 1951

Jan Novotný, *O bratrské družbě Čechů a Slováků za národního obrození*, Praha 1959

Lubomír Nový, *Filosofie T. G. Masaryka*, Praha 1962

Andrzej Nowicki, *Papieże przeciw Polsce. Doświadczenia dziesięciu stuleci naszych dziejów*, Warszawa 1949

O počiatkoch slovenských dejín. Sborník materiálov, ed. Peter Ratkoš, Bratislava 1965

Karl Obermann, *Deutschland von 1815 bis 1849 (Von der Gründung des Deutschen Reiches bis zur bürgerlich-demokratischen Revolution)*, Berlin 1963

Karl Obermann, *Die deutschen Arbeiter in der Revolution von 1848*, Berlin 1953

Wiesław Ochmański, *Zbójnictwo góralskie. Z dziejów walki klasowej na wsi góralskiej*, Kraków 1950

Karl-Heinz Otto, *Deutschland in der Epoche der Urgesellschaft (500000 v. u. Z. bis zum 5./6. Jh. u. Z.)*., Berlin 1961

Jan Pachta, *Pekař a pekařovština v českém dějepisectví*, Brno 1950

Josef Petráň, *Poddaný lid v Čechách na prahu třicetilete války*, Praha 1964

Wilhelm Pieck, *Reden und Aufsätze. Auswahl aus den Jahren 1908-1950*, Berlin 1950

Pierwsza Konferencja Metodologiczna Historyków Polskich. Przemówienia, referaty, dyskusja, eds. Stanisław Herbst, Witold Kula &Tadeusz Manteuffel, 2 vols., Warszawa 1953

Kazimierz Piwarski, *Kuria rzymska a polski ruch narodowo-wyzwoleńczy 1794-1863*, Warszawa 1955

Podstawy ideologiczne PZPR. Referat tow. Bolesława Bieruta wygłoszony w dniu 15 XII 1948 r. Koreferat tow. Józefa Cyrankiewicza wygłoszony w dn. 16 XII 1948 r. na Kongresie Polskiej Zjednoczonej Partii Robotniczej. Deklaracja ideowa PZPR, Warszawa 1952

Polska sztuka wojenna w czasach Odrodzenia, eds. Tadeusz Nowak & Adam Korta, Warszawa 1955

Karel Pomaizl, *Vznik ČSR 1918. Problém marxistické vědecké interpretace*, Praha 1965

Program podstaw marksizmu-leninizmu dla wszystkich Szkół Wyższych za wyjątkiem Technicznych i Rolnych, eds. Weronika Gostyńska, Emil Adler, Józef Siwek, Kazimierz Owoc & Aleksander Berler, Warszawa 1952

Jaroslav Purš, *Dělnické hnutí v českých zemích 1849-1867*, Praha 1961

Leopold von Ranke, *Historische Meisterwerke*, Hamburg [1932]

Peter Ratkoš, *Povstanie baníkov na Slovensku roku 1525-1526*, Bratislava 1963

Pavel Reiman, *Dělnické hnutí v českých zemích v letech 1889-1917*, Praha 1955

Revoluční dedičstvo rokov 1848-1849. Sborník článkov, ed. Ľudovít Holotík, Bratislava 1951

Rewolucja polska 1846 roku. Wybór źródeł, ed. Stefan Kieniewicz, Wrocław 1949

František Roubík, *Revoluční rok 1848 a rolnictvo*, Praha 1955

Adam Schaff, *Obiektywny charakter praw historii. Z zagadnień marksistowskiej metodologii historiografii*, Warszawa 1955

Adam Schaff, *Pogadanki o materializmie historycznym*, Warszawa 1949

Gerhard Schilfert, *Deutschland von 1648 bis 1789*, Berlin 1962

Hans Schleier, *Sybel und Treitschke. Antidemokratismus und Militarismus im historisch-politischen Denken großbourgeoiser Geschichtsideologen*, Berlin 1965

Josef Schleifstein, *Franz Mehring. Sein marxistisches Schaffen 1891-1919*, Berlin 1959

Friedrich Christoph Schlosser, *Weltgeschichte für das deutsche Volk*, vol. 1, Frankfurt/Main 1844

Marian Henryk Serejski, *Joachim Lelewel. Z dziejów postępowej myśli historycznej w Polsce*, Warszawa 1953

Marian Henryk Serejski, *Studia nad historiografią Polski, T. I, K. B. Hoffman*, Łódź 1953

Marian Henryk Serejski, *Zarys historii historiografii polskiej, T. I (od poł. XVIII w. do roku ok. 1860)*, Łódź 1954

Sesja naukowa w trzechsetną rocznicę zjednoczenia Ukrainy z Rosją 1654-1954, Warszawa 1954

Jaroslav Slavík, *Husité na Chebsku*, Cheb 1955

Slováci a ich národný vývin (Sborník materiálov z V. sjazdu slovenských historikov v Banskej Bystrici), Bratislava 1966

Slovenské Národné Povstanie. Sborník prác k 10. výročiu, ed. Ľudovít Holotík, Bratislava 1954

Władysław Smoleński, *Szkoły historyczne w Polsce. (Główne kierunki poglądów na przeszłość)*, Wrocław 1952

Władysław Smoleński, *Kuźnica Kołłątajowska. Studium historyczne*, Warszawa 1949

Józef Stalin, *Marksizm a kwestia narodowa. Kwestia narodowa a leninizm*, Warszawa 1949

Stanisław Staszic, *Uwagi nad życiem Jana Zamoyskiego*, Wrocław 1952

Max Steinmetz, *Deutschland von 1476 bis 1648*, Berlin 1967

Leo Stern, *Gegenwartsaufgaben der deutschen Geschichtsforschung*, Berlin 1952

Leo Stern & Horst Gericke, *Deutschland in der Feudalepoche von der Mitte des 11. Jh. bis zur Mitte des 13. Jh.*, Berlin 1964

Leo Stern & Hans-Joachim Bartmuß, *Deutschland in der Feudalepoche von der Wende des 5./6. Jh. zur Mitte des 11. Jh.*, Berlin 1963

Leo Stern, *Deutschland in der Feudalepoche von det Mitte des 13. Jh. Bis zum ausgehenden 15. Jh.*, Berlin 1965

Joachim Streisand, *Deutschland von 1789 bis 1815 (Von der Französischen Revolution bis zu den Befreiungskriegen und dem Wiener Kongreß)*, Berlin 1959

Joachim Streisand, *Geschichtliches Denken von der deutschen Frühaufklärung bis zur Klassik*, Berlin 1964

Bogdan Suchodolski, *Nauka polska w okresie Oświecenia*, Warszawa 1953

Heinrich von Sybel, *Die Begründung des Deutschen Reiches durch Wilhelm I. Vornehmlich nach den preußischen Staatackten*, vol. 1, München – Leipzig 1890

Krystyna Śreniowska, *Stanisław Zakrzewski. Przyczynek do charakterystyki prądów ideologicznych w historiografii polskiej 1893-1936*, Łódź 1956

Bedřich Šindelář, *Ohlas maďarské revoluce 1848-1849 na Moravě a Slezsku*, Praha 1957

Jozef Škultéty, *Za slovenský život*, Martin 1998

Jozef Škultéty, *Slovanská vzájimnosť v publicistike Jozefa Škultétyho (výber)*, Martin 1998

Zdeněk Šolle, *Ke vzniku první dělnické strany v naší zemi*, Praha 1953

Zdeněk Šolle, *Příspěvek k dějinám dělnického hnutí v Čechách v letech 1878-1882*, Praha 1960

Ľudovít Štúr – *život a dielo 1815-1856. Sborník materiálov z konference Historického ústavu Slovenskej akadémie vied*, Bratislava 1956

Ľudovít Štúr, *Wybór pism*, Wrocław 1983

Ľudovít Štúr, *Hlas k rodákom (Úvahy, články, polémiky a recenzie)*, Turčiansky sv. Martin 1943

Tadeusz Kościuszko w historii i tradycji, ed. Jan Stanisław Kopczewski, Warszawa 1968

Teksty źródłowe do dziejów chłopa śląskiego, vol. 1, eds. Józef Gierowski & Józef Leszczyński Wrocław 1956

Teksty źródłowe do historii Wrocławia, cz. II do końca XIX wieku, ed. Karol Maleczyński, Wrocław 1955

Ján Tibenský, *Chvály a obrany slovenského národa*, Bratislava 1965

Iwan Iwanowicz Udalcow, *Studia z dziejów walk narodowych w Czechach w r. 1848*, Warszawa 1953

Úlohy slovenskej historickej vedy v období socialistickej výstavby, ed. Ľudovít Holotík, Bratislava 1961

Rudolf Urbánek, *Z husitského věku*, Praha 1957

Branislav Varsik, *Husitské revolučné hnutie a Slovensko*, Bratislava 1965

Vlastimil Vávra, *Klamná cesta*, Praha 1958

Výbor z české literatury doby husitské, eds. Bohuslav Havránek, Josef Hrabák, Jiří Daňhelka et al., 2 vols., Praha 1963-1964

Vznik a vývoj lidově demokratického Československa. Sborník statí, ed. Václav Král, Praha 1961

Henryk Wereszycki, *Niewygasła przeszłość. Refleksje i polemiki*, Kraków 1987

Wiosna Ludów na ziemiach polskich, eds. Natalia Gąsiorowska-Grabowska, Stefan Kieniewicz, Anna Minkowska, Irena Pietrzak-Pawłowska, Leon Przemyski & Mieczysław Tobiasz, Warszawa 1948

Wiosna Ludów w Europie, vol. 2, *Zagadnienia ideologiczne*, eds. Natalia Gąsiorowska-Grabowska, Stefan Kieniewicz, Anna Minkowska, Irena Pietrzak-Pawłowska, Leon Przemyski & Mieczysław Tobiasz, Warszawa 1951

Jerzy Włodarczyk, *Tadeusz Korzon. Główne koncepcje historyczne i historiozoficzne*, Łódź 1958

Heinz Wohlgemuth, *Deutschland und die deutsche Arbeiterbewegung von der Jahrhundertwende bis 1917*, Berlin 1963

Zygmunt Wojciechowski, *Polska – Niemcy. Dziesięć wieków zmagania*, Poznań 1945

Kazimierz Wyka, *Teka Stańczyka na tle historii Galicji w latach 1849-1869*, Wrocław 1951

Wystawa Rewolucyjny ruch husycki (Muzeum Narodowe w Pradze – Muzeum Historyczne Miasta Stołecznego Warszawy. Listopad – grudzień 1959, Warszawa 1959

Z bojů za svobodu a socialismus. Úloha SSSR v osvobozeneckých bojích a budovatelském úsilí českého a slovenského lidu, ed. Jaroslav Vávra, Praha 1961

Z dejín československo-slovanských vzťahov, ed. Jozef Hrozienčik, Bratislava 1959

Z epoki Mickiewicza. Zeszyt specjalny "Przeglądu Historycznego" w rocznicę śmierci Adama Mickiewicza 1855-1955, eds. Stefan Kieniewicz, Izabela Bieżuńska-Małowist & Antoni Mączak, Wrocław 1956

Timoteus Čestmír Zelinka, *Husitskou Prahou*, Praha 1955

Zdeňku Nejedlému Československá Akademie Věd. Sborník prací k sedmdesátým pátým narozeninám, eds. Václav Husa, Bohuslav Havránek, Jan Kořan, Karol Rosenbaum & Otakar Zich, Praha 1953

Stefan Żółkiewski, *Stare i nowe literaturoznawstwo. Szkice krytyczno-naukowe*, Wrocław 1950

Secondary Sources

Sirkka Ahonen, *Clio sans uniform. A study of the post-Marxist transformation of the history curricula in East Germany and Estonia, 1986-1991*, Helsinki 1992

Helmut Alexander, *Geschichte, Partei und Wissenschaft. Liberale und demokratische Bewegungen in der Zeit der Restauration und im Vormärz aus der Sicht der DDR-Geschichtswissenschaft*, Frankfurt/Main 1988

Stefan Albrecht, *Geschichte der Großmährenforschung in den Tschechischen Ländern und in der Slowakei*, Praha 2003

Monika Baár, *Historians and nationalism. East-Central Europe in the nineteenth century*, Oxford 2010

Jacek Banaszkiewicz, *Polskie dzieje bajeczne Mistrza Wincentego Kadłubka*, Wrocław 1998

Simone Barck, Martina Langermann & Siegfried Lokatis, *Jedes Buch ein Abenteuer! Zensursystem und literarische Öffentlichkeiten in der DDR bis Ende der sechziger Jahre*, Berlin 1997

Michal Barnovský, "Niekoľko poznámok k výskumu povojnových dejín Slovenska v poslednom desaťročí," *HČSAV* 2002

Michal Bauer, "První kroky poúnorového režimu v ediční činnosti," *Tvar* 1997

Michal Bauer, "Jiráskovská akce," *Tvar* 1997

Begegnung und Konflikt. Schlaglichter auf das Verhältnis von Tschechen, Slowaken und Deutschen 1815-1989. Beiträge aus den Veröffentlichungen der Deutsch – Tschechischen und Deutsch – Slowakischen Historikerkommission, eds. Jörg K. Hoensch & Hans Lemberg, Essen 2001

Beruf und Berufung. Geschichtswissenschaft und Nationsbildung in Ostmittel- und Südosteuropa im 19. Und 20. Jahrhundert, eds. Markus Krzoska & Hans-Christian Maner, Münster 2005

Stanisław T. Bębenek, *Myślenie o przeszłości*, Warszawa 1981

Stanisław T. Bębenek, "Spory historyczne w polskiej prasie kulturalno-literackiej z lat 1945-1948," *DN* 1974

Stanisław T. Bębenek, "Problematyka historyczna w polskiej prasie społeczno-kulturalnej 1945-1966," *DN* 1978

Die Bildungs-, Wissenschafts- und Kulturpolitik in der Slowakei 1945-2004, eds. Beata Blehová & Peter Bachmeier, Frankfurt/Main 2004

Piotr Biliński, *Władysław Konopczyński. Historyk i polityk II Rzeczypospolitej (1880-1952)*, Warszawa 1999

Agnes Blänsdorf, "Die deutsche Geschichte in der Sicht der DDR. Ein Vergleich mit der Entwicklung in der Bundesrepublik Deutschland und in Österreich seit 1945," *GWU* 1988

Helmut Bleiber, "40 Jahre DDR-Geschichtswissenscheft – Leistungen und Grenzen," *Österreichische Osthefte* 33 (1991)

Katarzyna Błachowska, "Rosja w historiografii polskiej pierwszych lat powojennych (1945-1956)," in: *Klio polska. Studia i materiały z dziejów historiografii polskiej po II wojnie światowej*, ed. Andrzej Wierzbicki, Warszawa 2004

Katarzyna Błachowska, *Narodziny imperium. Rozwój terytorialny państwa carów w ujęciu historyków rosyjskich XVIII i XIX wieku*, Warszawa 2001

Katarzyna Błachowska, *Wiele historii jednego państwa. Obraz dziejów Wielkiego Księstwa Litewskiego do 1569 roku w ujęciu historyków polskich, rosyjskich, ukraińskich, litewskich i białoruskich w XIX wieku*, Warszawa 2010

Maria Bobrownicka, *Narkotyk mitu. Szkice o świadomości narodowej i kulturowej Słowian zachodnich i południowych*, Kraków 1995

Lucian Boia, *History and myth in Romanian consciousness*, Budapest – New York 2001

Michael Borgolte, "Eine Generation marxistische Mittelalterforschung in Deutschland. Erbe und Tradition aus der Sicht eines Neu-Humboldtianers," *GWU* 1993

Włodzimierz Borodziej, "'Ostforschung' aus der Sicht der polnischen Geschichtsschreibung," *ZfO-F*, 1997/3

Jaroslav Bouček, "Jan Slavík," *HaV* 1991

Thomas A. Brady Jr., *The Protestant reformation in German history*, Washington 1998

Jan Herman Brinks, *Die DDR-Geschichtswissenschaft auf dem Weg zur deutschen Einheit. Luther, Friedrich II und Bismarck als Paradigmen politischen Wandels*, Frankfurt/Main-New York 1992

Annette Buchholtz, "Der Studentenrat an der Universität Leipzig 1945-1951," *Das Hochschulwesen* 1990/2

Walter Bußmann, *Treitschke. Sein Welt- und Geschichtsbild*, Göttingen 1952

Herbert Butterfield, *Man on his past. The study of the history of historical scholarship*, Cambridge 1955

Herbert Butterfield, *History and human relations*, London 1951

Herbert Butterfield, *The Whig interpretation of history*, Cambridge 1931

Herbert Butterfield, *The discontinuities between the generations in history. Their effect on the transmission of political experience*, Cambridge 1972

Stanisław Bylina, "Polskie badania nad ruchami heretyckimi w średniowieczu," *PH* 1995

Valerián Bystrický, "K niektorým problémom vývoja historiografie na Slovensku v 90. rokoch 20. storočia," *HČSAV* 2002

Cenzura w PRL – relacje historyków, ed. Zbigniew Romek, Warszawa 2000

Marek Cetwiński, *Ideologia i poznanie. Społeczne funkcje mediewistyki śląskiej po 1945 roku*, Częstochowa 1993

Ivan Chalupecký, "Stav a úlohy výskumu novoveku," *HČSAV* 1991

John Connelly, *Captive university. The sovietisation of East German, Czech and Polish higher education 1945-1956*, Chapel Hill-London 2000

The culture of the Stalin period, ed. Hans Günther, London 1990

Hans Cymorek, *Georg von Below und die deutsche Geschichtswissenschaft um 1900*, Stuttgart 1998

Czechoslovakia Past and Present vol. 1, Political, International, Social and Economic Aspects, ed. Miloslav Rechcigl, jr, The Hague-Paris 1968

Jaroslav Čechura & Jana Šetřilová, "Josef Klik a II. sjezd československých historiků," *ČČH* 92/1994

Česká Akademie Věd a Umění 1891-1991. Sborník příspěvků k 100. výročí zahájení činnosti, eds. Jiří Pokorný & Jan Novotný, Praha 1993

Petr Čornej, *Lipanské ozvěny*, Praha 1995

Roumen Daskalov, *The Making of a Nation in the Balkans. Historiography of the Bulgarian Revival*, Budapest 2004

Die DDR als Geschichte. Fragen – Hypothesen – Perspektiven, eds. Jürgen Kocka & Martin Sabrow, Berlin 1994

Die DDR-Geschichtswissenschaft als Forschungsproblem, eds. Georg G. Iggers, Konrad H. Jarausch, Matthias Middell & Martin Sabrow, München 1998

Deutsche Geschichtswissenschaft nach dem Zweiten Weltkrieg (1945-1965), eds. Ernst Schulin & Elisabeth Müller-Luckner, München 1989

Deutsche Ostforschung und polnische Westforschung im Spannungsfeld von Wissenschaft und Politik. Disziplinen im Vergleich, eds. Jan M. Piskorski, Jörg Hackmann & Rudolf Jaworski, Osnabrück-Poznań 2002

Das deutsch – tschechische Verhältnis seit 1918, eds. Hans Lemberg & Gotthold Rhode, Stuttgart 1969

Deutsch – tschechische Beziehungen in der Schulliteratur und im populären Geschichtsbild, eds. Hans Lemberg & Ferdinand Seibt, Braunschweig 1980

Diktatur – Krieg – Vertreibung. Erinnerungskulturen in Tschechien, der Slowakei und Deutschland seit 1945, eds. Christoph Cornelißen, Roman Holec & Jiří Pešek, Essen 2005

Edmund Dmitrów, *Niemcy i okupacja hitlerowska w oczach Polaków. Poglądy i opinie z lat 1945-1948*, Warszawa 1987

Doświadczenia przeszłości. Niemcy w Europie Środkowo-Wschodniej w historiografii po 1945 roku. Erfahrungen der Vergangenheit. Deutsche in Ostmitteleuropa in der Historiographie nach 1945, eds. Jerzy Kłoczowski, Witold Matwiejczyk & Eduard Mühle, Lublin-Marburg 2000

Józef Dutkiewicz & Krystyna Śreniowska, *Zarys historii historiografii polskiej*, vol. 3, Łódź 1959

Stefan Ebenfeld, *Geschichte nach Plan? Die Instrumentalisierung der Geschichtswissenschaft in der DDR am Beispiel des Museums für Deutsche Geschichte in Berlin (1950 bis 1955)*, Marburg 2001

Rainer Eckert, "Die Widerstandsforschung über die NS-Zeit – ein methodisches Beispiel für die Erforschung widerständigen Verhaltens in der DDR?," *GWU* 1995

Irene Raab Epstein, *Gyula Szekfű. A Study in the Political Basis of Hungarian Historiography*, New York, 1987

Karl Dietrich Erdmann, *Die Ökumene der Historiker. Geschichte der Internationalen Historikerkongresse und des Comité International des Sciences Historiques*, Göttingen 1987

R. J. W. Evans, "A Czech historian in troubled times, J. V. Polišenský," *Past & Present. A journal of historical studies*, 176 (2002)

Jan Fiala & Andrej Romaňák, "Pavel Choc – historik a vlastenec," *HaV* 1991

Barbara Fijałkowska, *Borejsza i Różański. Przyczynek do dziejów stalinizmu w Polsce*, Olsztyn 1995

Barbara Fijałkowska, *Polityka i twórcy (1948-1959)*, Warszawa 1985

Marta Fik, *Kultura polska po Jałcie – kronika lat 1944-1981*, Londyn 1989

Alexander Fischer, "Neubeginn in der Geschichtswissenschaft. Zum Verhältnis von 'bürgerlichen' und marxistischen Historikern in der SBZ/DDR nach 1945," *GWU* 1980

Holger Fischer, *Politik und Geschichtswissenschaft in Ungarn. Die ungarische Geschichte von 1918 bis zur Gegenwart in der Historiographie seit 1956*, München 1982

Josef Foschepoth, *Reformation und Bauernkrieg im Geschichtsbild der DDR. Zur Methodologie eines gewandelten Geschichtsverständnisses*, Berlin 1976

František Graus – *člověk a historik. Sborník z pracovního semináře Výzkumného centra pro dějiny vědy konaného 10. prosince 2002*, eds. Zdeněk Beneš, Bohumil Jiroušek & Antonín Kostlán, Praha 2004

Julius Fučík, *Reportáž, psaná na oprátce. První úplné, kritické a komentované vydání*, Praha 1995

Jan Galandauer, "Česká vojenská tradice v proměnách času," *HaV* 1994

Andrzej Garlicki, *Stalinizm*, Warszawa 1993

Geschichte als Herrschaftsdiskurs. Der Umgang mit der Vergangenheit in der DDR, ed. Martin Sabrow, Köln 2000

Geschichte als Legitimation? Internationale Schulbuchrevision unter den Ausprüchen von Politik, Geschichtswissenschaft und Geschichtsbedürfnis, ed. Karl–Georg Faber, Braunschweig 1984

Geschichtsschreibung als Legitimationswissenschaft 1918-1945, ed. Peter Schöttler, Frankfurt/Main 1997

Geschichtsschreibung zu den böhmischen Ländern im 20. Jahrhundert. Wissenschaftstraditionen – Institutionen – Diskurse, ed. Christiane Brenner, München 2006

Geschichtswissenschaft in Deutschland. Traditionelle Positionen und gegenwärtige Aufgaben, ed. Bernd Faulenbach, München 1974

Pieter Geyl, *From Ranke to Toynbee. Five lectures on historians and historiographical problems*, Northampton/Massachusetts 1952

Gibt es ein deutsches Geschichtsbild? Konferenz der Ranke-Gesellschaft Vereinigung für Geschichte im öffentlichen Leben, ed. Georg von Rauch, Frankfurt/Main, Berlin, Bonn 1955

Horst Gies, "Die Rolle der Gefühle im Geschichtsunterricht des Dritten Reiches und der DDR," *GWU* 1995

Aleksander Gieysztor, Jerzy Maternicki & Henryk Samsonowicz, *Historycy warszawscy ostatnich dwóch stuleci*, Warszawa 1986

Trond Gilberg, *Nationalism and Communism in Romania. The Rise and Fall of Ceausescu's Personal Dictatorship*, Boulder 1990

Horst Glassl, *Die slowakische Geschichtswissenschaft nach 1945*, Wiesbaden 1971

Vladimír Goněc, "Národní dějiny – „politickovýchovný" účel, [pokleslá] beletrie či předmět kritické vědy?," *Česko-slovenská historická ročenka* 2000

G. P. Gooch, *History and Historians in the Nineteenth Century*, London 1952

Maciej Górny, *Między Marksem a Palackým. Historiografia w komunistycznej Czechosłowacji*, Warszawa 2001

Maciej Górny, *Przede wszystkim ma być naród. Marksistowskie historiografie w Europie Środkowo-Wschodniej*, Warszawa 2007

Maciej Górny, "Past in the future. National tradition and Czechoslovak Marxist historiography," *European Review of History* 2003/1

Maciej Górny, "Die Anfänge der ‚Nationalstaaten' in den marxistischen Historiographien Polens, der DDR und der Tschechoslowakei," *Inter Finitimos* 2005

Maciej Górny, "Historiographiegeschichte und marxistisches Erbe. Volksrepublik Polen, DDR und Tschechoslowakei im Vergleich," *Historie. Jahrbuch des Zentrums für Historische Forschung Berlin der Polnischen Akademie der Wissenschaften*, 2008/2009

Maciej Górny, ""Dialectical negation," East Central European Marxist historiography and the problem of the nation," *East Central Europe*, 2009

Maciej Górny, "Historical Writing in Poland, Czechoslovakia, and Hungary," in: *The Oxford History of Historical Writing*, vol. V: *Historical Writing since 1945*, eds. Axel Schneider, Daniel Woolf & Ian Hesketh, New York 2011

Andrzej Feliks Grabski, *Kształty historii*, Łódź 1985

Andrzej Feliks Grabski, *Dzieje historiografii*, Poznań 2003

Andrzej Feliks Grabski, *Zarys historii historiografii polskiej*, Poznań 2000

Andrzej Feliks Grabski, *Perspektywy przeszłości. Studia i szkice historiograficzne*, Lublin 1983

Andrzej Feliks Grabski, *Historiografia i polityka. Dzieje konkursu historycznego im. Juliana Ursyna Niemcewicza 1867-1922*, Warszawa 1979

Andrzej Feliks Grabski, *W kręgu kultu Naczelnika. Rapperswilskie inicjatywy kościuszkowskie (1894-1897)*, Warszawa 1981

Krzysztof Groniowski, "Seminarium Stefana Kieniewicza," *PH* 2000/3

A Guide to historiography in Slovakia, eds. Elena Mannová /David Paul Daniel, Bratislava 1995

Ingo Haar, *Historiker im Nationalsozialismus. Deutsche Geschichtswissenschaft und der „ Volkstumskampf" im Osten*, Göttingen 2000

Frank Hadler, "Historiografický mýtus Velké Moravy v 19. a 20. století," *ČMM* 2001

Josef Hanzal, *Cesty české historiografie 1945-1989*, Praha 1999

Josef Hanzal, "Proměny české historiografie 1945-1989," in: *VII. sjezd českých historiků Praha 24.-26. září 1993*, Praha 1994

Josef Hanzal, *Josef Pekař*, Praha 1992

Josef Hanzal, "Jan Slavík, historik, myslitel," ČČH 1995

Josef Hanzal, "Čeští historici před únorem 1948," ČČH 1993

Josef Hanzal, *Josef Pekař – život a dílo*, Praha 2002

Ľudovít Haraksim, "Povojnová historiografia obdobia národného obrodenia a národného hnutia," *HČSAV* 1991

Ľudovít Haraksim, "Úlóhy Slovenskej historickej spoločnosti pri spracovaní novších dejín," *HČSAV* 1990

Peter Haslinger, "Nationale oder transnationale Geschichte. Die Historiographie zur Slowakei im europäischen Kontext," *Bohemia* 2003

Miloš Havelka, *Dějiny a smysl. Obsahy, akcenty a posuny 'české otázky' 1895–1989*, Praha 2001

Marek Havrila, *Slovenská historiografia v rokoch 1945-1968*, Prešov 2004, at: www. pulib.sk/elpub/FF/Havrila1

Henryk Wereszycki (1898-1990). Historia w życiu historyka, eds. Elżbieta Orman & Antoni Cetnarowicz, Kraków 2001

Peter Heumos, "Geschichtswissenschaft und Politik in der Tschechoslowakei," *Jahrbücher für Geschichte Osteuropas* 26/1978 and 30/1982

Günther Heydemann, "Relativierung des Dogmas? Zur Entwicklung geschichtswissenschaftlicher Theorie und Methodologie in der DDR seit 1967", *GWU* 1980

Otto Hintze, *Soziologie und Geschichte. Gesammelte Abhandlungen zur Soziologie, Politik und Theorie der Geschichte*, Göttingen 1964

Maria Hirszowicz, *Pułapki zaangażowania. Intelektualiści w służbie komunizmu*, Warszawa 2001

Historia, mity, interpretacje, ed. Alina Barszczewska-Krupa, Łódź 1996

Historia, poznanie i przekaz, ed. Barbara Jakubowska, Rzeszów 2000

História a súčasnosť Univerzity Komenského v Bratislave 1919-2000, ed. Viliam Čsander, Bratislava 2000

Historik Daniel Rapant – život a dielo (1897-1988-1997), eds. Richard Marsina et al., Martin 1998

Historiker in der DDR, ed. Karl Heinrich Pohl, Göttingen 1997

Historikerkontroversen, ed. Hartmut Lehmann, Göttingen 2000

Historikertage im Vergleich, eds. Gerald Diesener & Matthias Middell, Leipzig 1996

Historiografia krajów Europy Środkowo-Wschodniej, eds. Jerzy Kłoczowski & Paweł Kras, Lublin 1997

Historiography between modernism and postmodernism. Contributions to the methodology of the historical research, ed. Jerzy Topolski, Amsterdam 1994

Historische Forschung und sozialistische Diktatur. Beiträge zur Geschichtswissenschaft der DDR, eds. Martin Sabrow & Peter Th. Walther, Leipzig 1995

Historische Institute im internationalen Vergleich, eds. Matthias Middell, Gabriele Lingelbach & Frank Hadler, Leipzig 2001

Historische Zeitschriften im internationalen Vergleich, ed. Matthias Middell, Leipzig 1999

Jörg K. Hoensch, *Studia Slovaca. Studien zur Geschichte der Slowaken und der Slowakei*, München 2000

Historismus in den Kulturwissenschaften. Geschichtskonzepte, historische Einschätzungen, Grundlagenprobleme, eds. Otto Gerhard Oexle & Jörn Rüsen, Köln – Weimar – Wien 1996

Anton Hönig, *Die slawische Mythologie in der tschechischen und slowakischen Literatur*, Augsburg 1976

Zdeněk Hrbata, *Romatismus a Čechy. Témata a symboly v literárnich a kulturních souvislostech*, Praha 1999

Karel Hrubý, "První desetiletí Československého časopisu historického (1953-1962)," *ČČH* 1999

Hure oder Muse? Klio in der DDR. Dokumente und Materialien des Unabhängigen Historiker-Verbandes, eds. Rainer Eckert, Ilko-Sascha Kowalczuk & Isolde Stark, Berlin 1994

Gondolf Hübinger, *Georg Gottfried Gervinus. Historisches Urteil und politische Kritik*, Göttingen 1984

Piotr Hübner, "Przebudowa nauk historycznych w Polsce (1947-1953)," *PH* 1987

Piotr Hübner, *Nauka polska po II wojnie światowej – idee i instytucje*, Warszawa 1987

Piotr Hübner, *Polityka naukowa w Polsce w latach 1944-1953. Geneza systemu*, 2 vols., Wrocław 1992

Georg G. Iggers, *Deutsche Geschichtswissenschaft. Eine Kritik der traditionellen Geschichtsauffassung von Herder bis zur Gegenwart*, Wien-Köln-Weimar 1997

Georg G. Iggers, *Geschichtswissenschaft im 20. Jahrhundert. Ein kritischer Überblick im internationalen Zusammenhang*, Göttingen 1996

Georg G. Iggers, *Historiography in the twentieth century. From scientific objectivity to the postmodern challenge*, Hanover – London 1997

Georg G. Iggers, *The German conception of history. The national tradition of historical thought from Herder to the present*, Middletown 1968

Georg G. Iggers, *New directions in European historiography*, Middletown 1983

Im geteilten Europa. Tschechen, Slowaken und Deutsche und ihre Staaten 1948-1989, eds. Hans Lemberg, Jan Křen & Dušan Kováč, Essen 1998

In memoriam Josefa Macka (1922-1991), eds. Miloslav Polívka & František Šmahel, Praha 1996

Interpretace ruské revoluce 1917, eds. Jiří Hanuš & Radomír Vlček, Brno 2008

Instytut Historii Polskiej Akademii Nauk 1953-1993, ed. Stefan K. Kuczyński, Warszawa 1993

Instytut Historii Polskiej Akademii Nauk 1953-2003, ed. Stefan K. Kuczyński, Warszawa 2003

Instytut Zachodni 50 lat, ed. Romualda Zwierzycka, Poznań 1994

Die Interdependenz von Geschichte und Politik in Osteuropa seit 1945. Historiker-Fachtagung der Deutschen Gesellschaft für Osteuropakunde e. V., Berlin vom 9.-11. 1976 in Bad Wiessee. Protokoll, ed. Günther Stökl, [München 1976]

Jozef Jablonický, *Glosy o historiografii SNP. Zneužívanie a falšovanie dejín SNP*, Bratislava 1994

Jozef Jablonický, "Slovenské národné povstanie a tri etapy jeho hodnotenia," *HČSAV* 1991

Jozef Jablonický, "Slovenské národné povstanie v historiografii v rokoch totality," in: *SNP v pamäti národa. Materiály z vedeckej konferencie k 50. výročiu SNP, Donovaly 26.-28. apríla 1994*, Bratislava 1994

Наталя Яковенко, *Нарис історії України з найдавніших часів до кінця XVIII століття*, Київ 1997

Jan Hus. Zwischen Zeiten, Völkern, Konfessionen. Vorträge des internationalen Symposiums in Bayreuth vom 22. bis 26. September 1993, ed. Ferdinand Seibt, München 1997

Halina Janaszek-Ivaničková, *Kochanek Sławy. Studium o Ľudovície Štúrze*, Katowice 1978

Maciej Janowski, "Three historians," *CEU History Department Yearbook* 2001-2002

Robert Jarocki, *Opowieść o Aleksandrze Gieysztorze*, Warszawa 2001

Dariusz Jarosz, *Polacy a stalinizm 1948-1956*, Warszawa 2000

Dariusz Jarosz, "O polskim stalinizmie – polemicznie," *Więź* 2002/2

Manfred Jäger, *Kultur und Politik in der DDR. Ein historischer Abriß*, Köln 1982

Jerzy Jedlicki, *Źle urodzeni czyli o doświadczeniu historycznym. Scripta i postscripta*, Londyn – Warszawa 1993

Ralph Jessen, *Akademische Elite und kommunistische Diktatur. Die ostdeutsche Hochschullehrschaft in der Ulbricht – Ära*, Göttingen 1999

Zdeněk Jirásek & Andrzej Małkiewicz, *Polska i Czechosłowacja w dobie stalinizmu (1948-1956). Studium porównawcze,* Warszawa 2005

Bohumil Jiroušek, *Josef Macek. Mezi historií a politikou,* Praha 2004

Bohumil Jiroušek, *Antonín Rezek,* České Budějovice 2002

K poctě Jaroslava Marka. Sborník prací k 70. narozeninám prof. dr. Jaroslava Marka, eds. Lubomír Slezák & Radomír Vlček, Praha 1996

Zdeněk Kalista, *Josef Pekař,* Praha 1994

Lýdia Kamencová, "Vznik Slovenskej historickej spoločnosti a prvá etapa jej činnosti (1946-1950)," *HČSAV* 1991

Ivan Kamenec, "Niekoľko poznámok o schopnosti (neschopnosti) k sebareflexii aleba naša nepripravenosť k polemickým diskusiám," *HČSAV* 2002

Ivan Kamenec, "Slovenské, české a československé dejiny, problem či pseudoproblém?," *Česko-slovenská historická ročenka* 2000

Ivan Kamenec, *Hľadanie a blúdenie v dejinách. Úvahy, štúdie a polemiky,* Bratislava 2000

Karel Kaplan, *Československo v letech 1948-1953,* vol. 2, *Zakladatelské období komunistického režimu,* Praha 1991

Karel Kaplan, *Největší politický proces. "M. Horáková a spol.,"* Brno 1995

Karel Kaplan & Pavel Kosatík, *Gottwaldovi muži,* Praha-Litomyšl 2004

Karel Kaplan & Dušan Tomášek, *O cenzuře v Československu v letech 1945-1956, studie,* Praha 1994

Kazimierz Tymieniecki (1887-1968). Dorobek i miejsce w mediewistyce polskiej, ed. Jerzy Strzelczyk, Poznań 1990

Mario Kessler, *Exilerfahrung in Wissenschaft und Politik. Remigrierte Historiker in der früher DDR,* Köln 2001

Stefan Kieniewicz, "'Kwartalnik Historyczny' w latach powojennych," *KH* 1989

Jarosław Kilias, *Naród a idea narodowa. Nacjonalizm T. G. Masaryka,* Warszawa 1998

Claudia Klemm, *Erinnert – umstritten – gefeiert. Die Revolution von 1848/49 in der deutschen Gedenkkultur,* Göttingen 2007

Klio ohne Fesseln? Historiographie im östlichen Europa nach dem Zusammenbruch des Kommunismus, eds. Alois Ivanišević et al., Wien – Frankfurt a. M. – Berlin 2003

Krise – Umbruch – Neubeginn. Eine kritische und selbstkritische Dokumentation der DDR-Geschichtswissenschaft 1989/90, eds. Rainer Eckert, Wolfgang Küttler & Gustav Seeber, Stuttgart 1992

Leszek Kołakowski, *Main currents of Marxism : the founders, the golden age, the breakdown,* transl. P.S. Falla, New York 2005

Leszek Kołakowski, *The presence of myth*, transl. Adam Czerniawski, Chicago 1989

Michal Kopeček & Miroslav Kunštát, "'Sudetoněmecká otázka' v české debatě po roce 1989," *SD* 2003/3

Michal Kopeček, "Ve službách dějin, ve jménu národa. Historie jako součást legitimizace komunistických režimů ve střední Evropě v letech 1948-1950," *SD* 2001/1

Michal Kopeček, *Hledání ztraceného smyslu revoluce. Počátky marxistického revizionismu ve Střední Evropě*, Praha 2008

Jiří Kořalka & Jiří Pokorný, "Česká společnost 19. a 20. století a čeští historikové (několik myšlenek k úvaze Dušana Třeštíka po 17. listopadu 1989)," *ČČH* 1990

Dietrich Koslowski, *Die SPD 1869-1900 in der Darstellung der DDR-Geschichtschreibung*, Frankfurt/Main 1977

Antonín Kostlán, "K vývoji českého dějepisectví v letech 1945-1948," *ČČH* 1994

Antonín Kostlán, *Druhý sjezd československých historiků (5.-11. října 1947) a jeho místo ve vývoji českého dějepisectví v letech 1935-1948*, Praha 1993

Dušan Kováč, "Slovensko - české vzťahy v historickom vedomí slovenskej spoločnosti," *Česko-slovenská historická ročenka* 2000

Dušan Kováč, *Dejiny Slovenska*, Praha 2000

Dušan Kováč, "Slovenská historiografia desať rokov po. Zámery a ich realizácia," *HČSAV* 2002

Ilko-Sascha Kowalczuk, "Die Historiker der DDR und der 17. Juni 1953," *GWU* 1993

Ilko-Sascha Kowalczuk, *Legitimation eines neuen Staates. Parteiarbeiter an der historischen Front. Geschichtswissenschaft in der SBZ/DDR 1945 bis 1961*, Berlin 1997

Markus Krzoska, *Für ein Polen an Oder und Ostsee. Zygmunt Wojciechowski (1900-1955) als Historiker und Publizist*, Osnabrück 2003

Jan Křen, *Bílá místa v našich dějinách*, Praha 1990

Jiří Křesťan, *Pojetí české otázky v díle Zdeňka Nejedlého*, Praha 1996

Marcin Kula, "Polska, narzucona i odrzucona komunistyczna wizja dziejów," *Borussia* 2003

Alexej Kusák, *Kultura a politika v Československu 1945-1956*, Praha 1998

František Kutnar & Jaroslav Marek, *Přehledné dějiny českého a slovenského dějepisectví. Od počátku národní kultury až do sklonku let třicátých 20. století*, Praha 1997

Hans Lades, "Zum Verhältnis der Geschichtswissenschaften in beiden deutschen Staaten," *GWU* 1980

Ulrich Langer, *Heinrich von Treitschke. Politische Biographie eines deutschen Nationalisten*, Düsseldorf 1998

Magdalena Lechowska, *Węgrzy patrzą na swą historię (1945-2003)*, Warszawa 2004

Richard D. Lewis, "Marxist historiography and the history profession in Poland, 1944-55," in: *Eastern Europe and the West. Selected papers from the Fourth World Congress for Soviet and East European Studies*, ed. John Morisonn, New York 1992

Lexikon současných českých historiků, eds. Jaroslav Pánek & Petr Vorel, Praha 1999

Ľubomír Lipták, "Poznámky o historiografii novších dejín," *HČSAV* 1990

Ľubomír Lipták, "Über den Ort der slowakischen Historiographie und der historischen Erfahrung," *Bohemia* 2003

Ľubomír Lipták, *Slovensko v 20. storočí*, Bratislava 2000

Ľubomír Lipták, *Changes of Changes. Society and Politics in Slovakia in the 20ᵗʰ Century*, Bratislava 2002

Ľubomír Lipták, "Pamätníky a pamäť povstania roku 1944 na Slovensku," *HČSAV* 1995

Ľubomír Lipták, "Slovenská historiografia obdobia po roku 1945," *HČSAV* 1991

Ľubomír Lipták, *Storočie dlhšie ako sto rokov. O dejinách a historiografii*, Bratislava 1999

Elena Londáková, "O kľúčových obdobiach slovenského kultúrneho vývoja po roku 1945," *HŠ* 2000

Herbert Ludat, "Die deutsch-polnische Vergangenheit in marxistischen Sicht," *ZfO* 1952

Michael Ludwig, *Tendenzen und Erträge der modernen polnischen Spätmittelalterforschung unter besonderer Berücksichtigung der Stadtgeschichte*, Gießen 1983

Robert Luft, "'Als die Wachsamkeit des Regimes nachliess'. Zur Beschäftigung mit der Vergangenheit des eigenen Faches in der Tschechischen Geschichtswissenschaft nach 1989," *Bohemia* 1994

Vladimír Macura, *Šťastný věk*, Praha 1992

Vladimír Macura, *Masarykovy boty a jiné semi(o)fejetony*, Praha 1993

Vladimír Macura, *Český sen*, Praha 1998

Vladimír Macura, *Znamení zrodu*, Praha 1995

Josef Macůrek, *Dějepisectví evropského východu*, Praha 1946

Czesław Madajczyk, *Klerk czy intelektualista zaangażowany? Świat polityki wobec twórców kultury i naukowców europejskich w pierwszej połowie XX wieku*, Poznań 1999

Piotr Madajczyk, "Polska myśl zachodnia w polityce komunistów polskich," *PZ* 1997

Elena Mannová, "Clio auf slowakisch. Probleme und neue Ansätze der Historiographie zu der Slowakei nach 1989," *Bohemia* 2003

Tadeusz Manteuffel, *Historyk wobec historii. Rozprawy nieznane. Pisma drobne. Wspomnienia*, Warszawa 1976

Tadeusz Manteuffel, "Warunki rozwoju nauki historycznej w dziesięcioleciu 1948-1958," *PH* 1995

Jaroslav Marek, *O historismu a dějepisectví*, Praha 1992

Jerzy Maternicki, *Historiografia polska XX wieku*, vol. 1, 1900-1918, Wrocław 1982

Die Mauern der Geschichte. Historiographie in Europa zwischen Diktatur und Demokratie, eds. Gustavo Corni/Martin Sabrow, Leipzig 1996

Max Weber und seine Zeitgenossen, eds. Wolfgang J. Mommsen & Wolfgang Schwenther, Göttingen – Zürich 1988

Zbigniew Mazur, *Obraz Niemiec w polskich podręcznikach szkolnych do nauczania historii 1945-1989*, Poznań 1995

Charles E. McClelland, *The German Historians and England. A Study in Nineteenth-Century Views*, Cambridge 1971

Zoltan G. Mesko, *The silent conspiracy, A communist model od political cleansing at the Slovak University in Bratislava after the Second World War*, Boulder 2003

Július Mésároš, "O zástojoch mojej generácie na povojnovom vývoji slovenskej historiografie," *HČSAV* 1990

Július Mésároš, "Reflexie o päťdesiatych a šesťdesiatych rokoch," *HČSAV* 1991

Július Mésároš, *Zložité hľadanie pravdy o slovenských dejinách. Výber štúdí, odborných polemic a článkov z polstoročnej výskumnej a publikačnej činnosti*, Bratislava 2004

Peter Meyers, *Friedrich II. von Preußen im Geschichtsbild der SBZ/DDR. Ein Beitrag zur Geschichte der Geschichtswissenschaft und der Geschichtsunterricht in der SBZ/DDR. Mit einer Methodik zur Analyse von Schulgeschichtsbüchern*, Braunschweig 1983

Magdalena Mikołajczyk, *Jak się pisało o historii... Problemy polityczne powojennej Polski w publikacjach drugiego obiegu lat siedemdziesiątych i osiemdziesiątych*, Kraków 1998

Ján Mlynárik, *Diaspora historiografie. Štúdie, články a dokumenty k dejinám československej historiografie v rokoch 1969-1989*, Praha 1998

Laurenz Müller, *Diktatur und Revolution. Reformation und Bauernkrieg in der Geschichtsschreibung des 'Dritten Reiches' und der DDR*, Stuttgart 2004

Nach dem Erdbeben. (Re-) Konstruktion ostdeutscher Geschichte und Geschichtswissenschaft, eds. Konrad H. Jarausch & Matthias Middell, Leipzig 1994

Die Nation schreiben. Geschichtswissenschaft im internationalen Vergleich, eds. Christoph Conrad & Sebastian Conrad, Göttingen 2002

The national idea as a research problem, ed. Jolanta Sujecka, Warszawa 2002

Nationale Geschichtskulturen – Bilanz, Ausstrahlung, Europabezogenheit, ed. Heinz Duchhardt, Mainz 2006

Balázs Németh, *Nationalism and Socialist Patriotism in the Hungarian Historiography between 1948 and 1956, and Ist Influence on the Post-1956 Era*, [PhD thesis, Budapest : CEU, Budapest College, 1995]

Ulrich Neuhäußer-Wespy, *Die SED und die Historie. Die Etablierung der marxistisch-leninistischen Geschichtswissenschaft der DDR in den fünfziger und sechziger Jahren*, Bonn 1996

Ulrich Neuhäußer-Wespy, "Zur Neuorientierung der DDR-Geschichtswissenschaft seit 1971," *GWU* 1980

Lutz Niethamer, *Deutschland danach. Postfaschistische Gesellschaft und nationales Gedächtnis*, Bonn 1999

Martin Nodl, "Možné přístupy ke studiu dějin české historické vědy v letech 1945-2000," *SD* 2001

Martin Nodl, *Dějepisectví mezi vědou a politikou. Úvahy o historiografii 19. a 20. století*, Brno 2007

O dějinách a politice. Janu Křenovi k sedmdesátinám, eds. Jiří Pešek & Oldřich Tůma, Ústí nad Labem 2001

Obraz Němců, Rakouská a Německá v české společnosti 19. a 20. století, eds. Jan Křen & Eva Broklová, Praha 1998

Od diktatúry k diktatúre. Slovensko v rokoch 1945-1953 (Zborník materiálov z vedeckej konferencie v Smoleniciach 6.-8. decembra 1994), ed. Michal Barnovský, Bratislava 1995

Osteuropa in der historischen Forschung der DDR, ed. Manfred Hellmann, 2 vols., Düsseldorf 1972

Paths of Continuity. Central European Historiography from the 1930s to the 1950s, eds. Hartmut Lehmann & James van Horn Melton, Cambridge 1994

Jan Pauer, *Moralisches Diskurs und die deutsch – tschechischen Beziehungen*, Bremen 1998

Tomasz Pawelec, *Myśl metodologiczna Marcelego Handelsmana*, Lublin 1994

Aleksander Pawlicki, *Kompletna szarość. Cenzura w latach 1965-1972. Instytucja i ludzie*, Warszawa 2001

Pekařovské studie, ed. Eva Kantůrková, Praha 1995

Maureen Perrie, *The Cult of Ivan the Terrible in Stalin's Russia*, Houndmills 2001

Josef Petráň, "Proměny české historiografie 1945-1989," in: *VII sjezd českých historiků Praha 24.-26. září 1993*, Praha 1994

György Péteri, *Academia and state socialism. Essays on the political history of academic life in post-1945 Hungary and Eastern Europe*, Highland Lakes/NJ 1998

Wojciech Piasek, *Antropologizowanie historii. Studium metodologiczne twórczości Witolda Kuli*, Poznań 2004

Karel Pichlík, Bohumír Klípa & Jitka Zabloudilová, *Českoslovenští legionáři (1914-1920)*, Praha 1996

Richard Georg Plaschka, *Von Palacký bis Pekař. Geschichtswissenschaft und Nationalbewußtsein bei den Tschechen*, Graz 1955

Milan Podrimavský, "Obraz národnej emancipácie v období 1848-1918," HČSAV 1991

Polacy wobec przemocy 1944-56, eds. Barbara Otwinowska & Jan Żaryn, Warszawa 1996

Zdeněk Pousta, *Dějiny Univerzity Karlovy 1918-1990*, Praha 1998

Vilém Prečan, *V kradeném čase. Výběr ze studií, článků a úvah z let 1973-1993*, Brno 1994

Proměny diskursu české marxistické historiografie (Kapitoly z historiografie 20. století), ed. Bohumil Jiroušek, České Budějovice 2008

Marin Pundeff, "Bulgarian Historiography 1942-1958," *The American Historical Review* 1961

Robert B. Pynsent, *Questions of identity: Czech and Slovak ideas of nationality and personality*, Budapest - London 1994

Jiří Rak, *Bývali Čechové*, Praha 1994

Ramy życia w Polsce. Praca zbiorowa zorganizowana przez Ośrodek Badań Europy Środkowej, eds. Stanisław Gryziewicz, Jan Jodzewicz, Leonard Rudowski & Wojciech Zaleski, special issue of *Kultura* 1952

Lutz Raphael, *Geschichtswissenschaft im Zeitalter der Extreme. Theorien, Methoden, Tendenzen von 1900 bis zur Gegenwart*, München 2003

Renate Reuther, *Die Weimarer Republik im Urteil der DDR-Geschichtswissenschaft – Kontinuität und Wandel*, Erlangen 1988

Zbigniew Romek, "Historycy radzieccy o historykach polskich. Uwagi o Zjeździe wrocławskim (1948) i konferencji otwockiej (1951/1952)," *Polska 1944/45-1989. Studia i materiały* 1999

Zbigniew Romek, *Cenzura a nauka historyczna w Polsce 1944-1970*, Warszawa 2010

Zbigniew Romek, "Nauka przeciw ideologii. Współpraca historyków polskich i radzieckich po II wojnie światowej," *DN* 2002/1

Zbigniew Romek, "Polsko-radzieckie dyskusje o Istorii Polszi v trech tomach w latach 1950-1959," *Klio polska. Studia i materały z dziejów historiografii polskiej po II wojnie światowej*, 2004

Andrew Rossos, "Czech Historiography," *Canadian Slavonic Papers* 1982

Ivan L. Rudnytsky, *Essays in modern Ukrainian history*, Cambridge/Mass. 1987

Helmut Rumpler, "Revolutionsgeschichtsforschung in der DDR," *GWU* 1980

Jacques Rupnik, "Politika vyrovnávání s komunistickou minulostí. Česká zkušenost," *SD* 2002/1

Ruské a sovětské dějiny v české poválečné historiografii, ed. Václav Veber, Praha 1996

Tadeusz Paweł Rutkowski, *Nauki historyczne w Polsce 1944-1970. Zagadnienia polityczne i organizacyjne*, Warszawa 2007

Tadeusz Paweł Rutkowski, *Polskie Towarzystwo Historyczne w latach 1945-1958. Zarys dziejów*, Toruń 2009

Jan Rychlík, "České, slovenské a československé dějiny – problém vzájemného vztahu v různých historických dobách," *Česko-slovenská historická ročenka* 2000

Martin Sabrow, *Das Diktat des Konsenses. Geschichtswissenschaft in der DDR 1949-1969*, München 2001

Karl-Heinz Schäfer, "1813 – Die Freiheitskriege in der Sicht der marxistischen Geschichtsschreibung der DDR," *GWU* 1970

Eva Schmidt–Hartmann, "Forty years of historiography under socialism in Czechoslovakia. Continuity and change in patterns of thought," *Bohemia* 1988

Michael C. Schneider, *Bildung für neue Eliten. Die Gründung der Arbeiter-und –Bauern-Fakultäten in der SBZ/DDR*, Dresden 1998

Johannes Schradi, *Die DDR-Geschichtswissenschaft und das bürgerliche Erbe. Das deutsche Bürgertum und die Revolution von 1848 im sozialistischen Geschichtsverständnis*, Frankfurt/Main 1984

Winfried Schulze, *Deutsche Geschichtswissenschaft nach 1945*, München 1989

Michał Sczaniecki, "Instytuty Ziem Zachodnich – ich działalność i miejsce w organizacji nauki polskiej," *PZ* 1995

Vincent Sedlák, "Slovenská historiografia k dejinám Slovenska v stredoveku," *HČSAV* 1991

Ferdinand Seibt, *Německo a Češi. Dějiny jednoho sousedství uprostřed Evropy*, Praha 1996

Ferdinand Seibt, *Bohemica, Probleme und Literatur seit 1945*, München 1970

Ferdinand Seibt, *Hussitica, Zur Struktur einer Revolution*, Köln 1965

Skryte oblicze systemu komunistycznego. U źródeł zła, eds. Roman Bäcker & Piort Hübner, Warszawa 1997

Vladimír Slámečka, *Science in Czechoslovakia*, New York-London 1963

Slovenská akadémia vied 1953-1973, eds. Milan Repáš, Vojtech Filkorn, Ján Gouda, Vojtech Kellö, Miroslav Murín & Alexander Ujváry, Bratislava 1973

Slovenská otázka v dejinách Česko-Slovenska (1945-1992). Zborník príspevkov z vedeckého kolokvia, ktoré sa konalo 20. októbra 1993, ed. Michal Barnovský, Bratislava 1994

Slovenská otázka v 20. Storočí, ed. Rudolf Chmel, Bratislava 1997

Henryk Słabek, *Intelektualistów obraz własny w świetle dokumentów autobiograficznych 1944-1989*, Warszawa 1997

Henryk Słabek, "Władza i intelektualiści," *DN* 2000

Słownik historyków polskich, ed. Maria Prosińska-Jackl, Warszawa 1993

The Sovietisation of Eastern Europe, New Perspectives on the Postwar Period, eds. Balázs Apor, Péter Apor & E.A. Rees, Washington (DC) 2008

Советская историография, ed. Ю. Н. Афанасьев, Москва 1996

Spor o smysl českých dějin 1895-1938, ed. Miloš Havelka, Praha 1995

Spor o smysl českých dějin 1938-1989. Posuny a akcenty české otázky, ed. Miloš Havelka, Praha 2006

Heinrich Ritter von Srbik, *Geist und Geschichte vom deutschen Humanismus bis zur Gegenwart*, 2 vols., Salzburg 1964

Tomáš Staněk, *Odsun Němců z Československa*, Praha 1991

Günther Stelzig, *Um ein gemeinsames Geschichtsbild? Die Zusammenarbeit der Historiker der DDR mit ihren Fachkollegen aus der UdSSR, aus Polen und der Tschechoslowakei im Rahmen der bilateralen Historikerkommissionen (1955-1984)*, Erlangen 1987

Rafał Stobiecki, *Bolszewizm a historia. Próba rekonstrukcji bolszewickiej filozofii dziejów*, Łódź 1998

Rafał Stobiecki, "Between continuity and discontinuity, a few comments on the post-war development of Polish historical research," *ZfO-F* 2001/2

Rafał Stobiecki, "Stalinizm w historiografii. Między radzieckim oryginałem a narodowymi kopiami," *Zeszyty Wiejskie* 2002

Rafał Stobiecki, "Między dogmatem ideologicznym a modernizacją. Marksizm a historiografia w Polsce po II wojnie światowej," *Historyka* 2002

Rafał Stobiecki, *Historia pod nadzorem. Spory o nowy model historii w Polsce (II połowa lat czterdziestych – początek lat pięćdziesiątych)*, Łódź 1993

Rafał Stobiecki, "Żanna Kormanowa. Szkic do portretu," in: *Niebem i sercem okryta. Studia historyczne dedykowane dr Jolancie Maliszewskiej*, ed. Mariusz Malinowski, Toruń 2002

Rafał Stobiecki, *Historiografia PRL. Ani dobra, ani mądra, ani piękna... ale skomplikowana*, Warszawa 2007

Günther Stökl, „Historiographie in der UdSSR und in den Ländern Ostmitteleuropas," in: *Sowjetisches Modell und nationale Prägung. Kontinuität und Wandel in Ostmitteleuropa nach dem Zweiten Weltkrieg*, ed. Hans Lemberg, Marburg/Lahn 1991

Grzegorz Strauchold, *Wrocław – okazjonalna stolica Polski. Wokół powojennych obchodów rocznic historycznych*, Wrocław 2003

Grzegorz Strauchold, *Myśl zachodnia i jej realizacja w Polsce Ludowej w latach 1947-1957*, Toruń 2003

Teresa Suleja, *Uniwersytet Wrocławski w okresie centralizmu stalinowskiego 1950-1955*, Wrocław 1995

Teresa Suleja, "Próby kształtowania „nowego człowieka" w czasach stalinowskich (na przykładzie Uniwersytetu Wrocławskiego 1949-1953)," *Sobótka* 2002/3

František Svátek, "Pokus o bilanci průběhu a výsledků „sporu historiků" v České republice na přelomu tisíciletí," *SD* 2001/1

Jerzy Szacki, *Historia myśli socjologicznej. Wydanie nowe*, Warszawa 2003

Środowiska historyczne II Rzeczypospolitej. Materiały konferencji naukowych w Krakowie i Lublinie 1984 i 1985, ed. Jerzy Maternicki, Warszawa 1986

František Šmahel, "Josef Macek," *ČČH* 1991-92

Anton Špiesz, "K problematike starších dejín Slovenska," *HČSAV* 1990

Ladislav Tajták, "K niektorým otázkam hodnotenia revolúcie 1848/1849 na Slovensku," *HČSAV* 2002

Janusz Tazbir, *Polska na zakrętach dziejów*, Warszawa 1997

Eduard Thaden, "Marxist historicism and the crises of Soviet historiography," *JfGO* 2003

Günther J. Trittel, "'Thomas Müntzer mit dem Schwerte Gedeonis" – Metamorphosen einer 'historischen Metapher'," *GWU* 1991

Dušan Třeštík, "České dějiny a čeští historikové po 17. listopadu," *ČČH* 1990

Dušan Třeštík, *Mýty kmene Čechů (7.-10. století). Tři studie ke „Starým pověstem českým"*, Praha 2003.

Jakub Tyszkiewicz, "Propaganda Ziem Odzyskanych w prasie PRL w l. 1945-1948," *PZ* 1995/4

Universities under dictatorship, eds. John Connelly & Michael Grüttner, University Park/PA 2005

Uniwersytet Jagielloński – Złota Księga Wydziału Historycznego, ed. Julian Dybiec, Kraków 2000

Uniwersytet Wrocławski w latach 1945-1955, ed. Franciszek Longchamps, vol. 1, Wrocław 1959

Otto Urban, *Česká společnost 1848-1918*, Praha 1982

Rudolf Urban, *Die Organisation der Wissenschaft in der Tschechoslowakei*, Marburg/Lahn 1957

Elisabeth Valkenier, "Sovietisation and liberalisation in Polish postwar historiography," *Journal of Central European Affairs* 1959

Steven Bela Vardy, *Modern Hungarian historiography*, Boulder 1976

Vladimír Varinský, "Aktuálne problémy slovenskej historiografie po novembri 1989 (kontroverzie z pohľadu ľudackej emigrácie)," *HČSAV* 2002

Verwaltete Vergangenheit. Geschichtskultur und Herrschaftslegitimation in der DDR, ed. Martin Sabrow, Leipzig 1997

Věda v Československu v letech 1953-1963. Sborník z konference (Praha, 23. – 24. listopadu 1999), eds. Hana Barvíková, Marek Ďurčanský & Pavel Kodera, Praha 2000

Věda v Československu v letech 1945-1953. Sborník z konference, eds. Blanka Zilynská, Petr Svobodný & Blanka Šachová Praha 1999

Vít Vlnas, *Jan Nepomucký, česká legenda*, Praha 1993

Thomas Vogtherr, "'Reformator' oder „frühbürgerlicher Revolutionär"? Martin Luther im Geschichtsbild der DDR," *GWU* 1988

Andrzej Walicki, "Marks i Engels o sprawie polskiej. Uwagi metodologiczne," in: *Powstanie listopadowe 1830-1831. Geneza – uwarunkowania – bilans – porównania*, eds. Jerzy Skowronek & Maria Żmigrodzka, Wrocław 1983

Hermann Weber, „Die Geschichte der DDR. Versuch einer vorläufigen Bilanz," *ZfG* 1993

Weimarer Klassik in der Ära Ulbricht, eds. Lothar Ehrlich, Gunther Mai & Ingeborg Cleve, Köln – Weimar – Wien 2000

Weimarer Klassik in der Ära Honecker, eds. Lothar Ehrlich, Gunther Mai & Ingeborg Cleve Köln – Weimar – Wien 2001

Węgry – Polska w Europie Środkowej. Historia – Literatura. Księga pamiątkowa ku czci Profesora Wacława Felczaka, eds. Antoni Cetnarowicz, Csaba Gyula Kiss & István Kovács, Kraków 1997

Andrzej Wierzbicki, *Naród – państwo w polskiej myśli historycznej dwudziestolecia międzywojennego*, Wrocław 1978

Andrzej Wierzbicki, *Historiografia polska doby romantyzmu*, Wrocław 1999

Andrzej Wierzbicki, *Konstytucja 3 Maja w historiografii polskiej*, Warszawa 1993

Matthias Willing, "Die DDR-Althistorie im Rückblick," *GWU* 1991

Tomáš Winkler, *Matica slovenská v rokoch 1945-1954. Z problémov a dokumentov ústredia MS*, Martin 1971

Lutz Winckler, "Die Novemberrevolution in der Geschichtsschreibung der DDR," *GWU* 1970

Joanna Wojdon, "Propaganda polityczna w podręcznikach dla szkół podstawowych Polski Ludowej (1944-1989)," *DN* 2000

Bertram D. Wolfe, "Agonia sowieckiej historiografii," *Kultura* 1953/1

Writing national histories. Western Europe since 1800, eds. Stefan Berger, Mark Donovan & Kevin Passmore, London – New York 1999

Serhy Yekelchyk, *Stalin's Empire of Memory. Russian–Ukrainian Relations in the Soviet Historical Imagination*, Toronto 2004

Andrzej Zahorski, *Spór o Stanisława Augusta*, Warszawa 1988

Marcin Zaremba, *Komunizm, legitymizacja, nacjonalizm. Nacjonalistyczna legitymizacja władzy komunistycznej w Polsce*, Warszawa 2001

Marcin Zaremba, "Próba legitymizacji władzy komunistycznej w latach 1944-1947 poprzez odwołanie się do treści narodowych," *Polska 1944/45-1989. Studia i materiały* 1997

Marína Zavacká, "Die slowakische Historiographie zur politischen Geschichte des 20. Jahrhunderts, die totalitären Regime," *Bohemia* 2003

Klaus Zernack, "Schwerpunkte und Entwocklungslinien der polnischen Geschichtswissenschaften nach 1945," *HZ* 1973/5

Klaus Zernack, *Mittelalterliches Polen. Probleme der polnischen Mediävistik auf dem Historikerkongreß in Krakau 1958*, Köln-Graz 1965

Klaus Zernack, *Preußens Ende und die ostdeutsche Geschichte*, Braunschweig 1989

Klaus Zernack, *Zwischen Kritik und Ideologie. Methodologische Probleme der polnischen Geschichtswissenschaft auf dem VII. polnischen Historikerkongreß in Breslau 1948*, Köln – Graz 1964

Zwischen Parteilichkeit und Professionalität. Bilanz der Geschichtswissenschaft der DDR, eds. Konrad H. Jarausch & Matthias Middell, Berlin 1991

Andrzej Zybertowicz, *Między dogmatem a programem badawczym. Problemy stosowania materializmu historycznego we współczesnej historiografii polskiej*, Warszawa – Poznań 1990

Joseph F. Žáček, *Palacký. The Historian as Scholar and Nationalist*, The Hague 1970

Index

Warsaw Studies in Contemporary History

Edited by Dariusz Stola / Machteld Venken

Vol.   1   Maciej Górny: The Nation Should Come First. Marxism and Historiography in East Central
Europe. 2013.

www.peterlang.de